Research Notes on Digital Business Transformation and Artificial Intelligence

Robert Leskovar and Borut Werber

# Research Notes on Digital Business Transformation and Artificial Intelligence

PETER LANG
Berlin · Bruxelles · Chennai · Lausanne · New York · Oxford

**Library of Congress Cataloging-in-Publication Data**
A CIP catalog record for this book has been applied for at the Library of Congress.

Library of Congress Control Number: 2025000546

**Bibliographic Information published by the Deutsche Nationalbibliothek**
The Deutsche Nationalbibliothek lists this publication in the Deutsche Nationalbibliografie; detailed bibliographic data is available in the internet at http://dnb.d-nb.de.

Cover Image: © Shutter_M/Shutterstock.com
Cover design by Peter Lang Group AG



ISBN 978-3-631-92432-7 (Print)
E-ISBN 978-3-631-92491-4 (E-PDF)
E-ISBN 978-3-631-92492-1 (E-PUB)
DOI 10.3726/b22722


Published by Peter Lang GmbH, Berlin (Germany)

info@peterlang.com



This publication has been peer reviewed.

www.peterlang.com

# Table of Contents

# Preface to »Research Notes on Digital Business Transformation and Artificial Intelligence«

The inception of the Research Notes on Digital Business Transformation and Artificial Intelligence began in 2023 with the simple idea of sharing our research findings with the academic community. Most of the authors were members of or close to the Department of Informatics, Faculty of Organisational Sciences at the University of Maribor. The game plan for the research was determined by global trends in the industry and scientific advances and breakthroughs in numerous fields. Digital business transformation and artificial intelligence were the magic words that aroused great interest in the scientific community. For the authors, these buzzwords were the natural extension of their research endeavours. Many of us began in the era of system dynamics, modelling and simulation, decision support systems, expert systems, reliability, security, e-business and e-commerce. Now it seems that they have merged into a complex with many interrelated components, where each one and the whole being important to the industry and the academic community.

This book is dedicated to all those, past and present, who have contributed to the above areas as researchers and mentors. Special recognition is due to our emeritus professors: the late Miroljub Kljajić for his pioneering research in the field of modelling, simulation and system dynamics, Vladislav Rajkovič for his fundamental research in the field of expert systems and decision support systems, and Jože Gričar, the founder of the Bled Conference on Electronic Data Interchange and Electronic Commerce.

We would also like to express our heartfelt thanks to our families and loved ones, whose support has been indispensable throughout this journey.

The authors gratefully acknowledge the financial support of the following institutions:

- Slovenian Research and Innovation Agency ( research core funding no. P5-0018),
- the Ministry of Higher Education, Science and Innovation of the Republic of Slovenia as part of the Next Generation EU National Recovery and Resilience Plan (grant no. 3330-22-3515; NOO no.: C3330-22-953012), and
- the Erasmus+ programme of the European Union (grant no. 2021-1-MK01-KA220-HED-000027646).

Specific acnowledgements are included in related chapters. Furthermore, this book would not have been possible without the kind and active support of Professor Iztok Podbregar, Dean of the Faculty of Organizational Sciences at the University of Maribor, and the reviewers Professor Michal Kvet (University of Žilina) and Professor Olga Cherednichenko (University of Lyon)

In preparing this book, we have tried to strike a balance between technological and organisational aspects and between depth and accessibility. Each chapter offers detailed insights while remaining comprehensible, self-contained and open to further quests. The contributions are the result of the collaboration of many experts, each bringing their unique perspective and expertise. We can only hope that the content will be providing teasers for both experienced researchers and newcomers to the field.

The journey begins with a deep dive into cellular automata and its role in enhancement of strategic allignment of business and IT. Chapter 2 offers practical insights for database designers and developers looking to utilise AI in their workflows. In the next chapter, research provides valuable insights into the societal dynamics shaping the adoption of microchip implants and their impact on digital transformation. The model for assessing data maturity among SMEs, empowering them to leverage data effectively in their operations is presented in Chapter 4. Chapter 5 discusses the legal framework and empirical findings on the opportunities and challenges of e-invoicing adoption. In Chapter 6, surveys and data analyses reveal the most important trends and preferences in online shopping. Chapter 7 provides a comprehensive overview of the revision of selected information security standards and their role in facilitating digital transformation through improved cybersecurity. Chapter 8 brings insight into the role of AI in predictive analytics and in preparing for future epidemic modelling and public health interventions. The final chapter presents new approaches and methods related to the functionality and security of facial recognition systems.

We hope that this book will serve as a valuable resource for many researchers and generate even more rigorous and high-profile ideas.

With sincere appreciation,

Robert Leskovar and Borut Werber
May, 2024

Robert Leskovar* and Blaž Kavčič**

# The quest for cellular automata: a case of strategic business IT alignment

**Abstract:** This research is a follow-up of the survey on the strategic alignment between business and IT (information technology) in Slovenia in 2021. Cellular automata are defined by a 4-tuple: the finite or infinite lattice, the finite set of cell states or values, the finite neighbourhood and the local transition function defined by the transition table/rule. A brief overview of the development in the field of cellular automata is presented. Some notable examples of significant contributions to various aspects of cellular automata are: rule 110, Wolfram's classification, synchronisation and pattern formation. In recent years, cellular automata have continued to evolve with the advances in technology and computing power. In period 2019–2022, more than 11 thousand scientific articles contributed to several disciplines, mainly in the fields of computer science, engineering, mathematics, physics, environmental science and science technology.The main part of this research presents experiments aimed at: a) developing CA based on the idea of partial differential equations (the focus is on experimenting with different values of gains, internal and external factors) and b) developing CA based on a finite set of rules and an offset caused by random noise (the focus is on experimenting with different rules). The research has shown that experiments with PDE-based CAs strongly depend on the determination of the gain and the function of the internal and external components. The experiment was conducted with five different values of gain, three functions of internal components and three functions of external components. The experiments with rule- based CAs involve the random generation of rules. In a time-limited experiment (60 seconds), 12 to 14 thousand random rules were generated. A subset of these rules had the property of leading the evolution of alignments from arbitrary initial states to arbitrary final states. The implications of the last finding are significant. The inclusion of machine learning algorithms would help to shorten the search time and narrow down the set of likely valid rules that determine the evolution of strategic business IT alignment in company.

**Keywords:** cellular automata, machine learning, artificial intelligence, strategic business alignment, digital business transformation

* University of Maribor, Faculty of organizational sciences, Kranj, Slovenia; e-mail: robert.leskovar@um.si

** University of Maribor, Faculty of organizational sciences, Kranj, Slovenia; e-mail: blaz.kavcic1@student.um.si

## 1. Introduction

An earlier study by Leskovar and Kavčič (2022) addressed the state of strategic alignment between business and IT (information technology) in Slovenia in 2021. It was inspired by the emerging interest in strategic alignment between business and IT and digital transformation (e.g. Gerow et al., 2014, Global institute for IT Management, 2019, Njanka et al., 2020, Verhoef et al., 2021, Erl and Stoffers, 2022). The translated Luftman questionnaire (2017) covers six areas: Communication, Measurement, IT Management, Partnership, IT Architecture and Skills. The authors received 68 surveys from Slovenian companies (the response rate was 4%). The statistical analysis of the survey includes frequencies, descriptive statistics, correlations and clustering. The calculation of the Cronbach's α coefficient using SPSS and R tools showed extremely high consistency. The classification of company orientations showed that the optimal number of clusters is two. These two clusters can be briefly described as "mature" and "less mature." Based on the survey, the authors constructed an algorithm that calculated the scores - the current states of the alignment areas. In addition, the authors proposed three scales to categorise the scores into 5 levels of compliance maturity. These levels were named similarly to the capability maturity levels of the CMMI model used in the software industry. Three modes of the discrete criterion conversion function were defined: a) strict, called KMax (logistic function), b) mild, called KMid (linear function), and c) minimalist, called KMin (shifted linear function). The idea of this article is that the alignment maturity levels could represent the states of a cellular automaton (CA) that can be used to search and predict the evolution of alignment domains for certain entities engaged in basic research (Leskovar and Kavčič, 2022). As a reminder, CA is defined as a 4-tuple:

$$CA = (Z, S, N, f)$$

where:

- Z is the finite or infinite lattice
- S is a finite set of cell states or values
- N is the finite neighbourhood and
- f is the local transition function, defined by the transition table/rule.

For the observed topic, namely the strategic business IT alignment, it would be possible to define a two-dimensional grid with real geographic locations. Unfortunately, the small number of responses returned would make the grid too sparse. Therefore, we decided to construct a one-dimensional CA where the current cell has two neighbouring cells (alignments). The initial finite set of cell states had five named and defined intervals. For this investigation, we have added another one that is close to "zero". So we have six states. We have also limited the number of neighbours to two - left and right of the current neighbour. Since there are six alignment areas, we can define 120 possible pairs of neighbours of the current cell. Local transition functions usually depend on the previous state and are based on the perspective of partial differential equations. The new state also depends on the change caused by the difference between the abstract left and right neighbours. More often, however, the transition from the current state to the new state is defined as a simple rule in the form:

$$if\ (L = l\ \&\ R = r\ \&\ C = c)\ then\ N = n$$

In this research we will present a brief overview of the development of cellular automata. Then we will proceed with the development of a CA that would be able to simulate behavior of alignment areas in the Luftman questionnaire. We will quest the idea of incorporating partial differential equations and a rule-based approach to the development of cellular automata. The experimental part of the research will present parts of the R language code and the results derived from it.

# 2. Overview of cellular automata development

## 2.1 Notes on past development

By generally accepted definition, a cellular automata (pl. cellular automata, abbreviated CA) is a computational system defined as a set of cells that change state in parallel based on a transition rule applied to each cell and a finite number of its neighbours. CA can be represented as a graph in which vertices correspond to cells and edges connect adjacent cells to define their state. CA is inherently suitable for parallel implementations.

CA research spans several decades. The concept of cellular automata was first introduced by mathematician John von Neumann and physicist Stanislaw Ulam in the 1940s. They were interested in developing mathematical models to simulate self-replicating systems. Initially, research on cellular automata focussed on simple, abstract models consisting of a lattice of cells, each of which could exist in a finite number of states. The behaviour of these cells was determined by a set of rules that specified how the state of a cell would evolve over time based on the states of neighbouring cells. This idea was inspired by the study of biological systems in which individual cells interact with their immediate environment (e.g. Wiener, 1946). In the early years, cellular automata were mainly studied for their mathematical properties and used as tools to explore fundamental concepts of data processing, complexity theory and the theory of dynamical systems (e.g. Shannon, 1956, Von Neuman, 1966, Codd, 1968, Zuse n.d.). As computing power increased over the years, researchers were able to study more complex cellular automaton systems and explore their applications in various fields. In the 1980s and 1990s, cellular automata found practical applications in areas such as computer graphics, image processing and cryptography. They have also been used as models for the study of physical phenomena such as fluid dynamics and traffic flow. Cellular automata have proven to be valuable tools for the study of emergent behaviour and complex systems. They have been used to simulate phenomena ranging from the growth of crystals to the behavior of crowds. Cellular automata are also used in the field of artificial life, where researchers are trying to understand the processes that lead to life-like behaviour. Outstanding contributions to research with cellular automata should be recognised:

- John von Neumann and Stanislaw Ulam: both laid the foundation for cellular automata with their work on self-replicating systems in the 1940s. They introduced the concept of cellular automata and researched their mathematical properties.
- John Conway: John Conway's Game of Life, introduced in 1970, is perhaps the best known and most influential cellular automaton. It demonstrated complex emergent behavior from simple rules and inspired countless researchers to explore the field further.
- Stephen Wolfram: He has made significant contributions to the study of cellular automata. In his 2002 book "A New Kind of Science", Wolfram presented a comprehensive study of cellular automata and their impact on a variety of scientific disciplines.
- Tommaso Toffoli and Norman Margolus: In the 1980s, they developed the concept of "billiard ball" cellular automata, which introduced the idea of local reversible transformations within the rules of cellular automata. This work expanded the scope of cellular automata and their applications.
- Christopher Langton: He is an outstanding figure in the field of artificial life and cellular automata. His research focused on the study of self-organisation, complexity and evolution within cellular automaton systems.
- Edward Fredkin: He made significant contributions to the theory and application of cellular automata. He explored the concept of reversible computation and its relationship to cellular automata, paving the way for research in reversible computation and computational irreducibility.

- Wolfram Research: Founded by Stephen Wolfram, has been influential in advancing the field of cellular automata. It has developed software tools such as Mathematica and Wolfram Alpha that have enabled researchers and enthusiasts to explore and experiment with cellular automata on a large scale.

Some notable examples of significant contributions to various aspects of cellular automata are:

- Rule 110: Rule 110 was discovered by Wolfram. It applies to a one-dimensional cellular automaton that is Turing-complete, i.e. it can simulate any computable function. This result demonstrates the computational universality of cellular automata.
- Wolfram's classification: Stephen Wolfram classified a wide range of one-dimensional cellular automaton rules based on their behaviour and complexity. This classification system provided a framework for understanding the behavior of different types of cellular automata.
- Synchronisation and pattern formation: Researchers have studied the ability of cellular automata to exhibit synchronised behaviour and create intricate patterns. This research has implications for fields such as physics, chemistry and biology, where pattern formation is a crucial phenomenon.
- Applications in physics and mathematics: Cellular automata have been used to model physical systems and phenomena such as fluid flow, magnetism and quantum mechanics. They have also been used in mathematical research, e.g. in the study of tilings, fractals and chaos theory.

These examples represent only a fraction of the influential research in the field of cellular automata. The field continues to evolve with ongoing studies, and new contributions are constantly emerging as researchers explore the potential of cellular automata in various domains.

## 2.2 Recent development

In recent years, cellular automata have evolved with advances in technology and computing power. Researchers are now exploring more sophisticated variants, including three-dimensional cellular automata and non-uniform cellular automata, which allow for more realistic modelling of complex systems. Overall, the history of cellular automata is characterised by continuous research into their mathematical properties, computational capabilities and practical applications. They have proven to be a powerful tool for understanding and simulating a variety of phenomena and have made significant contributions to the fields of mathematics, computer science, physics, biology and many others.

Web of Science (2023) states that in the period 2019–2022, the keyword "cellular automata" was used in more than 11 thousand scientific articles in various disciplines (see Table 1).

*Table 1: Articles on CA by scientific discipline between 2019–2022*

| Scientific discipline | Percent of articles |
|---|---|
| Computer Science | 13,39 |
| Engineering | 12,04 |
| Mathematics | 11,39 |
| Physics | 8,66 |
| Environmental Sciences Ecology | 6,75 |
| Science Technology Other Topics | 6,44 |
| Materials Science | 4,35 |
| Geography | 3,85 |
| Mathematical Computational Biology | 3,82 |
| Biodiversity Conservation | 3,27 |
| Mechanics | 2,88 |
| Transportation | 2,28 |
| Geochemistry Geophysics | 2,10 |
| Chemistry | 2,09 |
| Business Economics | 2,08 |
| Communication | 1,72 |
| Telecommunications | 1,68 |
| Meteorology Atmospheric Sciences | 1,66 |
| Physical Sciences Other Topics | 1,60 |
| Water Resources | 1,53 |
| Metallurgy Metallurgical Engineering | 1,39 |
| Automation Control Systems | 1,37 |
| Geology | 1,36 |
| Public Administration | 1,19 |
| Agriculture | 1,12 |

Traditional scientific disciplines predominate (computer science, engineering, mathematics and physics), but there are also signs that cellular automata are being studied in virtually all scientific disciplines. Artificial intelligence and machine learning are of particular interest due to the nature of cellular automata.

## 2.3 Cellular automata and artificial intelligence

Artificial intelligence (AI) and cellular automata (CA) have some common ground (they deal with dynamic and complex systems), although they are completely different fields. AI focuses on the development of intelligent machines with the ability to learn from the past and predict the future. Machine learning (ML) algorithms are the building blocks of artificial intelligence as they provide experience-like feedback. Cellular automata as mathematical models can simulate the behaviour of complex systems (predict the future) by using simple rules. These rules enable computation and can appear very unconventional, cryptic and meaningless at first glance. By generating huge data sets, CA can provide input for ML algorithms to:

- develop more effective strategies for environmental management, e.g. in relation to forest fires, flooding, the spread of pollutants in air, soil and water and rising sea levels
- better predict the growth of cities
- advanced theoretical studies of complex systems
- real applications in industry (e.g. production planning problems in manufacturing systems)
- more safety in transport, more efficient logistics
- Growth of human tissue, either for reconstruction or removal
- Balancing network traffic and power grids with an agent-based model (ABM).
- Spread/erasure of cultures, languages, movements, initiatives in society

For this research, we will design experiments that apply some machine learning concepts.

## 2.4 One dimensional (1D) cellular automata and rule 110

The array of cells in 1D CA is represented as a row (see Fig. 1.). Rule developers usually consider two neighbours on each side, but it is possible to define a wider neighbourhood. A border cell can have only one or two neighbours by applying a circular configuration.

*Figure 1: Scheme of one-dimensional cellular automata with one left and one right neighbour.*

| L state | C state | R state |
|---|---|---|
| l | c | r |

The steps of CA evolution are represented as discrete time intervals or generations. In CA, all cells are simultaneously mapped into new states. Conventional computers update sequentially, but this requires more memory. In computer languages, one-dimensional CA can be implemented as vectors, matrices or classes. The rules of a one-dimensional CA can be defined as a lookup table or as an expression.

A well-known example of a one-dimensional CA is Rule 110 (see Fig. 2), which was discovered by Stephen Wolfram. Rule 110 uses a rule table with eight patterns and determines the new state of a cell based on the current states of the cell and its immediate neighbours.

*Figure 2: One dimensional cellular automata Rule 110.*

| 111 | 110 | 101 | 100 | 011 | 010 | 001 | 000 |
|---|---|---|---|---|---|---|---|
| 0 | 1 | 1 | 0 | 1 | 1 | 1 | 0 |

The binary value $01101110_2$ is decimal $110_{10}$. Rule 110 can also be expressed as equation:

$$x_{t+1}^{i} = x_t^{i} + x_t^{i-1}(1 - x_t^{i} * x_t^{i+1})$$

Rule 110 has a remarkable property - it is Turing-complete, which means that it can simulate any computable function. Since our problem domain requires 6 state CA, we can ask whether the binary rule 110 can be mapped into cellular automata with 6 states. For simplicity, we use numbers from 0 to 5 to represent the states. In rule 110, the neighbourhood consists of the current cell and its two neighbours on the left and right. Luftman's model has 6 areas, so there are 120 alternatives to form a neighbourhood, assuming that each cell has exactly 2 neighbours. In rule 110 there are 8 transition rules based on the states of the neighbourhood cells. To map Rule 110 to a cellular automaton with 6 states, we need to define the transition rules for all possible combinations of states. For a CA with 6 states, the total number of rules would be much higher than eight. Currently, there is no evidence of an attempt to analytically map rule 110 to a similar rule for 6 state CA. A direct comparison of rule 110 and the expected rule for 6-state 6 CA is complicated by the lack of comparison criteria. Rule 110 is known for its complexity and its ability to perform universal calculations. An eventual discovery of a similar rule for 6-state CA would likely contribute to many applications in economics and advances in the social sciences. In this case, we have 6 possible states for each cell (0 to 5). The neighbourhood consists of three cells. So there are a total of $6^3$=216 possible combinations of triples and 1296 quadriples. Each assignment can lead to different behaviours and patterns in the automaton, so there are a multitude of possibilities to explore.

## 3. Methodology

The ideas are implemented in the R language. The experimental part of this research is performed on laptop with decent performance.

The problem can be defined as a quest for a 6 state CA founded on Luftman's areas of alignment, which together form the strategic business IT alignment. The areas of alignment are: Communication, Measurement, IT Management, Partnership, Architecture and Human Resource Skills. Initial values of the alignments were identified in research by Leskovar and Kavčič (2022). Further research includes the exploration of:

- CA, based on the idea of partial differential equations, and
- CA, based on a finite set of rules and an offset caused by random noise.

The goals are:

- To develop CA based on the idea of partial differential equations. The focus is on experimenting with different values of gains, internal and external factors.
- To develop a CA based on a finite set of rules and an offset caused by random noise. The focus is on experimenting with different rules, which can be totalitaristic, probabilistic or hybrid.

The obvious limitation of this research is completeness, caused by enormous complexity of the subject, insufficient computer resources and the preference for experimental work over analytical rigour.

The ideas are implemented in the R language. The experimental part of this research is conducted on a laptop with decent performance.

## 4. Experiments

### 4.1 Experiment 1: design of CA, based on idea of partial differential equations

The ratio to start with the idea of partial differential equations can be justified by the nature of partial differential equations. The new state depends on the current state and the difference between input and output. Input and output can therefore be treated as neighbours, which corresponds to the basic idea of CA. The current state, which is usually represented by an upper and lower bounded continuous variable, can be mapped as the current state of CA. The transition rule is applied as the difference between the input and the output. So we have the essential elements of CA: states, neighbours and rules. The PDE is defined:

$$state_{t+1} = state_t + gain * (internal_t - external_t)$$

Time has discrete values and increments can be treated as real time slots (day, week, month, year). The state refers to one of the six alignment areas. The initial state (actually a human expert estimate) of the alignment area is calculated based on the responses to the Luftman questionnaire. Gain determines the factor by which the difference between internal and external components is multiplied. Three alternatives were defined for each of the internal and external components and five values were defined for gain. The total number of variants is thus 45.

### *4.1.1 Initial states of CA - answers to luftman's questionaire*

The data source is Excel spreadsheet which was derived in previous research. The spreadsheet has 68 rows (68 companies) and 7 columns: id of company (values from 1 to 68) and 6 alignment areas (Communication, Measurement, IT Management, Partnership, Architecture and Human resources skills).

### *4.1.2 Reading initial states of CA*

The following code sequence in R loads the required libraries: plot.matrix for ploting results, vtree for creating tree diagrams, readxl for reading xlsx format of spreadsheet, sqldf for creating add-hoc queries on data frames, xtable for preparing Latex ready tables, ploty for 3D plots and gtools for permutations. After reading in the data, a new dataframe is created and the columns are named. The last command prints Latex ready table with the initial CA data.

```
library(plot.matrix)
library(vtree)
library(readxl)
library(sqldf)
library(xtable)
library(plotly)
library(gtools)
initial_CA <- read_excel("Initial_CA_Alignment.xlsx")
a<-as.matrix(initial_CA, nrow = 68, ncol= 7, byrow = TRUE)
colnames(a) <- c('Company', 'Communication', 'Measuring', 'IT management', 'Partnership',
'IT Architecture', 'Skills')
```

### 4.1.3 Gain

Gain is defined as a 5-element vector with values between 0 and 1.

```
gain_f <- c(0.10, 0.25, 0.50, 0.75, 0.90)
```

### 4.1.4 Internal components

Internal components are defined threefold:

a) mean value of target alignment area including all history of target alignment area and all population of companies. The expression in R is defined as:

```
mean(result[1:t,j,1:n_matrix])
```

where result is 3D matrix in the form (time = y axis, alignment area = x axis and company = z axis):

- 1:t is y segment of 3D matrix
- j is target alignment area and
- 1:n_matrix is z segment of 3D matrix

b) mean value of all alignment areas in previous step for specific company. Expression in R is defined as:

```
mean(result[t-1,1:algn,i]
```

where result is 3D matrix in the form (time = y axis, alignment area = x axis and company = z axis):

- t-1 is y previous time slot of 3D matrix
- 1:algn are all alignment areas and
- i is z company

c) variance of previous time slot of all alignment areas and target company. Expression in R is defined as:

```
var(result [t-1,1:n_algn,i])
```

where result is 3D matrix in the form (time = y axis, alignment area = x axis and company = z axis):

- t-1 is y previous time slot of 3D matrix
- 1:n_algn are all alignment areas and
- i is z company

### *4.1.5 External components*

The external components are implemented as three time series - scenarios. They are defined in ten discrete points in time with lag of six slots of time units. This could effectively span time series over five years if the time unit was one month and the lag between forecasts six months. Negative values of the external components increase the alignment areas, while positive values decrease the alignment areas. A regression function is calculated based on point-in-time forecasts. The most suitable function is automatically selected from the polinomial functions with a degree between one and eight. The best fited function is automaticaly selected. Forecasted scenario is ploted on line graph.

The first scenario, called OECD (not to be confused with the Organisation for Economic Co-operation and Development), mainly predicts the decline of the alignment areas. This scenario could be described as pessimistic. The second scenario, called UMAR (not to be confused with the Institute for Macroeconomic Analysis and Development), predicts a sharp increase/decrease. In other words, it could be described as a realistic scenario. The third or almost optimistic scenario called Eurostat (not to be confused with the Statistical Office of the European Commission) predicts a positive effect in the first half and a negative effect in the second half of the 5-year period.

R code presents:

- the definition of the function which find best fited polinomial and plot it
- the setting of three forecats in 10 time point and
- setting the best fit regression polinomial to month prediction.

```
frcst_vector <- function (frcst, ttl)
{
 polinom1 <- lm(y~x, data=frcst)
 polinom2 <- lm(y~poly(x,2,raw=TRUE), data=frcst)
 polinom3 <- lm(y~poly(x,3,raw=TRUE), data=frcst)
 polinom4 <- lm(y~poly(x,4,raw=TRUE), data=frcst)
 polinom5 <- lm(y~poly(x,5,raw=TRUE), data=frcst)
 polinom6 <- lm(y~poly(x,6,raw=TRUE), data=frcst)
 polinom7 <- lm(y~poly(x,7,raw=TRUE), data=frcst)
 polinom8 <- lm(y~poly(x,8,raw=TRUE), data=frcst)
# izračun R2 in določitev modela, ki se najbolje prilega
r2 <- c(summary(polinom1)$adj.r.squared,
     summary(polinom2)$adj.r.squared,
     summary(polinom3)$adj.r.squared,
```

```
    summary(polinom4)$adj.r.squared,
    summary(polinom5)$adj.r.squared,
    summary(polinom6)$adj.r.squared,
    summary(polinom7)$adj.r.squared,
    summary(polinom8)$adj.r.squared)
 plot(frcst$x, frcst$y,
   ylim = c((min(frcst$y)- 0.1), (max(frcst$y) + 0.1)))
 x_os <- seq(1, 60, length=60)

  print(paste("Best fit polinomial: ", which.max(r2)))
 best_fit <- lm(y~poly(x,which.max(r2),raw=TRUE), data=frcst)
 lines(x_os, predict(best_fit,
             data.frame(x=x_os)),
     col='tomato',
     main=paste("Forecast: ",
           ttl, " polinom. degr. : ",
           which.max(r2)))
 frcst_fit <- as.data.frame(predict(best_fit, data.frame(x=x_os)))

 return(frcst_fit)
}
frcst1 <- data.frame(x=c(1,6,12,24,30,36,42,48,54,60),
               y=c(0.85, 0.92, 0.83, 0.90, 0.75,
                 0.89, 0.82, 0.96, 0.94, 0.84))
frcst2 <- data.frame(x=c(1,6,12,24,30,36,42,48,54,60),
               y=c(0.85,-0.52, 0.43,-0.60, 0.65,
                 -0.55, 0.52,-0.66, 0.74,-0.84))
frcst3 <- data.frame(x=c(1,6,12,24,30,36,42,48,54,60),
               y=c(-0.85,-0.52,-0.43,-0.60, 0.65,
                 0.55, 0.52, 0.66, 0.74, 0.84))
frcst_tag <- c("OECD", "UMAR","Eurostat")

frcst_fit1 <- frcst_vector(frcst1,"OECD")
frcst_fit2 <- frcst_vector(frcst2,"UMAR")
frcst_fit3 <- frcst_vector(frcst3,"Eurostat")
frcst_fit <-cbind(frcst_fit1,frcst_fit2,frcst_fit3)
colnames(frcst_fit) <- frcst_tag
```

### *4.1.6 Presentation of cartesian product of alternative triples*

This portion of the R code implemetation is auxilary and merely serves as visual presentation. Internal components are named “Mean 1”, “Mean 2” and “Variance”.

External components have abbreviated names “PES”, “OPT”, “REAL”. Vector of gain values is defined in previous portion of the R code.

```
internal <- c("Mean 1 ","Mean 2","Variance")
external <- c("PES","REA","OPT")
data_cp1 <- expand.grid(gain_f, internal, external)
colnames(data_cp1) <- c("G","I","E")
vtree(data_cp1,"G","I","E", horiz=FALSE)
```

### 4.1.7 *Formation of 3D matrix*

Dimension of the matrix are: time (y plane = 60), alignment areas (x plane = 6) and company (z plane = number of rows in input spreadsheet; 68). 3D matrix is named “result”. After 3D matrix initialization initial values from spreadsheet is inserted in time 1 for all companies. Names of other variables are self descriptive. This part of R code is essential.

```
tmax <- 60
n_algn <- 6
n_matrix <- nrow(initial_CA)
n_cells <- tmax*n_algn*n_matrix
result <- array(c(rep(0.0,n_cells)),
          dim=c(tmax,n_algn,n_matrix))
for(i in 1:n_matrix) {
 for (j in 1:n_algn) {
     result[1,j,i] <- a[i,(j+1)]
 }
}
```

### 4.1.8 *Implementation of CA based on PDE*

Computing the CA states is implemented as multiple loops:

- for all gain variants
- for all external component variants
- for all internal component variants
- for all time slots
- for all alignment areas and
- for all companies

If previous calculation is stored in csv file then data is simply read. Plot function returns 68 matrix plots (for each company) with gain=0.75, external “REAL” scenario and internal “Mean 2” scenario. This part of R code is essential.

```
clmn <- c('gain','external','internal','company', 'time',
       'Comms', 'Measur', 'IT_Mgt', 'Partn', 'IT_Arch', 'Skills')
hdf = data.frame(matrix(nrow = 0, ncol = length(clmn)))
csv_ime = "CA_Luftman.csv"
if (file.exists(csv_ime)) {
 print("File exists")
 hdf <- read.csv(csv_ime)
 } else {
for (ifaktor in 1:length(gain_f)) { ## 5 variants
for (ifrcst in 1:ncol(frcst_fit)) {     ## 3 variants
for (inotr in 1:3) {                    ## 3 variants
 for (t in 2:tmax) {              ## t
  for(i in 1:n_matrix) {             ## 68 companies
   for (j in 1:n_algn) {           ## 6 alignments
    interni <-  mean(result[1:t,j,n_matrix])
    if (inotr == 1) {interni <-  mean(result[1:t,j,1:n_matrix])}
    if (inotr == 2) {interni <-  mean(result[t-1,1:n_algn,i])}
    if (inotr == 3) {interni <-  var(result[t-1,1:n_algn,i])}
    eksterni <- frcst_fit[t,ifrcst]
    sprememba <- gain_f[ifaktor]*(interni-eksterni)
    novo_stanje <- result[(t-1),j,i] + sprememba
    if (novo_stanje < 0) { novo_stanje <- 0}
    if (novo_stanje > 1) { novo_stanje <- 1}
    result[t,j,i] <- novo_stanje
   }
   vrstica <- c(ifaktor, ifrcst, inotr, i, t,
                result[t,1,i],
                result[t,2,i],
                result[t,3,i],
                result[t,4,i],
                result[t,5,i],
                result[t,6,i])
   hdf[nrow(hdf) + 1,] <- vrstica
  }
 }
}}
 print(paste("factor completed", ifaktor, Sys.time()))
}
 colnames(hdf) <- clmn
 write.csv(hdf, file = csv_ime,
        quote = FALSE, row.names = FALSE)
}
```

### *4.1.9 Presentation of all companies under same conditions (gain, int, ext)*

This section presents the outcomes of CA for each company under same conditions.

```
pgn <- 1
pex <- 2
pin <- 2
for(i in 1:n_matrix) {
  sqlcom1 <- paste("select gain, external, internal,",
  "company, time, Comms, Measur, IT_Mgt, Partn, IT_Arch,",
  "Skills from hdf where gain=", pgn, " and external = ", pex,
  " and internal = ", pin, " and company = ", i, " and time = 2")
  r <- sqldf(sqlcom1)
  gttlgf <- r[1,1]
  gttlex <- r[1,2]
  gttlin <- r[1,3]
  gttl <- paste("Company: ", i,
            "/ GF: ", gain_f[gttlgf],
            " /Ext.: ", external[gttlex],
            "  Int.: ", internal[gttlin])
  sqlcom2 <- paste("select Comms, Measur, IT_Mgt, Partn, IT_Arch,",
  "Skills  from hdf where gain=", pgn, " and external = ", pex,
  " and internal = ", pin, " and company = ", i, " order by time")
  r <- sqldf(sqlcom2)
  ccell <- as.matrix(r)
  class(ccell)
  par(mar=c(5.1, 4.1, 4.1, 4.1))
  plot(ccell, border=NA, breaks=6, main=gttl,
     las=3, col=topo.colors,
   key=list(side=4,  font=2, cex.axis=0.75), fmt.key="%.2f",
   polygon.key=NULL, axis.key=NULL, spacing.key=c(3,2,2),
   xlab="alignment", ylab="time",
   digits=4, text.cell=list(cex=0.5))
}
```

Sample plots are presented on Figures 3, 4 and 5.

*Figure 3: Alignment areas for company 4 under given conditions.*

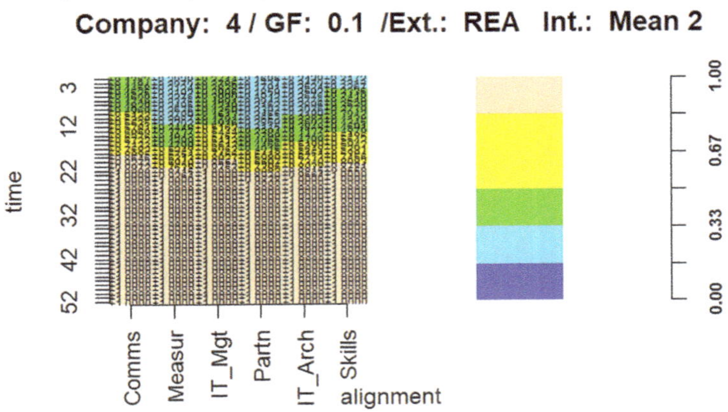


*Figure 4: Alignment areas for company 43 under given conditions.*

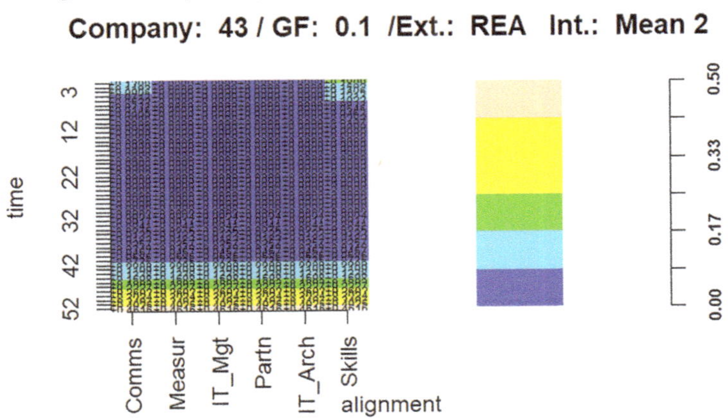

*Figure 5: Alignment areas for company 68 under given conditions.*

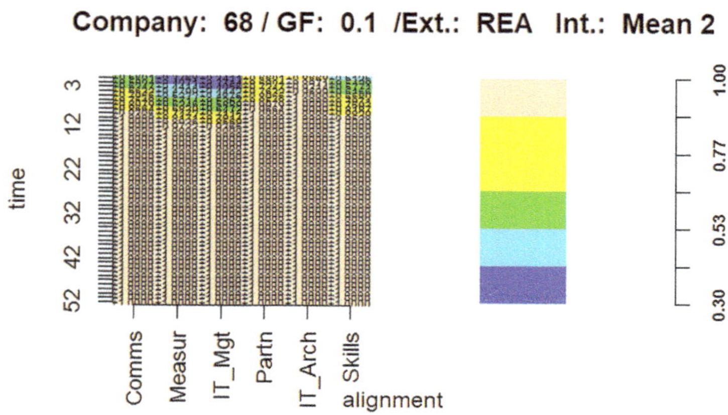


### 4.1.10 *Presentation of selected company under all combination of conditions (gain, int, ext)*

This section presents the outcomes of selected company under all combination of conditions (gain, int, ext).

```
pcomp <- 1
for (ifaktor in 1:length(gain_f)) { ## 5 variants
for (ifrcst in 1:ncol(frcst_fit)) {     ## 3 variants
for (inotr in 1:3) {                    ## 3 variants
  gttlgf <- ifaktor
  gttlex <- ifrcst
  gttlin <- inotr
  gttl <- paste("Company: ", i,
           "/ GF: ", gain_f[gttlgf],
           " /Ext.: ", external[gttlex],
           "  Int.: ", internal[gttlin])
  sqlcom2 <- paste("select Comms, Measur, IT_Mgt, Partn, IT_Arch,",
  "Skills  from hdf where gain=", gttlgf, " and external = ", gttlex,
  " and internal = ", gttlin, " and company = ", pcomp, " order by time")
  r <- sqldf(sqlcom2)
  ccell <- as.matrix(r)
  class(ccell)
  par(mar=c(5.1, 4.1, 4.1, 4.1))
  plot(ccell, border=NA, breaks=6, main=gttl,
     las=3, col=topo.colors,
```

```
  key=list(side=4,  font=2, cex.axis=0.75), fmt.key="%.2f",
  polygon.key=NULL, axis.key=NULL, spacing.key=c(3,2,2),
  xlab="alignment", ylab="time",
  digits=4, text.cell=list(cex=0.5))
}}}
```

Sample plots are presented on Figures 6, 7 and 8.

*Figure 6: Alignment areas for company 6 under given conditions.*

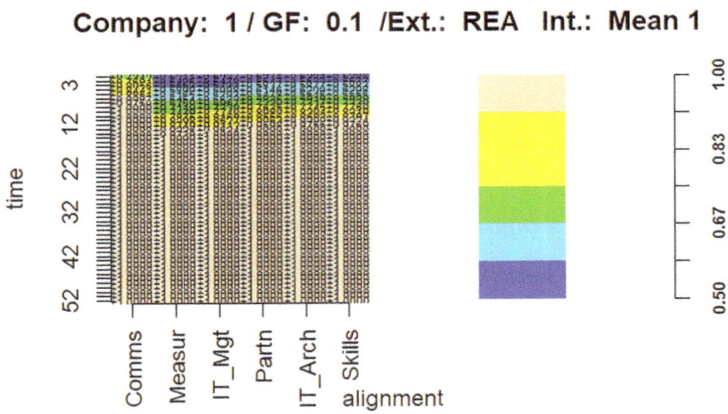


*Figure 7: Alignment areas for company 1 under given conditions.*

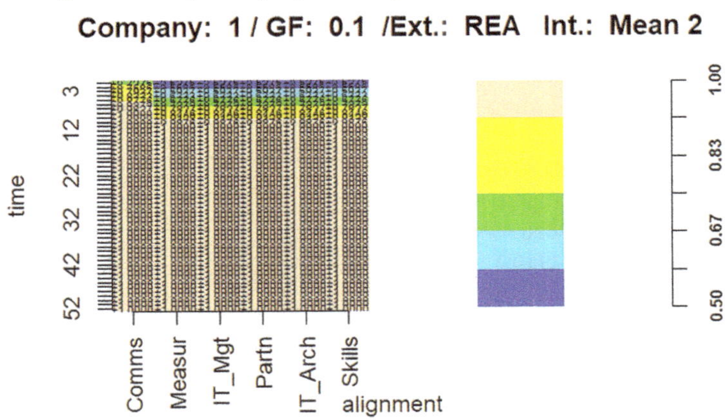

*Figure 8: Alignment areas for company 1 under given conditions.*

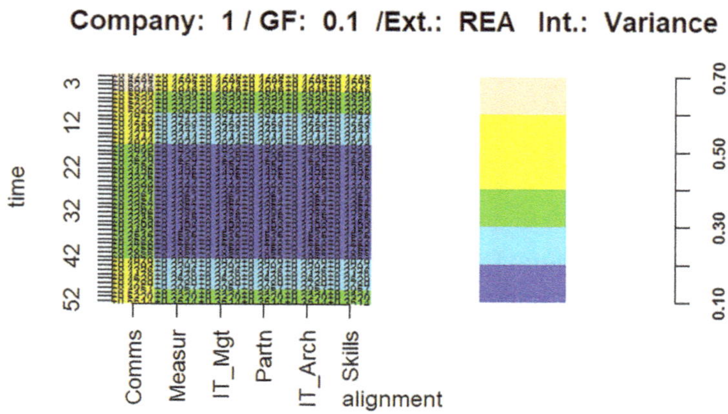


## 4.2 Experiment 2: design of CA, based on rules

### *4.2.1 Conversion of continuous values into discrete states of CA*

Function CA_stateC2D requires two arguments: continuous value and criteria of conversion. Criteria of conversion is specified as integers with distinct meaning: Kmax=1, Kmid=2 and Kmin=3. The code converts extreme values to allowed lower and upper values.

```
CA_stateC2D <- function (inp,criteria)
{
if(criteria < 1 & criteria > 3) {criteria <- 1}
if (inp > 1) {inp <- 1}
if (inp < 0) {inp <- 0}

# maximalistic criteria
if (criteria == 1) {
 if (inp == 1)              {rval <- 5}
 if (inp >= 0.8 & inp < 1.0) {rval <- 4}
 if (inp >= 0.6 & inp < 0.8) {rval <- 3}
 if (inp >= 0.4 & inp < 0.6) {rval <- 2}
 if (inp >= 0.2 & inp < 0.4) {rval <- 1}
 if (inp < 0.2)             {rval <- 0}
}
```

```
# logistic function derived criteria
if (criteria == 2) {
  if (inp >= 0.84 & inp <= 1.0) {rval <- 5}
  if (inp >= 0.68 & inp < 0.84) {rval <- 4}
  if (inp >= 0.52 & inp < 0.68) {rval <- 3}
  if (inp >= 0.36 & inp < 0.52) {rval <- 2}
  if (inp >= 0.2 & inp < 0.36)  {rval <- 1}
  if (inp < 0.2)                {rval <- 0}
}
# minimalistic criteria
if (criteria == 3) {}
  if (inp >= 0.80 & inp <= 1.0) {rval <- 5}
  if (inp >= 0.60 & inp < 0.80) {rval <- 4}
  if (inp >= 0.40 & inp < 0.60) {rval <- 3}
  if (inp >= 0.20 & inp < 0.40) {rval <- 2}
  if (inp >= 0.10 & inp < 0.20) {rval <- 1}
  if (inp < 0.10)               {rval <- 0}
  return(rval)
}
```

### *4.2.2 Implementation of CA based on finite set of rules and offset, caused by random noise*

Let us create a Cartesian product of input states (inpstate), output states (outstate) and current states (cutstate), each with a cardinality of 6 (0,1,2,3,4,5). The resulting set has a cardinality of 216, which is the number of triples. However, each rule is described by four values. In R, the rules are implemented as a matrix with 216 rows and four columns: $left_{state}$, $right_{state}$, $current_{state}$ and $new_{state}$. To speed up the evaluation of these rules, we can select the $new_{state}$ by addressing the nth row and the fourth column. The row index is computed:

$$row_{index} = left_{state} + 6{*}right_{state} + 36{*}current_{state}$$

and

$$new_{state} = cprod[row_{index}, 4]$$

### *4.2.3 Experimental set of 216 rules*

The sample set always assigns the new state as the current state, with 17 exceptions. The following code implements this description.

```
inpstate <- c(0,1,2,3,4,5)
prep216  <- expand.grid(inpstate, inpstate,inpstate)
# bind fourth column with values equal to third column
# columns represent Left, Right and Current value
# fourth column present New state
cprod <-cbind(prep216,prep216[1:nrow(prep216),3])
colnames(cprod)    <- c('L','R','C','N')
# Exceptions to N <- C:
cprod[1,4]   <- 1 # If the C== 0 and LR == 0, N <- 1
cprod[37,4]  <- 2 # If the C== 1 and LR == 0, N <- 2
cprod[44,4]  <- 3 # If the C== 1 and LR == 1, N <- 3
cprod[51,4]  <- 4 # If the C== 1 and LR == 2, N <- 4
cprod[80,4]  <- 4 # If the C== 2 and LR == 1, N <- 4
cprod[87,4]  <- 5 # If the C== 2 and LR == 2, N <- 5
cprod[109,4] <- 1 # If the C== 3 and LR == 0, N <- 1
cprod[116,4] <- 2 # If the C== 3 and LR == 1, N <- 2
cprod[123,4] <- 4 # If the C== 3 and LR == 2, N <- 4
cprod[130,4] <- 5 # If the C== 3 and LR == 3, N <- 5
cprod[152,4] <- 5 # If the C== 4 and LR == 1, N <- 5
cprod[159,4] <- 5 # If the C== 4 and LR == 2, N <- 5
cprod[181,4] <- 1 # If the C== 5 and LR == 0, N <- 1
cprod[188,4] <- 2 # If the C== 5 and LR == 1, N <- 2
cprod[195,4] <- 4 # If the C== 5 and LR == 2, N <- 4
cprod[202,4] <- 5 # If the C== 5 and LR == 3, N <- 5
cprod[216,4] <- 4 # If the C== 5 and LR == 4, N <- 4
```

Resulting matrix is presented in the Table 2.

### 4.2.4 *The code before executing experimental set of rules on CA*

The next portion of the code:

- creates matrix *b*,
- sets initial states in 3D matrix resultd by conversion of continuous values to CA domain (0, 1, 2, 3, 4, 5)
- sets some constants (simulation time, number of alignment areas, number of companies, number of cells in 3D matrix),
- defines function *CA_CurrRule* which returns index of the row in rules matrix
- defines function *CA_6to8* which expands alignment vector with left and right neighbour to 1st and 6th value of alignment
- defines two vectors of strings for Slovene and English alignment areas.

*Table 2: Experimental set of 216 rules*

| rule# | L | R | C | N | rule# | L | R | C | N | rule# | L | R | C | N | rule# | L | R | C | N | rule# | L | R | C | N | rule# | L | R | C | N |
|---|---|---|---|---|---|---|---|---|---|---|---|---|---|---|---|---|---|---|---|---|---|---|---|---|---|---|---|---|---|
| 1 | 0 | 0 | 0 | 1 | 37 | 0 | 0 | 1 | 2 | 73 | 0 | 0 | 2 | 2 | 109 | 0 | 0 | 3 | 1 | 145 | 0 | 0 | 4 | 4 | 181 | 0 | 0 | 5 | 1 |
| 2 | 1 | 0 | 0 | 0 | 38 | 1 | 0 | 1 | 1 | 74 | 1 | 0 | 2 | 2 | 110 | 1 | 0 | 3 | 3 | 146 | 1 | 0 | 4 | 4 | 182 | 1 | 0 | 5 | 5 |
| 3 | 2 | 0 | 0 | 0 | 39 | 2 | 0 | 1 | 1 | 75 | 2 | 0 | 2 | 2 | 111 | 2 | 0 | 3 | 3 | 147 | 2 | 0 | 4 | 4 | 183 | 2 | 0 | 5 | 5 |
| 4 | 3 | 0 | 0 | 0 | 40 | 3 | 0 | 1 | 1 | 76 | 3 | 0 | 2 | 2 | 112 | 3 | 0 | 3 | 3 | 148 | 3 | 0 | 4 | 4 | 184 | 3 | 0 | 5 | 5 |
| 5 | 4 | 0 | 0 | 0 | 41 | 4 | 0 | 1 | 1 | 77 | 4 | 0 | 2 | 2 | 113 | 4 | 0 | 3 | 3 | 149 | 4 | 0 | 4 | 4 | 185 | 4 | 0 | 5 | 5 |
| 6 | 5 | 0 | 0 | 0 | 42 | 5 | 0 | 1 | 1 | 78 | 5 | 0 | 2 | 2 | 114 | 5 | 0 | 3 | 3 | 150 | 5 | 0 | 4 | 4 | 186 | 5 | 0 | 5 | 5 |
| 7 | 0 | 1 | 0 | 0 | 43 | 0 | 1 | 1 | 1 | 79 | 0 | 1 | 2 | 2 | 115 | 0 | 1 | 3 | 3 | 151 | 0 | 1 | 4 | 4 | 187 | 0 | 1 | 5 | 5 |
| 8 | 1 | 1 | 0 | 0 | 44 | 1 | 1 | 1 | 3 | 80 | 1 | 1 | 2 | 4 | 116 | 1 | 1 | 3 | 2 | 152 | 1 | 1 | 4 | 5 | 188 | 1 | 1 | 5 | 2 |
| 9 | 2 | 1 | 0 | 0 | 45 | 2 | 1 | 1 | 1 | 81 | 2 | 1 | 2 | 2 | 117 | 2 | 1 | 3 | 3 | 153 | 2 | 1 | 4 | 4 | 189 | 2 | 1 | 5 | 5 |
| 10 | 3 | 1 | 0 | 0 | 46 | 3 | 1 | 1 | 1 | 82 | 3 | 1 | 2 | 2 | 118 | 3 | 1 | 3 | 3 | 154 | 3 | 1 | 4 | 4 | 190 | 3 | 1 | 5 | 5 |
| 11 | 4 | 1 | 0 | 0 | 47 | 4 | 1 | 1 | 1 | 83 | 4 | 1 | 2 | 2 | 119 | 4 | 1 | 3 | 3 | 155 | 4 | 1 | 4 | 4 | 191 | 4 | 1 | 5 | 5 |
| 12 | 5 | 1 | 0 | 0 | 48 | 5 | 1 | 1 | 1 | 84 | 5 | 1 | 2 | 2 | 120 | 5 | 1 | 3 | 3 | 156 | 5 | 1 | 4 | 4 | 192 | 5 | 1 | 5 | 5 |
| 13 | 0 | 2 | 0 | 0 | 49 | 0 | 2 | 1 | 1 | 85 | 0 | 2 | 2 | 2 | 121 | 0 | 2 | 3 | 3 | 157 | 0 | 2 | 4 | 4 | 193 | 0 | 2 | 5 | 5 |
| 14 | 1 | 2 | 0 | 0 | 50 | 1 | 2 | 1 | 1 | 86 | 1 | 2 | 2 | 2 | 122 | 1 | 2 | 3 | 3 | 158 | 1 | 2 | 4 | 4 | 194 | 1 | 2 | 5 | 5 |
| 15 | 2 | 2 | 0 | 0 | 51 | 2 | 2 | 1 | 4 | 87 | 2 | 2 | 2 | 5 | 123 | 2 | 2 | 3 | 4 | 159 | 2 | 2 | 4 | 5 | 195 | 2 | 2 | 5 | 4 |
| 16 | 3 | 2 | 0 | 0 | 52 | 3 | 2 | 1 | 1 | 88 | 3 | 2 | 2 | 2 | 124 | 3 | 2 | 3 | 3 | 160 | 3 | 2 | 4 | 4 | 196 | 3 | 2 | 5 | 5 |
| 17 | 4 | 2 | 0 | 0 | 53 | 4 | 2 | 1 | 1 | 89 | 4 | 2 | 2 | 2 | 125 | 4 | 2 | 3 | 3 | 161 | 4 | 2 | 4 | 4 | 197 | 4 | 2 | 5 | 5 |
| 18 | 5 | 2 | 0 | 0 | 54 | 5 | 2 | 1 | 1 | 90 | 5 | 2 | 2 | 2 | 126 | 5 | 2 | 3 | 3 | 162 | 5 | 2 | 4 | 4 | 198 | 5 | 2 | 5 | 5 |
| 19 | 0 | 3 | 0 | 0 | 55 | 0 | 3 | 1 | 1 | 91 | 0 | 3 | 2 | 2 | 127 | 0 | 3 | 3 | 3 | 163 | 0 | 3 | 4 | 4 | 199 | 0 | 3 | 5 | 5 |
| 20 | 1 | 3 | 0 | 0 | 56 | 1 | 3 | 1 | 1 | 92 | 1 | 3 | 2 | 2 | 128 | 1 | 3 | 3 | 3 | 164 | 1 | 3 | 4 | 4 | 200 | 1 | 3 | 5 | 5 |
| 21 | 2 | 3 | 0 | 0 | 57 | 2 | 3 | 1 | 1 | 93 | 2 | 3 | 2 | 2 | 129 | 2 | 3 | 3 | 3 | 165 | 2 | 3 | 4 | 4 | 201 | 2 | 3 | 5 | 5 |
| 22 | 3 | 3 | 0 | 0 | 58 | 3 | 3 | 1 | 1 | 94 | 3 | 3 | 2 | 2 | 130 | 3 | 3 | 3 | 5 | 166 | 3 | 3 | 4 | 4 | 202 | 3 | 3 | 5 | 5 |
| 23 | 4 | 3 | 0 | 0 | 59 | 4 | 3 | 1 | 1 | 95 | 4 | 3 | 2 | 2 | 131 | 4 | 3 | 3 | 3 | 167 | 4 | 3 | 4 | 4 | 203 | 4 | 3 | 5 | 5 |
| 24 | 5 | 3 | 0 | 0 | 60 | 5 | 3 | 1 | 1 | 96 | 5 | 3 | 2 | 2 | 132 | 5 | 3 | 3 | 3 | 168 | 5 | 3 | 4 | 4 | 204 | 5 | 3 | 5 | 5 |
| 25 | 0 | 4 | 0 | 0 | 61 | 0 | 4 | 1 | 1 | 97 | 0 | 4 | 2 | 2 | 133 | 0 | 4 | 3 | 3 | 169 | 0 | 4 | 4 | 4 | 205 | 0 | 4 | 5 | 5 |
| 26 | 1 | 4 | 0 | 0 | 62 | 1 | 4 | 1 | 1 | 98 | 1 | 4 | 2 | 2 | 134 | 1 | 4 | 3 | 3 | 170 | 1 | 4 | 4 | 4 | 206 | 1 | 4 | 5 | 5 |
| 27 | 2 | 4 | 0 | 0 | 63 | 2 | 4 | 1 | 1 | 99 | 2 | 4 | 2 | 2 | 135 | 2 | 4 | 3 | 3 | 171 | 2 | 4 | 4 | 4 | 207 | 2 | 4 | 5 | 5 |
| 28 | 3 | 4 | 0 | 0 | 64 | 3 | 4 | 1 | 1 | 100 | 3 | 4 | 2 | 2 | 136 | 3 | 4 | 3 | 3 | 172 | 3 | 4 | 4 | 4 | 208 | 3 | 4 | 5 | 5 |
| 29 | 4 | 4 | 0 | 0 | 65 | 4 | 4 | 1 | 1 | 101 | 4 | 4 | 2 | 2 | 137 | 4 | 4 | 3 | 3 | 173 | 4 | 4 | 4 | 4 | 209 | 4 | 4 | 5 | 5 |
| 30 | 5 | 4 | 0 | 0 | 66 | 5 | 4 | 1 | 1 | 102 | 5 | 4 | 2 | 2 | 138 | 5 | 4 | 3 | 3 | 174 | 5 | 4 | 4 | 4 | 210 | 5 | 4 | 5 | 5 |
| 31 | 0 | 5 | 0 | 0 | 67 | 0 | 5 | 1 | 1 | 103 | 0 | 5 | 2 | 2 | 139 | 0 | 5 | 3 | 3 | 175 | 0 | 5 | 4 | 4 | 211 | 0 | 5 | 5 | 5 |
| 32 | 1 | 5 | 0 | 0 | 68 | 1 | 5 | 1 | 1 | 104 | 1 | 5 | 2 | 2 | 140 | 1 | 5 | 3 | 3 | 176 | 1 | 5 | 4 | 4 | 212 | 1 | 5 | 5 | 5 |
| 33 | 2 | 5 | 0 | 0 | 69 | 2 | 5 | 1 | 1 | 105 | 2 | 5 | 2 | 2 | 141 | 2 | 5 | 3 | 3 | 177 | 2 | 5 | 4 | 4 | 213 | 2 | 5 | 5 | 5 |
| 34 | 3 | 5 | 0 | 0 | 70 | 3 | 5 | 1 | 1 | 106 | 3 | 5 | 2 | 2 | 142 | 3 | 5 | 3 | 3 | 178 | 3 | 5 | 4 | 4 | 214 | 3 | 5 | 5 | 5 |
| 35 | 4 | 5 | 0 | 0 | 71 | 4 | 5 | 1 | 1 | 107 | 4 | 5 | 2 | 2 | 143 | 4 | 5 | 3 | 3 | 179 | 4 | 5 | 4 | 4 | 215 | 4 | 5 | 5 | 5 |
| 36 | 5 | 5 | 0 | 0 | 72 | 5 | 5 | 1 | 1 | 108 | 5 | 5 | 2 | 2 | 144 | 5 | 5 | 3 | 3 | 180 | 5 | 5 | 4 | 4 | 216 | 5 | 5 | 5 | 4 |

```
b <- as.matrix(initial_CA, nrow = 68, ncol= 7, byrow = TRUE)
tmax <- 60
n_algn <- 6
n_matrix <- nrow(initial_CA)
n_cells <- tmax*n_algn*n_matrix

# 3D matrix: (row=time step, column= n-th alignment, z=company)
resultd <- array(c(rep(0.0,n_cells)),
          dim=c(tmax,n_algn,n_matrix))
```

```
# initial values derived from questionnaire: row 1 in resultd
for(i in 1:n_matrix) {
 for (j in 1:n_algn) {
     resultd[1,j,i] <- CA_stateC2D(b[i,(j+1)],2)
 }
}

# function CA_CurrRule returns index of the row in rules matrix
CA_CurrRule <- function (rules,l,r,c) {
 i <- l+(6*r)+(36*c)
 return(rules[i,4])
}

# expands alignment vector with left and right neighbour
# to 1st and 6th value of alignment
CA_6to8 <- function (alignment) {
 expanded_alignment <- c(alignment[6],alignment,alignment[1])
 return(expanded_alignment)
}
alignment_si <- c('Komuniciranje', 'Merjenje', 'Upravljanje IT', 'Partnerstvo', 'Arhitektura IT', 'Veščine')
alignment_en <- c('Communication', 'Measuring', 'IT management', 'Partnership', 'IT Architecture', 'Skills')
```

### 4.2.5 *CA execution and ploting*

The following portion of code execute three embedded “for” loops:

- for all companies
- for all steps
- for all alignment areas

Random noise is implemented for a set of alignment areas in the same company at a given time. The first random generator for the normal distribution is activated. If the p-value is greater than the specified value, the uniform distribution of integers in the range from 0 to 3 is activated and its value is assigned to the new state. Otherwise, a new state is generated according to a predefined rule. The following example code activates random noise in 5% of the transitions and 95% of the transitions are defined by rules. Plot function generates matrix plots for all companies.

```
## z,p table: 2;0.95/2.326;0.99/3.09;0.999/4.753;0.999999/
for(i in 1:n_matrix) {          ## 68 companies n_matrix
 for (t in 2:tmax)  {           ## time step
```

```
alignment <- CA_6to8(resultd[t-1,1:6,i])
for (j in 1:6) {          ## 6 alignments
if (rnorm(1) < 2) {
  ruleindex <-  1 + alignment[j] + 6*alignment[j+2] + 36*alignment[j+1]
  resultd[t,j,i] <- cprod[ruleindex,4]}
else {resultd[t,j,i] <- floor(runif(1, min=0, max=3))}
  }
}
ccell <- matrix(resultd[1:tmax,1:n_algn,i], ncol=6) # num. mat.obj
colnames(ccell) <- c('Comm.', 'Measur', 'IT Mgt', 'Partn', 'IT Arch', 'Skills')
class(ccell)
par(mar=c(5.1, 4.1, 4.1, 4.1)) # adapt margins
plot(ccell, border=NA, digits=NA,
  breaks= c(0,1,2,3,4,5), main=paste("Company #", i),
  las=3, col=topo.colors,
  key=list(side=4,  font=1, cex.axis=0.75),
  polygon.key=NULL, axis.key=NULL, spacing.key=c(4,2,2),
  xlab='Alignment', ylab="korak",
  text.cell=list(cex=0.5))

}
```

Figures 9, 10 and 11 show the behavior of the alignment areas for three companies, which are controlled by experimental rules in 95% of the cases and by random noise in 5% of the cases.

*Figure 9: Alignment areas for company 1 under given experimental rules.*

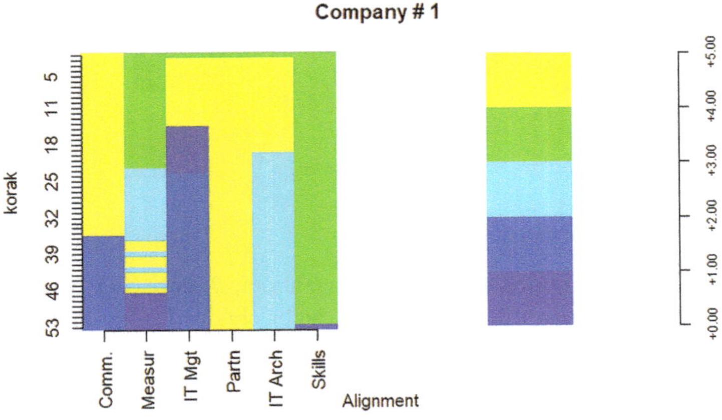

*Figure 10: Alignment areas for company 36 under given experimental rules.*

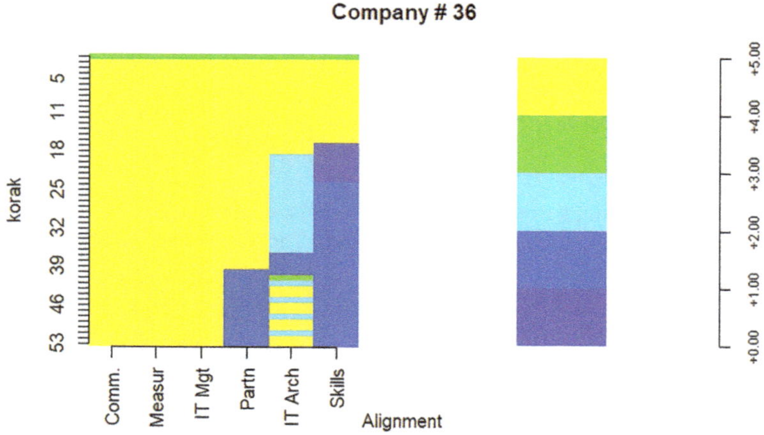


*Figure 11: Alignment areas for company 62 under given experimental rules.*

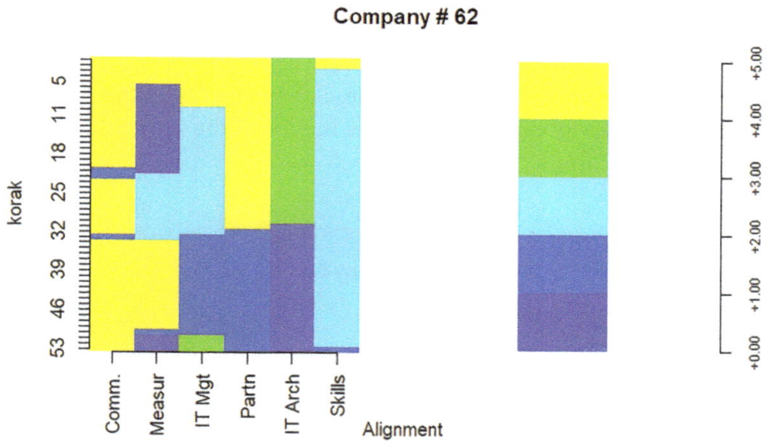


### *4.2.6 Neighbors to the central cell*

If we consider only one left and one right neighbour, we have (n-1)! pairs - in our case 120. Permutations of two neighbours can be obtained easily determined for each central cell (e.g. cell is 0).

```
atable <- permutations(n=5,r=2,v=c(1,2,3,4,5),repeats.allowed=F)
colnames(atable) <- c('Left','Right')
```

When defining more than two neighbours, the rules can be defined as the closures or non-closures. In closure configuration, the proximity to the central cell would not matter. We took no further experiments with the permutation of neighbours.

### *4.2.7 Generating random rules and applying to specific company*

In the following experiments, rules are generated randomly. The number of randomly generated by uniform distribution generator with the limits 1 to 216. The actual number of distinct rules is less than the number generated, as the index of the rule number can be generated multiple times.

The example code shows the result of applying randomly generated rules to company number 1. The matrix representation can show the new behaviour of the observed alignment areas of the specified company.

```
inpstate <- c(0,1,2,3,4,5)
prep216  <- expand.grid(inpstate, inpstate,inpstate)
# bind fourth column with values equal to third column
# columns represent Left, Right and Current value
# fourth column present New state
cprod <-cbind(prep216,prep216[1:nrow(prep216),3])
colnames(cprod)    <- c('L','R','C','N')
# set company
icomp = 1
# Generate exceptions to N <- C:
# number_of_rules to change is runif between 1 to 32
number_of_rules <- floor(runif(1, min=1, max=216))
for (i in 1:number_of_rules) {
 # modify random rule with random value
 rn <- floor(runif(1, min=1, max=216))
 rval <- floor(runif(1, min=0, max=5))
 cprod[rn,4] <- rval
 }

for (t in 2:tmax)  {                ## time step
    alig <- CA_6to8(resultd[t-1,1:n_algn,icomp])
    for (j in 1:n_algn) {            ## 6 alignments
     ridx <-  1 + alig[j] + 6*alig[j+2] + 36*alig[j+1]
     resultd[t,j,icomp] <- cprod[ridx,4]}
    }
```

Fig. 12 presents company 1 under set of experimental rules with addition to new random rules.

*Figure 12: Alignment areas for company 1 under given experimental and 144 random modified rules.*

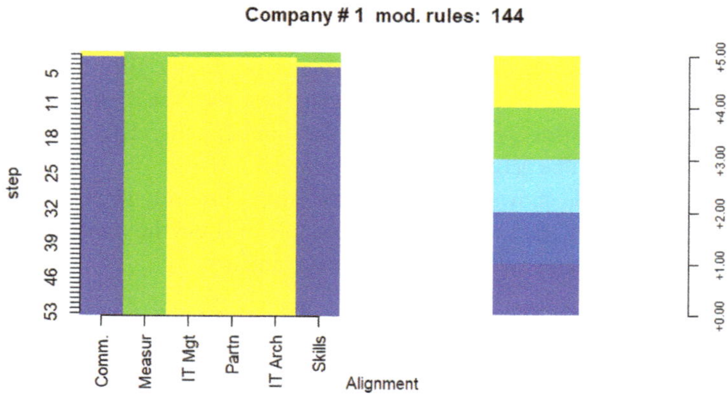


## *4.2.8 Search procedure for best fited CA rules under time constraints*

Estimation of real states of the alignments can be obtained by new questionaire. We anticipate that new estimation of alignments are presented as a 1D matrix:

$$E_t^j = (e_t^{(1,j)}, \ldots e_t^{(k-1,j)})$$

where $E$ is 1D matrix of alignment estimations in time $t$ for company $j$ where $k$ denotes the number of CA possible states.

Criteria for best fit set of CA rules is given by:

$$\min \sum_{m=1}^{k-1} (c_t^{(m,j)} - e_t^{(m,j)})^2$$

**Set step to real time equivalent**

Since time is discrete in CA, we have the difficult task of converting steps into time equivalents. Let us assume that 2 weeks is the shortest time slot for a CA change. If we process 53 steps, that would mean approximately two years. We received the first estimate of adjustments in June 2021 and the second was attempted in June 2023 for a limited number of companies (7). As we were unsuccessful with the interviews and questionnaires, the new states of alignments were simulated with random numbers. We set the target step for the two-year period at 53.

**Set random values for final states at n=53**

For testing purposes, let us re-estimate the random number in the range [0, 1, 2, 3, 4, 5] for all companies.

```
target_step <- 53
resulte <- array(c(rep(0.0,n_cells)),
            dim=c(tmax,n_algn,n_matrix))

for (i in 1 : nrow(a)) {
  for (j in 1 : 6) {
    resulte[target_step,j,i] <-  floor(runif(1, min=0, max=5))
  }
}
```

The set of all rules for 6 state cellular automata is $6*(6+6*6+6*6*6)=1296$ while the set of all possible paths to final state 53 is $1296^{53}=9.291056*10^{164}$. Large number, obviously. Now it is the time to test search procedure for the selected company.

```
# create estimated states instead of questionaire!
resulte <- array(c(rep(0.0,n_algn*n_matrix)), # 3D matrix (1x6x68)
            dim=c(1,n_algn,n_matrix))

for (i in 1 : n_matrix) {                # generate random resulte
  for (j in 1 : n_algn) {
    resulte[1,j,i] <-  floor(runif(1, min=0, max=5))
  }
}
# simulate random set of rules for max_secs for company icomp
icomp = 1
start_t <- Sys.time()
stop_t  <- start_t
max_secs <- 60
tmax <- 53
new_min <- 126
n_iter <- 0
while (as.numeric(difftime(stop_t,start_t,units="secs")) < max_secs) {
  # General rule: N=C, except for number_of_rules rules
```

```
  # number_of_changes in rules runif between 1 to nmodif
  # modify random nthrule rule with random nthval value
  cprod <-cbind(prep216,prep216[1:nrow(prep216),3])
  number_of_rules <- floor(runif(1, min=22, max=180))
  for (i in 1:number_of_rules) {
   nthrule <- floor(runif(1, min=1, max=216))
   nthval <- floor(runif(1,  min=0, max=5))
   cprod[nthrule,4] <- nthval
  }

  for (t in 2:tmax)  {              ## time step
   alig <- CA_6to8(resultd[t-1,1:n_algn,icomp])
   for (j in 1:n_algn) {            ## 6 alignments
    ridx <-  1 + alig[j] + 6*alig[j+2] + 36*alig[j+1]
    resultd[t,j,icomp] <- cprod[ridx,4]}
  }
  # compute criteria
  criteria <- sum((resultd[tmax,1:6,icomp]- resulte[1,1:6,icomp])^2)
          (sum((resultd[53,1:6,icomp]- resultd[54,1:6,icomp])^2))
  if ( criteria < new_min) {
   new_min <- criteria
   new_rules216 <- cprod
   new_mod_rules <- number_of_rules
   new_resultd <- resultd
  }

  n_iter <- n_iter + 1
  stop_t <- Sys.time()
}
print(difftime(stop_t,start_t,units="secs"))
print(paste('No. of attempts:', n_iter))
colnames(new_rules216)    <- c('L','R','C','N')
print(xtable(new_rules216, type="Latex",
    caption='Best rules'))

print(paste('The above set of rules generates sq.dif.:', new_min))
# let the 54th step present new estimation
# to visualy detect the difference
new_resultd[54,1:6,icomp] <- resulte[1,1:6,icomp]
print(sum((new_resultd[53,1:6,icomp]- resultd[54,1:6,icomp])^2))
```

```
atable <- as.data.frame(new_resultd[53:54,1:6,icomp])
colnames(atable) <- alignment_en
rownames(atable) <- c('CA derived','New estimation')
print(xtable(atable, type="Latex",
        caption='Comparison of states for final step'))
View(atable)
ccell <- matrix(new_resultd[1:54,1:n_algn,icomp], ncol=6) # num. mat.obj
colnames(ccell) <- c('Comm.', 'Measur', 'IT Mgt', 'Partn', 'IT Arch', 'Skills')
class(ccell)
par(mar=c(5.1, 4.1, 4.1, 4.1)) # adapt margins
plot(ccell, border=NA, digits=NA,
   breaks= c(0,1,2,3,4,5), main=paste("Company #", icomp,
                        " mod. rules: ",
                        new_mod_rules,
                        " sum sq.dif.:", new_min),
   las=3, col=topo.colors,
   key=list(side=4,  font=1, cex.axis=0.75),
   polygon.key=NULL, axis.key=NULL, spacing.key=c(4,2,2),
   xlab='Alignment', ylab="step",
   text.cell=list(cex=0.5))
```

Several runs of the above code were performed. In just 1 minute, about 12–14 thousand random rule sets were generated and tested for one company. The code ran on an Intel(R) Core(TM) i7-11800H @ 2.30GHz. The surprise was that the best sum of squared differences between the states generated by CA and the randomly generated "estimates" was consistently around 1. Basically, this means that the rule search procedure did an excellent job regardless of the type of estimate (real or randomly generated). Table 3 and Figure 13 show the case where 164 modified rules that were randomly generated match almost exactly with the "estimated" states in step 53, which themselves were also randomly generated. The small green spot with the IT management alignment in Figure 13 shows the difference between simulated and estimated states, which in this case is only one. But as I said, the search procedure has found an acceptable set of rules that lead CA to the estimated state. And if so, then the examined set of CA rules has a strong predictive value. Table 3 shows only the final step (53), while Fig. 13 shows the matrix plot for the first 53 steps and the added "estimated" states

*Table 3: States of alignment areas: CA derived vs. new estimatation in time 53*

| | Communication | Measuring | IT management | Partnership | IT Architecture | Skills |
|---|---|---|---|---|---|---|
| CA derived | 2 | 2 | 2 | 2 | 1 | 0 |
| New estimation | 2 | 2 | 3 | 2 | 1 | 0 |

*Figure 13: States of alignment areas: CA derived (53 steps) and new estimatation in time 53 in 60 seconds.*

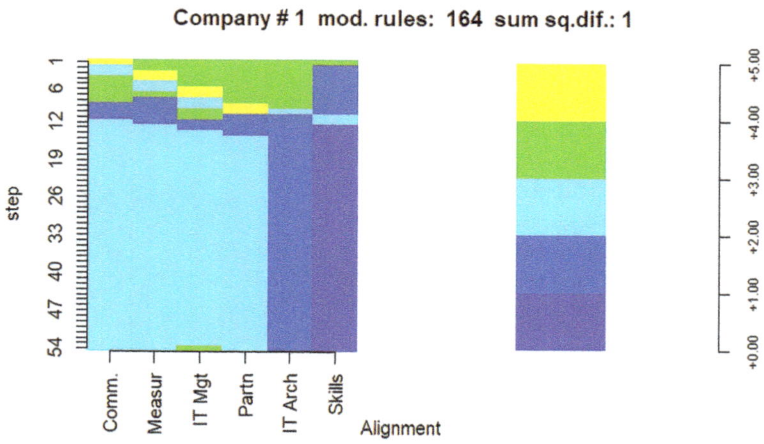


A detailed examination of the generated set of rules revealed that despite 164 attempts, only 57 of them were unique (see Table 4).

The presented search procedure could be considerably improved by the parallel execution of several sets of random rules, the prevention of the execution of already tested rule sets and the generation of only unique modifications of the rules.

Further experiments with extended execution time (from 60 to 300) were generally not much more accurate (see Table 5). However, the best generated rules were 96% -100% accurate in reproducing the estimated states in time 53.

*Table 4: Set of rules that generated 96% occurate target states*

| rule# | L | R | C | N | rule# | L | R | C | N | rule# | L | R | C | N | rule# | L | R | C | N | rule# | L | R | C | N | rule# | L | R | C | N |
|---|---|---|---|---|---|---|---|---|---|---|---|---|---|---|---|---|---|---|---|---|---|---|---|---|---|---|---|---|---|
| 1 | 0 | 0 | 0 | 0 | 37 | 0 | 0 | 1 | 2 | 73 | 0 | 0 | 2 | 2 | 109 | 0 | 0 | 3 | 3 | 145 | 0 | 0 | 4 | 2 | 181 | 0 | 0 | 5 | 5 |
| 2 | 1 | 0 | 0 | 3 | 38 | 1 | 0 | 1 | 1 | 74 | 1 | 0 | 2 | 2 | 110 | 1 | 0 | 3 | 2 | 146 | 1 | 0 | 4 | 0 | 182 | 1 | 0 | 5 | 5 |
| 3 | 2 | 0 | 0 | 0 | 39 | 2 | 0 | 1 | 3 | 75 | 2 | 0 | 2 | 2 | 111 | 2 | 0 | 3 | 3 | 147 | 2 | 0 | 4 | 4 | 183 | 2 | 0 | 5 | 5 |
| 4 | 3 | 0 | 0 | 0 | 40 | 3 | 0 | 1 | 1 | 76 | 3 | 0 | 2 | 2 | 112 | 3 | 0 | 3 | 3 | 148 | 3 | 0 | 4 | 4 | 184 | 3 | 0 | 5 | 5 |
| 5 | 4 | 0 | 0 | 0 | 41 | 4 | 0 | 1 | 1 | 77 | 4 | 0 | 2 | 3 | 113 | 4 | 0 | 3 | 3 | 149 | 4 | 0 | 4 | 4 | 185 | 4 | 0 | 5 | 5 |
| 6 | 5 | 0 | 0 | 0 | 42 | 5 | 0 | 1 | 1 | 78 | 5 | 0 | 2 | 2 | 114 | 5 | 0 | 3 | 3 | 150 | 5 | 0 | 4 | 4 | 186 | 5 | 0 | 5 | 5 |
| 7 | 0 | 1 | 0 | 0 | 43 | 0 | 1 | 1 | 1 | 79 | 0 | 1 | 2 | 2 | 115 | 0 | 1 | 3 | 1 | 151 | 0 | 1 | 4 | 2 | 187 | 0 | 1 | 5 | 5 |
| 8 | 1 | 1 | 0 | 3 | 44 | 1 | 1 | 1 | 2 | 80 | 1 | 1 | 2 | 4 | 116 | 1 | 1 | 3 | 1 | 152 | 1 | 1 | 4 | 3 | 188 | 1 | 1 | 5 | 2 |
| 9 | 2 | 1 | 0 | 0 | 45 | 2 | 1 | 1 | 1 | 81 | 2 | 1 | 2 | 2 | 117 | 2 | 1 | 3 | 2 | 153 | 2 | 1 | 4 | 4 | 189 | 2 | 1 | 5 | 3 |
| 10 | 3 | 1 | 0 | 0 | 46 | 3 | 1 | 1 | 1 | 82 | 3 | 1 | 2 | 2 | 118 | 3 | 1 | 3 | 3 | 154 | 3 | 1 | 4 | 4 | 190 | 3 | 1 | 5 | 5 |
| 11 | 4 | 1 | 0 | 0 | 47 | 4 | 1 | 1 | 1 | 83 | 4 | 1 | 2 | 2 | 119 | 4 | 1 | 3 | 4 | 155 | 4 | 1 | 4 | 4 | 191 | 4 | 1 | 5 | 5 |
| 12 | 5 | 1 | 0 | 0 | 48 | 5 | 1 | 1 | 1 | 84 | 5 | 1 | 2 | 2 | 120 | 5 | 1 | 3 | 3 | 156 | 5 | 1 | 4 | 4 | 192 | 5 | 1 | 5 | 1 |
| 13 | 0 | 2 | 0 | 0 | 49 | 0 | 2 | 1 | 1 | 85 | 0 | 2 | 2 | 2 | 121 | 0 | 2 | 3 | 3 | 157 | 0 | 2 | 4 | 0 | 193 | 0 | 2 | 5 | 4 |
| 14 | 1 | 2 | 0 | 0 | 50 | 1 | 2 | 1 | 1 | 86 | 1 | 2 | 2 | 2 | 122 | 1 | 2 | 3 | 3 | 158 | 1 | 2 | 4 | 4 | 194 | 1 | 2 | 5 | 5 |
| 15 | 2 | 2 | 0 | 0 | 51 | 2 | 2 | 1 | 1 | 87 | 2 | 2 | 2 | 4 | 123 | 2 | 2 | 3 | 3 | 159 | 2 | 2 | 4 | 4 | 195 | 2 | 2 | 5 | 5 |
| 16 | 3 | 2 | 0 | 0 | 52 | 3 | 2 | 1 | 2 | 88 | 3 | 2 | 2 | 2 | 124 | 3 | 2 | 3 | 3 | 160 | 3 | 2 | 4 | 3 | 196 | 3 | 2 | 5 | 5 |
| 17 | 4 | 2 | 0 | 0 | 53 | 4 | 2 | 1 | 4 | 89 | 4 | 2 | 2 | 2 | 125 | 4 | 2 | 3 | 1 | 161 | 4 | 2 | 4 | 4 | 197 | 4 | 2 | 5 | 5 |
| 18 | 5 | 2 | 0 | 0 | 54 | 5 | 2 | 1 | 1 | 90 | 5 | 2 | 2 | 2 | 126 | 5 | 2 | 3 | 2 | 162 | 5 | 2 | 4 | 1 | 198 | 5 | 2 | 5 | 5 |
| 19 | 0 | 3 | 0 | 0 | 55 | 0 | 3 | 1 | 1 | 91 | 0 | 3 | 2 | 2 | 127 | 0 | 3 | 3 | 3 | 163 | 0 | 3 | 4 | 2 | 199 | 0 | 3 | 5 | 4 |
| 20 | 1 | 3 | 0 | 0 | 56 | 1 | 3 | 1 | 1 | 92 | 1 | 3 | 2 | 2 | 128 | 1 | 3 | 3 | 3 | 164 | 1 | 3 | 4 | 1 | 200 | 1 | 3 | 5 | 5 |
| 21 | 2 | 3 | 0 | 0 | 57 | 2 | 3 | 1 | 1 | 93 | 2 | 3 | 2 | 2 | 129 | 2 | 3 | 3 | 3 | 165 | 2 | 3 | 4 | 1 | 201 | 2 | 3 | 5 | 2 |
| 22 | 3 | 3 | 0 | 4 | 58 | 3 | 3 | 1 | 1 | 94 | 3 | 3 | 2 | 2 | 130 | 3 | 3 | 3 | 3 | 166 | 3 | 3 | 4 | 4 | 202 | 3 | 3 | 5 | 5 |
| 23 | 4 | 3 | 0 | 0 | 59 | 4 | 3 | 1 | 1 | 95 | 4 | 3 | 2 | 2 | 131 | 4 | 3 | 3 | 3 | 167 | 4 | 3 | 4 | 4 | 203 | 4 | 3 | 5 | 4 |
| 24 | 5 | 3 | 0 | 0 | 60 | 5 | 3 | 1 | 1 | 96 | 5 | 3 | 2 | 2 | 132 | 5 | 3 | 3 | 3 | 168 | 5 | 3 | 4 | 4 | 204 | 5 | 3 | 5 | 3 |
| 25 | 0 | 4 | 0 | 0 | 61 | 0 | 4 | 1 | 1 | 97 | 0 | 4 | 2 | 2 | 133 | 0 | 4 | 3 | 4 | 169 | 0 | 4 | 4 | 4 | 205 | 0 | 4 | 5 | 5 |
| 26 | 1 | 4 | 0 | 0 | 62 | 1 | 4 | 1 | 0 | 98 | 1 | 4 | 2 | 2 | 134 | 1 | 4 | 3 | 3 | 170 | 1 | 4 | 4 | 1 | 206 | 1 | 4 | 5 | 5 |
| 27 | 2 | 4 | 0 | 0 | 63 | 2 | 4 | 1 | 1 | 99 | 2 | 4 | 2 | 2 | 135 | 2 | 4 | 3 | 4 | 171 | 2 | 4 | 4 | 4 | 207 | 2 | 4 | 5 | 2 |
| 28 | 3 | 4 | 0 | 0 | 64 | 3 | 4 | 1 | 1 | 100 | 3 | 4 | 2 | 2 | 136 | 3 | 4 | 3 | 3 | 172 | 3 | 4 | 4 | 4 | 208 | 3 | 4 | 5 | 0 |
| 29 | 4 | 4 | 0 | 0 | 65 | 4 | 4 | 1 | 1 | 101 | 4 | 4 | 2 | 2 | 137 | 4 | 4 | 3 | 3 | 173 | 4 | 4 | 4 | 4 | 209 | 4 | 4 | 5 | 3 |
| 30 | 5 | 4 | 0 | 2 | 66 | 5 | 4 | 1 | 1 | 102 | 5 | 4 | 2 | 2 | 138 | 5 | 4 | 3 | 3 | 174 | 5 | 4 | 4 | 1 | 210 | 5 | 4 | 5 | 4 |
| 31 | 0 | 5 | 0 | 0 | 67 | 0 | 5 | 1 | 1 | 103 | 0 | 5 | 2 | 2 | 139 | 0 | 5 | 3 | 3 | 175 | 0 | 5 | 4 | 2 | 211 | 0 | 5 | 5 | 2 |
| 32 | 1 | 5 | 0 | 4 | 68 | 1 | 5 | 1 | 1 | 104 | 1 | 5 | 2 | 2 | 140 | 1 | 5 | 3 | 3 | 176 | 1 | 5 | 4 | 2 | 212 | 1 | 5 | 5 | 5 |
| 33 | 2 | 5 | 0 | 0 | 69 | 2 | 5 | 1 | 4 | 105 | 2 | 5 | 2 | 2 | 141 | 2 | 5 | 3 | 4 | 177 | 2 | 5 | 4 | 4 | 213 | 2 | 5 | 5 | 5 |
| 34 | 3 | 5 | 0 | 1 | 70 | 3 | 5 | 1 | 1 | 106 | 3 | 5 | 2 | 2 | 142 | 3 | 5 | 3 | 3 | 178 | 3 | 5 | 4 | 4 | 214 | 3 | 5 | 5 | 5 |
| 35 | 4 | 5 | 0 | 0 | 71 | 4 | 5 | 1 | 2 | 107 | 4 | 5 | 2 | 2 | 143 | 4 | 5 | 3 | 2 | 179 | 4 | 5 | 4 | 0 | 215 | 4 | 5 | 5 | 5 |
| 36 | 5 | 5 | 0 | 0 | 72 | 5 | 5 | 1 | 1 | 108 | 5 | 5 | 2 | 2 | 144 | 5 | 5 | 3 | 1 | 180 | 5 | 5 | 4 | 4 | 216 | 5 | 5 | 5 | 5 |

*Table 5: Run for 300 seconds*

| | Communication | Measuring | IT management | Partnership | IT Architecture | Skills |
|---|---|---|---|---|---|---|
| CA derived | 1 | 1 | 3 | 4 | 0 | 1 |
| New estimation | 1 | 2 | 3 | 4 | 0 | 1 |

*Figure 14: States of alignment areas: CA derived (53 steps) and new estimatation in time 53 in 300 seconds.*

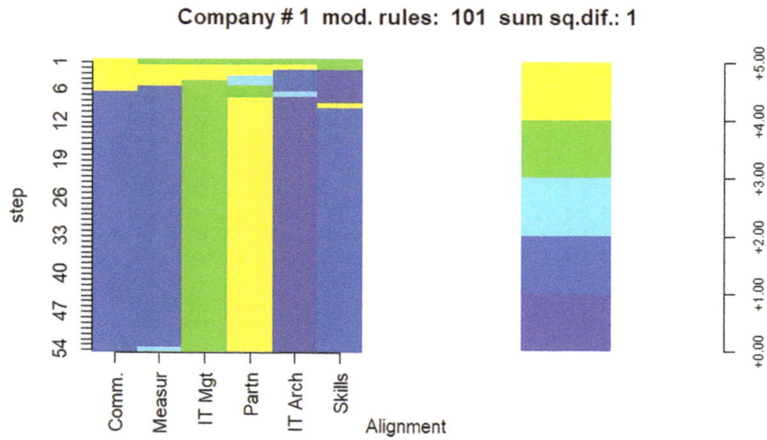


Figure 15 shows an example of perfect match of CA generated states with the "estimated" for time 53 and Table 6 present the rules applied to CA for company 68.

*Figure 15: An example of perfect match of CA generated states with the "estimated" for time 53.*

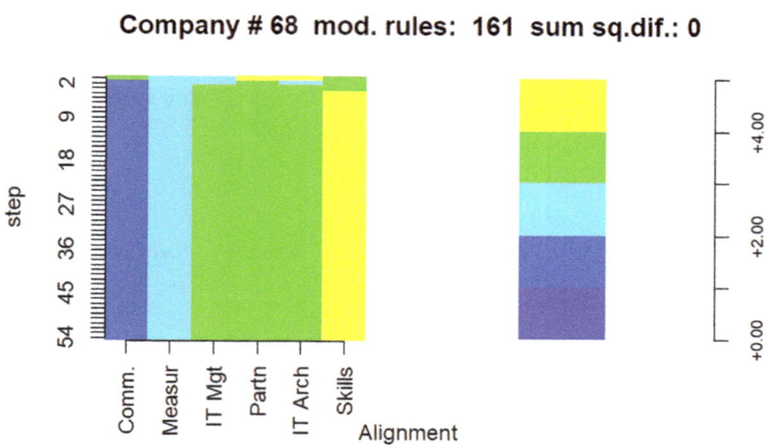

*Table 6: Rules for company 68 with perfect match of CA generated states with the "estimated" for time 53*

| rule# | L | R | C | N | rule# | L | R | C | N | rule# | L | R | C | N | rule# | L | R | C | N | rule# | L | R | C | N | rule# | L | R | C | N |
|---|---|---|---|---|---|---|---|---|---|---|---|---|---|---|---|---|---|---|---|---|---|---|---|---|---|---|---|---|---|
| 1 | 0 | 0 | 0 | 4 | 37 | 0 | 0 | 1 | 1 | 73 | 0 | 0 | 2 | 0 | 109 | 0 | 0 | 3 | 0 | 145 | 0 | 0 | 4 | 4 | 181 | 0 | 0 | 5 | 3 |
| 2 | 1 | 0 | 0 | 0 | 38 | 1 | 0 | 1 | 1 | 74 | 1 | 0 | 2 | 3 | 110 | 1 | 0 | 3 | 4 | 146 | 1 | 0 | 4 | 4 | 182 | 1 | 0 | 5 | 5 |
| 3 | 2 | 0 | 0 | 0 | 39 | 2 | 0 | 1 | 3 | 75 | 2 | 0 | 2 | 3 | 111 | 2 | 0 | 3 | 3 | 147 | 2 | 0 | 4 | 2 | 183 | 2 | 0 | 5 | 3 |
| 4 | 3 | 0 | 0 | 0 | 40 | 3 | 0 | 1 | 4 | 76 | 3 | 0 | 2 | 3 | 112 | 3 | 0 | 3 | 1 | 148 | 3 | 0 | 4 | 4 | 184 | 3 | 0 | 5 | 3 |
| 5 | 4 | 0 | 0 | 0 | 41 | 4 | 0 | 1 | 1 | 77 | 4 | 0 | 2 | 2 | 113 | 4 | 0 | 3 | 3 | 149 | 4 | 0 | 4 | 4 | 185 | 4 | 0 | 5 | 0 |
| 6 | 5 | 0 | 0 | 0 | 42 | 5 | 0 | 1 | 4 | 78 | 5 | 0 | 2 | 3 | 114 | 5 | 0 | 3 | 3 | 150 | 5 | 0 | 4 | 4 | 186 | 5 | 0 | 5 | 4 |
| 7 | 0 | 1 | 0 | 0 | 43 | 0 | 1 | 1 | 1 | 79 | 0 | 1 | 2 | 4 | 115 | 0 | 1 | 3 | 3 | 151 | 0 | 1 | 4 | 0 | 187 | 0 | 1 | 5 | 1 |
| 8 | 1 | 1 | 0 | 1 | 44 | 1 | 1 | 1 | 1 | 80 | 1 | 1 | 2 | 2 | 116 | 1 | 1 | 3 | 0 | 152 | 1 | 1 | 4 | 4 | 188 | 1 | 1 | 5 | 5 |
| 9 | 2 | 1 | 0 | 2 | 45 | 2 | 1 | 1 | 4 | 81 | 2 | 1 | 2 | 1 | 117 | 2 | 1 | 3 | 3 | 153 | 2 | 1 | 4 | 0 | 189 | 2 | 1 | 5 | 5 |
| 10 | 3 | 1 | 0 | 4 | 46 | 3 | 1 | 1 | 4 | 82 | 3 | 1 | 2 | 2 | 118 | 3 | 1 | 3 | 3 | 154 | 3 | 1 | 4 | 1 | 190 | 3 | 1 | 5 | 1 |
| 11 | 4 | 1 | 0 | 0 | 47 | 4 | 1 | 1 | 1 | 83 | 4 | 1 | 2 | 4 | 119 | 4 | 1 | 3 | 4 | 155 | 4 | 1 | 4 | 1 | 191 | 4 | 1 | 5 | 5 |
| 12 | 5 | 1 | 0 | 0 | 48 | 5 | 1 | 1 | 1 | 84 | 5 | 1 | 2 | 1 | 120 | 5 | 1 | 3 | 3 | 156 | 5 | 1 | 4 | 4 | 192 | 5 | 1 | 5 | 2 |
| 13 | 0 | 2 | 0 | 0 | 49 | 0 | 2 | 1 | 1 | 85 | 0 | 2 | 2 | 2 | 121 | 0 | 2 | 3 | 3 | 157 | 0 | 2 | 4 | 3 | 193 | 0 | 2 | 5 | 1 |
| 14 | 1 | 2 | 0 | 4 | 50 | 1 | 2 | 1 | 1 | 86 | 1 | 2 | 2 | 2 | 122 | 1 | 2 | 3 | 3 | 158 | 1 | 2 | 4 | 3 | 194 | 1 | 2 | 5 | 3 |
| 15 | 2 | 2 | 0 | 0 | 51 | 2 | 2 | 1 | 4 | 87 | 2 | 2 | 2 | 2 | 123 | 2 | 2 | 3 | 3 | 159 | 2 | 2 | 4 | 4 | 195 | 2 | 2 | 5 | 5 |
| 16 | 3 | 2 | 0 | 3 | 52 | 3 | 2 | 1 | 1 | 88 | 3 | 2 | 2 | 1 | 124 | 3 | 2 | 3 | 1 | 160 | 3 | 2 | 4 | 2 | 196 | 3 | 2 | 5 | 3 |
| 17 | 4 | 2 | 0 | 0 | 53 | 4 | 2 | 1 | 1 | 89 | 4 | 2 | 2 | 3 | 125 | 4 | 2 | 3 | 2 | 161 | 4 | 2 | 4 | 3 | 197 | 4 | 2 | 5 | 5 |
| 18 | 5 | 2 | 0 | 3 | 54 | 5 | 2 | 1 | 1 | 90 | 5 | 2 | 2 | 2 | 126 | 5 | 2 | 3 | 1 | 162 | 5 | 2 | 4 | 4 | 198 | 5 | 2 | 5 | 5 |
| 19 | 0 | 3 | 0 | 0 | 55 | 0 | 3 | 1 | 3 | 91 | 0 | 3 | 2 | 2 | 127 | 0 | 3 | 3 | 0 | 163 | 0 | 3 | 4 | 4 | 199 | 0 | 3 | 5 | 4 |
| 20 | 1 | 3 | 0 | 0 | 56 | 1 | 3 | 1 | 3 | 92 | 1 | 3 | 2 | 4 | 128 | 1 | 3 | 3 | 0 | 164 | 1 | 3 | 4 | 2 | 200 | 1 | 3 | 5 | 0 |
| 21 | 2 | 3 | 0 | 0 | 57 | 2 | 3 | 1 | 1 | 93 | 2 | 3 | 2 | 2 | 129 | 2 | 3 | 3 | 3 | 165 | 2 | 3 | 4 | 4 | 201 | 2 | 3 | 5 | 5 |
| 22 | 3 | 3 | 0 | 0 | 58 | 3 | 3 | 1 | 4 | 94 | 3 | 3 | 2 | 2 | 130 | 3 | 3 | 3 | 3 | 166 | 3 | 3 | 4 | 0 | 202 | 3 | 3 | 5 | 5 |
| 23 | 4 | 3 | 0 | 1 | 59 | 4 | 3 | 1 | 1 | 95 | 4 | 3 | 2 | 1 | 131 | 4 | 3 | 3 | 3 | 167 | 4 | 3 | 4 | 4 | 203 | 4 | 3 | 5 | 5 |
| 24 | 5 | 3 | 0 | 4 | 60 | 5 | 3 | 1 | 0 | 96 | 5 | 3 | 2 | 3 | 132 | 5 | 3 | 3 | 3 | 168 | 5 | 3 | 4 | 0 | 204 | 5 | 3 | 5 | 4 |
| 25 | 0 | 4 | 0 | 0 | 61 | 0 | 4 | 1 | 1 | 97 | 0 | 4 | 2 | 2 | 133 | 0 | 4 | 3 | 3 | 169 | 0 | 4 | 4 | 4 | 205 | 0 | 4 | 5 | 5 |
| 26 | 1 | 4 | 0 | 3 | 62 | 1 | 4 | 1 | 2 | 98 | 1 | 4 | 2 | 2 | 134 | 1 | 4 | 3 | 1 | 170 | 1 | 4 | 4 | 1 | 206 | 1 | 4 | 5 | 5 |
| 27 | 2 | 4 | 0 | 0 | 63 | 2 | 4 | 1 | 1 | 99 | 2 | 4 | 2 | 3 | 135 | 2 | 4 | 3 | 2 | 171 | 2 | 4 | 4 | 2 | 207 | 2 | 4 | 5 | 5 |
| 28 | 3 | 4 | 0 | 4 | 64 | 3 | 4 | 1 | 0 | 100 | 3 | 4 | 2 | 2 | 136 | 3 | 4 | 3 | 3 | 172 | 3 | 4 | 4 | 4 | 208 | 3 | 4 | 5 | 5 |
| 29 | 4 | 4 | 0 | 0 | 65 | 4 | 4 | 1 | 4 | 101 | 4 | 4 | 2 | 4 | 137 | 4 | 4 | 3 | 4 | 173 | 4 | 4 | 4 | 4 | 209 | 4 | 4 | 5 | 1 |
| 30 | 5 | 4 | 0 | 0 | 66 | 5 | 4 | 1 | 1 | 102 | 5 | 4 | 2 | 2 | 138 | 5 | 4 | 3 | 3 | 174 | 5 | 4 | 4 | 1 | 210 | 5 | 4 | 5 | 0 |
| 31 | 0 | 5 | 0 | 0 | 67 | 0 | 5 | 1 | 0 | 103 | 0 | 5 | 2 | 4 | 139 | 0 | 5 | 3 | 3 | 175 | 0 | 5 | 4 | 0 | 211 | 0 | 5 | 5 | 5 |
| 32 | 1 | 5 | 0 | 0 | 68 | 1 | 5 | 1 | 1 | 104 | 1 | 5 | 2 | 2 | 140 | 1 | 5 | 3 | 3 | 176 | 1 | 5 | 4 | 0 | 212 | 1 | 5 | 5 | 3 |
| 33 | 2 | 5 | 0 | 1 | 69 | 2 | 5 | 1 | 1 | 105 | 2 | 5 | 2 | 2 | 141 | 2 | 5 | 3 | 3 | 177 | 2 | 5 | 4 | 3 | 213 | 2 | 5 | 5 | 4 |
| 34 | 3 | 5 | 0 | 1 | 70 | 3 | 5 | 1 | 2 | 106 | 3 | 5 | 2 | 1 | 142 | 3 | 5 | 3 | 3 | 178 | 3 | 5 | 4 | 3 | 214 | 3 | 5 | 5 | 4 |
| 35 | 4 | 5 | 0 | 0 | 71 | 4 | 5 | 1 | 2 | 107 | 4 | 5 | 2 | 2 | 143 | 4 | 5 | 3 | 2 | 179 | 4 | 5 | 4 | 2 | 215 | 4 | 5 | 5 | 0 |
| 36 | 5 | 5 | 0 | 0 | 72 | 5 | 5 | 1 | 1 | 108 | 5 | 5 | 2 | 2 | 144 | 5 | 5 | 3 | 3 | 180 | 5 | 5 | 4 | 4 | 216 | 5 | 5 | 5 | 5 |

A further examination of the distribution of the number of randomly generated rules shows that a uniform distribution is obeyed (see Fig. 16) and that the distribution of the criteria (sum of the squares of the differences) is normal-like (see Fig. 17). As expected, only a small percentage of the generated rules would control CA in such a way that the criterion is less than 5 (target state is missed by less than 17%).

*Figure 16: Distribution of number of randomly generated rules in interval from 22 to 180.*

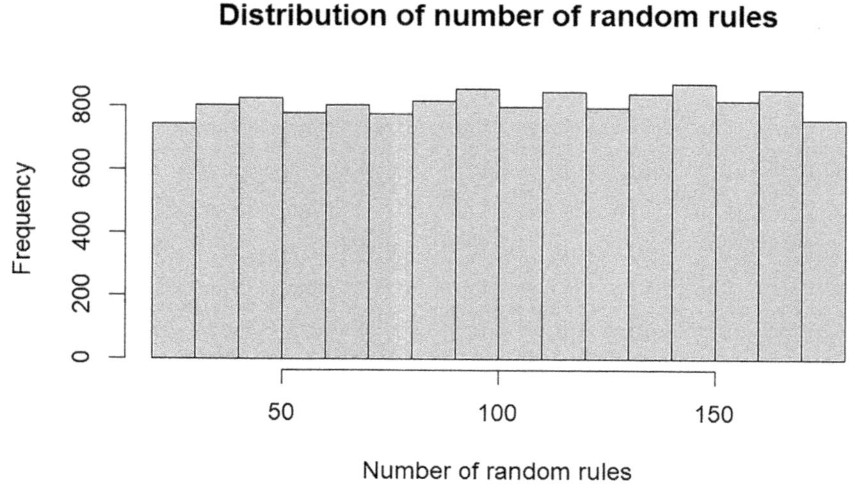


*Figure 17: Distribution of sums of squared differences between CA computed states 53 and "estimated" states for step 53.*

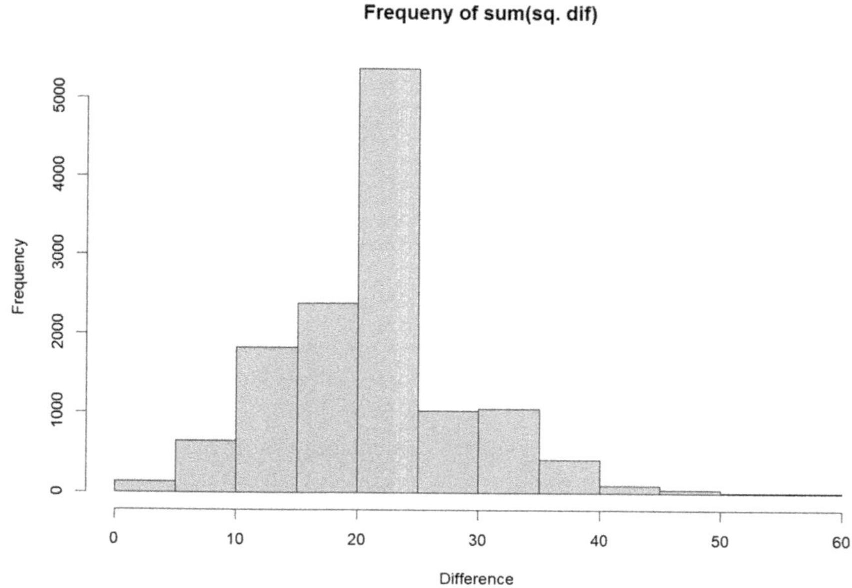

## 5. Discussion and conclusions

Two approaches to build a cellular automata were tested in this research:

- Inspired on the idea of partial differential equations
- Inspired on rules for CA.

### 5.1 PDE founded CAs

Experiments with PDE-based CAs depend heavily on the determination:

- Gain is a real number and we only tested 5 different values (0.1, 0.25, 0.50, 075 and 0.90). The effects of the gain value are characterised as linear. Decreasing or increasing the gain has a linear effect on the alignment areas. There is no hidden non-linear behaviour, even if values outside the interval (0–1) are specified.
- The functions of the internal components are defined as: A) Mean value of the target alignment area considering the entire history of the target alignment area and the entire population of companies, B) mean value of all alignment areas in the previous step for a given company, and C) variance of all alignment areas in the previous step for a given company. In all cases, the prior alignment value is considered twice, firstly as the exact value and secondly as the term of the difference. This could be eliminated by selecting all alignments other than the target alignment. However, we expect the impact on the new score to be relatively small, at the expense of additional CPU utilisation.
- Functions of external components: In this research, three time series were defined by setting only ten time points and then determining the best-fit polynomial by regression. This procedure actually saved time for human experts who might be involved in the development of scenarios. The disadvantage of this approach is that the time points are usually not exactly hit by the polynomial. While some external factors behave more stepwise (e.g. law enforcement), others are more continuous (e.g. inflation). The decision to calculate regression functions therefore makes sense. Another problem with the external components is their dimensionless nature. It is not expressed in monetary units, not in the inflation rate and not as a GDP rate. This makes modelling more of an art than a science.

One advantage of PDE-based CAs is the ability to refine and compose the internal and external components more precisely, but this also turns to be a sword of Damocles. As the complexity of the functions increases, so does the likelihood of modelling non-essential components.

## 5.2 Rule founded CAs

The experiments with rule CAs resulted with some caveats:

- There are only 216 possible rules and 1296 different outcomes under normal conditions. But what happens when more simultaneous outcomes are possible? Perhaps the introduction of probability would bring some rationality to the issue, but it would not settle the problem. How would CA evolve? When stochastic cellular automata were first introduced (in the 1970s), there were no experimental facilities such as quantum computers. With the advent of quantum computers, stochastic cellular automata are finally being rediscovered.
- The quest for mapping rule 110 to 6 state CA has been presented, but there are still unfinished tasks. Is not the ratio between the transition to a new state the same? In rule 110, the ratio is 3/8, which means that the new state is different than the current state. So, with a little analogy, can we infere that 81 changed states make the behaviour of 6 state CA a complete Turing machine? In this way we can make extensive analytical and experimental efforts to solve this mapping.
- When planning experiments, we always have one question in mind: How to determine how long a step in cellular automaton evolution actually takes in real units of time? Is it a day, a week, two weeks, a month, a year? The only thing we know is that the mapping between step and real time occurs. One approach is that we estimate the alignment areas twice in time. Then, by applying valid CA rules, we can make a conversion between steps and real time. However, this leads us to a new question: what is a valid CA set of rules?
- Finding a set of rules that leads CA from a known initial state, which is actually an estimated past (we used a questionnaire), to a state in the future, which is actually an estimated "new" past, was a mental journey. The first thing we did was to abstract the estimated "new" past by random generation. We found that randomly generated values of the estimated "new" past effectively replaced the need for a second survey. In our search for a suitable set of rules, we had another surprise: in a time-limited experiment, a 12 to 14 thousand random rules contained a subset of good candidates which meet condition "criteria

<= 5". By defining the criteria as the sum of the squared differences of the alignments at two different time points, we were able to find satisfactory good rule sets. This small subset of rule sets can mimic the control that guides the process from arbitrary initial states to arbitrary final states.

The implications of the last point are significant. We can determine a set of rules that have the potential to be valid for a particular company. Fig. 18 presents the scheme of incorporating machine learning into search algorithm for CA rules which best simulate the behavior of specific company.

*Figure 18: Conceptual scheme for coupling CA and machine learning.*

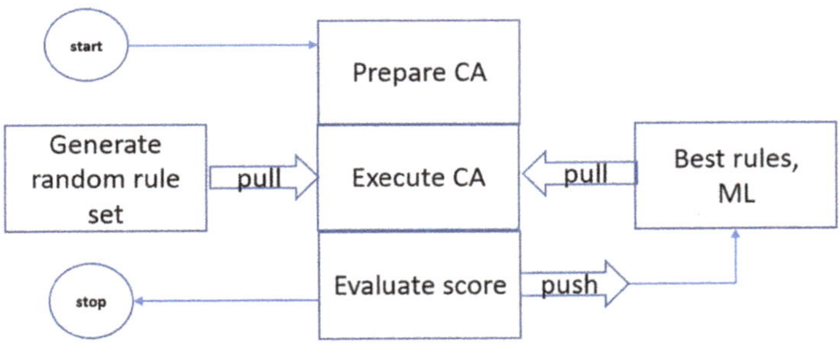


An empirical study on a larger scale would clarify some open issues related to step-to-time mapping. Further empirical data and machine learning algorithms would help to narrow down the set of likely valid rules - the rules that improve the predictability of the maturity of strategic alignment between IT and business.

## Acknowledgement

The authors acknowledge the partial support from the Slovenian Research and Innovation Agency, research core funding No. P5-0018.

## Bibliography

Codd, E. F. (1968). Cellular Automata. Academic Press, Inc., New York, London.

Cosentino, C., Vescio, B., & Amato, F. (2013). Cellular Automata. In W. Dubitzky, O. Wolkenhauer, K.-H. Cho, & H. Yokota (Eds.), Encyclopedia of Systems Biology (pp. 381–385). doi: 10.1007/978-1-4419-9863-7_989

Erl, T. and Stoffers, R. (2022). A Field Guide to Digital Transformation. Addison Wesley Publishing Company Incorporated. ISBN 9780137571840.

Gerow, J. E., Grover, V., Thatcher, J. B. in Roth, P. J. (2014). Looking toward the Future of IT-Business Strategic Alignment through the Past: A meta-analysis. MIS Quarterly, 38(4), 1059–1085.

Global institute for IT Management (2019). An Analysis of IT-Business Alignment on Company Performance: A Balanced Score Card Evaluation.

Leskovar R., Kavčič B. (2022). Stanje strateške skladnosti poslovanja in IT v Sloveniji. In Kljajić Borštnar M., Pucihar A. (Eds.), Znanstveno-raziskovalni izzivi na poti digitalne preobrazbe (pp. 183–231). doi: 10.18690/um.fov.6.2022.8

Luftman J. (2017). Enhancing the Measurement of Information Technology (IT) Business Alignment and Its Influence on Company performance, Journal of Information Technology

Martinez, S. J., Mendoza, I. M., Martinez, G. J., & Ninagawa, S. (2019). Universal One-Dimensional Cellular Automata Derived for Turing Machines and its Dynamical Behaviour. ArXiv [Nlin.CG]. Retrieved from http://arxiv.org/abs/1907.04211

Njanka, S. Q., Sandula, G., & Colomo-Palacios, R. (2021). IT-Business alignment: A systematic literature review. Procedia Computer Science, 181(2020), 333–340. https://doi.org/10.1016/j.procs.2021.01.154

Shannon, C. E. (1956). A Universal Turing Machine with Two Internal States. In C. E. Shannon & J. McCarthy (Eds.), Automata Studies. (AM-34), Volume 34 (pp. 157–166). doi: 10.1515/9781400882618-007

Verhoef, P. C., Broekhuizen, T., Bart, Y., Bhattacharya, A., Qi Dong, J., Fabian, N., & Haenlein, M. (2021). Digital transformation: A multidisciplinary reflection and research agenda. Journal of Business Research, 122 (July 2018), 889–901. https://doi.org/10.1016/j.jbusres.2019.09.022

Von Neumann, J. (1966). Theory of self-reproducing automata. Urbana and London: University of Illinois Press.

Wiener, N., & A, R. (1946). The mathematical formulation of the problem of conduction of impulses in a network of connected excitable elements, specifically in cardiac muscle. Archivos Del Instituto de Cardiologia de Mexico, 3, 205–265.

Wolfram, S. (2002). A New Kind of Science. Retrieved from https://www.wolframscience.com

Zuse, K. (n.d.). The computing universe. International Journal of Theoretical Physics, 589–600. doi: 10.1007/BF02650187

Borut Werber* and Uroš Rajkovič**

# Database normalization – can ChatGPT manage it?

**Abstract:** Relational database design is a critical aspect of building effective software solutions that handle complex data relationships. A well-designed database enables efficient data storage, retrieval, and manipulation. Normalization is a process that helps to eliminate data redundancies and inconsistencies while improving data integrity and accuracy. The goal of normalization is to organize data into logical groups that reflect the relationships between entities and reduce data duplication.

Normalization is typically divided into several levels or normal forms, including First Normal Form (1NF), Second Normal Form (2NF), and Third Normal Form (3NF). Each level represents a higher degree of data normalization and provides a more robust data model. The process of normalization involves identifying the functional dependencies between attributes in a relation, decomposing the relation into smaller, more manageable relations, and establishing relationships between the resulting tables. To illustrate the process of normalization, we presented a practical example of a relational database design for a library system. We started with an unnormalized relation that contained significant data redundancies and inconsistencies. Then we applied the normalization process and brought the relation to Third Normal Form, resulting in a more efficient and reliable data model.

To test the use of AI for database design and normalisation we used ChatGPT version 3.5. We use the same description of case scenario and Chat GPT did find the right solution. Then we check if he understands database design and normalisation rules, so the answer is not just copy of solution from internet. We were very satisfied with ChatGPT answers on specific questions that can be answered only by person who is expert in database design and normalisation. We can confirm that ChatGPT would pass our exam with excellence. Overall, a well-designed database is essential for effective software solutions that manage complex data relationships. Normalization is a key aspect of database design that enables data organization, integrity, and consistency. By following the normalization process and building a robust data model, developers can create software solutions that provide efficient and reliable data management. We proved that AI, in this case ChatGPT can help database designers to successful do their work.

**Keywords:** relational database, normalization, educational process, artificial intelligence, ChatGPT

---

* University of Maribor, Faculty of organizational sciences, Kranj, Slovenia; e-mail: borut.werber@um.si

** University of Maribor, Faculty of organizational sciences, Kranj, Slovenia; e-mail: uros.rajkovic@um.si

# 1. Introduction

When it comes to designing a database, many factors need to be considered to ensure it is efficient, scalable, and maintainable. The data model must be carefully planned, taking into account the needs of both experts and end-users. Unfortunately, in many cases, end-users themselves are responsible for designing the data model, leading to complications and issues with data storage and retrieval. This is where normalization comes in. It is a technique used to organize data in a database to minimize redundancy and dependency. By doing so, normalization ensures that data is stored logically and efficiently, allowing for easy maintenance and scalability. It is more than two decades ago we included practical question in master level exam of Information Systems where students must do normalization according to description of sales representative business cases. Results were much lower than expected since almost 80% of students did not answer correct. We were interested if Artificial Intelligence (AI) in this case ChatGPT can help with this task.

In this chapter, we will explore the basics of normalization, starting with an introduction to key database terms and concepts. We will discuss the different types of databases available, with a particular focus on relational databases, which are the most commonly used. We will then delve into the different normal forms and their rules, the process called normalization. Finally, we will provide practical examples and guidance on how to apply normalization to your database design and compere the answer given by ChatGPT version 3.5. Whether you are a novice database designer or an experienced database administrator, this chapter will provide you with a solid foundation in normalization, enabling you to design efficient and maintainable databases.

A database is an essential tool for organizing and managing data in a structured way, making it easy to access, update, and retrieve information. Databases can be used to store all types of data, from customer information to financial records and product inventories.

There are many types of databases available, each with its own unique features and benefits. Some of the most common types of databases include (Arjun, 2019):

- Relational databases: These databases are structured around tables with predefined relationships between them. Data is stored in rows and columns, and each row represents a unique record or entity. Relational databases are widely used in applications such as banking, inventory management, and customer relationship management.
- Object-oriented databases: These databases store data in objects, making them ideal for complex data structures. They allow developers to represent complex

relationships between data points and are widely employed in applications such as geographic information systems and computer-aided design.

- Graph databases: These databases use graph structures to store and manage data, making them ideal for analysing relationships between data points. They are commonly used in social networking applications, recommendation engines, and fraud detection systems.
- Cloud databases: These are databases that are hosted on cloud platforms, allowing for easy access and scalability. They are designed to handle large volumes of data and are commonly used in big data applications.
- NoSQL databases: These databases are also designed to handle large volumes of unstructured data, making them ideal for big data applications. They are typically utilised in applications such as social networking, real-time analytics, and internet of things (IoT) applications.
- Columnar databases: These databases store data in columns rather than rows, making them ideal for analytics and reporting. They are ideal for applications such as business intelligence and data warehousing.
- In-memory databases: These databases store data in memory rather than on disk, making them ideal for applications that require fast access to data. They are often used in applications such as high-frequency trading and real-time analytics.
- Time-series databases: These databases are designed to handle time-stamped data, making them ideal for applications that track changes over time. They are frequently tylised in applications such as financial trading, energy management, and IoT.
- Hierarchical databases: These databases store data in a hierarchical structure, making them ideal for applications that require a tree-like structure. They are often used in applications such as file systems, network directories, and XML documents.
- Network databases: These databases store data in a network structure, making them ideal for applications that require complex relationships between data points. They find application in supply chain management and social networking applications.
- Distributed databases: These are databases that are distributed across multiple servers, making them ideal for applications that require high availability and scalability. They are commonly used in applications such as e-commerce, content delivery networks, and mobile applications.
- Multidimensional databases: These databases store data in multiple dimensions, making them ideal for data warehousing and analytics. They are used in applications such as business intelligence and financial reporting.

- Document databases: These databases store data in JSON-like documents, making them ideal for applications that handle unstructured data. They are employed in a variety of applications such as content management systems, e-commerce, and mobile applications.
- NewSQL databases: A NewSQL or a newron database is a type of database that uses artificial neural networks to store and retrieve data. These databases are designed to handle complex data structures, making them ideal for applications that require machine learning and artificial intelligence. They are typically used in applications such as fraud detection, recommendation engines, and personalized marketing.

When relational database is used it is important to use adequate software that can retrieve the data and organize databases. *Structured Query Language* (SQL) is most known software used for creating, design and retrieve data, tables, queries, forms and reports from relational databases. It was first time introduced in 1979 in form of Oracle, the first relational database program to use SQL (Hall, 2023, Leskovar et al., 2024).

To understand the importance and spread of relational databases use in practice it is important to know the distinct between SQL databases and NoSQL databases. The name NoSQL doesn't mean that there is no SQL, its means Not Only SQL, so this software solution or product use more than one storage mechanisms that could be used according on the needs (Kanade et al., 2014; Patel & Eltaieb, 2015).

Now that we have a better understanding of what databases are and the different types available, let us dive deeper into normalization and its importance in database design.

## 2. Introduction to data normalization

Database normalization is a crucial process that involves organizing a database into tables and columns in a way that reduces data redundancy and dependency, and ensures data accuracy and integrity. By dividing large tables into smaller ones and defining relationships between them, normalization simplifies and improves the structure of a database. This process is a key component of relational database design and helps improve the performance and scalability of the database. It also minimizes data anomalies, which can lead to data inconsistency and errors when data is modified.

The concept of normalization dates back to 1970 when Edgar F. Codd introduced the first normal form (1NF) for the relation model with a normal form for the time-varying collection of relationships (Codd, 1983). Since then, researchers have proposed similar principles for object-oriented data models (Merunka et al.,

2009) hierarchical-document data models (Kanade et al., 2014), and hierarchical-XML data models (Mocean et al., 2007). Today, there are ten different levels and six normal forms, but in most cases, only the first three are used (Bhattacharyya, 2020).

Despite the importance of normalization, many students struggle with this field of expertise even after being introduced to the normalization process twice before enrolling in a master's degree program. Additionally, some faculties have omitted this knowledge since other database systems were introduced that do not require database normalization. However, statistics show that the first four database systems used in the present day are relational database systems (Oracle, MySQL, Microsoft SQL Server, Postgre SQL), and they are increasing in popularity (https://db-engines.com/en/ranking). To bridge this knowledge gap, we have decided to present normalization in this chapter using examples and a description of the steps required to normalize a database to the third normal form.

Before delving into the normalization process, it is essential to understand key concepts such as entities, attributes, keys, and relations (Shelly et al., 2008; Werber, 2023). An entity refers to a distinct object or concept in the real world, such as a person, place, or thing. Attributes describe the characteristics of an entity, such as a person's name or age. Keys are unique identifiers that distinguish one entity from another, while relations describe the connections between entities.

## 2.1 Database fundamentals: entities, attributes, tuples, relations, and keys

An **entity** in a relational database is a fundamental building block that represents a real-world object, concept, or event. It is a unique and identifiable entity that has a set of attributes or properties that describe it. Entities can be tangible, such as a person or product, or intangible, such as a transaction or event.

Entities are typically represented in a database as tables, where each table represents a specific entity and its associated attributes. For instance, a PRODUCT entity could have a table that includes columns for the product name, type, unit of measure, price, and other relevant attributes.

Entities are essential for organizing and structuring data in a relational database. They allow for efficient data management, querying, and retrieval, as well as ensuring data integrity and accuracy.

An **attribute** is a characteristic or feature of an entity that describes the entity in more detail. In a relational database, an attribute is a column in a table that contains information about the entity. Attributes are essential elements of an entity, and they provide the necessary context to understand the entity fully. An attribute is indivisible from a content perspective, which means it cannot be further broken down into smaller parts. However, it is possible to divide an attribute into sub-attributes, depending on the needs of the user or the client's requirements. For example, the address of a person can be an attribute, which may be further divided into street name, house number, and zip code. The level of breakdown depends on the granularity required by the application.

In a relational database, a **tuple** represents a specific instance of an entity and is composed of a set of attributes that define the characteristics of the entity. Each attribute or field in the tuple stores a specific piece of information about the entity. For example, a tuple in a PRODUCT table could represent a specific product, such as a laptop, and contain attributes such as product name, price, manufacturer, and description.

Tuples are the basic building blocks of a relational database and are used to store and retrieve data. They are also known as records or rows, and multiple tuples can be stored in a table. The order of the attributes in a tuple is usually not significant, and tuples can be sorted based on the values in one or more attributes. The number of tuples in a table can vary depending on the amount of data being stored.

In a relational database, a **relation** is a table that stores data related to a specific entity or concept. A relation consists of a set of attributes that describe the properties of the entity, and each row in the table represents a unique instance of that entity. Relations are used to establish relationships between different entities, and the data in the tables can be queried and manipulated using various database operations. In other words, a relation is a collection of tuples that share a common set of attributes. The concept of a relation is a fundamental aspect of the relational database model, and is the basis for organizing and storing data in a structured and efficient manner.

In order to understand and create relationships between tables or relations, it is important to have a solid understanding of the concept of keys. Keys play a crucial role in identifying and linking data across tables. In the next subchapter, we will delve deeper into the different types of keys and their importance in relational databases.

## 2.2 Keys

A key is an attribute or a set of attributes that uniquely identifies a record in a database table. The employee number, for example, enables the output of all data on a specific employee. It is used to store and retrieve data from a database. Keys are divided into primary, candidate, external and composite keys.

A **super key** is a set of attributes that can uniquely identify a record in a table. A super key may contain more attributes than necessary to uniquely identify a record. For example, in an employee table, a super key could be a combination of employee number, name, and birthdate.

A **candidate key** is a minimal super key, meaning it contains the fewest possible attributes needed to uniquely identify a record in a table. For example, in an employee table, a candidate key could be the employee number or the social security number.

A **primary key** is a candidate key that has been selected to uniquely identify each record in a table. A primary key is used to reference other tables in a relational database. A relational database prevents two identical primary key values from being used. Examples of primary keys include employee number, product number, order number, citizen identification number, and tax number. When multiple candidate keys exist for a table, one is chosen as the primary key and the others are referred to as **alternate keys**.

In a relational database, a composite key is a key that consists of two or more attributes that together form a primary key of a relation. Each column in the composite key is called a component of the key. Composite keys are used to uniquely identify each record in a table, ensuring that no two records have the same combination of values.

The use of composite keys becomes necessary when it is not possible to uniquely determine the appearance of an entity with the help of one attribute alone. In a database of car rentals, a composite key consisting of the rental start date, rental end date, and the car's license plate number might be used to uniquely identify each rental agreement. This combination of attributes ensures that each rental agreement is uniquely identifiable in the database, as two rental agreements for the same car cannot have the same start and end dates.

In cases where a composite key is not used, a single attribute is used as a primary key. This is called a simple key. Simple keys are often used when the data in a table can be uniquely identified with the help of a single attribute.

When choosing between a simple key and a composite key, it is important to consider the trade-offs involved. A simple key is generally easier to work with, as it requires only a single attribute to be considered. However, if the data in a table cannot be uniquely identified with a single attribute, a composite key becomes necessary.

In some cases, it is not possible to uniquely determine the appearance of an entity with the help of one attribute, but it is also not necessary to use a composite key. In such cases, a foreign key can be used to reference a unique record in another table. The opposite of a composite key is a simple key or a single attribute key.

A **foreign or secondary key** is an essential component in establishing relationships between tables in a relational database. It enables the database to link information across tables, ensuring the accuracy and consistency of data. A foreign key is created by referencing the primary key of another table, thereby establishing a relationship between the two tables.

The foreign key constraint ensures that any data entered into the table referencing the primary key of another table must correspond to a valid entry in that table. This ensures that data in related tables remains consistent and up-to-date. If a foreign key references a primary key that does not exist, the database will not allow the record to be inserted or updated.

Foreign keys are important for maintaining data integrity in a relational database. They allow data to be stored in separate tables, reducing redundancy and making it easier to manage data. By linking tables together using foreign keys, you can easily retrieve information from multiple tables at once. This enables you to create complex queries and generate reports that combine information from multiple tables.

The opposite of a foreign key is a primary key. While a foreign key references a primary key in another table, a primary key is an attribute in a table that uniquely identifies each record in the table. Primary keys are used to establish relationships between tables, and are referenced by foreign keys in other tables.

In summary, keys play a crucial role in relational databases by uniquely identifying records in tables and allowing for relationships between tables.

## 2.3 Establishing relationships between tables/relations

In the context of databases, a relationship refers to the association between two or more entities, which can be tables, fields, or other objects. Relationships are established using primary and foreign keys that link related entities, and they play a critical role in organizing and retrieving data efficiently.

There are several types of relationships in relational databases, including one-to-one (1:1), one-to-many (1:N), and many-to-many (N:N). A one-to-one relationship exists when one row in a table corresponds to only one row in another table. An example of such a relationship is the connection between an order and an invoice, assuming that there is only one invoice for each order. Another example could be the relationship between fishing licenses and their types (annual, guest, or time-limited).

**One-to-one relationships** are relatively rare and are typically replaced by combining related entities into a single table and selectively displaying the relevant attributes. In a one-to-many relationship, one row in one table can be associated with multiple rows in another table. In a many-to-many relationship, multiple rows in one table can be associated with multiple rows in another table.

To represent relationships in a database diagram, a one-to-one relationship is indicated by a line with 1's on both ends (Figure 1). Other types of relationships are represented by different symbols and lines. Understanding the different types of relationships is crucial for designing a well-structured database that can efficiently handle complex data queries.

*Figure 1: One to one relationship.*

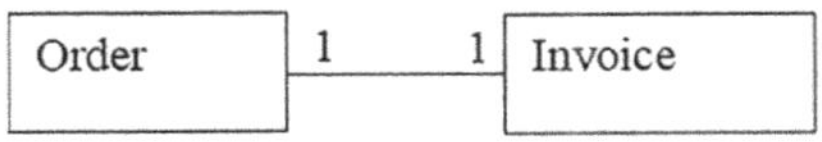


A **one-to-many relationship** is represented as a line and the symbols 1 and infinity (∞) on the opposite side (Figure 2). This is the connection we strive for, as it allows us to easily work with data. For example, one competitive skier can have several pairs of skis, but these skis belong only to him. In a company, the head of the department is the superior of several employees, but each employee has only one head of the department. In a manufacturing scenario, one manufacturer can produce several products, but each product is produced by only one manufacturer.

*Figure 2: One to many relationship.*

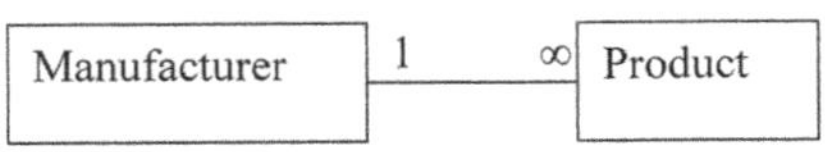


A **many-to-many relationship** is represented by a connecting line with infinity signs (∞) at both ends (Figure 3). This is a link that we cannot implement directly in a relational database. Therefore, we eliminate it by inserting a new entity in the place of such a link, in which we enter keys from neighbouring entities and combine them into a compound key or add a new primary key and thus form an **open variant** (also known as a junction table or bridge table).

For example, in the film industry, an actor can act in multiple films, and multiple actors can play in one film. The relation between ACTOR and MOVIE is therefore many-to-many, which is unfavourable for us because in this case, the program would always list all actors and all movies. Instead, we can create a new entity called ROLE, which links actors and movies, and this will allow us to better organize and access the data.

*Figure 3: Many to many relationship.*

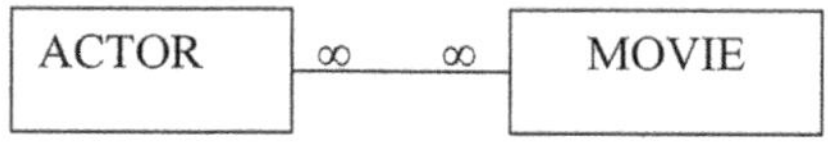


As previously discussed, in situations where a many-to-many relationship exists between two entities, we can create a new entity to serve as a bridge between them. Let us call this new entity "Actor in the Movie". There are two options to consider when creating this new entity, with the more common one being the closed variant.

In the **closed variant**, we insert the foreign key for the Actor ID from the Actor entity and the Movie ID from the Movie entity into the Actor in the Movie entity. The two foreign keys are used to form a composite key, which is marked with a bold, underlined font and an asterisk (*) (Figure 4). However, the limitation of this approach is that we cannot record the same actor in the same movie more than once.

*Figure 4: Closed variant relationship.*

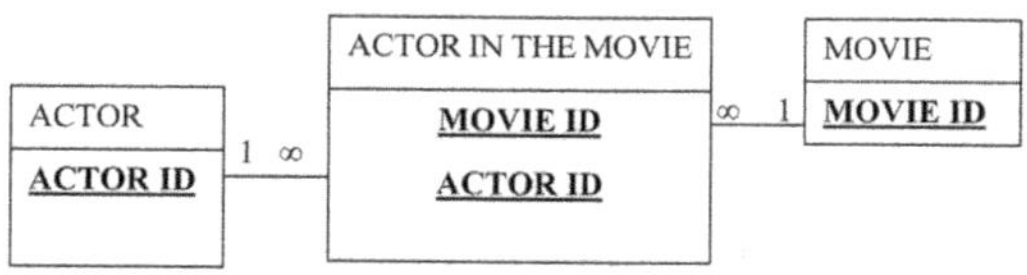


To address this limitation, we can create an **open variant** using a new primary key, which we'll call "Role ID". We still use the Movie ID and Actor ID as foreign keys, but this time they are not part of the composite key (Figure 5). Instead, we assign a sequential number to the Role ID, which automatically increases for each new record. This allows us to have multiple records for the same actor in the same movie, as demonstrated by actors such as Woody Allen or Eddie Murphy.

It's important to note that the choice between the closed and open variant will depend on the specific requirements of the client. A thorough analysis of these requirements can help avoid complications and changes to the database structure later on.

*Figure 5: Open variant relationship.*

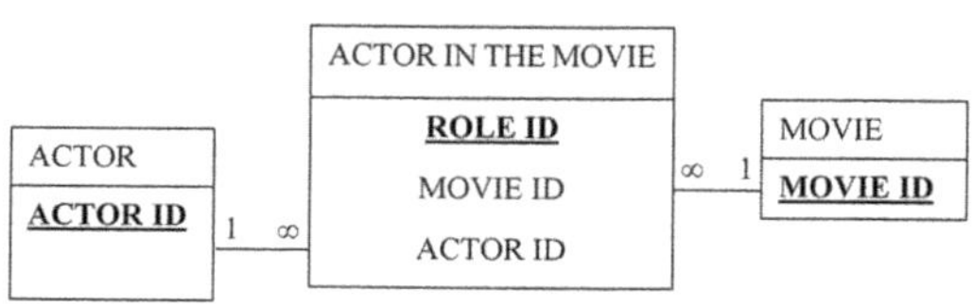

To illustrate the difference between closed and open variants, consider an example where the same actor appears in the same movie multiple times, such as Allen Woody or Eddie Murphy. In the closed variant, a composite key consisting of the movie ID and actor ID is used to uniquely identify each record in the "actor in the movie" entity. However, if we try to enter the same movie ID and actor ID combination again, as shown in the example where film ID is 1 and actor ID is 1, the relational database will report a duplication of keys and reject the input (Figure 6).

*Figure 6: Detecting error in records.*

| MOVIE ID | ACTOR ID | Composite key |
|---|---|---|
| 1 | 1 | ☑ |
| 1 | ~~1~~ | ☒ (error!) |

On the other hand, the open variant allows for the same actor to appear multiple times in the same movie by using a new primary key, such as ROLE ID, which is not part of the composite key. The foreign keys, movie ID and actor ID, can be repeated in the open variant, while the primary key ROLE ID ensures that there is no duplication of primary keys with its auto-increment feature (Figure 7).

*Figure 7: Proof of concept in records.*

| ROLE ID | MOVIE ID | ACTOR ID | |
|---|---|---|---|
| 1 | 1 | 1 | ☑ |
| 2 | 1 | 1 | ☑ |

It's important to note that the choice between closed and open variants should be based on the specific requirements of the client's software solution. Conducting a detailed analysis of the client's requirements can help avoid complications and changes to the database structure later on.

## 2.4 Determining entity relationships and primary keys

In order to illustrate the principles of database normalization, we will use a simplified example of a product sales system that involves sales representatives (Werber, 2023). In practice, we may encounter two scenarios. In the first scenario, there may already be existing documents and forms that are used in the business event that we want to automate with a computer program. By describing the business events and functions, the task will be easier to accomplish. In the second scenario, the forms and documents may not exist, and we will solely rely on the description of business functions and the client's requirements. This option is more challenging, and therefore, a detailed and precise description is crucial.

To demonstrate the functionality of individual components, commands, and functions, we will use a hypothetical scenario of a product sales system that utilizes sales representatives. Unfortunately, the company is in the process of being established, and the necessary forms and documents are not yet available. Our task is to create a user interface for recording orders for customers who can place orders for multiple products in a single transaction. Each customer is assigned to a single sales representative. The sales representative visits the customer at their home to obtain their personal information, such as their permanent address and credit rating for the new order.

The credit rating is represented by a numerical value ranging from 0 to 4, where 0 indicates no credit rating, 1 represents 1–3 purchases, 2 indicates 4–6 purchases, 3 represents 7–9 purchases, and 4 represents 10 or more purchases. The credit rating can be used as a percentage discount on the total order. The sales representatives are employed by the company, and therefore, we are also interested in their full address and the commission percentage that they are entitled to. The commission is represented in percentages ranging from 1 to 99 and is determined based on the representative's performance.

We offer a wide range of products from different manufacturers, and each product has a unique two-letter code that represents its type. For instance, FP represents food products, CP indicates chemical products, TP denotes technical products, TE represents textile products, etc. Additionally, each product has a unit of measure code consisting of a maximum of three letters, such as KG for kilogram, PAK for package, PCE for piece, L for litre, KIT for kit, etc.

In order to facilitate the distribution of products, the products are stored in four warehouses, numbered 1 to 4, and divided by the type of product. There are warehouses for pre-storage products, textiles, technical, and chemical products. The customer can order several different products, including multiple individual products, in one order, but the order should prevent ordering the same product twice. This helps prevent incorrect entry of orders and duplication of orders within the same order.

Each product is supplied at a certain purchase price and sold with an appropriate margin and value-added tax (VAT) rate. There are three possible VAT rates: reduced (9.5%), basic (22%), and tax-exempt (0%). It is important to note that tax rates can change over time, so the system should be flexible enough to adjust accordingly.

Each order should record the order date and the validity date, which is typically 8 days greater than the order date. The software solution should enable order history so that the originally recorded values are preserved even if there are changes to the price, tax, or margin. The system should also calculate and print out the value of each line in the order, including tax, and the total sum of the entire order, including tax, as well as the value of the total tax and the breakdown of taxes by levels.

Based on the given requirements, we can identify four entities: products, customers, sales representatives (agents), and orders. Each entity should have suitable attributes defined based on the written instructions and client's requirements. To ensure accurate work, it is essential to read the instructions several times and plan accordingly.

Entity: Sales representative
Attributes: Repr last name, Repr first name, Repr address, Commission

Entity: Customer
Attributes: Customer's last name, Customer's name, Customer's address, Credit rating

Entity: Product
Attributes: Product name, Product type, Unit of measure, Quantity per unit, Warehouse

Entity: Order
Attributes: Order date, Validity date, product name, number of products, price, tax, margin.

Having identified the entities and their respective attributes, the next step is to determine the primary keys for each entity. A primary key must be unique and able to uniquely identify each instance of an entity. In cases where there is no attribute that can serve as a primary key, a new attribute must be created.

For the Sales Representative entity, the last name of the representative might seem like an obvious choice for a primary key. However, using the last name alone could lead to duplicate keys in the database, as multiple representatives could share the same last name. Similarly, while a uniform identity number of a citizen could theoretically serve as a primary key due to its uniqueness, its use is impractical due to the potential for errors and data privacy concerns under GDPR.

After careful consideration, a new attribute called Repr ID is selected as the primary key for the Sales Representative entity. The same process is followed for the Customer, Product, and Order entities, resulting in the determination of Customer ID, Product ID, and Order ID.

Entity: Repr
Primary Key: Repr ID
Attributes: Repr last name, Repr first name, Repr address, Commission

Entity: Customer
Primary Key: Customer ID
Attributes: Customer's last name, Customer's name, Customer's address, Credit rating

Entity: Product
Primary key: Product ID
Attributes: Product name, Product type, Unit of measure, Quantity per unit, Warehouse

Entity: Order
Primary key: Order ID
Attributes: Order date, Validity date, product name, number of products, price, tax, margin.

The next step is to test the primary keys by asking if they can accurately identify each instance of an entity. For example, can the Repr ID be used to determine the sales representative's location and commission? If the answer is yes, then the primary key is suitable for the entity.

Furthermore, relationships between entities must be established. For instance, when considering the Order entity, the question is asked: "Who is ordering?" The answer is the customer. How many orders can a customer have? One or more. To which customer does an order belong? To one customer. Based on these answers, relations and keys can be established, linking the Order entity to the Customer entity (Figure 8).

*Figure 8: Customer order relationship.*

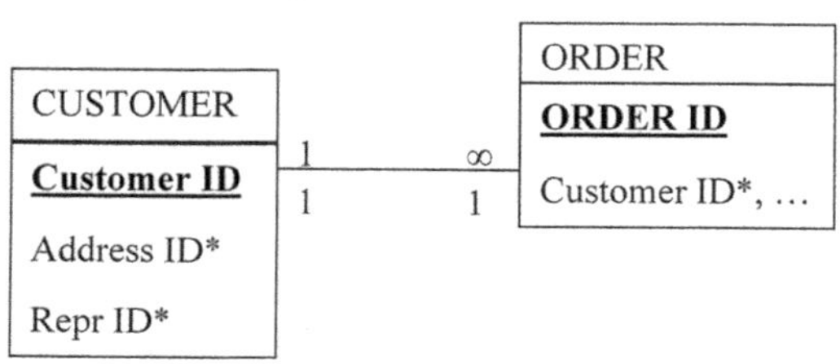

After establishing the relationship between the Customer and Order entities, we move on to the relationship between the Order and Product entities. We discover that a product can be a part of multiple orders and one order can contain several different products. This indicates a many-to-many relationship, which is not convenient for our purposes (Figure 9). To resolve this, we introduce a new entity called Order line, which acts as an intermediary between Order and Product. The Order line entity combines the Order ID and Product ID into a composite key, which forms a closed variant (Figure 10). The customer's requirements dictate that this is the appropriate choice since the customer can order multiple products in one order and even the same product more than once.

*Figure 9: Customer order 'many to many' relationship.*

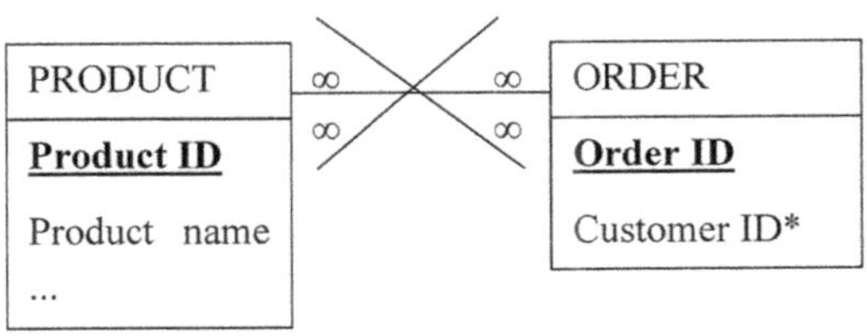


*Figure 10: Customer order relationship closed variant.*

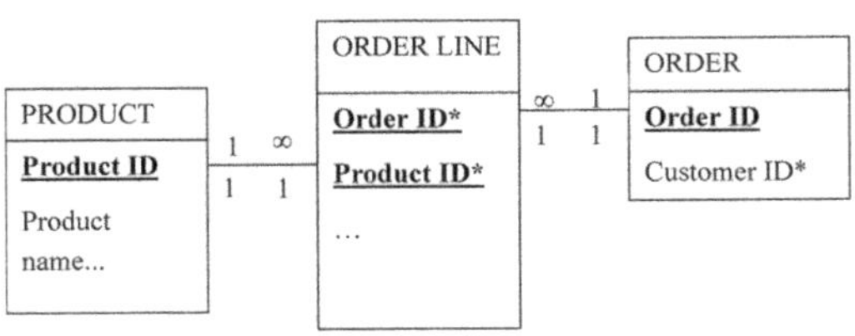


Now, the question arises as to where to include the other attributes of the Order, such as price, margin, and tax. Since the price of a product is specific to each product, we include it in the Order line entity, which is linked to the Product entity. Similarly, the tax rate is tied to the product, so we do the same. However, for the Margin attribute, we require additional information. If we assume that the margin is the same for all products, we could include it in the Order entity. However, in our case, this assumption is not valid, so we include the Margin attribute in the Order line entity.

Where should we write the other attributes from the Order, such as price, margin and tax? The price depends on the individual product, so we write it down in the Order Item, which is linked to the Product. The VAT rate is tied to the product, so we do the same. Margin? Additional information is required here. Do we have the same margin for all products? If we agreed to this, we could write the Margin attribute to the Order entity, because in our case it is not the case, we write the Margin to the Order line.

## 2.5 Normalization in database design

To reorder data in a way that optimizes the structure, ensures data integrity and consistency, and speeds up data processing, researchers have proposed rules that describe the levels of normalization, called Normal Forms (NF). There are six normal forms, but in most cases, only the first three are used. In theory, we can find different definitions of normal forms, but they all aim to describe the same rule using different words.

To distinguish between normal and un-normal forms, we also define the Zeroth Normal Form (0NF) (Table 1). Zeroth Normal Form is not a formal normal form, but it is sometimes used to refer to an unnormalized table that does not meet the requirements of the first normal form (1NF). In other words, a table in 0NF violates the basic rules of database normalization. A table in 0NF may contain repeating groups and non-atomic values that make it difficult to maintain data integrity and consistency.

A repeating group is a set of two or more columns in a table that contains similar information. This type of data redundancy is common in unnormalized tables and can cause problems in data processing and maintenance.

Atomic values, on the other hand, are indivisible values that cannot be further decomposed into smaller parts. In the context of database normalization, we strive to ensure that each attribute (or column) in a table contains atomic values to avoid redundancy and inconsistencies in the data.

*Table 1: Example of 0NF*

| Record | Order number | Order date | Product ID | Product description | Number ordered |
|---|---|---|---|---|---|
| 1 | 2301 | 01012023 | 102<br>107<br>235 | Pencil<br>Ink<br>Rubber | 4<br>2<br>3 |
| 2 | 2302 | 02012023 | 205<br>102 | Ruler<br>Pencil | 5<br>12 |
| 3 | 2303 | 02012023 | 102 | Pencil | 7 |

The concept of repeating groups and atomic values can be further explained. Repeating groups refer to the presence of multiple related values in a single record that should instead be represented as separate records. In the given example, the first and second records contain repeating groups because they each include multiple products that are not directly tied to the order number. Each product has its own unique primary key, the Product ID.

Moving on to the first normal form (1NF) (Table 2), it is a standard for organizing relational database tables that ensures that no repeating groups are present in any of its columns. The data in each column of a 1NF table should only contain atomic, indivisible values. Each row in the table should be unique, meaning that there should be no duplicate entries. Adhering to this standard helps to ensure that the data is organized efficiently and accurately, which in turn simplifies querying and manipulation of the data.

*Table 2: Example of 1NF*

| Record | Order number | Order date | Product ID | Product description | Number ordered |
|---|---|---|---|---|---|
| 1 | 2301 | 01012023 | 102 | Pencil | 4 |
| 2 | 2301 | 01012023 | 107 | Ink | 2 |
| 3 | 2301 | 01012023 | 235 | Rubber | 3 |
| 4 | 2302 | 02012023 | 205 | Ruler | 5 |
| 5 | 2302 | 02012023 | 102 | Pencil | 12 |
| 6 | 2303 | 02012023 | 102 | Pencil | 7 |

We can observe that each record in the table has a combination primary key comprising the Order number and Product ID, allowing us to uniquely identify each row. Furthermore, we can see that there are no repeating groups in the table.

Moving on to the Second Normal Form (2NF), a table is considered to be in 2NF if it meets the requirements of 1NF and every non-key column is fully dependent on the primary key. This implies that every non-key column should be functionally dependent on the entire primary key and not on any part of it.

Applying this to the previous table, we can divide the data into three tables. The first table, which we can name Orders (Table 3), will contain Order number and Order date, as only Order date depends on the primary key (Order number).

*Table 3: Example of 2NF for table Order*

| Record | Order number | Order date |
|---|---|---|
| 1 | 2301 | 01012023 |
| 2 | 2302 | 02012023 |
| 3 | 2303 | 02012023 |

The second table, which we named Products (Table 4), contains information about the products such as their Product ID and Product description. The primary key for this table is the Product ID, which uniquely identifies each product.

*Table 4: Example of 2NF for table Product*

| Record | Product ID | Product description |
|---|---|---|
| 1 | 102 | Pencil |
| 2 | 107 | Ink |
| 3 | 235 | Rubber |
| 4 | 205 | Ruller |

The third table, which we named Orders-line (Table 5), contains records of ordered items. It is a join table that links the Orders table and Products table. It consists of a composite key based on the combination of two keys: Order Number and Product ID. This means that for each product that is ordered, there will be a separate record in the Orders-line table.

*Table 5: Example of 2NF for table Order line*

| Record | Order Number | Product ID | Number ordered |
|---|---|---|---|
| 1 | 2301 | 102 | 4 |
| 2 | 2301 | 107 | 2 |
| 3 | 2301 | 235 | 3 |
| 4 | 2302 | 205 | 5 |
| 4 | 2302 | 102 | 12 |
| 4 | 2303 | 102 | 7 |

It can be inferred that the primary key in all three 2NF tables (Orders, Products, and Orders-line) is functionally dependent on all fields. For a table to be in third normal form (3NF), it must meet the criteria of 2NF and ensure that there are no transitive dependencies between non-key columns. In other words, if a non-key column depends on another non-key column, it should be moved to a separate table.

To illustrate 3NF, let's examine a different table from the same sales representative system example. In this table, data from both customers and representatives are combined (Table 6). To determine whether the Rep ID or the Cust ID should be included in the other table as a foreign key, one should consider that one representative can have multiple customers, but one customer can only have one representative. Therefore, in this example, the Rep ID should be included in the Customer table as a foreign key.

This table is in 1NF because there are no repeating groups. It is also in 2NF because the primary key is a single key. However, there is still an issue as the sales representative's name depends on the Sales representative ID.

*Table 6: Example of 3NF for table Order*

| Record | Cust ID | Cust Name | Cust Surname | Cust address | Repr ID | Repr name |
|---|---|---|---|---|---|---|
| 1 | 105 | John | Doe | 7 Bullevar str.,NH | 11 | Mark, Weber |
| 2 | 216 | Anne | Frank | 350 West 39th St, NY | 23 | Andy, Opkin |
| 3 | 117 | John | Ficguard | 1 South Franklin, Chicago, IL | 15 | Susan, Obama |
| 4 | 301 | Patric | Swayse | 11519 Market Street, Huston, TX | 7 | Mark, Twain |

Based on the analysis, it is clear that the Sales representative name is dependent only on the Sales representative ID and not on the Customer ID. Therefore, it is necessary to separate the table of sales representatives from the table of customers. In the Customer table (Table 7), the primary key is Cust ID, while in the Sales representative table (Table 8), the primary key is Rep ID.

*Table 7: Example I of 3NF for table Customer*

| Record | Cust ID | Cust Name | Cust Surname | Cust address | Repr ID |
|---|---|---|---|---|---|
| 1 | 105 | John | Doe | 7 Bullevar str., NH, 03031 | 11 |
| 2 | 216 | Anne | Frank | 350 West 39th St, NY, 10001 | 23 |
| 3 | 117 | John | Ficguard | 1 South Franklin, Chicago, IL,60606 | 15 |
| 4 | 301 | Patric | Swayse | 11519 Market Street, Huston, TX, 75015 | 7 |

*Table 8: Example of 3NF for table Customer representative*

| Record | Repr ID | Repr name |
|---|---|---|
| 1 | 11 | Mark, Weber |
| 2 | 23 | Andy, Opkin |
| 3 | 15 | Susan, Obama |
| 4 | 7 | Mark, Twain |

*Figure 11: Customer Sales representative relationship.*

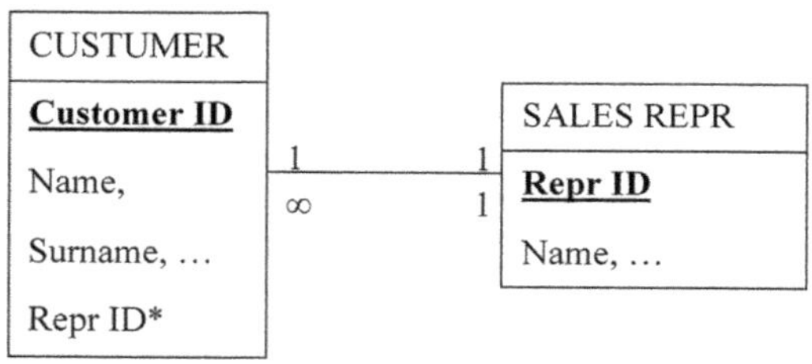


While it may be theoretically correct that after separating the table into two (Customer and Sales representative) (Figure 11), there are no non-key fields that depend on another non-key field, there are still practical issues that need to be addressed. For instance, the address field is not simple, as it consists of street number, town, state, and zip code. Furthermore, a large building can have numerous occupants with the same address. To address this, we can create an Address ID (Table 10) and separate it from the Customer table (Table 9). This will enable us to group data based on City, State, and Zip code more effectively.

*Table 9: Example II of 3NF for table Customer*

| Record | Cust ID | Cust Name | Cust Surname | Cust Address ID | Repr ID |
|---|---|---|---|---|---|
| 1 | 105 | John | Doe | 27 | 11 |
| 2 | 216 | Anne | Frank | 345 | 23 |
| 3 | 117 | John | Ficguard | 55 | 15 |
| 4 | 301 | Patric | Swayse | 73 | 7 |

*Table 10: Example of 3NF for table Address*

| Record | Address ID | Address |
|---|---|---|
| 1 | 27 | 7 Bullevar str., NH, 03031 |
| 2 | 345 | 350 West 39th St, NY, 10001 |
| 3 | 55 | 1 South Franklin, Chicago, IL, 60606 |
| 4 | 73 | 11519 Market Street, Huston, TX, 75015 |

Similarly, the Sales representative table also needs to be addressed (Figure 12). To ensure that each Sales representative belongs to only one address, we can create a relational rule stating "One sales representative is from one address, and each address has zero or can have more representatives." In line with the relational rule, the primary key is written where the label of the relation is one, while the foreign key of the entity in the relation is written where the label is many (∞). This will help to ensure that the data is properly organized and that there are no dependencies between non-key fields.

*Figure 12: Representative address relationship.*

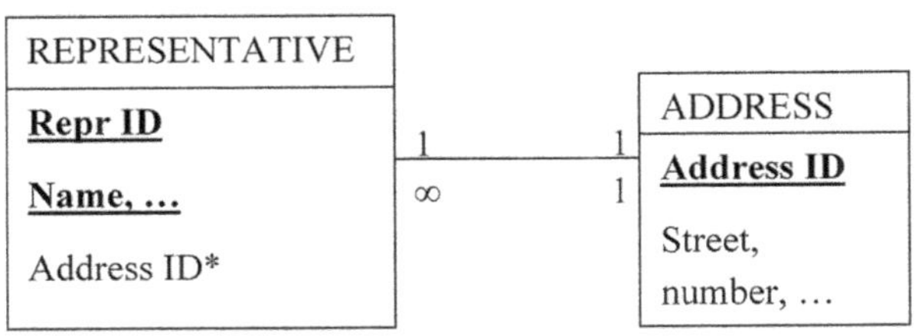


After analysing the relationships between entities in the sales representative system, we have successfully normalized the tables up to the third normal form. However, there are still some issues that need to be addressed to ensure the database's efficiency and accuracy.

One of the challenges we encountered was the address field, which includes the street number, town, state, and zip code. This field can pose problems, especially when several people live in the same building with the same address. To address this issue, we decided to generate an Address ID and separate it from the Customer entity. By doing so, we have two tables, namely the Customer and Address tables, which are related by the Address ID foreign key.

Similarly, we also identified the need to separate the Sales Representative entity from the Address entity. By writing the Address ID as a foreign key in the Sales Representative entity, we have established a one-to-many relationship between them.

In addition to these relational issues, we also examined the attributes of the entities in the system. For instance, the Customer entity has a Credit attribute that takes values between 0 and 5. Rather than expecting users to remember what each value means, we proposed the creation of a new entity called Customer Credit, which would contain the Credit ID Number and Credit Description. This would make it easier for users to understand the meaning of the Credit attribute.

However, it's worth noting that not all attributes need to be converted into separate entities. For example, if an attribute is a simple code that doesn't change over time, we can use a combo box or list box component offered by the database software. This is known as a dead code book, and it can only be modified by the programmer. Although it simplifies the database, we should carefully consider whether it's the right approach for our specific needs.

Overall, by normalizing the tables and addressing the various issues, we can ensure that the sales representative system's database is optimized for efficiency and accuracy.

Continuing, we see that the Product entity contains several attributes such as Product Type, Unit of Measure, VAT Rate, and Warehouse. These attributes need to be properly organized to ensure efficient data storage and retrieval. To achieve this, we will replace the missing entities with appropriate software components based on the data format to be recorded, such as Combo box, List box, or Option buttons.

However, there is also a requirement for retaining event history, which means that the software solution must allow users to issue an order identical to the original, even several years after the event. This requirement can be challenging, especially if the data is constantly changing.

Another important factor to consider is the normalization rules, which dictate that calculated fields should not be stored in the database. This means that we cannot write down totals of values, taxes, and other calculations. Instead, we must ensure that these sums are calculated in real-time based on the existing data.

For instance, let's consider the price of a product. In the current solution, the price is written in the Order line, and the user is required to know and enter the price when placing an order. However, the price of a product can change over time, and we don't want to change the records of previous sales prices. Therefore, we need to organize the attributes of the Product entity and the Order line entity properly.

In order to further refine our database schema, we need to consider the issue of inventory management. The company needs to track the quantity of each product it has in stock and be able to update this information in real time as products are sold and restocked. To achieve this, we will create a new entity called Inventory, which will have a one-to-one relationship with the Product entity.

The Inventory entity will have attributes such as Quantity on Hand, Re-order Level, and Re-order Quantity. Quantity on Hand represents the current number of units of the product that are in stock. Re-order Level is the minimum quantity of the product that should be in stock at any given time, and Re-order Quantity is the number of units that should be ordered when the inventory falls below the re-order level.

We will also need to add a new entity called Supplier to our database schema. This entity will have attributes such as Supplier ID, Name, Address, Contact Person, and Phone Number. Each product in our database will have a corresponding supplier, which will be linked through a foreign key.

Finally, we need to consider security and access control. We do not want just anyone to be able to access and modify our database. Therefore, we will create a new entity called User, which will have attributes such as User ID, Username, Password, and Access Level. The Access Level attribute will determine the level of access that each user has to the database. For example, a manager may have full access to all tables in the database, while a salesperson may only have access to the Order and Customer tables.

By incorporating these additional entities and attributes into our database schema, we can create a more comprehensive and secure system that meets the company's needs. The final schema of our database (Figure 13) will be a well-structured and normalized model that accurately reflects the company's data requirements, and provides a solid foundation for future growth and development.

*Figure 13: Database model solution.*

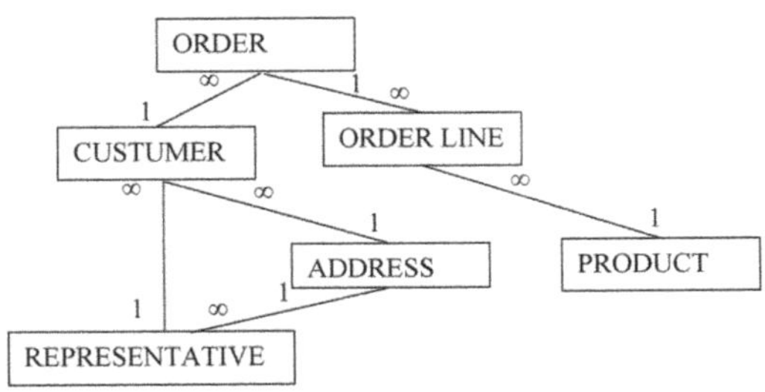


Even though we have completed the normalization of the database manually in our example, specialized data normalization software known as Case tools can help automate the process. However, the more complex the tool, the more expensive it becomes. Oracle, for instance, provides such a tool that is accessible to users, but it requires prior knowledge of normalization for successful use. In essence, the program requests information from the user regarding the composition of entities, their keys, and the relationships between entities. If the user lacks familiarity with these terms, the program will not effectively perform the normalization and connection of entities.

## 2.6 Use of ChatGPT for database normalisation and design

Before delving into the utilization of ChatGPT, there are several inquiries we need to address. Initially, what exactly does ChatGPT represent? It can be established that ChatGPT was developed by OpenAI in 2022 and is an acronym for Generative Pre-trained Transformer. Primarily, as a natural language processing (NLP) model, it facilitates human-like response-generation capabilities across various domains of human interest (Ngo, 2023).

Secondly, can we draw parallels between human intelligence and the realms of deep learning (DL) and machine learning (ML)? Despite the fervour surrounding novel technologies, we will inevitably confront limitations. In certain scenarios, the responses from multimillion-dollar systems may falter when faced with rudimentary queries. Conversely, such systems possess the capacity to learn akin to humans and progressively enhance their performance over time. However, their advancement is constrained by factors such as the availability of data and algorithms, the limitations imposed by their designers and developers, and ethical considerations (Baeza-Yates & Villoslada, 2022). We must say that the first results six months ago with ChatGPT were not encouraged. After six months the system has learned and when we give him exact description of studied case as is on page 16 the ChatGPT give us this answer:

ChatGPT: To design a database schema (entity-relationship diagram) for the given scenario, we can identify the following entities and their attributes:

1. Products:
    - Product Code (Primary Key)
    - Product Name
    - Unit of Measure Code
    - Purchase Price
    - Margin
    - VAT Rate

- Warehouse Number
- Available Quantity

2. Customers:
   - Customer ID (Primary Key)
   - Customer Name
   - Permanent Address
   - Credit Rating
   - Sales Representative ID (Foreign Key)
   - Discount Percentage
3. Sales Representatives (Agents):
   - Sales Representative ID (Primary Key)
   - Full Name
   - Address
   - Commission Percentage
4. Orders:
   - Order ID (Primary Key)
   - Customer ID (Foreign Key)
   - Sales Representative ID (Foreign Key)
   - Order Date
   - Validity Date
   - Total Order Value
   - Total Tax Value
5. Order Details (to represent line items in an order):
   - Order Detail ID (Primary Key)
   - Order ID (Foreign Key)
   - Product Code (Foreign Key)
   - Quantity
   - Line Item Value
   - Line Item Tax Value

We can see that the answer is almost fully in consistency with our second proposed solution (Figure 5: Open variant relationship). The only difference is that we separated Address table as Customer and Sales representative can live in the same town, district, street. So we ask ChatGPT: Why did you not separated table address since Customer and Sales representative have their address with the same attributes? His answer was as this:

ChatGPT: Separating the "Address" attribute into a separate table is a valid design choice and can provide advantages in terms of data normalization and maintainability. It's known as the practice of using a separate "Address" table to manage addresses for various entities like customers and sales representatives. This approach is especially useful when multiple entities share the same attributes for addresses.

With this modification:

1. The "Address" entity includes a unique "Address ID" as its primary key and a reference to the entity type (whether it's a customer or sales representative). This allows you to associate addresses with the respective entities.
2. Both "Customers" and "Sales Representatives" have a foreign key reference to the "Address" table. This ensures that each entity can have its own address, and if there are multiple customers or sales representatives at the same address, you can reuse the same address entry.
3. This approach promotes data normalization, as you store address information only once and reference it from various entities, reducing data duplication and ensuring consistency.
4. It also simplifies maintenance because if an address needs to be updated, you only need to update it in one place (the "Address" table), and it automatically reflects in all related entities.

In summary, separating the "Address" attribute into a separate table is a sound database design practice, especially when multiple entities share the same attributes for addresses. It promotes data integrity and maintainability.

Then we tested does ChatGPT understands normalisation and database rules or the database solution is just copy of given solution found in internet. To check that we ask him: Can you explain why we need Line Item Value in Order detail instead of using Purchase price from Products?

His answer was:

ChatGPT: Certainly! The "Line Item Value" attribute in the "Order Details" entity is included to store the calculated value of each line item in an order. While it's true that you can calculate the line item value using the "Purchase Price" from the "Products" entity, there are several reasons why it's beneficial to store this value separately:

1. **Data Integrity and Historical Accuracy**: Storing the calculated "Line Item Value" ensures that the order's historical accuracy is preserved. If the purchase price of a product changes in the future, the order's historical data would still reflect the actual price at the time of the purchase. This is crucial for auditing, reporting, and maintaining the accuracy of past orders.
2. **Tax Calculation**: The "Line Item Value" can also be used to calculate the tax on each line item. Different products may have different VAT rates, and the total tax for an order depends on the individual line item values. Storing this value simplifies tax calculation and reporting.
3. **Discounts and Promotions**: In some scenarios, discounts or promotions might be applied at the line item level, such as a bulk discount on a specific product. Having the "Line Item Value" allows you to accurately calculate discounts and promotions for each line item separately.
4. **Performance Optimization**: Retrieving historical order data for reporting purposes can be more efficient when the line item values are precalculated and stored. It reduces the need for complex calculations during data retrieval, especially when dealing with a large dataset.
5. **Flexibility**: Storing the line item value provides flexibility to handle cases where the purchase price might vary within the same order. For example, if you have a negotiated price for a specific quantity of a product within an order, you can record the appropriate line item value for that specific quantity.

In summary, while it is possible to calculate the line item value on-the-fly using the purchase price from the "Products" entity, storing this value separately in the "Order Details" entity enhances data accuracy, simplifies tax calculations, and provides flexibility for handling various scenarios related to pricing, discounts, and historical data integrity.

Separating the "Address" attribute into a separate table is a valid design choice and can provide advantages in terms of data normalization and maintainability. It's known as the practice of using a separate "Address" table to manage addresses for various entities like customers and sales representatives. This approach is especially useful when multiple entities share the same attributes for addresses.

We can conclude that this version of ChatGPT (3.5) can deal with database design and normalisation. The answer were concise and correct and the explanation show that system is using database and normalisation rules. If for many years CASE tools for database design and normalisation were used only by large business because of high prices, now ChatGPT can help design databases to all interested subjects. We also saw that primary knowledge is needed to know how to ask ChatGPT to get right answers.

This concludes our practical illustration of the normalization process on a given example with use of ChatGPT.

## 3. Conclusion

In conclusion, proper database design is essential to ensure the integrity and efficiency of data storage and retrieval. Normalization is a crucial process for achieving this goal, as it helps eliminate data redundancies and inconsistencies, minimizes data update anomalies, and improves query performance. Normalization also enables easier maintenance and modification of the database schema as the application evolves over time.

By following the rules of normalization and establishing appropriate relationships between entities, it is possible to design a well-structured and efficient database that can effectively support the desired functionality of the application. It is important to note that normalization should not be seen as a one-time task, but rather an ongoing process that should be revisited as the data requirements of the application change over time.

Furthermore, understanding the different types of relationships between entities, such as one-to-one, one-to-many, and many-to-many, is crucial in establishing appropriate foreign key constraints and ensuring data consistency. Properly defining relationships between entities helps to ensure that data is not duplicated unnecessarily and that updates are performed in a consistent manner.

In modern times AI is developed to such level we can use it in database design and normalisation. Decades ago, CASE tools were developed as predecessor and were used only by privileged developer in large businesses that could afford this software for hundreds of dollars. With ChatGPT version 3.5 the use of AI is available to all users. Unfortunately, it is like when you buy hi tech wash machine, you must know the basics of washing to use it.

In summary, designing a normalized and well-structured database with appropriate relationships is critical to the success of any software application that relies on data storage and retrieval. It requires careful consideration of the application's data requirements and ongoing attention to ensure that the database schema continues to meet those requirements as they evolve over time. Propriate use of AI can contribute to our success.

## Acknowledgement

The authors acknowledge the partial support from the Slovenian Research and Innovation Agency, research core funding No. P5-0018.

## Bibliography

Arjun, P. (2019). *Types of Database Management Systems*. Febrero 11. https://www.c-sharpcorner.com/UploadFile/65fc13/types-of-database-management-systems/

Baeza-Yates, R., & Villoslada, P. (2022). Human vs. Artificial Intelligence. *Proceedings - 2022 IEEE 4th International Conference on Cognitive Machine Intelligence, CogMI 2022*, 40–48. https://doi.org/10.1109/CogMI56440.2022.00016

Bhattacharyya, M. (2020). Database Management Systems, Database Normalization. *Indian Statistical Institute*. https://www.isical.ac.in/~malaybhattacharyya/Courses/DBMS/Spring2020/Class V.pdf

Codd, E. F. (1983). A Relational Model of Data for Large Shared Data Banks. *Communications of the ACM*, *26*(1), 64–69. https://doi.org/10.1145/357980.358007

Hall, M. (2023). *Oracle Corporation*. Encyclopedia Britannica. https://www.britannica.com/topic/Oracle-Corporation

Kanade, A., Gopal, A., & Kanade, S. (2014). A study of normalization and embedding in MongoDB. In *Souvenir of the 2014 IEEE International Advance Computing Conference, IACC 2014* (pp. 416–421). https://doi.org/10.1109/IAdCC.2014.6779360

Leskovar, R., Rajkovič, U., & Baggia, A. (2024). Intranet news for employees. In: Leskovar, R. (ed.), Baggia, A. (ed.). Low code programming with APEX: how to and practical cases. 1st edition. Maribor: University of Maribor, University Press, pp. 221–230.

Merunka, V., Brožek, J., Šebek, M., & Polák, J. (2009). BORM - Business object relation modeling. *15th Americas Conference on Information Systems 2009, AMCIS 2009*, *10*, 6847–6864.

Mocean, L., Buchmann, R., & El, P. Ş. (2007). *About Hierarchical Xml Structures, Replacement of Relational Data Structures in Construction and Implementation of Erp Systems*. *1*(1), 53–57.

Ngo, T. T. A. (2023). The Perception by University Students of the Use of ChatGPT in Education. *International Journal of Emerging Technologies in Learning*, *18*(17), 4–19. https://doi.org/10.3991/ijet.v18i17.39019

Patel, T., & Eltaieb, T. (2015). Relational Database vs NoSQL. *Journal of Multidisciplinary Engineering Science and Technology (JMEST)*, *2*(4), 691–695. www.jmest.org

Shelly, G. B., Cashman, T. J., & Rosenblatt, H. J. (2008). *Systems analysis and design*. 702. https://books.google.com/books/about/Systems_Analysis_and_Design.html?hl=sl&id=i_7EnA2cS5sC

Werber, B. (2023). *Skripta MS Access - naprednejša uporaba*. Univerza v Mariboru, Fakulteta za organizacijske vede. https://estudij.um.si/pluginfile.php/606727/mod_folder/content/0/Skripta MS Access V5.pdf?forcedownload=1

Alenka Baggia*, Borut Werber** and Anja Žnidaršič***

# What about microchip implants? Digital transformation of the human body

**Abstract:** Despite technological advances, microchip implants remain a controversial issue. Perceptions of their usefulness and rejection of their use have been further influenced by the recent COVID -19 pandemic. In the present study, we aimed to determine what factors influence user acceptance of microchip implants with passive near-field communication and radio frequency identification. The survey was conducted in five countries in the Eastern European region. SEM was used to analyse the data obtained from the online survey. Nearly a decade of research in microchip implant acceptance has expanded the basic model of technology acceptance to include three additional factors identified after the COVID-19 pandemic in this study. Using the proposed procedures and fit indices, we found that the measurement model fits the sample data well. All fourteen postulated hypotheses were confirmed. Intention to use microchip implants depends on perceived usefulness, ease of use, and trust in the technology. Younger respondents are more inclined to use the technology. Perceived usefulness of microchip implants is influenced by perceptions of their usefulness in the event of pandemic, while on the other hand, perceived trust in the technology and health concerns along with implantation-related pain have negative effects on perceived usefulness. The safety of the technology increases trust in microchip implants. In contrast, belief in conspiracy theories and threats to privacy rights decrease trust. There is a relationship between belief in fake news and conspiracy theories. Overall, the proposed extended technology acceptance model shows good insight into the acceptance of microchip implants. Despite some changes in the general perception of the usefulness of microchip implants in pandemic, the future of this technology is not clear. Currently, the acceptance of microchip implants is highly dependent on progress in their successful applications, especially in the healthcare sector, where the use of artificial intelligence has significantly expanded the possibilities of their use. All in all, regulatory requirements must be prepared to prevent the misuse of microchip implants and thus increase confidence in this technology.

**Keywords:** microchip implant, artificial intelligence, technology acceptance, SEM model, privacy, health concerns, technology safety

---

* University of Maribor, Faculty of organizational sciences, Kranj, Slovenia; e-mail: alenka.baggia@um.si

** University of Maribor, Faculty of organizational sciences, Kranj, Slovenia; e-mail: borut.werber@um.si

*** University of Maribor, Faculty of organizational sciences, Kranj, Slovenia; e-mail: anja.znidarsic@um.si

## 1. Introduction

In recent decades, technology has expanded the possibilities of human identification. With the help of computers, biometric science has developed various more or less reliable systems such as voice recognition, facial, fingerprint, palm or iris scanning (Shaheed et al., 2021). In search of a more secure and reliable solution for mass deployment, the use of passive radio frequency identification (RFID) microchip implants (MIs) has been proposed (Perakslis & Michael, 2012; Sarfraz, 2019). These MIs consist of three components: the transmitter microchip, a capacitor, and the antenna coil (Sarwar et al., 2019). The microchip implant (MI) is injected under the skin, does not move around in the body, and has been shown to have no side effects. As always when a new technology is proposed there are technology enthusiasts and sworn opponents of the innovation who see a conspiracy in every aspect of its use. Despite the differing opinions, according to (Franks and Smith 2021), it is apparent, that human microchip implantation may be an inevitable part of the future. In addition, with the use of artificial intelligence, their design, functionality, security, and reliability can additionally be enhanced (Al Mansouri & Alnajjar, 2023). Buttazzo (2023) reports on different types of microchips, installed inside the body to prevent epileptic attacks or help patients with Parkinson's disease. The most common concerns about the use of MI are health, the right to privacy, and the threat to privacy posed by government surveillance of people. In general, we can divide the use of MI into several groups such as personal identification, health care, payment and shopping, and household use. There are several studies that examine the use of MI from different points of view, and only some of them use data from more than one country. From the data published in recent years we can conclude that the use of MI is increasing, especially in the business sector where business owners have introduced MI as an additional way for employees to access business facilities, shared multifunction devices, food vending machines, parking lots, and the like. Despite recent attempts and successful adoption of MI in practice there is a dearth of studies on the factors that influence the willingness to adopt MI. In addition, the factor model proposed by (Gangadharbatla, 2020) was evaluated using only basic statistics, while the models proposed by (Žnidaršič et al., 2021) and (Shafeie et al., 2022) were based on smaller samples. Based on these findings, we focused our study on a broader population of five Eastern European countries (Poland, Croatia, Slovenia, Ukraine, and Russia) to determine the factors influencing the adoption of MI using an extended model based on the Technology Acceptance Model (TAM). The proposed model of willingness to use MI for various purposes included the impact of the COVID-19 pandemic and other factors that might influence willingness to use a MI, e.g., conspiracy theories and fake news.

The following section presents the theoretical background of MI. Research findings on the acceptance of MI and MI are discussed, as well as the use of MI and possible threats. The research methodology section begins by introducing the research model and measurement items. The characteristics of the sample and data analysis are explained. The results section presents the general attitude towards MIs and the evaluation of the proposed model. The discussion and conclusions section presents the results and future directions.

## 2. Microchip implants

MI are small RFID devices that are inserted subcutaneously into a living object for a variety of purposes. Initially, they were mainly used to identify animals, while recently their use in humans has become more popular (Rodriguez, 2019). In addition to identification, MIs have also been successfully used as medical devices such as pacemakers, temperature or blood pressure monitors (Eltorai et al., 2016). There are two basic types of MIs in terms of power supply (Yang et al., 2020). Active MI use batteries for power, while passive MIs use coil antennas to transmit the power from the reader. MIs may also have specialised sensors to sense temperature, pressure, and various chemicals. The human MI is usually encapsulated in a silica glass capsule the size of a grain of rice and is inserted into the skin above the thumb (Banafa, 2022). The glass capsule is coated with a special layer to prevent movement of the microchip within the body (K. Michael et al., 2008). MIs use the Near Field Communication (NFC) protocol for data transmission and can therefore only be read from a short distance, a maximum of 20 cm (Japertas & Jankuniene, 2020).

### 2.1 Acceptance of microchip implants

MIs are often perceived as a controversial technology and generally seen as a thread to individuals. As a result, research on the acceptability of MIs has not kept pace with their technological advances, despite their obvious usefulness in certain fields, particularly medicine. The first study on public acceptance of MIs was conducted in 2008, and the results showed that the majority of respondents would not be implanted (Smith, 2008). The study among Indian millennials (Perakslis & Michael, 2012) and a cross-national study (Perakslis et al., 2014) both found that willingness to adopt MI is slowly increasing and varies by country and generation. On the other hand, the study conducted among small business owners (K. Michael et al., 2017) found that in most cases they are favourable to the idea of an ID implant for employees. According to (Franks & Smith, 2021), when asked about their willingness to use a human-implanted microchip, nearly a quarter (23%) of respondents stated they would try the technology, showing a slight increase over the results of research conducted in 2018. Interestingly, (Franks and Smith 2021) described that recent identity crime victims were more than twice as willing as non-victims to have an MI implanted to protect their data (42% vs. 20%). More recent studies (Gangadharbatla, 2020; Shafeie et al., 2022; Žnidaršič et al., 2021) have used technology acceptance models to identify factors influencing MI acceptance. In addition, Shafeie et al. (2023) applied machine learning classifiers to recognize health risk concerns regarding the MIs.

## 2.2 Use of microchip implants

Four types of use of MI can be derived from the literature review: medical purposes, personal identification, shopping and payments, and access control. Currently, the most widely accepted and widespread use of MI is for medical purposes. MIs as pacemakers are now very common, and patients no longer hesitate when offered this option to improve their health (Shafeie et al., 2022). Other uses of MIs are less common. (Sundaresan et al. 2015) describes the use of MI to identify unconscious patients and retrieve their medical history to perform proper procedures and treatments based on the retrieved data. In conjunction with sensors, MIs can be used to measure and report body temperature, blood oxygen, blood pressure, sugar, or use various chemicals in the body, enabling telemedicine (Eltorai et al., 2016). MIs with additional containers for medications can be used for blood glucose control (Sundaresan et al., 2015) or even birth control (Shafeie et al., 2022). In addition, (Reicher et al. 2007) reported a case in which the MI was used as an indicator of successful catheter insertion into the trachea.

In recent years, the use of MIs for other purposes is also increasing. Since the initial trials of MI use research by Professor Warwick (K. Michael & Michael, 2013), the number of people using MI has increased since the FDA approved the procedure in 2004 (Rotter et al., 2008). After the Asian tsunami disaster, MIs were used to identify the bodies and allow smoother processing according to the disaster victim identification procedure (Meyer et al., 2006). In Australia, a study was conducted to replace military personnel identifiers with MIs (Nicholls, 2017). Not only people, but also dentures have been implanted with MIs to enable faster identification in a senior facility (Venkat et al., 2019). These are just a few of the examples of using MI for identification, and there are many more. In purchasing processes, MIs could replace contactless payment cards or wearable devices (K. Michael & Michael, 2013). MI can be used as a means of controlling access to restricted areas and premises of high importance (Gillenson, 2019). As (Gazziro et al. 2010) outlines, MIs can also be used to control access to weapons. Cases of using MI for employee access control have been reported (Banafa, 2022; Rodriguez, 2019; Siibak & Otsus, 2022), as well as using MI for smart home management (e.g., to open doors, computers, phones), as in the case of Professor Warwick in 1998 (Rotter et al., 2008).

In all the cases presented, we can see plenty of advantages of MI use: you cannot lose them, they are not easy to steal, and since they are passive devices, the battery cannot run down. Also, there is no need to remember passwords or other access codes. Nevertheless, we must not neglect the negative aspects of using MI, which are presented in the following subsection.

## 2.3 Potential threats from the use of microchip implants

Since the first attempts to use MI in humans, the issue of privacy has been discussed. According to previous research, one of the main barriers to using MI is the fear of surveillance. In many MI acceptance studies, individuals have expressed concern that governments or even their employers will monitor them by tracking their MI (Pettersson, 2017; Rodriguez, 2019; Shafeie et al., 2022). For the MIs covered in this research, there is no reasonable basis for these fears. MI is a passive device that cannot track location unless it is read at close range by an external device, which then transmits the data further. Therefore, the thread of uncontrolled data transmission is similar to technology we already use on a daily basis, such as mobile devices (Harkin et al., 2019), social media activity (Wilson et al., 2021) or card payments (Lauer, 2020).

Unlike the voluntary use of MI, companies that require employees to use a MI invade their privacy and, more importantly, their bodies. Some sources referenced by (Shafeie et al., 2022) claim that implanted employees can claim intentional discrimination. Although (Rodriguez, 2019) reports only a few examples of employers providing body microchips to their employees in the United States and Sweden, the number of companies using this technology continues to grow. The most recent report of microchips in the workplace was found in Estonia (Siibak & Otsus, 2020). According to (Lobban 2022), only 11 states in the US. have laws prohibiting mandatory microchipping of humans, while the other states in the US. only require informed consent from individuals prior to implantation. To our knowledge, the European Union (EU) has not developed a privacy regime for MI users. In 2018, the European Parliament published a study on the use of MI for workers (Graveling et al., 2018). Despite the wide range of potential uses, legal restrictions, ethical considerations, safety risks, and potential health concerns identified in the study

(Graveling et al. 2018), there is no strict ban on MI use for workers. Similar to various software applications (Perera et al., 2019), the General Data Protection Regulation (GDPR) must be considered when implementing MI in the EU. EU legislation does not include provisions for potential liability for health problems of workers who have been implanted with microchips at the request of their employer.

In addition to privacy concerns, health concerns about microchips are often discussed. MI is a foreign body in the human body. Microchip implantation is generally considered safe when performed by qualified medical professionals in a sterile environment using proper techniques and equipment. However, as with any medical procedure, there are always potential risks and complications that should be carefully considered. The risk of infection or development of malignancy is among the greatest concerns when it comes to the use of MI. According to (Albrecht 2010), eleven cases of sarcoma and other cases in animals were reported in scientific journals between 1990 and 2006. On the other hand, (Lai et al. 2016) reported the use of MI for the treatment of cancer cells. Therefore, the decision to use MI in humans should be based on a detailed analysis of the advantages and disadvantages in each individual case (e.g., if life-saving drugs were administered, the advantages would likely outweigh the possibility of side effects). Based on current scientific knowledge, there are no known cases of adverse reactions to MIs in humans. MIs are commonly used in pets, and there have been occasional reports of complications such as infection or movement of the chip in the body. However, such complications are rare and usually minor, while the problem of movement in the body could be solved by the special non-slip layer (Graveling et al., 2018). As for other medical interventions, no major problems were found in the literature. According to (Fram et al. 2020), magnetic resonance imaging of patients with MIs is likely to be safe. Although no actual study was performed with MI, based on previous studies on other subdermal implants, there is a risk of allergic reaction to some of the materials in the MI coating or tissue infection due to skin injury.

Overall, the safety of MIs depends on a number of factors, including the skill of the healthcare provider performing the procedure, the materials used in the implant, and the individual's overall health status. It's important to discuss the potential risks and benefits of MIs with a qualified healthcare provider before making a decision.

## 3. Research methodology

The purpose of this study is to identify the factors that influence our decision to adopt the MI. The conceptual model of the factors is shown in Figure 1. Previous literature suggests that these factors include a wide range of usability and apprehension due to potential threats. Therefore, in this study, an extended model TAM is proposed to answer the question of acceptability of MI.

Based on previous studies, we built a model to predict behavioural intentions to use MIs based on TAM, as shown in Figure 1. In this research, we followed a similar research protocol as in our previous studies (Werber et al., 2018; Žnidaršič et al., 2021). The extended model based on TAM adopts the components of TAM (Venkatesh & Davis, 2000): Perceived Ease of Use (PEU), Perceived Usefulness (PU), and Behavioural Intention to Use (BIU). In the previous round of the study in 2016, we included four constructs: Perceived Trust (PT), Privacy Right (PR), Privacy Threat (PT) and Health Concerns (HC), as well as three individual predictors Age, perception of Technology Safety, and Painful Procedure (Žnidaršič et al., 2021). In the present 2021 study, three additional constructs were added to the model: Conspiracy Theory (CT), Fake News (FN), and Microchips in Pandemic (MP).

*Figure 1: The proposed acceptance model for behavioural intentions to use microchip implants.*

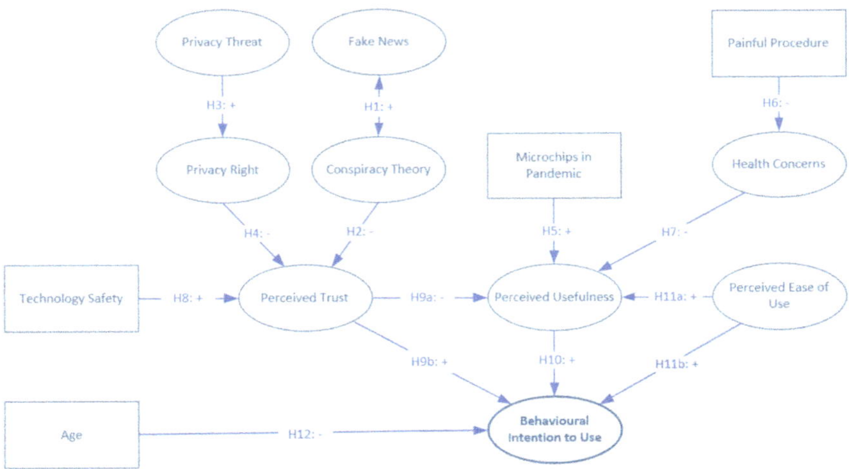


To examine the relationships between our constructs, the fourteen hypotheses shown in Figure 1 were generated. In addition, hypothesized positive or negative effects between the constructs are presented.

The measurement of the questionnaire items pertaining to HC, PP, PT, PR, PTh, TS, PEU, CT, FN, and MP was conducted on a 5-point scale (ranging from "strongly disagree" to "strongly agree"), while the items concerning PU were measured on a 5-point scale of acceptance (ranging from "very bad idea" to "very good idea"). The calculation of BIU was derived as the sum of five indicators measured with binary "yes/no" options. Age was measured as a numeric variable. Table 1 lists the constructs, measurement items and sources.

*Table 1: Measurement items*

| Constructs | Measurement Items | Sources |
|---|---|---|
| **Behavioural Intention to Use** | BIU1: Number of different potential subcutaneous MIs uses. | (Davis, 1989; Venkatesh et al., 2012; Venkatesh & Davis, 2000; Werber et al., 2018) |
| **Technology Safety** | TS1: MIs technology is safe enough to be used in humans. | (Perakslis et al., 2014) |
| **Perceived Trust** | PT1: The state will ensure the security and the protection of human rights (security of identity documents, passport, identity theft, tracking via GPS, no records should be archived without the consent of the person observed).<br>PT2: Banks will provide security (payment, discretion of operation, transactions, etc.).<br>PT3: The healthcare system will provide security (personal data, medical data, information on treatments, organ donation, etc.). | (Graveling et al., 2018; Smith, 2008) |
| **Perceived Usefulness** | MIs could be used for:<br>PU1: monitoring the health of the user.<br>PU2: warning about potential health problems or complications.<br>PU3: storing a user's medical info to be used in an emergency.<br>PU4: storing information about organ donation.<br>PU5: saving life (e.g., unconsciousness, cardiac pacemaker, insulin dispenser). | (Davis, 1989; Katz & Rice, 2009; Werber et al., 2018) |
| **Perceived Ease of Use** | PEU1: MIs are always available.<br>PEU2: MIs cannot be lost.<br>PEU3: MIs can integrate multiple functions at the same time. | (Davis, 1989; Venkatesh et al., 2012; Venkatesh & Davis, 2000; Werber et al., 2018) |
| **Conspiracy Theory** | CT1: Authorities plan to use a corona virus vaccine to inject MI.<br>CT2: Governments have a secret plan to use MI for unauthorised surveillance or supervision.<br>CT3: There is a relation between 5G technology and the spread of Covid-19. | (Gagliardone et al., 2021; Gu et al., 2021; Halpern et al., 2019; Imhoff et al., 2018; Ullah et al., 2021) |

| Constructs | Measurement Items | Sources |
|---|---|---|
| **Privacy Right** | PR1: No one should be able to gather or disclose your personal information without your consent.<br>PR2: People should have the right to control their personal information. | (Graveling et al., 2018; Lockton & Rosenberg, 2005) |
| **Microchips in Pandemics** | MP1: In my opinion, global pandemic management could benefit from microchip implant usage. | (Aji et al., 2020; Al-Maroof et al., 2020) |
| **Health Concerns** | HC1: MIs can be threatening to my health because of the possibility of movement in my body.<br>HC2: MIs may affect my emotional behaviour (control of human behaviour, etc.).<br>HC3: MIs can be threatening to my health because of possible allergies.<br>HC4: MIs can be threatening to my health because of their impact on the nervous system. | (Albrecht, 2010; Foster & Jaeger, 2007; Gillenson, 2019; Graveling et al., 2018; Katz & Rice, 2009; Rotter et al., 2008; van der Togt et al., 2011) |
| **Fake news** | FN1: Drinking hot water, methanol or alcohol has been recommended as a proven cure for Covid-19.<br>FN2: Coronavirus can be transmitted by houseflies, mosquito bites or domestic animals. | (Halpern et al., 2019; Ullah et al., 2021) |
| **Privacy Threat** | PTh1: Organizations and agencies ask you for too much personal information.<br>PTh2: The present use of computers is an actual threat to personal privacy in the country.<br>PTh3: I am concerned about threats to my privacy in the country today. | (Bansal et al., 2015) |
| **Painful Procedure** | PP1: Implanting MI is a painful procedure. | (M. G. Michael & Michael, 2010) |

## 3.1 Sample and data collection

In order to investigate the acceptance of MIs, the survey was conducted in spring 2021 in five countries: Poland, Croatia, Slovenia, Ukraine and Russia. A convenience sample of the general population was used. Data were used from 1995 respondents who answered at least some of the questions in the questionnaire. A quarter of the respondents (25.76%) were from Poland, 18.50% from Croatia, 20.30% from Slovenia, 20.10% from Ukraine, and 15.34% from Russia (Table 2). The youngest respondents were 18 years old, while the highest age was 91 years. The average age of respondents was 37.81 years with a standard deviation of 16.67 years. The frequency distribution of the age of the respondents is shown in Table 2.

*Table 2: Characteristics of the sample*

| Demographic characteristic | | Frequency | Percentage (%) |
|---|---|---|---|
| **Country** | Poland | 512 | 25.76 |
| | Croatia | 369 | 18.50 |
| | Slovenia | 405 | 20.30 |
| | Ukraine | 401 | 20.10 |
| | Russia | 306 | 15.34 |
| **Gender** | Female | 1123 | 56.52 |
| | Male | 864 | 43.48 |
| **Age** | 18 – 20 years old | 349 | 17.59 |
| | 21 – 30 years old | 482 | 24.29 |
| | 31 – 40 years old | 355 | 17.89 |
| | 41 – 50 years old | 342 | 17.24 |
| | 51 – 60 years old | 234 | 11.79 |
| | 61 – 70 years old | 130 | 6.55 |
| | 71 years old and above | 92 | 4.64 |
| **Status** | Student | 631 | 31.68 |
| | Employed | 1055 | 52.96 |
| | Unemployed | 95 | 4.77 |
| | Retired | 211 | 10.59 |
| **Education level** | Elementary school or less | 34 | 1.71 |
| | Vocational school | 71 | 3.56 |
| | Four-year secondary school | 568 | 28.51 |
| | College | 228 | 11.45 |
| | First Bologna cycle | 360 | 18.07 |
| | Second Bologna cycle | 444 | 22.29 |
| | Third Bologna cycle | 287 | 14.41 |

## 3.2 Data analysis, validity and reliability

The model shown in Figure 1 describes the relationships and impacts between the constructs. Data obtained from the survey were analysed using the standard two-stage approach at SEM (Schumacker & Lomax, 2010), with the first stage validating the measurement model. Confirmatory Factor Analysis (CFA) was used to determine how well the measured questionnaire items reflected the theoretical constructs. Construct validity of the measurement model was assessed by examining convergent and discriminant validity. Three criteria were examined to assess convergent validity: Estimates of standardised factor loadings should not exceed 0.5, Composite Reliability (CR) for each construct should exceed 0.7, and Average Variance Extracted (AVE) for each construct should exceed 0.5 (Fornell & Larcker, 1981; Koufteros, 1999).

In the second step, SEM was used to test for structural impacts between constructs. To describe the relationships between constructs, the unstandardized (B) and standardized path coefficients ($\beta$), z-values, and significance level were calculated and reported. A coefficient of determination ($R^2$) was calculated for each endogenous construct, representing the percentage of variance explained for the variable by its set of predictors.

The overall fit of the measurement and structural model was assessed based on a number of the most common fit indices:

- The comparative fit index (*CFI*) and the Tucker-Lewis Index (*TLI*) should be at least 0.9 (Koufteros, 1999). The root mean square error of approximation (*RMSEA*) value should be below 0.06 (Teo & Zhou, 2014), or at least less than 0.08 (MacCallum et al., 1996),
- The standardised root mean square residual (*SRMR*) should be at least less than 0.08 (Hu & Bentler, 1999).

Several researchers (Cheung and Rensvold 2002) point out that some goodness-of-fit indices (*GFI*) are affected by the model complexity (e.g., *CFI*, but not *RMSEA*). Therefore, widely accepted criteria for goodness of fit indices (e.g., $CFI = 0.90$) should be judged with caution in complex models, and models should not be rejected based on a single fail in one index.

All analyses, CFA and SEM, were performed using the R-package lavaan (Rosseel, 2021) and semTools (Jorgensen et al., 2020). The following section presents the results according to the described analysis procedure.

## 4. Results

The percentages of respondents willing to use a MI for various purposes are shown in Table 3. The highest percentage of respondents (37.19%) would use an MI for health care purposes and the lowest percentage of respondents (15.89%) would have MI for shopping and payment. The variable "number of potential MI uses" was calculated as the sum of five dichotomous variables on the different MI uses, and its mean value was 1.23 and $SD = 1.73$ (Table 4).

The following section provides details of the descriptive statistics (*M*, i.e. the mean, and *SD*, i.e. the standard deviation) for the 29 continuous variables that were included in the research model. These are presented in Table 4. The findings indicate that on average, the highest levels of agreement among respondents in the case of

*Table 3: Willingness to implant a microchip (N = 1995)*

| Would you insert MI | Positive response |
|---|---|
| …for health care purposes (identification, storage of medical data, information on organ donations, etc.)? | 37.19% |
| …for identification purposes (ID card, passport, driving license, etc.)? | 21.80% |
| …for shopping and payment purposes (debit cards, credit cards, profit cards, etc.)? | 15.89% |
| …for everyday use at home (unlocking of house or apartment, car, computer, mobile phone, etc.)? | 16.35% |
| …if you had been assured that GPS tracking and positioning would not be possible? | 25.76% |

PR construct were observed for the variables "No one should be able to collect or disclose your personal information without your consent" ($M = 4.56$, $SD = 0.74$), and "People should have the right to control their personal information" ($M = 4.55$, $SD = 0.74$). On average, the statement from the FN construct that drinking hot water, methanol, or alcohol is recommended as a proven cure for COVID-19 receives the greatest disagreement ($M = 2.86$, $SD = 0.99$).

*Table 4: Descriptive statistics of the items for the model constructs (N = 1995)*

| Constructs | Items | M | SD | Constructs | Items | M | SD |
|---|---|---|---|---|---|---|---|
| PR | PR1 | 4.56 | 0.735 | PU | PU1 | 3.38 | 1.224 |
| | PR2 | 4.55 | 0.740 | | PU2 | 3.55 | 1.208 |
| PTh | PTh1 | 3.94 | 0.966 | | PU3 | 3.46 | 1.213 |
| | PTh2 | 3.96 | 0.950 | | PU4 | 3.18 | 1.231 |
| | PTh3 | 3.77 | 1.042 | | PU5 | 3.62 | 1.186 |
| TS | TS1 | 2.53 | 1.073 | PEU | PEU1 | 3.05 | 1.088 |
| MP | MP1 | 2.77 | 1.181 | | PEU2 | 3.52 | 1.074 |
| HC | HC1 | 3.29 | 1.169 | | PEU3 | 3.70 | 0.967 |
| | HC2 | 3.09 | 1.278 | CT | CT1 | 2.25 | 1.173 |
| | HC3 | 3.48 | 1.137 | | CT2 | 2.75 | 1.290 |
| | HC4 | 3.39 | 1.168 | | CT3 | 2.13 | 1.140 |
| PP | PP1 | 3.10 | 1.091 | FN | FN1 | 1.86 | 0.995 |
| PT | PT1 | 2.47 | 1.181 | | FN2 | 2.06 | 0.983 |
| | PT2 | 2.78 | 1.184 | BIU | BIU1 | 1.23 | 1.730 |
| | PT3 | 2.79 | 1.195 | | | | |

## 4.1 Measurement model assessment

In order to establish construct validity — the extent to which a set of measured items reflects the theoretical construct — convergent validity and discriminant validity were assessed.

The outcomes of the evaluation are outlined in Table 5. The analysis indicates that the factor loadings for these items exceed 0.5, suggesting that the measurement model has convergent validity (see Table 5). Furthermore, the *AVE* for eight constructs exceeds the threshold of 0.5, thereby demonstrating that the measurement model has convergent validity. The results obtained demonstrate the convergent validity for the set of latent variables and the corresponding items in the measurement model. In other words, the results indicate that all included items are significantly related to the specified latent variable.

An examination of the discriminant validity of the measurement model was conducted by comparing the square root of *AVE* for each construct with the correlations between the corresponding constructs (Table 5). As demonstrated in the right panel of Table 5, the correlations between eight constructs (and five measured variables within the structural model) are presented, with the diagonal elements corresponding to the square root of *AVE* values. The values of the square root of *AVE* for each construct were found to exceed the respective correlations between constructs. Consequently, it may be inferred that discriminant validity exists for all constructs.

Cronbach's alpha coefficients (Table 5) for eight constructs ranged from 0.80 to 0.95 indicating high internal reliability (Field, 2018; Hair et al., 2019). The coefficient for FN is slightly lower but still acceptable (Cronbach's alpha = 0.66).

The overall fit of the measurement model was assessed using a number of commonly used fit indices. The $\chi^2$ value was 971.15 at 247 degrees of freedom. *CFI*, *TLI* and *SRMR* indicate good model fit (*CFI* = 0.969, *TLI* = 0.962, *SRMR* = 0.034). The *RMSEA* value is equal to 0.038 and the upper limit of the 90% confidence interval of the *RMSEA* (0.036, 0.041) is less than 0.06 suggesting good model fit (MacCallum et al., 1996). From the calculated fit indices, it can be concluded that the measurement model fits the sample data well.

## 4.2 Testing the structural model

According to the research model (Figure 1), four measured variables and 14 structural paths were added to nine constructs. The structural paths are consistent with the proposed hypotheses. First, the overall model was evaluated.

The fit of the structural model was good according to the set of indices examined: $\chi^2 = 3259.81$, $df = 385$, $CFI = 0.894$, $TLI = 0.881$, and $RMSEA = 0.061$

*Table 5: Cronbach's Alpha, Composite reliability (CR), average variance extracted (AVE), square root of AVE and correlations between constructs*

| | PR | PTh | TS[a] | MP[a] | HC | PP[a] | PT | PU | PEU | CT | FN | Age[a] | BIU[a] |
|---|---|---|---|---|---|---|---|---|---|---|---|---|---|
| **Cronbach's Alpha** | 0.862 | 0.802 | / | / | 0.898 | / | 0.891 | 0.950 | 0.804 | 0.850 | 0.657 | / | / |
| **CR** | 0.864 | 0.806 | / | / | 0.900 | / | 0.892 | 0.950 | 0.804 | 0.851 | 0.679 | / | / |
| **AVE** | 0.761 | 0.580 | / | / | 0.693 | / | 0.734 | 0.792 | 0.578 | 0.656 | 0.522 | / | / |
| **Correlations** | | | | | | | | | | | | | |
| | **PR** | **PTh** | **TS[a]** | **MP[a]** | **HC** | **PP[a]** | **PT** | **PU** | **PEU** | **CT** | **FN** | **Age[a]** | **BIU[a]** |
| **PR** | 0.872 | | | | | | | | | | | | |
| **PTh** | 0.544 | 0.761 | | | | | | | | | | | |
| **TS[a]** | −0.086 | −0.229 | / | | | | | | | | | | |
| **MP[a]** | −0.049 | −0.154 | 0.401 | / | | | | | | | | | |
| **HC** | 0.159 | 0.313 | −0.587 | −0.303 | 0.833 | | | | | | | | |
| **PP[a]** | 0.103 | 0.149 | −0.316 | −0.150 | 0.604 | / | | | | | | | |
| **PT** | −0.107 | −0.274 | 0.419 | 0.447 | −0.316 | −0.120 | 0.857 | | | | | | |
| **PU** | 0.051 | −0.131 | 0.531 | 0.479 | −0.436 | −0.226 | 0.576 | 0.890 | | | | | |
| **PEU** | 0.149 | 0.035 | 0.393 | 0.337 | −0.345 | −0.189 | 0.397 | 0.538 | 0.760 | | | | |
| **CT** | 0.020 | 0.251 | −0.355 | −0.184 | 0.530 | 0.318 | −0.209 | −0.376 | −0.319 | 0.760 | | | |
| **FN** | −0.169 | 0.041 | −0.107 | 0.003 | 0.292 | 0.197 | 0.055 | −0.120 | −0.236 | 0.698 | 0.723 | | |
| **Age[a]** | −0.111 | 0.021 | −0.050 | −0.030 | −0.007 | 0.005 | −0.074 | −0.144 | 0.066 | −0.023 | −0.010 | / | |
| **BIU[a]** | −0.008 | −0.208 | 0.455 | 0.400 | −0.161 | −0.371 | 0.445 | 0.539 | 0.338 | −0.250 | −0.060 | −0.222 | / |

[a]The individual variables TS, MP, PP, Age, and BIU are presented in the table solely to compare the square root of the AVE of each construct with correlations between the corresponding construct and all other constucts and individual measured variables. For individual measured variables the Cronbach's Alpha, CR, and AVE are not applicable.

(90% $CI; 0.059, 0.063$). Table 6 shows the results for the unstandardized coefficients ($B$), the standardized coefficients ($\beta$) and the corresponding $z$-values, which reflect the relationships between the latent variables in terms of magnitude and statistical significance. A graphical overview of the confirmed hypotheses and the coefficient of determination ($R^2$) for each endogenous construct is shown in Figure 2.

*Table 6: Summary of hypothesis tests for the structural model*

| Hypotheses & Paths | Expected Sign | $\beta$ | z | p | Confirmed? |
|---|---|---|---|---|---|
| H1: FN ↔ CT | + | 0.691 | 20.510 | 0.000 | Yes |
| H2: CT → PT | – | −0.070 | −2.371 | 0.018 | Yes |
| H3: PTh → PR | + | 0.551 | 14.926 | 0.000 | Yes |
| H4: PR → PT | – | −0.081 | −2.967 | 0.003 | Yes |
| H5: MP → PU | + | 0.233 | 8.990 | 0.000 | Yes |
| H6: PP → HC | + | 0.606 | 24.146 | 0.000 | Yes |
| H7: HC → PU | – | −0.200 | −7.786 | 0.000 | Yes |
| H8: TS → PT | + | 0.409 | 14.641 | 0.000 | Yes |
| H9a: PT → PU | + | 0.380 | 12.575 | 0.000 | Yes |
| H9b: PT → BIU | + | 0.210 | 7.772 | 0.000 | Yes |
| H10: PU → BIU | + | 0.350 | 14.734 | 0.000 | Yes |
| H11a: PEU → PU | + | 0.324 | 9.960 | 0.000 | Yes |
| H11b: PEU → BIU | + | 0.072 | 2.977 | 0.003 | Yes |
| H12: Age → BIU | – | −0.169 | −9.160 | 0.000 | Yes |

The TAM theory posits the notion of positive effects of PEU and PU on BIU (in this case H11a and H10). The findings have substantiated both hypotheses at the 1% significance level. In addition to PEU and PU, BIU is also influenced by PT (H9b) and Age (H12). The collective contribution of these factors to the variance of BIU was determined to be 28.5%. The TAM model further predicts a positive impact of PEU on PU ($\beta = 0.324$).

The original TAM model was augmented with six constructs and four external variables, as illustrated in Figure 1. The hypothesis indicating the positive impact of PTh on PR was confirmed at the 1 % significance level, with the result $\beta = 0.551$. Conversely, the negative impact of PR on PT (H4) was confirmed ($\beta = -0.081$).

In addition, the analysis revealed that the predictor variable PU is influenced by three significant indicators, namely HC, PT, and MP, and that these three variables collectively accounted for 39.8% of the total variance observed in the data. The strongest impact is the one of PT ($\beta = 0.380$). In addition, PP has a significant negative impact on HC (H6), and TS has a significant positive impact on PT (H8).

CT and FN are positively correlated ($r = 0.691$) and CT has statistically significant negative impact on PT ($\beta = -0.070$) at the 5% significance level.

*Figure 2: The model for behavioural intentions regarding the use of microchip implants.*

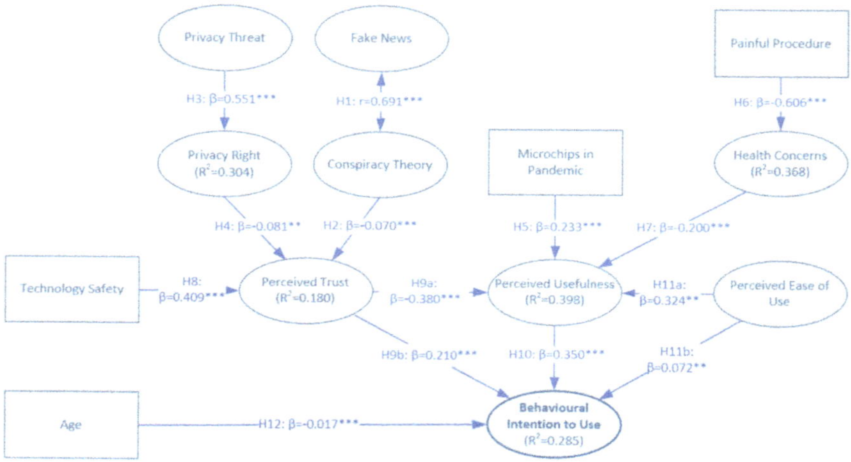


## 5. Discussion and conclusions

Microchip implants are implanted in a person's body, usually in the hand or arm. These devices contain information that can be read by a scanner so that the person's identity or medical information can be quickly retrieved. While microchip implants have been used in animals for many years, their use in humans is relatively new and controversial.

There are many arguments for and against the use of microchip implants in humans. Supporters of the technology point to the many potential benefits. For example, they argue that microchip implants could be used to store medical data, allowing physicians and other health professionals to quickly access a person's medical history and make more informed decisions about his or her treatment (Eltorai et al., 2016; Sundaresan et al., 2015). In addition, microchip implants could be used to store identification information, which would make it easier for law enforcement to identify individuals in emergency situations (Meyer et al., 2006).

However, opponents of microchip implants, raise a number of concerns. According to (Pettersson 2017; Rodriguez 2019) one of the biggest concerns is privacy. Some worry that microchip implants could be used to track a person's movements or monitor their activities. Others worry that the information contained in the chip could be accessed by hackers or other malicious actors, compromising the privacy and security of the individual. Another concern is the risk of misuse. For example, microchip implants could be used as a surveillance or monitoring tool, allowing governments or corporations to monitor or manipulate people's behaviour.

Despite these concerns, some people are already opting for microchip implantation. In some cases, people are interested in the technology and want to experiment with it (K. Michael et al., 2017), or they see the potential benefits of the technology and are willing to accept the risks (Morris, 2016). In toher cases, employers recommend the use of microchip implants to their employees (Siibak & Otsus, 2022).

In this study, we identified a number of factors that influence microchip implant acceptance. Nearly a decade of studying microchip implant acceptance has given us deep insight into how it has evolved and changed over time, influenced by various events, research advances, and regulations. A total of 12 factors influencing microchip acceptance were included in the research model. Due to changes in the general perception of technology and health in recent years after the COVID-19 pandemic, the constructs of fake news, conspiracy theory, and microchips in pandemic were added to the basic model presented by (Žnidaršič et al., 2021). In addition, the study was extended to five different countries in the Eastern European region. All proposed hypotheses were confirmed. Perceived usefulness, ease of use, trust, and age have a significant impact on the intention to use microchip implants. While the first three constructs have a positive impact, the impact of age is negative, indicating that younger people are more willing to use microchip implants.

Further on, usefulness depends on perceptions of the usefulness of microchip implants in pandemics and health concerns, which in turn are influenced by perceptions of the pain related to the implantation. On the other hand, trust in technology is influenced by perceptions of the technology safety, while it decreases when the right to privacy and conspiracy theories are added. The right to privacy is influenced by threats to privacy. Belief in conspiracy theories is closely related to fake news, which also negatively affects perceived trust in the microchip implant technology.

Despite the large sample which included participants from five different countries, this study is limited to the Eastern European region. Therefore, future studies should include samples from other regions and cultures. Also, studies could identify differences in responses according to these demographic characteristics.

All in all, by providing insight into the factors that influence the readiness to adopt MI, our study has highlighted the potential threats and opportunities for decision makers or other stakeholders of MI technology. In this way, actions can be taken to improve the level of adoption of MI using a variety of approaches. For example, researching the safety of MI, conducting additional testing, further improving the technology, and disseminating the results to the general public would significantly improve perceived confidence in the technology and reduce health concerns. Special consideration should be made to the use of artificial intelligence with microchip implants, which holds the potential for enhanced communication, cognitive abilities, and medical advancements.

Ultimately, the acceptance of microchip implants in the future will depend on a variety of factors, including their usefulness, effectiveness, safety, and privacy protections, as illustrated in the model. As technology continues to evolve, it will be important for individuals, governments, and other stakeholders to carefully consider these issues and weigh the potential benefits and risks of microchip implants.

## Acknowledgement

This research was supported by the Slovenian Research and Innovation Agency; Program No. P5-0018 – Decision Support Systems in Digital Business.

The authors would like to thank Lukasz Zakonnik from the Department of Computer Science in Economics, University of Łódź, Maryna Vovk from the National Technical University "Kharkiv Polytechnic Institute", Vanja Bevanda from the Faculty of Economics and Tourism "Dr. Mijo Mirković", Juraj Dobrila University of Pula, as well as Daria Maltseva and Stanislav Moissev from the HSE University Moscow, for their valuable assistance in data collection.

## Bibliography

Aji, H. M., Berakon, I., & Md Husin, M. (2020). COVID-19 and e-wallet usage intention: A multigroup analysis between Indonesia and Malaysia. *Cogent Business and Management*, *7*(1), 1–16. https://doi.org/10.1080/23311975.2020.1804181

Al Mansouri, L. M. K., & Alnajjar, F. (2023). A Survey on the Emerging Trend of Human Microchip Implants And Their Potential. *2023 Advances in Science and Engineering Technology International Conferences (ASET)*, 1–5. https://doi.org/10.1109/ASET56582.2023.10180565

Albrecht, K. (2010). Microchip-induced tumors in laboratory rodents and dogs: A review of the literature 1990–2006. *2010 IEEE International Symposium on Technology and Society*, 337–349. https://doi.org/10.1109/ISTAS.2010.5514622

Al-Maroof, R. S., Salloum, S. A., Hassanien, A. E., & Shaalan, K. (2020). Fear from COVID-19 and technology adoption: the impact of Google Meet during Coronavirus pandemic. *Interactive Learning Environments*, 1–16. https://doi.org/10.1080/10494820.2020.1830121

Banafa, A. (2022). Microchips in humans: Consumer-friendly app, or new frontier in surveillance? *Bulletin of the Atomic Scientists*, *78*(5), 256–260. https://doi.org/10.1080/00963402.2022.2109330

Bansal, G., Zahedi, F. M., & Gefen, D. (2015). Do context and personality matter? Trust and privacy concerns in disclosing private information online. *Information & Management*, *53*(1), 1–21. https://doi.org/10.1016/j.im.2015.08.001

Buttazzo, G. (2023). Rise of artificial general intelligence: risks and opportunities. Frontiers in Artificial Intelligence, 6. https://doi.org/10.3389/frai.2023.1226990

Cheung, G. W., & Rensvold, R. B. (2002). Evaluating goodness-of-fit indexes for testing measurement invariance. *Structural Equation Modeling*, *9*(2), 233–255. https://doi.org/10.1207/S15328007SEM0902_5

Davis, F. D. (1989). Perceived Usefulness, Perceived Ease Of Use, And User Acceptance. *MIS Quarterly*, *13*(3), 319–339. https://doi.org/10.2307/249008

Eltorai, A. E. M., Fox, H., McGurrin, E., & Guang, S. (2016). Microchips in Medicine: Current and Future Applications. *BioMed Research International*, *2016*, 1743472. https://doi.org/10.1155/2016/1743472

Field, A. (2018). *Discovering Statistics Using IBM SPSS Statistics* (5th ed.). SAGE Publications.

Fornell, C., & Larcker, D. F. (1981). Evaluating Structural Equation Models with Unobservable Variables and Measurement Error. *Journal of Marketing Research*, *18*(1), 39–50. https://doi.org/10.2307/3151312

Foster, K. R., & Jaeger, J. (2007). RFID inside: The murky ethics of implanted chips. *IEEE Spectrum*, *44*(3), 24–29. https://doi.org/10.1109/MSPEC.2007.323430

Fram, B. R., Rivlin, M., & Beredjiklian, P. K. (2020). On Emerging Technology: What to Know When Your Patient Has a Microchip in His Hand. *Journal of Hand Surgery*, *45*(7), 645–649. https://doi.org/10.1016/j.jhsa.2020.01.008

Franks, C., & Smith, R. G. (2021). Changing perceptions of biometric technologies. In *AIS Research Report no. 20*. https://doi.org/10.52922/rr78146

Gagliardone, I., Diepeveen, S., Findlay, K., Olaniran, S., Pohjonen, M., & Tallam, E. (2021). Demystifying the COVID-19 Infodemic: Conspiracies, Context, and the Agency of Users. *Social Media + Society*, *7*(3), 1–16. https://doi.org/10.1177/20563051211044233

Gangadharbatla, H. (2020). Biohacking: An exploratory study to understand the factors influencing the adoption of embedded technologies within the human body. *Heliyon*, *6*(5), e03931. https://doi.org/10.1016/j.heliyon.2020.e03931

Gazziro, M. A., Almeida, L. O. B., Pedrazzani, C. D., & Machado, C. G. C. F. (2010). Smart Gun with Implantable RFID Match System – A practical approach. *Advances in Control, Chemical Engineering, Civil Engineering and Mechanical Engineering: European Conference of Chemical Engineering*, *3*, 223–226.

Gillenson, M. L. (2019). I' ve got you under my skin: the past, present, and future use of RFID technology in people and animals. *Journal of Information Technology Management*, *XXX*(2), 19–29.

Graveling, R., Winski, T., & Dixon, K. (2018). The use of chip implants for workers. In *Study for the EMPL Committee*.

Gu, F., Wu, Y., Hu, X., Guo, J., Yang, X., & Zhao, X. (2021). The Role of Conspiracy Theories in the Spread of COVID-19 across the United States. *International Journal of Environmental Research and Public Health*, *18*(7), 3843. https://doi.org/10.3390/ijerph18073843

Hair, J. F., Black, W. C., Babin, B. J., & Anderson, R. E. (2019). *Multivariate Data Analysis* (8th ed.). Cengage Learning.

Halpern, D., Valenzuela, S., Katz, J., & Miranda, J. P. (2019). *From Belief in Conspiracy Theories to Trust in Others: Which Factors Influence Exposure, Believing and Sharing Fake News BT - Social Computing and Social Media. Design, Human Behavior and Analytics* (G. Meiselwitz, Ed.; pp. 217–232). Springer International Publishing.

Harkin, D., Molnar, A., & Vowles, E. (2019). The commodification of mobile phone surveillance: An analysis of the consumer spyware industry. *Crime, Media, Culture*, *16*(1), 33–60. https://doi.org/10.1177/1741659018820562

Hu, L., & Bentler, P. M. (1999). Cutoff criteria for fit indexes in covariance structure analysis: Conventional criteria versus new alternatives. *Structural Equation Modeling*, *6*(1), 1–55. https://doi.org/10.1080/10705519909540118

Imhoff, R., Lamberty, P., & Klein, O. (2018). Using Power as a Negative Cue: How Conspiracy Mentality Affects Epistemic Trust in Sources of Historical Knowledge. *Personality and Social Psychology Bulletin*, *44*(9), 1364–1379. https://doi.org/10.1177/0146167218768779

Japertas, S., & Jankuniene, R. (2020). *NFC Vulnerabilities Investigation*.

Jorgensen, T. D., S, P., Schoemann, A. M., Rosseel, Y., Miller, P., Quick, C., Garnier-Villarreal, M., Selig, J., Boulton, A., Preacher, K., Coffmann, D., Rhemtulla, M., Robitzsch, A., Enders, C., Arslan, R., Clinton, B., Panko, P., Merkle, E., Chesnut, S., … Ben-Shachar, M. S. (2020). *Useful Tools for Structural Equation Modeling.*

Katz, J. E., & Rice, R. E. (2009). Public views of mobile medical devices and services: A US national survey of consumer sentiments towards RFID healthcare technology. *International Journal of Medical Informatics, 78*, 104–114. https://doi.org/10.1016/j.ijmedinf.2008.06.001

Koufteros, X. A. (1999). Testing a model of pull production: a paradigm for manufacturing research using structural equation modeling. *Journal of Operations Management, 17*(4), 467–488. https://doi.org/10.1016/S0272-6963(99)00002-9

Lai, H. C., Chan, H. W., & Singh, N. P. (2016). Effects of radiation from a radiofrequency identification (RFID) microchip on human cancer cells. *International Journal of Radiation Biology, 92*(3), 156–161. https://doi.org/10.3109/09553002.2016.1135264

Lauer, J. (2020). Plastic surveillance: Payment cards and the history of transactional data, 1888 to present. *Big Data & Society, 7*(1), 2053951720907632. https://doi.org/10.1177/2053951720907632

Lobban, K. (2022). The Anomaly That Is Privacy: Data Privacy Concerns Related to the Rise of Microchip Implants in Humans Comments. *Catholic University Journal of Law and Technology, 30*(2), 65–90.

Lockton, V., & Rosenberg, R. S. (2005). RFID: The next serious threat to privacy. *Ethics and Information Technology, 7*(4), 221–231. https://doi.org/10.1007/s10676-006-0014-2

MacCallum, R. C., Browne, M. W., & Sugawara, H. M. (1996). Power analysis and determination of sample size for covariance structure modeling. *Psychological Methods, 1*(2), 130–149. https://doi.org/10.1037/1082-989X.1.2.130

Meyer, H. J., Chansue, N., & Monticelli, F. (2006). Implantation of radio frequency identification device (RFID) microchip in disaster victim identification (DVI). *Forensic Science International, 157*(2–3), 168–171. https://doi.org/10.1016/j.forsciint.2005.10.001

Michael, K., Aloudat, A., Michael, M. G., & Perakslis, C. (2017). You Want to do What with RFID? Perceptions of radio-frequency identification implants for employee identification in the workplace. *IEEE Consumer Electronics Magazine, 6*(3), 111–117. https://doi.org/10.1109/MCE.2017.2684978

Michael, K., & Michael, M. G. (2013). The future prospects of embedded microchips in humans as unique identifiers: The risks versus the rewards. *Media, Culture and Society, 35*(1), 78–86. https://doi.org/10.1177/0163443712464561

Michael, K., Michael, M. G., & Ip, R. (2008). *Microchip implants for humans as unique identifiers: a case study on VeriChip.*

Michael, M. G., & Michael, K. (2010). Toward a State of Überveillance [Special Section Introduction]. *IEEE Technology and Society Magazine, 29*(2), 9–16. https://doi.org/10.1109/MTS.2010.937024

Morris, H. (2016). Microchip implanted in man's hand allows him to pass through airport security. In *Traveller.*

Nicholls, R. (2017). Implanting Military RFID: Rights and Wrongs. *IEEE Technology and Society Magazine, 36*(1), 48–51. https://doi.org/10.1109/MTS.2017.2654288

Perakslis, C., & Michael, K. (2012). Indian Millennials: Are microchip implants a more secure technology for identification and access control? *Proceedings of the 2012 IEEE Conference on Technology and Society in Asia, T and SA 2012,* 1–9. https://doi.org/10.1109/TSAsia.2012.6397977

Perakslis, C., Michael, K., Michael, M. G., & Gable, R. (2014). Perceived barriers for implanting microchips in humans: A transnational study. *2014 IEEE Conference on Norbert Wiener in the 21st Century (21CW),* 1–8. https://doi.org/10.1109/NORBERT.2014.6893929

Perera, H., Hussain, W., Mougouei, D., Shams, R. A., Nurwidyantoro, A., & Whittle, J. (2019). Towards Integrating Human Values into Software: Mapping Principles and Rights of GDPR to Values. *2019 IEEE 27th International Requirements Engineering Conference (RE),* 404–409. https://doi.org/10.1109/RE.2019.00053

Pettersson, M. (2017). *Microchip implants and you: A study of the public perceptions of microchip implants.* UMEA Universitet.

Reicher, J., Reicher, D., & Reicher, M. (2007). Use of Radio Frequency Identification (RFID) Tags in Bedside Monitoring of Endotracheal Tube Position. *Journal of Clinical Monitoring and Computing, 21*(3), 155–158. https://doi.org/10.1007/s10877-007-9069-9

Rodriguez, D. A. (2019). Chipping in at work: Privacy concerns related to the use of body microchip ("RFID") implants in the employer-employee context. *Iowa Law Review, 104*(3), 1581–1611.

Rosseel, Y. (2021). The lavaan tutorial. In *The lavaan tutorial.*

Rotter, P., Daskala, B., & Compano, R. (2008). RFID implants: Opportunities and and challenges for identifying people. *IEEE Technology and Society Magazine, 27*(2), 24–32. https://doi.org/10.1109/mts.2008.924862

Sarfraz, N. (2019). Adermatoglyphia: Barriers to Biometric Identification and the Need for a Standardized Alternative. *Cureus, 11*(2), e4040–e4040. https://doi.org/10.7759/cureus.4040

Sarwar, N., Khan, F. N., Ali, A., Rafique, H., Hussain, I., & Irshad, A. (2019). Microchip with Advance Human Monitoring Technique and RFTS. In I. S. Bajwa, F. Kamareddine, & A. Costa (Eds.), *Intelligent Technologies and Applications* (pp. 560–570). Springer Singapore. https://doi.org//10.1007/978-981-13-6052-7_48

Schumacker, R. E., & Lomax, R. G. (2010). *A beginner's guide to structural equation modeling*. Routledge/Taylor & Francis Group.

Shafeie, S., Chaudhry, B. M., & Mohamed, M. (2022). Modeling Subcutaneous Microchip Implant Acceptance in the General Population: A Cross-Sectional Survey about Concerns and Expectations. *Informatics, 9*(1). https://doi.org/10.3390/informatics9010024

Shafeie, S., Mohamed, M., Issa, T.B., Chaudhry, B.M. (2023). Using Machine Learning to Model Potential Users with Health Risk Concerns Regarding Microchip Implants. In: Degen, H., Ntoa, S. (eds) Artificial Intelligence in HCI. HCII 2023. Lecture Notes in Computer Science(), vol 14051. Springer, Cham. https://doi.org/10.1007/978-3-031-35894-4_42

Shaheed, K., Mao, A., Qureshi, I., Kumar, M., Abbas, Q., Ullah, I., & Zhang, X. (2021). A Systematic Review on Physiological-Based Biometric Recognition Systems: Current and Future Trends. *Archives of Computational Methods in Engineering, 28*(7), 4917–4960. https://doi.org/10.1007/s11831-021-09560-3

Siibak, A., & Otsus, M. (2020). "You Either Love It Immediately, or You Hate It" Reflections and Experiences of Estonian Employees With Microchip Implants. *AoIR Selected Papers of Internet Research, October*. https://doi.org/10.5210/spir.v2020i0.11329

Siibak, A., & Otsus, M. (2022). Tracing the Innovation – Decision Process for Adopting Microchip Implants: Reflections and Experiences of Estonian Employees. *Somatechnics, 12*(3), 200–220. https://doi.org/10.3366/soma.2022.0388

Smith, C. (2008). Human microchip implantation. *Journal of Technology Management and Innovation, 3*(3), 151–156. https://doi.org/10.4067/S0718-27242008000100015

Sundaresan, S., Doss, R., & Zhou, W. (2015). *RFID in Healthcare – Current Trends and the Future BT - Mobile Health: A Technology Road Map* (S. Adibi, Ed.; pp. 839–870). Springer International Publishing. https://doi.org/10.1007/978-3-319-12817-7_36

Teo, T., & Zhou, M. (2014). Explaining the intention to use technology among university students: a structural equation modeling approach. *Journal of Computing in Higher Education, 26*(2), 124–142. https://doi.org/10.1007/s12528-014-9080-3

Ullah, I., Khan, K. S., Tahir, M. J., Ahmed, A., & Harapan, H. (2021). Myths and conspiracy theories on vaccines and COVID-19: Potential effect on global vaccine refusals. *Vacunas, 22*(2), 93–97. https://doi.org/10.1016/j.vacun.2021.01.001

van der Togt, R., Bakker, Piet. J. M., & Jaspers, M. W. M. (2011). A framework for performance and data quality assessment of Radio Frequency IDentification (RFID) systems in health care settings. *Journal of Biomedical Informatics, 44*(2), 372–383. https://doi.org/10.1016/j.jbi.2010.12.004

Venkat, R., Adchaya, A. S., Muthukumar, B., & Manipal, S. (2019). In-Vitro Study to Check the Viability of Fixed Partial Dentures with Built-in Passive RFIDs-A Forensic Dentistry Tool. *Journal of Clinical and Diagnostic Research, 13*(10), 8–13. https://doi.org/10.7860/jcdr/2019/42412.13186

Venkatesh, V., & Davis, F. D. (2000). A Theoretical Extension of the Technology Acceptance Model : Four Longitudinal Field Studies. *Management Science, 46*(2), 186–204. https://doi.org/10.1287/mnsc.46.2.186.11926

Venkatesh, V., Thong, J., & Xu, X. (2012). Consumer Acceptance and Use of Information Technology: Extending the Unified Theory. *MIS Quaterly, 36*(1), 157–178.

Werber, B., Baggia, A., & Žnidaršič, A. (2018). Factors Affecting the Intentions to Use RFID Subcutaneous Microchip Implants for Healthcare Purposes. *Organizacija, 51*(2), 121–133. https://doi.org/10.2478/orga-2018-0010

Wilson, A. E., Lehmann, C. U., Saleh, S. N., Hanna, J., & Medford, R. J. (2021). Social media: A new tool for outbreak surveillance. *Antimicrobial Stewardship & Healthcare Epidemiology, 1*(1), e50. https://doi.org/10.1017/ash.2021.225

Yang, Y., Luo, X., Chu, X., & Zhou, M.-T. (2020). *IoT Technologies and Applications BT - Fog-Enabled Intelligent IoT Systems* (Y. Yang, X. Luo, X. Chu, & M.-T. Zhou, Eds.; pp. 1–37). Springer International Publishing. https://doi.org/10.1007/978-3-030-23185-9_1

Žnidaršič, A., Baggia, A., Pavliček, A., Fischer, J., Rostanski, M., & Werber, B. (2021). Are we Ready to Use Microchip Implants? An International Crosssectional Study. *Organizacija, 54*(4), 275–292. https://doi.org/10.2478/orga-2021-0019

Blaž Gašperlin*, Andreja Pucihar** and Mirjana Kljajić Borštnar***

# Data maturity assessment of SMEs and definition of measurement scales

**Abstract:** The ubiquity of digital technologies has enabled a vast amount of data to be collected, analyzed and used to support daily business operations. The organization's maturity in data utilization can be described as ability to collect, manage and use data to make informed decisions and create new value. Small and medium-sized enterprises (SMEs) often have greater challenges in data utilization compared to large enterprises. To address this problem, we propose a model to assess data maturity of SMEs. Based on the assessment, the SMEs will be able to plan their actions towards data maturity better. For this purpose, we have identified a set of criteria and measurement scales that will serve as an input into the multiple criteria decision model following DEX methodology.

**Keywords:** data maturity, assessment, DEX, measurement scales, SMEs, artificial intelligence

## 1. Introduction

The development and use of digital technologies have enabled easier communication, connectivity and changed how organizations do business and provide a value to the customers through the changes in their business processes, products and service offerings (Rachinger et al., 2019; Vial, 2019). With the use of digital technologies, the amount of data has begun to increase and is now becoming the main driver for organizations' development and a source for quick response to business environment changes and market needs. At the forefront of these changes are decisions, which must often be quick, but above all accurate and based on data. Due to the fast-paced changes from traditional to digital business, a data and its management is becoming increasingly important (Kraus et al., 2022).

Data is the foundation of any information system that the organization uses to support its activities and decisions. In addition, data also plays an important role

* University of Maribor, Faculty of organizational sciences, Kranj, Slovenia; e-mail: blaz.gasperlin@um.si

** University of Maribor, Faculty of organizational sciences, Kranj, Slovenia; e-mail: andreja.pucihar@um.si

*** University of Maribor, Faculty of Organizational Sciences, Kranj, Slovenia, e-mail: mirjana.kljajic@um.si

in the development of advanced digital technologies such as distributed ledger technology (i.e. Blockchain) (Nofer et al., 2017; Xu et al., 2019), augmented reality (Al-Ansi et al., 2023; Y. Chen et al., 2019), and quantum computing (Gill et al., 2022; Rietsche et al., 2022), as well as artificial intelligence (AI) (Canhoto & Clear, 2019; Collins et al., 2021), where data is the foundation for artificial intelligence learning (Sundblad, 2018). Artificial intelligence algorithms require data to function and learn. The larger the data set available for learning, the better the result with fewer errors (Collins et al., 2021). Data must be cleaned and structured before it is used in artificial intelligence algorithms, otherwise we will not get the desired results. Although an AI system performs a learning process with a basic training data set, an AI system continuously learns throughout its lifecycle (De Silva & Alahakoon, 2022). For this purpose, new data is always needed.

Due to exponential data growth, organizations are dealing with an ever-growing amount of data that, if not managed properly, can lead to information overload and information chaos (Arnold et al., 2023). Therefore, the role of data and its management are becoming increasingly important.

The proper data management, good control and overview of the data, can make the organization more competitive and increase organization's added value (Eroğlu & Çakmak, 2018). According to Eroğlu & Çakmak (2018) advanced and successful organizations build, organize, store, and utilize their information assets in the most efficient manner, which is related with the ability to rapidly integrate information with new products and technologies, and establish a successful information management practices. Carillo (2017) based on findings of (Lavalle et al., 2011) defined this as a *data transformation*, describing a transformation from a traditional to a data-driven business. As described by (Carillo, 2017) a data-driven business can be defined as an entity whose business operations and decisions are based around the collection, storage and analysis of data in real-time and predictive manner, allowing to turn data into actionable insights at all organizational levels. Rogers (2020), based on the review of (Cech et al., 2018; Chen & Nath, 2018; Farah, 2017) defined data maturity as the ability of an organization to collect, store, transform and report on data, while also being able to build processes that require data-based decision-making. Others (Marchildon et al., 2018) understands data maturity as a property of data governance and the extent to which an organization has developed and applied the processes, policies, practices and structures necessary to optimize the collection, storage, use and dissemination of its data as an organizational resource.

Based on the description and definitions presented above such enterprises can be described as data mature, as they have developed capabilities to collect, store, transform, analyze, interpret and use the data to perform daily activities and make decisions based on data, but most important to create value from the data and create competitive advantage (Kljajič Borštnar et al., 2022; Rogers, 2020).

A tool that helps to assess the current situation (as-is) of an organization and to identify organization weaknesses and its strengths is defined as a maturity model. Proença & Borbinha (2016) defined a maturity model as "*a technique to assess business processes or certain aspect of organization*". Newer definition provided by (Stoiber et al., 2023) define maturity model as "*a valuable management tool for assessing and managing capabilities, creating a basis for their identification, prioritization and further development*". A maturity models can have a different maturity levels applied, but often consists of five maturity levels (Initial, Managed, Defined, Quantitatively Managed and Optimizing) (Proença & Borbinha, 2016). The maturity levels proposed in the maturity models are often derived from the Capability Maturity Model (CMMI) (Humphrey, 1988), which represents a basis for the development of today's maturity models. Based on the results of the as-is analysis, the recommendations for improvements can be derived and appropriate actions defined to create or improve capabilities to achieve higher maturity level (Becker et al., 2009; Stoiber et al., 2023).

The absence of a good data management is often present among the small and medium-sized enterprises (SMEs). Among the SMEs, there is still a perception that data is not as critical as compared to a large, usually more digitally mature enterprises (Harie, 2021). With an effective data management, organization can reach a better productivity (better data organization and easier and faster data search), reduced data loss and security risks, better adaptability to market needs, optimization of costs (Almazmomi et al., 2021), accurate data-based decisions and increase the revenue created through monetization of products and services (Faroukhi et al., 2020; Hanafizadeh & Harati Nik, 2020), enabling a new value creation and increase of competitiveness. According to (Gür, Guggenberger, et al., 2021) the role of data for organizations increases constantly and becomes crucial for developing data-driven services, business models, and innovation. The authors also emphasize that the large variety and amount of data available today, offers the potential to create and sustain competitive advantages, which can be achieved by effective data management.

Compared to large enterprises, SMEs often have greater challenges related with a good data utilization, which is often due to a lack of resources (financial, human, time), and appropriate skills (M. Iqbal et al., 2018; Parra et al., 2019). The fundamental problem is that the majority of SMEs do not exploit the potential of data for decision-making, which translates into less responsiveness to the dynamic demands of the environment and less competitiveness (Pascucci et al., 2023;

Tabesh et al., 2019). The previous research show (Gašperlin et al., 2021; Mohamed & Weber, 2020; Saura et al., 2023) that data in organizations is mainly used to support daily business operations, while the utilization of data to generate a new value still remains low, resulting in a low level of data maturity. SMEs represent 98,9% of all the enterprises, employ nearly 70% of people and generate more than 50% of the revenue of all enterprises (Muller et al., 2022). It is often said, that they are »the backbone« of the European economy. An important part of achieving the desired state of digitalization is directly connected to data and its utilization. Therefore, it is of great importance to help SMEs understand and improve, not only in their digital maturity, but also in the efficient utilization of data. To address this problem, we propose a model to assess data maturity of SMEs. Based on the assessment against a set of criteria, describing the data maturity, SMEs will be able to plan their actions towards data maturity better. This will help SMEs to understand where they are and what they need to do to improve their operations based on data. For this purpose, a number of data maturity models have already been proposed and developed, but they mainly refer to large companies (Hornick, 2020; Marchildon et al., 2018; O'Donovan et al., 2016), are either too extensive or incomplete in the proposed criteria (Limpeeticharoenchot et al., 2022), or too static in their structure (CMMI Institute, 2019; Deloitte, 2021) and do not address the specifics of SMEs. Therefore, the development of a comprehensive model for the data maturity assessment of SMEs is needed.

If we want to assess data maturity comprehensively, this requires to define a set of criteria and define the measurement scales. However, the definition of the measurement scales is not a trivial problem. In the DEX method, criteria values consist of words or numeric intervals. The measurement scales are mostly ordered from least to most desirable values (e.g. bad, good, very good, excellent) (Bohanec et al., 2013). In the case of the DEX method, this is not necessary, but it is welcome, as it is used in the next phase when checking the consistency of decision rules and can significantly speed up the process of capturing utility functions (Bohanec, 2006). For this reason, it is important to properly define the measurement scales and to assign the right values.

## 2. Background and theoretical findings

Even though an urge to develop to a data mature organization is becoming highlighted nowadays, effective utilization of data and its management can still be a big challenge for small and medium-sized enterprises. Kemppainen et al. (2022) emphasize that it is not always clear how to collect and utilize information strategically, which is one of the challenges that hinders the SMEs' progress on a data maturity level and to transform from a data immature to a data mature or data-driven enterprise. To help SMEs to assess their level of data maturity, different data maturity models and measurement scales have been proposed (Mert Onuralp Gökalp et al., 2022; Grossman, 2018; Spruit & Pietzka, 2015a). The proposed models in the literature are addressing different fields from Industry 4.0 (Gajdzik, 2022; Mert Onuralp Gökalp, Gökalp, Kayabay, et al., 2021), to assessing the big data maturity (Farzaneh et al., 2019; Okuyucu & Yavuz, 2020) and data analytics (Mach-Król, 2022; Nda et al., 2020; Perales-Manrique et al., 2019). Some of the models are also focused more on technical aspects, for example on the maturity assessment of artificial intelligence (W. Chen et al., 2022; Yablonsky, 2021).

Most of the data maturity models have their structure and measurement scales derived from the capability maturity assessment model (CMMI) (Mert Onuralp Gökalp, Gökalp, Gökalp, et al., 2021; Olszak & Mach-Król, 2018; Perales-Manrique et al., 2019), which represents the basis for further development of today's maturity models and uses a wide known five level maturity scale (Initial, Managed, Defined, Quantitatively Managed and Optimizing) (Humphrey, 1988). As observed by (Perales-Manrique et al., 2019), there are different maturity models, each with its own characteristics, structure and scope on which they are focusing on to assess the data maturity.

(Perales-Manrique et al., 2019) have proposed a data analytics maturity model, with a focus on organizations in financial sector. The models' aim was to assess the maturity of the data analytics among the two SMEs and one large enterprise, based on five criteria (technology, governance, data management, culture and analytics itself). The proposed model measures data analytics maturity based on five maturity levels (i.e. basic, functional, competitive, outstanding and continuous improvement). Parra et al. (2019) have developed a model specifically for SMEs, to evaluate and determine the level of their competence, readiness and maturity in the use of information to support decision-making. The proposed model also measures data maturity based on five maturity levels (i.e. Uninitiated, Awareness, Proactive adopting, Integral embracement and Completely embedded).

There are also models that are measured on a 5 or 6 maturity levels (i.e. incomplete, performed, managed, established, predictable and innovating), as in (Mert O Gökalp et al., 2021), where the authors proposed a Data Drivenness Process Capability Determination Model (DDPCDM) based on the ISO/IEC 330xx family of standards. Same authors have published another article (Mert Onuralp Gökalp, Gökalp, Kayabay, et al., 2021), where they have proposed a theoretically grounded Data Science Maturity Model (DSMM) for manufacturing organizations to assess their existing strengths and weaknesses, perform a gap analysis, and draw a roadmap for continuous improvements in their progress towards data-driven manufacturing. The proposed model measures the data maturity based on 6 maturity levels (from Not performed to Innovating), twenty-eight data science processes and 6 process areas (Organization, Strategy Management, Data Analytics, Data Governance, Technology Management, and Supporting processes).

In the literature, we can also find the models that have four level scale, such as in (Limpeeticharoenchot et al., 2022), where the authors wanted to assess the maturity level of the big data use in Thai SMEs. The model assesses maturity based on four capabilities: organizational and attitude factors, information technology, data analytics technology and people readiness. For each capability, the authors have defined criteria and assigned values to each of criteria. For example, in assessing the use of software for data analysis (i.e. Excel, business intelligence, data mining software) the following values were applied: use; do not use; and do not know; and similarly, in the case when the SMEs were asked, if they analyze the data (i.e transaction data, financial data, customer feedback) the values were as follows: analyze; do not analyze; and do not have. Despite the maturity levels applied to assess the big data maturity use, the levels in the proposed model are defined in the form of numerical assessment (from 1 to 4), which is not so clear to understand (i.e. the maturity level 4.75), as compared to qualitative assessment, where the values are symbolic, described by words (i.e. bad, good, very good), which are simpler to understand and offer transparent interpretation of the final assessment (Bohanec, 2006; Kljajić Borštnar & Pucihar, 2022).

Others, (Høj Brasen et al., 2021) have addressed data maturity from a perspective of data use in relation to the maintenance strategy. The aim of the study was to know, how Danish SMEs are maintaining a production line, through the use of production data and maintenance approach. Based on the previous models in the literature, the authors proposed three levels to assess the maturity related to data use (low/initial, medium/established and high/advanced) and similar the levels applied to the maintenance strategy (ad hoc, predetermined, condition-based). For each level of maturity, the authors provide a description of what is covered at each level of maturity and also partly indicating the possibility of setting up measurement scales for assessing maturity in the use of data, (i.e. not collecting or using data from production; individualistic planning based on experience, rather than data; collecting data from all production equipment). Similarly, (Höck et al., 2020), within the context of data maturity focused on the data re-use and data quality, where they proposed a Quality Maturity Matrix (QMM), which helps the user to judge the appropriateness of the data for a possible re-use. The proposed matrix is described with a five maturity levels (from Level 1 to 5) and is linked to the five phases: concept, production/processing, project collaboration/intended use, long-term archiving, and impact re-use.

## 3. Methodology

The aim of this paper is to prepare a list of measurement scales to assess the data maturity of SMEs. For this purpose, we reviewed the literature of existing data maturity models, its criteria and their measurement scales.

As a research approach, we used the design science research - DSR (Hevner et al., 2004) (Figure 1). DSR is described by three main research cycles (rigor cycle, relevance cycle, and design and development cycle) (Hevner, 2007). The result represents a developed artifact (i.e. construct, model, method), in our case this will be a multi-criteria model for evaluating the data maturity of SMEs, where we follow the methodology of modeling the multi-criteria decision-making knowledge of the DEX qualitative method (Bohanec et al., 2013). In this paper, we focus on the second step in the DEX methodology, i.e. the formulation and definition of measurement scales that describe the value of each criteria in the preliminary list, which we have defined in previous research (Gašperlin et al., 2023).

DEX is a qualitative decision support methodology for the evaluation and analysis of decision alternatives (Bohanec et al., 2013). It represents a combination of the numerical multi-criteria decision modeling with rule-based expert systems. The DEX methodology offers simpler understanding and more transparent interpretation of the final assessment (Bohanec, 2006; Kljajić Borštnar & Pucihar, 2022), where the values are symbolic, described by words (i.e. bad, good, very good), as compared to other methods (e.g. AHP, ELECTRE), where the numerical assessment are used (i.e. the maturity level 4.75) and the assessment is not so transparent. The DEX methodology consists of a sequence of steps, which includes the identification and definition of the decision problem, identification of criteria, structuring the criteria and definition of measurement scales, followed by determination of criteria value scales and utility functions in the form of decision rule tables (Bohanec et al., 2013; Kljajić Borštnar & Pucihar, 2022). The output represents a tree of criteria (attributes), with the root of the tree that combines all the criteria into one final score of the alternative. In our case, this is the level of data maturity assessment of an individual SME.

*Figure 1: Design science research methodology – adapted from (Hevner, 2007).*

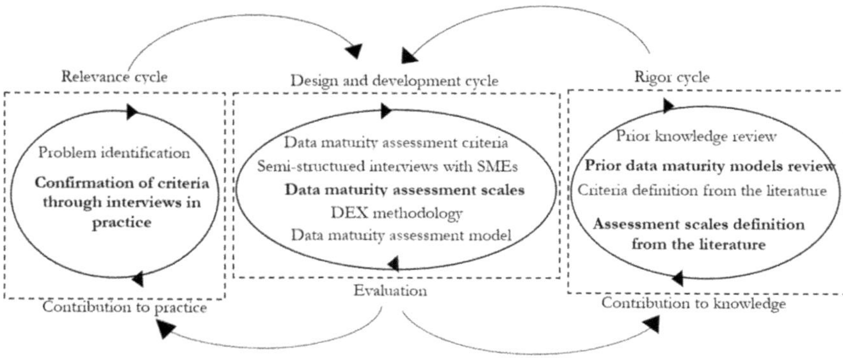


The search was performed in the Web of Science (WoS) and Scopus databases. We used the search queries "data maturity model", "data maturity assessment" and "data maturity model" AND "SMEs" and searched by all search fields. We started with the search in the Scopus database. Since we wanted to find as many papers as possible that would be relevant to our research, we expanded the search with the additional queries ("data maturity assessment model") and ("data maturity scale") and the combination of the query "data maturity" and other keywords: "data maturity AND scale", "data maturity" AND "assessment", "data maturity" AND "assessment" AND "scale" and "data maturity" AND "assessment" AND "SMEs". The number of papers found by a specific search string or keyword can be seen in Figure 2. In the beginning set of papers, we screened the titles and abstracts and eliminated all papers that did not address data maturity, did not contain measurement scales, and papers that were duplicated. From the 617 papers in the Scopus database, we eliminated 374 papers that were not relevant in terms of content and selected 243 papers for further review. Among the papers included for further review, those papers, whose full content was not available (9 papers), were not written in English (2 papers), were duplicated (71 such papers) or were not linked to the data maturity assessment or models (166 papers) were also excluded from further analysis. We repeated the search with the same queries in the WoS database, where we got a significantly lower number of results (57 papers). After the review of the papers in the WoS database, we did not select any papers for further review because all the papers were a duplicate with those found in the Scopus database. After reviewing the literature in the Scopus and Web of Science databases, we reviewed data maturity models developed by research institutions and organizations (Gartner, Stanford, IBM, CMMI, Deloitte, Accenture, TDWI).

In the end, we identified a total of 19 papers relevant to our research, including eight models of research institutions. Figure 2 shows the review process with databases and search queries for each database.

*Figure 2: Literature review process.*

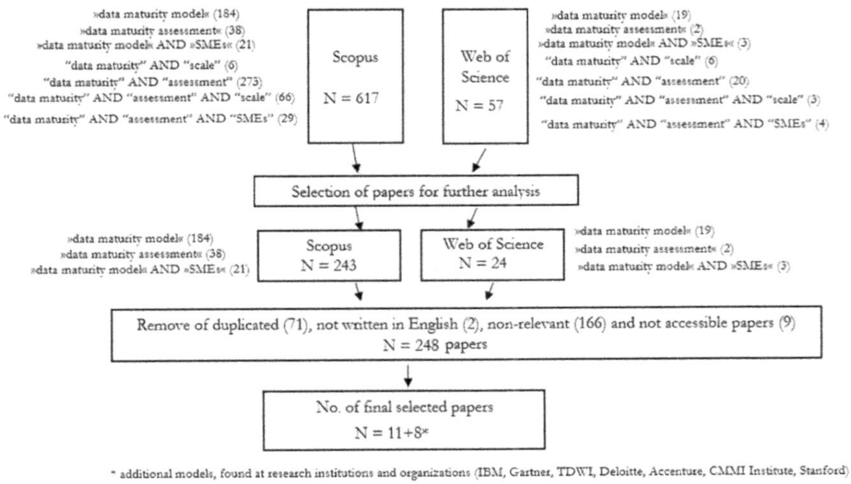


In Figure 3, we have gathered the data maturity models relevant for this research, which we have reviewed in the literature and their measurement scales. In addition, the models of consulting companies and organizations (IBM, Gartner, Stanford TDWI, Deloitte, Accenture, CMMI) are also shown, which are often mentioned in the literature and are used to help in further development of data maturity models.

## 4. Data maturity criteria and measurement scales for assessing data maturity of small and medium-sized enterprises

In this part, we present selected criteria for evaluating the data maturity of SMEs and the measurement scales (domain values) for each of the criterion.

A measurement scales (domain values) are represented as ordered sets of qualitative (descriptive) discrete values, which are assigned to each criterion, describing the characteristics of alternatives (Milavec Kapun et al., 2022). The alternatives

*Figure 3: List of relevant data maturity models and maturity levels identified in the literature.*

| | Data maturity model | Author(s) | Maturity level(s) | | | | | |
|---|---|---|---|---|---|---|---|---|
| 1 | Gartner Enterprise Information Management (EIM) Maturity Model (2008) | (Gartner, 2008) | Unaware | Aware | Reactive | Proactive | Managed | Effective |
| 2 | Gartner Maturity Model for Data and Analytics (2017) | (Gartner, 2017) | Basic | Opportunistic | Systematic | Differentiating | Transformational | |
| 3 | Stanford Data Governance Maturity Model (2011) | (Stanford, 2011) | 1 | 2 | 3 | 4 | 5 | |
| 4 | IBM Data Governance Maturity Model (2007) | (IBM, 2007) | Initial | Managed | Defined | Quantitatively managed | Optimizing | |
| 5 | CMMI Data Management Maturity (DMM) Model (2014) | (CMMI, 2014) | Performed | Managed | Defined | Measured | Optimized | |
| 6 | Data Maturity Model (2021) | (Deloitte, 2021) | Basic | Beginner | Intermediate | Advanced | Master | |
| 7 | Accenture Data Maturity model (2018) | (Accenture, 2018) | Ad-hoc | Organize | Tactical | Critical | Industrial | |
| 8 | TDWI Big Data Maturity Model (2014) | (TDWI, 2014) | Nascent | Pre-adoption | Early adoption | Corporate adoption | Mature/Visionary | |
| 9 | A Data Analytics Maturity Model for Financial Sector Companies (2021) | (Perales-Manrique et al., 2019) | Basic | Functional | Competitive | Outstanding | Continuous improvement | |
| 10 | Temporal Big Data Maturity Model (TBDMM) framework (2018) | Olszak et al., 2018) | Atemporal | Pre-temporal | Partly temporal | Predominantly temporal | Temporal | |
| 11 | CHROMA model | (Parra, 2017) | Uninitiated | Awareness | Proactive adopting | Integral embracement | Completely embedded | |
| 12 | Big Data maturity model (BDMM) (2016) | (Comuzzi & Patel, 2016) | 1 | 2 | 3 | 4 | 5 | |
| 13 | Data Drivenness Process Capability Determination Model (DDPCDM) (2021) | (Gokalp et al., 2021) | Incomplete | Performed | Managed | Established | Predictable | Innovating |
| 14 | Data Science Maturity Model (DSMM) for manufacturing organizations (2021) | (Gokalp et al., 2021) | Incomplete | Performed | Managed | Established | Predictable | Innovating |
| 15 | Big data maturity model (BDMM) (2022) | (Limpeeticharoenchot et al., 2022) | 1 | 2 | 3 | 4 | | |
| 16 | Master data management maturity model (MD3M) (2015) | (Spruit&Pietzka, 2015) | Initial | Repeatable | Defined process | Managed & Measurable | Optimized | |
| 17 | Fuzzy ELECTRE model | (Peña et al., 2019) | Inexistent | Exploring | Analyzing | Integrating | Innovating | |
| 18 | Industrial AI (I-AI) maturity model | (Chen et al, 2022) | Planning | Specification | Integration | Optimization | Leading | |
| 19 | Data analytics maturity assessment framework (DAMAF) | (Gokalp et al., 2021) | Initial | Managed | Defined | Quantitatively managed | Optimizing | |

will in our case represent the SMEs, with which we will conduct a semi-structured interview to validate the selected criteria and measurement scales. According to the recommendations of the DEX method, we have ordered the values of the measurement scales from the least desirable to most desirable values. According to (Bohanec, 2006), such arrangement is not necessary, but it significantly increases the understandability of the model and helps to capture utility functions more easily in the later stage of the model development. When defining the number of values taken by an individual criterion, it is recommended that this number be as small as possible, but enough that we can describe all significantly different decision situations.

For the clarity, based on the (Moonen et al., 2019), we have divided the selected criteria and measurement scales in three tables by three groups of capabilities (organizational, data management and technical capabilities). Organizational capabilities refer to capabilities of the organization to use organizational resources to perform a task or activity (Akaegbu & Usoro, 2017). Data management capabilities refer to the capabilities of coordinating and using the data information resources (Brinkhues et al., 2014), while technical capabilities indicate the capability of implementing, using and developing the technology to provide products and services (Omar et al., 2012).

We begin with the presentation of the group of criteria and measurement scales related to the organizational capabilities (Table 1), followed by the presentation of criteria and measurement scales related to the data management capabilities (Table 2) and conclude with the third group related to the technical capabilities in Table 3.

The tables are structured as follows: first we provide a criterion and its description based on the literature reviewed. Based on the criteria description and reviewed literature, we have defined and assigned the measurement scale (value) to each of the criterion.

*Table 1: Criteria and measurement scales related to organizational capabilities*

| Criterion | Description | Measurement scale (Values) |
|---|---|---|
| **Leadership style**<br>(Halper, 2020; Peña et al., 2018), (Schmidt et al., 2023), (Kljajić Borštnar & Pucihar, 2021), (Windt et al., 2019), (Gierlich-Joas & Hess, 2020), (Schmidt et al., 2023), (Parra et al., 2019) | Defines the leadership behavior and aspirations towards data-driven culture and to becoming a data-driven organization | • Leadership is hierarchical, where the management of the organization and all of the decisions are left to the company's management<br>• Leadership is hierarchical with collaboration, where the decisions are made together with the heads of individual departments<br>• Leadership is collaborative and supportive, where the decisions are made together with the heads of individual departments and considering the opinions of the employees |
| **Training**<br>(Coleman et al., 2016; Mert Onuralp Gökalp et al., 2022; Kljajić Borštnar & Pucihar, 2021; Peña et al., 2018) | Assesses whether enterprise organize any trainings in data management field (i.e. data security, data quality, data analytics) | • There aren't any trainings organized in data management field (i.e. data security, data quality, data analytics - Not organized;<br>• There aren't any trainings organized in data management field (i.e. data security, data quality, data analytics, but employees are acquainted with internal data management acts and regulations;<br>• There aren't any trainings organized in data management field, but the employees are encouraged to attend trainings that interests them - Constant improvement;<br>• There is a regular systematic and planned approach to internal and external trainings in data management field for our employees |

(Continued)

*Table 1: (Continued)*

| Criterion | Description | Measurement scale (Values) |
|---|---|---|
| **Skills**<br>(Comuzzi & Patel, 2016; Mert O Gökalp et al., 2021; Lismont et al., 2017; Peña et al., 2018; Schmidt et al., 2023) | Assesses the level of analytical skills of employees in data management | • Employees have no analytical skills developed, because they don't need them<br>• Employees have basic analytical skills to manage the data and prepare simple reports in Excel;<br>• Employees have advanced analytical skills, which includes advanced use of Excel (i.e. a pivot table design, data drill-down) and the knowledge of using data analytics and business intelligence tools to prepare complex reports;<br>• We have a data management expert(s) employed, who have knowledge of advanced statistical, data analytics and business intelligence tools (i.e. SPSS, MATLAB, Power BI, SAS Business Intelligence) and knowledge of artificial intelligence and machine learning to prepare complex data visualization reports and predictions |
| **Roles**<br>(Hornick, 2020), (Peña et al., 2018), (Comuzzi & Patel, 2016), (Mert O Gökalp et al., 2021) | Assesses the roles or positions established that support data management activities within the enterprise | • No data management roles exist within the enterprise;<br>• General data management roles exist and are established, such as database administrators and IT administrators<br>• Data experts are employed, such as data analytics teams, data analysts, data managers and data engineers<br>• Chief analytics officer or chief data officer, or chief information officer are employed that has accountability for value creation by means of the organization's data and analytics assets, as well as the data and analytics ecosystem. |
| **Strategy**<br>(Chandler, 1962; Comuzzi & Patel, 2016; Davenport & DalleMule, 2017; Mert Onuralp Gökalp et al., 2022; Grossman, 2018; Gür, Spiekermann, et al., 2021; Mitra et al., 2019) | Assesses the strategic role of the data - whether data are recognized as an important resource in the business strategy for creating the company's added value | • Strategic role of data is not recognized and not used as a source for new value creation<br>• Strategic role of data is recognized, but only in individual areas, such as sales, marketing, development;<br>• The data is recognized and used as a strategic resource to create added value and innovations at the level of entire enterprise |

| Criterion | Description | Measurement scale (Values) |
|---|---|---|
| **Data governance**<br><br>(Mert Onuralp Gökalp et al., 2022; Koltay, 2016; Saputra et al., 2018) | Assesses whether the data governance document exists and is used within the enterprise | • No data governance document exists within the enterprise, because we don't need it<br>• We are aware of importance to have a data governance document, but such document not yet exists<br>• Only internal acts and guidelines for data governance exists and are used to manage the data<br>• A formally written data governance documents exists and are in use (i.e. data governance act, ISO standards, DAMA-DM BOK). |
| **Investments in IT architecture and infrastructure**<br><br>(Mert O Gökalp et al., 2021; Kljajić Borštnar & Pucihar, 2021; Mitra et al., 2019) | Share of annual revenue investments in information architecture and infrastructure | • No investments in IT architecture and IT infrastructure;<br>• Less than 2% of annual revenue is invested in IT architecture and IT infrastructure;<br>• 2% to 5% of annual revenue is invested in IT architecture and IT infrastructure;<br>• More than 5% of annual revenue is invested in IT architecture and IT infrastructure |
| **Outsourcing of IT infrastructure**<br><br>(Deloitte, 2021; Ishizaka et al., 2019; Lismont et al., 2017; Moonen et al., 2019) | Assesses whether the company hires external experts for data management or is completely independent | • Outsourcing to another organization - we do not have our own IT department, nor a person who would take care of IT infrastructure, external contractors take care of this;<br>• Partner with another organization - We take care of IT infrastructure ourselves (i.e. taking care of the databases, servers, information systems), the rest (data analytics, statistical data processing, data visualization) is taken care of by external contractors;<br>• In our company, we take care of the IT infrastructure ourselves and are independent in data management activities (data analytics, statistical data processing, data visualization) and do not need external contractors |

*(Continued)*

*Table 1: (Continued)*

| Criterion | Description | Measurement scale (Values) |
|---|---|---|
| **Mindset**<br><br>(Accenture, 2018; Halper, 2020; Mitra et al., 2019; Parra et al., 2019) | Assesses the level of data driven mindset incorporated within the enterprise | • Risk averse mindset – we are avoiding the uncertainty and risk-taking as we are concerned about consequences of failure;<br>• Channel or technology centricity mindset – we are focused on development of the product from perspective of technology or product and does not consider customer needs<br>• Customer centricity mindset – we are focused on the customer needs and develop our product and service offerings based on customer insights to develop and provide tailored solutions for customers<br>• Continuous innovation – we promote continuous innovation and improvements to keep pace with evolving technology development to develop and provide new product and service offerings to our customers |
| **Organizational culture**<br><br>(Mitra et al., 2019; Parra et al., 2019; Rogers, 2020) | Defines the level of culture developed to support experi-mentation, new products and services development | • We are focusing only on running the business and business processes, no experimentation is present within the enterprise<br>• We support experimentation within the goals of the enterprise and assigned business tasks<br>• Continuous innovation – Innovation is wanted in our company and is also supported outside of the company |
| **Data awareness**<br><br>(Hornick, 2020; Stanford, 2013) | Employees awareness of the available data management tools and their possibilities | • Employees are not aware of which data management tools are available<br>• Employees are aware of which data management tools are available, but they do not see the advantages of using them and do not use them<br>• Employees are aware of available tools, their possibilities and the benefits and are using them to support business tasks<br>• Employees are aware of available tools, technologies and their possibilities, use them and propose new solutions |

| Criterion | Description | Measurement scale (Values) |
|---|---|---|
| **Collaboration**<br>(Hagen & Hess, 2020; Hornick, 2020; Mitra et al., 2019; Moonen et al., 2019) | Defines the support of collaboration among employees towards the better management of data | • There is no collaboration among the employees towards better management of data<br>• Only the collaboration within individual departments exists, but not collaboration with different departments<br>• We support collaboration within different departments, and encourage employees to collaborate together (Cross-department collaboration)<br>• We support open collaboration among the employees and across entire enterprise |
| **Team work**<br>(Mert O Gökalp et al., 2021; Vidgen et al., 2017) | The extent of team work support within the organization | • There is no team work established within the enterprise<br>• Team-work is present within individual departments<br>• Cross-department team-work<br>• Team work is established across entire enterprise |
| **Open communication**<br>(Hagen & Hess, 2020; Hornick, 2020; Moonen et al., 2019; Peña et al., 2018) | The extent of the open communication support within the enterprise | • No open communication is supported within the enterprise<br>• We only support communication within individual departments<br>• We support cross-department team communication as well as employees to connect and help each other<br>• Completely open communication, where all the propositions are communicated on regular meetings |
| **Management support**<br>(CMMI Institute, 2019; Coleman et al., 2016; Mert O Gökalp et al., 2021; Parra et al., 2019; Peña et al., 2018; Vidgen et al., 2017) | The extent of management support for open communication, collaboration, and encouragement of employees to better manage their data | • There is no management support present for employees to better manage their data<br>• We are aware of importance to have a good data management, and are encouraging the employees to explore the possibilities for better data management<br>• We are supporting employees to analyze and integrate data from data sources and business processes to gain knowledge and an integrated understanding of them<br>• We constantly support our employees to propose and improve data management practices with regular meetings and informal discussion, support them to attend data management trainings and use data to innovate and create new products and services |

In the following, we describe each criterion from Table 1 in more detail:

**Leadership**
One of the first criterion to consider to assess the data maturity of SMEs is leadership. Parra et al. (2019) describe leadership as the conditions of leadership, commitment and willingness to delegate authority functions with different degrees of power and autonomy that must exist in all levels of the organization to consolidate a data-driven decision-making culture throughout the company. Other authors (Halper, 2020) refers to the leadership from a data analytic perspective and refers to the leadership as the extent the leadership support and evangelize a successful analytics program. As proposed by (Windt et al., 2019), to establish a data-driven leadership the following aspects also need to be followed, such as constant communication and explanation of the value of being data-driven, which is promoted through the establishment of data-driven culture. Data-driven culture is further directly connected with the establishment of direction, in this case direction towards data-driven organization and with the motivation of people for organizational change. According to (Windt et al., 2019) communication and explanation of the benefits of being data-driven makes the organization more aware, enabling the establishment of the analytical mindset and culture, where data-driven insights and encouragement of evidence-based decision making are adopted throughout entire organization. In the context of becoming the data driven organization, leadership must therefore develop a capability of analytical decision-making and promote a passion for data-driven decision making on the level of entire organization.

Based on these descriptions, we understand that data-driven leadership can be defined through different perspectives (non-data driven leadership, data-driven aspired leadership and data-driven leadership) and through the involvement towards data driven culture, where data is managed as a corporate asset on a level of entire enterprise. Based on the literature and the review of the data maturity models in Figure 3, we defined to the leadership criterion three values - no data driven aspiration, data driven aspired, and data driven oriented leadership:

- No data-driven aspiration leadership refers to no interest or aspiration of using the data as a strategic resource to support a data-driven culture throughout the enterprise. Leadership is in this stage hierarchical, where the management of the organization and all of the decisions are left to the company's management
- Data-driven aspired leadership start to recognize the potential value of the data and start to incorporating the data as a strategic resource. Leadership is in this stage hierarchical, but prepared to collaborate, where the decisions are made together with the heads of individual departments

- Data-driven leadership has developed a strong data-driven mindset and use data as a strategic resource at the level of the entire enterprise. Leadership is in this stage collaborative and supportive, where the decisions are made together with the heads of individual departments and considering the opinions of the employees

**Training**

Training was identified as a next important criterion and is directly connected to skills. The training provides a standardized and repeatable roadmap for employees to acquire, develop and integrate their data management skills to perform data management tasks and activities and helps to establish a data-driven culture within the organization (Mert Onuralp Gökalp et al., 2022). In other words, it refers to the extent to which the company organizes training for its employees so that they acquire the appropriate skills for data management.

According to (Coleman et al., 2016) training can be organized from a technological aspect, where the focus is on development of technical skills and knowledge, such is the knowledge of statistics and database management or from the view of the management aspect, where focus is on having people, that are able to see where to use the analytical capabilities, who ask provocative questions and, who can think of interesting experiments to be run and at the end who are really data-based decision makers.

**Skills**

Skills refers to the level of data management knowledge and skills the employees has developed to be able to collect, store, analyze and use the data to perform data management tasks and activities (Mert Onuralp Gökalp et al., 2022; Parra et al., 2019; Peña et al., 2018). According to (Comuzzi & Patel, 2016) the skills should not only be technical but also analytical to understand the business applications of data.

Based on the definition above we divided the skills to basic, advanced and expert data management skills.

The basic data management skills are related to limited set of skills, meaning the employees only have skills to track basic business indicators (i.e. KPI – Key Performance Indicators) to support daily business operations and using the spreadsheets basic analytic software to analyze the data (i.e. Excel).

Advanced skills refer to employees that have a deeper understanding and knowledge on data, and know how to use the advanced data analytic tools (e.g. Power BI, Tableau, SAS Business analytics), to perform advanced reporting and visualization of data and not only spreadsheets (i.e. Excel).

Expert knowledge and skills means that a data management expert skills are present within the organization and are related to the ability to prepare data, write code, use machine learning algorithms and to visualize and communicate results to both technical and nontechnical audiences.

**Roles**

In Table 1, roles as a criterion relates to the roles that are established within the enterprise. According to (Hornick, 2020) roles can be defined as »a set of connected behaviors, rights, obligations, beliefs, and norms as conceptualized by people in a social situation.«. Hornick (2020) mention several roles that have become more common in recent years (i.e. data scientist, chief data officer, chief data science officer, and data librarian).

In our case, we define the roles from the organizational structure point of view, as the roles that an organization has established to support data management tasks and activities.

The criteria values are defined from the least desirable (e.g. no data management roles exist) to most desirable state (employment of a chief analytics officer or chief data officer, or chief information officer). If no data management roles are defined within the organization it cannot progress towards better data management and to progress on data maturity.

**Strategy**

Strategy is most important criterion to consider when addressing the data maturity of SMEs. We must differentiate between the organizational and data management strategy. The organizational strategy as defined by (Chandler, 1962, p. 13) refers to the determination of the company's basic long-term goals and the definition of the course of action and the allocation of resources necessary to realize these goals. Similarly, data strategy refers to the long-term decisions an organization makes about how a company uses its data to take actions that fulfill its organizational vision and mission (Grossman, 2018).

In this context, we define strategy from a view of a strategic role of the data - whether data are recognized as an important resource in the business strategy for creating the company's added value or not. Based on that description, we have defined three criteria values:

- Strategic role of data is not recognized– the data are not recognized as an important resource in the business strategy for creating the company's added value
- Strategic role of data is recognized but in individual areas – the data are recognized and included as an important resource only in several business areas (e.g. production, accounting, sales, procurement, …)
- Strategic role of data is recognized at the level of entire enterprise - the data are recognized as an important resource in the business strategy for creating the company's added value

**Data governance**

Data governance is the exercise in the term of planning, monitoring, and enforcement of authority and control in the top of data management assets (Saputra et al., 2018, pp. 325, 326). The data governance function guideshow all other data management functions are performed. It refers to the organizational bodies, rules, decision rights, and accountabilities of people and information systems as they perform information-related processes (Saputra et al., 2018, pp. 326).

The data governance process area plays a significant role in providing insights about the metadata of the collected, stored and processed data to prevent security, privacy, quality and management issues (Mert Onuralp Gökalp et al., 2022, pp. 560).

**Investments in information technology (IT) architecture and infrastructure**

To become a data driven organizations it is also necessary to assess the level of financial resources the enterprise invests to support information infrastructure and information technologies (Kljajić Borštnar & Pucihar, 2021; Mitra et al., 2019).

This criterion relates to the share of annual revenue, that enterprise invests in information technologies (IT) and consequently in information architecture and infrastructure.

**Outsourcing of IT infrastructure**

Outsourcing is by definition provided by (Ishizaka et al., 2019) a business agreement, domestic or international (known as offshoring), and strategic management initiative for gaining a competitive advantage of a firm by contracting out their existing internal and/or external non-value added functions, and/or value-added functions, and/or core competencies to competent supplier(s) to produce products and/or services efficiently and effectively for the outsourcing firm.

In the context of data maturity assessment, we define outsourcing as an extent of data management services that are provided by external contractors (e.g. outsource enterprise). Based on this definition, we have defined four criteria values: (Hiring of skilled staff; Outsourcing to another organization; Partner with another organization; and Independent in data management (upskill of current employees)):

Outsourcing to another organization - we do not have our own IT department, nor a person who would take care of IT infrastructure, external contractors take care of this;

Partner with another organization - We take care of IT infrastructure ourselves (i.e. taking care of the databases, servers, information systems), the rest (data analytics, statistical data processing, data visualization) is taken care of by external contractors;

Independent in data management (upskill of current employees) – The organization is independent in provisioning data management activities and services. Employees take care of the IT infrastructure by themselves, are independent in data management activities (data analytics, statistical data processing, data visualization) and do not need any of the external contractors.

**Mindset**

According to (Mitra et al., 2019) one of the components for data driven organization and important part of data strategy is data driven mindset, which is directly connected to culture and relates to the use of data to identify problems and opportunities to consequently make better decisions. Parra et al. (2019) emphasize that for addressing a business problem a broader mindset is needed, where one of the solutions represent the capability to innovate.

Based on the description above, we have defined mindset from a data driven perspective and refer to it as a level of data driven mindset, that is incorporated within the enterprise. To differentiate from different levels of mindset, based on the (Mitra et al., 2019), we have defined four criteria values: risk averse mindset; channel centricity mindset; customer centricity mindset and continuous innovation.

Risk averse mindset means that organization avoids uncertainty and risk-taking, as it is concerned with the consequences of failure.

Channel centricity mindset means that organization is only focused on the product and service development from the technology perspective and customer needs, and not on customer feedback and insights. While in the customer centricity mindset, customer feedback and insights are also considered in the development of products and services. The best option is continuous innovation, where enterprise continuously promote innovation and improvements to keep pace with evolving technology development to develop and provide new product and service offerings to its customers.

**Data awareness**

Awareness is another criterion that represents the driver for better data management within the organization. According to (Hornick, 2020) data awareness refers to know (to be aware) which data exists in an enterprise and to understand its content. Hornick (2020) also emphasize that problem in organizations often represents data silos, where one part of enterprise in unaware of the existence of data in another. In this way the full potential and value of data is not utilized.

Based on the definition above, we define data awareness as employee's awareness of the available data management tools and their possibilities. We have defined four criteria values starting from low awareness, to medium and high awareness.

- No awareness is present, where employees are unaware of the data tools available in the enterprise
- Low awareness is present, where employees are aware of the additional data tools available, but they do not see the advantages of using them and do not use them. Employees seek the additional information by contacting the people in different departments.
- Medium awareness means that employees are aware of the data tools available in the organization and knows the benefits of using them to support business tasks
- High awareness of the available data management tools and their possibilities means that employees are aware of available tools, technologies and their possibilities, use them and propose new solutions

**Collaboration and team work**

To enable the success to manage the data better and to progress to a data driven organization it is often required the multiple individuals in different roles (IT and database administrators, application developers, business and data analysts, data engineers, domain experts) collaborate together to achieve a common goal and establish team work approach (Hornick, 2020). In other words, to achieve a culture that is collaborative (Mitra et al., 2019).

Based on the description above we define a collaboration as a measure of how the organization support collaboration among employees towards the better management of data. Based on this definition we defined four criteria values:

- No collaboration supported – in the organization there is no collaboration. The improvement for better data management are left to the individuals.
- Collaboration within individual departments – collaboration is starting to form within the individual departments, but there is no broader collaboration in the form of cross department collaboration.
- Cross-department collaboration – employees are starting to connect with other departments to brainstorm and solve any data management issues, but the collaboration is still not established on the level of entire organization.
- Open collaboration across entire enterprise – the collaboration among the employees is highly supported and is established on the level of entire organization.

The same criteria values also apply for the team work and open communication.

**Management support**

Management support is a crucial for further progress to improve the management of data and to progress toward a data driven organization. The management allocates the human, time and financial resources (budget) to support data management infrastructure, initiative for data strategy development, data-driven culture and use of data as a strategic resource to decision making (Coleman et al., 2016; Parra et al., 2019; Peña et al., 2018; Vidgen et al., 2017). To assess the level of management support to employees towards effective data management, we have defined four criteria values (no support, low management support, medium management support and high management support).

- No support means that management does not provide any support for better data management and does not support any open communication, collaboration, and encouragement of employees to better manage their data.
- Low level support means that management is starting to recognize the importance of effective data management and start to support employees through the allocating the financial resources for data management infrastructure and start promoting data-driven culture.
- Medium level support means that management recognizes the importance of effective data management by supporting employees with the establishment of open communication, collaboration, and encouragement of employees to better manage their data. The management in this stage supports their employees through organization of data management trainings.
- High management support the management is motivated and committed to provide effective data management by establishing data management strategies and resources for employees to establish efficient data management practices.

In Table 2 the criteria and measurement scales related to data management capabilities are presented. Additional description of each criterion is provided below Table 2.

*Table 2: Criteria and measurement scales related to data management capabilities*

| Criterion | Description | Measurement scale (Values) |
|---|---|---|
| **Data processing**<br><br>(Coleman et al., 2016), (Gajdzik, 2022; Godoy et al., 2021; R. Iqbal et al., 2019), (Huang, 2019; Paunović, 2008) | Defines whether the data are processed within the enterprise and for which purpose | • No processing of data is established within the enterprise<br>• Only processing of business data and KPIs is established and performed<br>• Processing of business data and KPIs is established, but we are also planning to process the data from other data sources (i.e. social media, sensors, web sources)<br>• Processing of business data and KPIs is established, as well as processing of data from the social media, sensors, and other web sources |

| Criterion | Description | Measurement scale (Values) |
|---|---|---|
| **Data management policies** (Accenture, 2018; CMMI Institute, 2019; Coleman et al., 2016; Grossman, 2018; Halper, 2020; Koltay, 2016; Parra et al., 2019; Peña et al., 2018) | Assesses the establishment of data management policies and guidelines | • No data management policies or guidelines are established within the enterprise, nor they are prescribed;<br>• No data management policies or guidelines are established but we are planning to establish them;<br>• Data management policies and guidelines are established, but only for certain business areas – i.e. data quality assurance;<br>• Data management policies and guidelines are established across entire enterprise and applied through internal regulations and ISO standards |
| **Data security & data privacy** (Halper, 2020; Rath & Kumar, 2021; Spruit & Pietzka, 2015a) | Assesses the establishment of data protection policies and security mechanisms | • No data protection policies and security mechanisms are present or used within the enterprise to provide data security<br>• We are aware of data security importance, but no data protection policies and security mechanisms are present or used within the enterprise to provide data security<br>• Data protection policies and security mechanisms to provide data security are established, but only used in some enterprise business areas (accounting, human resources)<br>• Ensuring data security is very important to us, so we have the necessary data protection policies and security mechanisms established throughout entire enterprise (i.e. backups and data loss prevention solutions, encryption to prevent unauthorized users from reading files) |
| **Data quality strategy** (CMMI Institute, 2019), (Günther et al., 2019), (Parra et al., 2019), (Peña et al., 2018), (Kerr, 2000; Kerr et al., 2009) | Assesses the establishment of a data quality strategy through which enterprise ensure the quality of data | • No data quality strategy is established, because we don't think we need one;<br>• We are aware of data quality strategy importance, but it is yet to be established (in plan);<br>• Data quality strategy has been started to identify all the data quality issues in the data and to set the goals and objectives for the measurement of data quality<br>• Data quality strategy is established as part of business strategy through definition of goals and objectives, and established metrics and international ISO standards (i.e. ISO 8000-1:2022) to assure that data is fit for purpose, and meets future business needs |

*(Continued)*

*Table 2: (Continued)*

| Criterion | Description | Measurement scale (Values) |
|---|---|---|
| **Data quality assessment**<br>(Ardagna et al., 2018; CMMI Institute, 2019; Dravis, 2004; Günther et al., 2019; Kilkenny & Robinson, 2018) | Assesses the establishment of a data quality assurance process within the enterprise | • No data quality assessment is performed within the enterprise;<br>• We are aware of data quality assessment importance, but we do not need it;<br>• No data quality assessment is performed within the enterprise, but we are planning to do so (in plan);<br>• Data quality assessment is performed on regularly basis to provide the necessary validity of data (i.e. accuracy, completeness, reliability, relevance, and timeliness of data) and post monitoring reports; |
| **Decision-making sources**<br>(Baesens et al., 2016; Hornick, 2020; Kljajić Borštnar & Pucihar, 2021; Mazumdar et al., 2019; Nijzink, 2020; Sais et al., 2022) | Defines, which data sources enterprise use, when making strategic decisions (i.e. internal data sources, external data sources, public data sources or combination of all of the above) | • Decisions are made only on the basis of internal data sources (i.e. spreadsheets, databases, business reports) to organize, analyze, and visualize internal data (i.e. data from sales, marketing, finance, human resources, customer service, and others)<br>• Decisions are made partly on internal (i.e. spreadsheets, databases, business reports) and partly on external data sources (surveys, interviews, social-media (i.e. Facebook, LinkedIn, Instagram) to collect, organize, analyze, visualize and interpret the data;<br>• We use all the data sources available to support our decisions with accurate and relevant information, including internal, external and publicly available data sources, including open data repositories and portals |
| **Decision-making style**<br>(Davids et al., 2016; Kljajić Borštnar & Pucihar, 2021; Palmiero et al., 2020; Parra et al., 2019) | Describes the way the decisions are made (intuition; partly use of data, partly intuition; data-driven decisions) | • Decisions are made only based on intuition and past experiences (Intuition driven decision-making);<br>• Decisions are made based on intuition and past experiences as well as on the information gathered through data from business reports (Intuition-driven + Data-driven decision-making);<br>• Decision are made based on the data from business reports and cooperation with department heads (Data-driven decision-making) |

| Criterion | Description | Measurement scale (Values) |
|---|---|---|
| **Data innovation**<br><br>(Babu et al., 2021; Gandhi et al., 2018; Geissdoerfer et al., 2018; Hanafizadeh & Harati Nik, 2020; Rachinger et al., 2019; Thomke, 2001) | Assesses the extent the data are used to increase the enterprise added value and to innovate (processes, products, services, business models) | • No data innovation exists within the enterprise<br>• Data is used in a generic manner to support daily business operations and activities of the enterprise<br>• Data is used in an experimental manner to support some strategic initiatives and start to experiment with the data to optimize business processes and understanding the value the data can offer<br>• Data is used as a strategic resource for the development and creation of new product and service offerings as well for the new business model creation |

**Data processing**

According to (Huang, 2019) data processing refers to the extraction of information through organizing, indexing and manipulating data. When data is processed, information are created which provides valuable relationships and patterns that can help solve problems of interest. Similar definition is provided by (Paunović, 2008) who defines data processing as the process of data management, which enables creation of valid, useful information from the collected data and includes classification, computation, coding and updating of the data.

In the context of data maturity assessment, we want to assess whether the data are processed within the enterprise and for which purpose. Based on the provided definitions above, we have defined a measurement scale from the least desirable value, where no data processing is established within the enterprise to most desirable value, where enterprise process the business data and KPIs established, as well as the data from the social media, sensors, and other web sources (i.e. web page, web store).

**Data management policies**

Data management policies relate to the set of data management policies that organization need to have established to comply with the laws and regulations, to protect its data and to follow standards for effective data management (Coleman et al., 2016; Parra et al., 2019; Peña et al., 2018).

Based on this definition, we define data management policies as the data management policies established and prescribed within the enterprise in the form of guidelines and standards to be followed to establish efficient data management practices which entails the principles of FAIR principles (Wilkinson et al., 2018, 2019) (i.e. data to be findable, accessible, interoperable and reusable) and good control over the data (Alazie & Tsigie, 2019) through entire data lifecycle (from collecting the data to its destruction) (Shah et al., 2021).

**Data security and data privacy**

The data security relates to the protection of data the organization has established against unauthorized access, intrusion into the information system, alienation (theft) of data and abuse, as well as other security incidents (Spruit & Pietzka, 2015b).

While the data privacy (also known as information privacy) is an intangible apprehension of an individual and indicates an individual right to keep the personal information and matters secret and have control over the information (Rath & Kumar, 2021).

Within the context of the definitions provided above and in the context of data maturity assessment, we want to assess, what data protection policies and security mechanisms the enterprise has established to provide data security and maintain privacy. The least desirable value indicates that enterprise has no any data protection policies or security mechanisms established. The slightly better value represents the option that the enterprise is aware of the security importance, but no data protection policies or security mechanisms is established. The next value indicates that data protection policies are established, but only in individual business areas (i.e. human resources, accounting). The best value is establishment of data protection policies and security mechanisms on the level of entire enterprise to provide high level of data security and privacy.

**Data quality strategy**

Since organizations depend on data, which are produced during the operation of the business and business processes, a comprehensive data management program must be established, which can be achieved also through establishment of a data quality strategy (Kerr, 2000; Kerr et al., 2009).

Data quality strategy can be defined as an integrated, organization-wide strategy to achieve and maintain the level of data quality required to support the business goals and objectives (CMMI Institute, 2019; Günther et al., 2019; Parra et al., 2019).

**Data quality assessment**

Data quality assessment provides a systematic approach to measure and evaluate data quality according to processes, techniques, and against data quality rules (Ardagna et al., 2018; CMMI Institute, 2019; Günther et al., 2019).

According to (Günther et al., 2019) and (Kilkenny & Robinson, 2018) there are several data quality dimensions to consider:

Accuracy - evaluates whether the data is correct, reliable and certified free of errors

Completeness - evaluates if a data set includes all data necessary to represent every meaningful state of the represented real-world system

Consistency - refers to the extent whether the data are always presented in the same format and are compatible with previous data

Timeliness – is influenced by system volatility (rate of change) and time of data update and can be described as the extent to which the age of the data is appropriate for the task

Relevancy - evaluates whether available data types are relevant for the intended use and if they satisfy the user needs

In accordance with the definition and description provided and within the context of data maturity assessment, we want to assess whether the enterprise has established a data quality assurance process to provide a quality data. For this purpose, we have defined the following criteria values:

- No data quality assessment is performed within the enterprise;
- We are aware of data quality assessment importance, but we do not need it;
- No data quality assessment is performed within the enterprise, but we are planning to do so (in plan);
- Data quality assessment is performed on regularly basis to provide the necessary validity of data (i.e. accuracy, completeness, reliability, relevance, and timeliness of data) and post monitoring reports;

**Decision-making sources**

Data sources are directly connected to the data storage. According to (Mazumdar et al., 2019) and (Sais et al., 2022) data can be generated through various sources (databases of the enterprise, social media (i.e. Facebook, Twitter) and sensor devices) that can generate a huge amount of data, therefore we must provide a proper storage, that would allow the efficient retrieval of data when needed (Mazumdar et al., 2019).

In the context of data maturity we define data sources as a kind of the data sources the organization use to collect the data for business – internal data sources (i.e. internal databases, data from business report, data from ERP and CRM), the combination of internal and external data sources, such as data collected from social media and open data repositories and combination of internal, external and publicly available data (i.e. public statistic, government data sources) together represents the source for decision-making.

**Decision-making style**

Decision-making style can be defined as the processes that individuals follow in making decisions, where the style could be of different forms (e.g. rational, intuitive, dependent, avoidant, and spontaneous) (Davids et al., 2016; Palmiero et al., 2020).

According to (Davids et al., 2016) decision making styles can often differ how individuals gather information concerning the decision to be made and also how they consider the possible alternatives to resolve the conflicting situation to make a decision.

Based on the definition provided, we define decision making style as the way the organization uses its data to make decisions. In the context of data maturity assessment, we define decision making style from the strategic decision point of view referring to on what basis organization decides, whether it is intuition-driven and base its decision only on feeling and experience, disregarding the data, whether it combines experience with data, or if it wants to experiment, where the data represents a strategic resource to support decisions.

**Data innovation**

Data value creation (also known as data innovation or data monetization) refers to the various approaches that can be used to create added value for a business through the exploitation of data (Babu et al., 2021; Gandhi et al., 2018; Hanafizadeh & Harati Nik, 2020).

As last, the criteria and measurement scales related to technical capabilities are presented in Table 3. Additional description of each criterion is provided below Table 3.

*Table 3: Criteria and measurement scales related to technical capabilities*

| Criterion | Description | Measurement scale (Values) |
|---|---|---|
| **Enterprise software solutions**<br><br>(Moonen et al., 2019), (Coleman et al., 2016), (Gil-Gomez et al., 2020; Ruivo et al., 2014, 2017), (Marolt, 2018), (Kljajić Borštnar & Pucihar, 2021);(Molina-Castillo et al., 2022) | Enterprise software solutions used to support enterprise to business and operate (such as accounting programs, sales and marketing programs, human resource programs, ERP and CRM) | • Use of e-mail and basic software solutions (i.e. Microsoft Office);<br>• Use of only partial software solutions (i.e. use of only accounting program);<br>• Use of basic (standard) software solutions (accounting programs, sales and marketing support programs and human resource management programs);<br>• Use of enterprise software solutions ERP and CRM – i.e. SAP, Pantheon, Vasco, SAOP, Minimax or similar; |

| Criterion | Description | Measurement scale (Values) |
|---|---|---|
| **IT infrastructure**<br><br>(Jabbouri et al., 2016), (IBM,2023), (Al-Sabaawi & Alyouzbak, 2022), (Rahaman & Arif, 2018), (Widajanti & Ratnawati, 2020) | Type of established IT infrastructure to support enterprise to business and operate (i.e. use of personal computers, servers, desktop, mobile, cloud services) | • Use of only personal computers<br>• Use of personal computers and servers (client-server architecture)<br>• Use of servers and cloud solutions<br>• Use of cloud services |
| **Data architecture**<br><br>(Iyamu, 2019; Kaidalova et al., 2018; Sherman, 2015; TOGAF, 2018; van den Hoven, 2003) | Assesses the type of data architecture established within the enterprise | • No data architecture is present or established within the enterprise<br>• Basic data architecture is established within the enterprise including databases, servers, computers (on-premise)<br>• Hybrid data architecture is established – on-premise and in cloud to integrate data across domains, between departments or geographies and business functions breaking down data silos, having access to each other's data<br>• Entire data infrastructure is established through cloud (cloud-based data architecture) |
| **Social media (i.e. Facebook, LinkedIn, Instagram)**<br><br>(Appel et al., 2020; Carr & Hayes, 2015; F. Li et al., 2021) Borštnar & Pucihar, 2021) | Assesses the level of social media use within the enterprise (use of Facebook, LinkedIn, Instagram) and its purpose (marketing activities, advertising and building | • Social media are not used<br>• Social media are used minimally only as addition to support marketing activities (distribution of news)<br>• Social media are used as a marketing tool for advertising and building relationships with customers (segmentation of custom-ers, creation of informative content)<br>• Social media are used as a part of the enterprise business strategy to expand geographic reach to our customers, strengthen the brand of the organization and to include customers in marketing communication process, where they become creator, collaborator and commentator of messages that helps us to promote our products and services and enhance customer experience |

*(Continued)*

*Table 3: (Continued)*

| Criterion | Description | Measurement scale (Values) |
|---|---|---|
| **Cloud computing**<br><br>(Al-Ruithe et al., 2018, 2019; Golightly et al., 2022; Guangming et al., 2017; Hassan et al., 2022; Mell & Grance, 2011; Parashar et al., 2013; Srilakshmi et al., 2013; Sunyaev, 2020) | Assesses the level of cloud computing use within the enterprise | • Cloud computing is not used<br>• Cloud computing is used minimally, for providing additional safety of organizational data, due to standards or due to the business area in which the enterprise works<br>• Cloud computing is used, but for specific solutions and projects, when we collaborate with our suppliers or business partners<br>• Cloud computing is used in most of our business processes and is part of the enterprise strategy |
| **Artificial intelligence, Internet of Thing (IoT), robotics and digital twins**<br><br>(Ahmad Khan & Khaled, 2018; Canhoto & Clear, 2019; Gimpel, 2020; Gölzer & Philipp, 2018; H.-J. Uhlemann et al., 2017; Lee et al., 2019; J. Li et al., 2019; Nofer et al., 2017; OECD, 2022; Peña et al., 2018; Sadiq et al., 2021; Soori et al., 2023; Xu et al., 2019) | Assesses the level of advanced technologies use within the enterprise (i.e. artificial intelligence, IoT, robotics, digital twins, blockchain) | • Advanced technologies (i.e. artificial intelligence, internet of things, robotics, digital twins, blockchain) are not used within the enterprise<br>• The use of advanced technologies (i.e. artificial intelligence, internet of things, robotics, digital twins, blockchain) is planned in near future<br>• The use of advanced technologies (i.e. artificial intelligence, internet of things, robotics, digital twins, blockchain) is used, but in limited scope (used as needed)<br>• We have a good knowledge of the advanced technologies (i.e. artificial intelligence, internet of things, robotics, digital twins, blockchain) where one or more of them is already used within the enterprise |
| **Data analytics**<br><br>(Cao, 2017; Coleman et al., 2016; Karaboga et al., 2019; Lavalle et al., 2011; Monino, 2021; O'Donovan et al., 2016; Sarker, 2021; Vijesh Joe et al., 2020) | Assesses the level of data analytics established within the enterprise for analysis of business data | • There is no data analytics present within the enterprise<br>• Data analytics is used to monitor and improve basic business functions and KPIs (purchasing, sales, production, accounting, finance, staffing, etc.)<br>• Data analytics is used to support basic business functions and KPIs and to support decision-making on operational and tactical level<br>• Data analytics is used to monitor and improve basic business functions and KPIs and to support decision-making on all levels of enterprise |

| Criterion | Description | Measurement scale (Values) |
|---|---|---|
| **Data analytics tools** (Deloitte, 2021; Mikalef et al., 2018; Moonen et al., 2019; Parra et al., 2019; Sarker, 2021) | Assesses the implementation of business intelligence (BI) and data analytic tools used within the enterprise for analysis of business data | • Business intelligence tools are not used within the enterprise<br>• Use of basic statistical, data analytics and BI tools such as Excel to analyze the business data<br>• Use of advanced data analytic tools (i.e. MS PowerBI, SAS Business Intelligence, Oracle Analytics Cloud, Qlik View, Qlik Sense) to analyze the business data<br>• Use of advanced data analytic and BI tolls, such as artificial intelligence to discover hidden patterns and knowledge within data and databases |
| **Digital channels (i.e. Web page, online store, electronic marketplaces)** (Chaparro-Peláez et al., 2022; Grieger, 2003; Lemon & Verhoef, 2016; Spiekermann, 2019; Stahl et al., 2016; Stankovska et al., 2016; Wang & Archer, 2007; Wolf & Steul-Fischer, 2022) | To extent the organization use the digital channels within the enterprise (i.e. Web page, web store, electronic marketplaces) to support communication and interaction with customers | • No digital channels are used within the enterprise<br>• A web page is established to enable digital presence of the enterprise and to provide interaction and communication with the customers<br>• Online store is established and used to communicate and interact with customers and to provide services and product offerings the enterprise has<br>• Electronic marketplaces (i.e. Amazon, eBay, AliExpress) and data portals are established and used to communicate and interact with customers and to provide services and product offerings the enterprise has |
| **Paperless office (digitalization level)** (Briscoe, 2022; Chao, 2015; Harwood, 2006; Verhoef et al., 2019; Vial, 2019; Yousufi, 2023) | Assesses the extent of transition to paperless business established within the organization also known as digitalization process | • Paperless office not established;<br>• Paperless office not yet implemented, but in plan;<br>• Partial establishment of paperless office – paperless business only established in some business areas – i.e. Accounting;<br>• Paperless office is implemented at a level of entire enterprise |

*(Continued)*

*Table 3: (Continued)*

| Criterion | Description | Measurement scale (Values) |
|---|---|---|
| **Document and data exchange with business partners and suppliers**<br>(Costa & Miguel, 2020; Elsaify & Hasan, 2021; Otto & Jarke, 2019), (Kljajić Borštnar & Pucihar, 2021), (Quach et al., 2022) | Assesses how the documents are shared and exchanged with business partners and suppliers | • Documents are shared through e-mail and physical contact<br>• All standard business documents (purchase order, invoice, delivery note) are exchanged and shared electronically in digital form<br>• Within the enterprise are established connected information systems, which enables insights into business partners IS systems – i.e. insights in product stock<br>• The entire supply chain is electronically connected through IS system that is established within the enterprise and connected with business partners IS systems |
| **Access to business data within the enterprise**<br>(R. Iqbal et al., 2019; Nijzink, 2020) | Assesses how the employees can access the business data for their work within the enterprise | • Within the enterprise, employees access the business data only through individual departments (data silos)<br>• Within the enterprise, employees access the business data through the company's servers<br>• Within the enterprise, employees access the business data through the company's servers and cloud (i.e. SharePoint, Microsoft Teams)<br>• Within the enterprise, employees access all the business data through the cloud (i.e. SharePoint, Microsoft Teams, Microsoft One Drive) |
| **Data storage arrangement within the enterprise**<br>(Blumzon & Pănescu, 2020; Halper, 2020; IBM, 2023b; Mazumdar et al., 2019; Sriramoju, 2019; Stanford, 2013) | Assesses how the data are stored within the enterprise | • Data are stored only on paper<br>• Data are stored locally on company servers and on multiple Network Attached Storage (NAS) systems that are duplicated and in different locations (Network storage (NAS) systems and servers);<br>• Data are stored on local servers, network attached storage (NAS) systems as well as in the cloud<br>• All the data are stored in the cloud |

| Criterion | Description | Measurement scale (Values) |
|---|---|---|
| **E-Archiving (also known as electronic or digital archiving)**<br>(Ragaisis et al., 2012; Sutanto & Nuryani, 2020), (Hornick, 2020) | Assesses the establishment of e-archiving within the enterprise | • E-archiving is not established within the enterprise<br>• E-archiving not yet established within the enterprise, but it is planned to be established<br>• E-archiving is established, but only due to the legal requirements<br>• E-archiving is established at the level of the entire enterprise – all the data and documents are electronically stored and archived to provide instant access and review to necessary information when needed |

**Enterprise software solutions**

Due to the growing amount of data, managing the data efficiently is becoming difficult. To be able to manage the data efficiently this requires a well-developed capabilities to process, analyze, understand, interpret and use the results (Monino, 2021). A prerequisite for the transition to a digitally mature organization is not only related to the use of digital technologies, but to also ensure a successful data management, for which we need a suitable software solution.

Enterprise software solutions such as accounting programs, sales and marketing support programs, and human resource management (HRM) programs are the basis for capturing, managing, transmitting and storing the data. This ensures the entire life cycle of data management. If this is not the case, a comprehensive approach to data management and using the data to support decision-making is not possible.

**Basic enterprise software solutions**

While the basic enterprise software solutions such as accounting programs, sales and marketing support programs, and human resources management (HRM) programs provide a basis for enterprise basic business functions and operations (i.e. issuing invoices, managing the number of employees, paying salaries, …), the use of comprehensive enterprise software solutions such as CRM and ERP is gaining importance among companies.

In the following a more detailed description about what is ERP and CRM and what is their main purpose.

**Customer Relationship Management (CRM)**

Customer relationship management or CRM represents a set of software tools that enhances a company's capability to coordinate marketing and service strategies to reach and retain partnerships and helps to address the customer needs and demands, and improve customer satisfaction (Gil-Gomez et al., 2020; Marolt, 2018; Ruivo et al., 2017)

According to (Gil-Gomez et al., 2020) the implementation and use of CRM in SMEs brings direct benefits in terms of both financial performance and daily business activity (i.e. increased customer loyalty, a more effective marketing strategy, improved customer service and support, greater efficiency, and cost reduction).

**Enterprise Resource Planning (ERP)**

Enterprise resource planning (ERP) is an enterprise software solution that is able to identify, collect, integrate, structure, and process data of different kinds of departments within the enterprise, and provide employees with the information they need in an appropriate and timely manner (Molina-Castillo et al., 2022). ERP integrates and coordinates inter-organizational processes involving suppliers and customers, improving the information flows and reducing time and costs in communication (Molina-Castillo et al., 2022).

A CRM systems encompass the external part of the extended enterprise, ERP encompasses the internal part (Ruivo et al., 2017). Based on the description and definitions provided, we describe the *Enterprise software solutions* criterion as an enterprise software solutions that are used to support enterprise business and operations (such as accounting programs, sales and marketing programs, human resource programs, ERP and CRM), where we want to assess what enterprise software solutions organization use to support business tasks, processes and operations, whether it uses only basic software solutions (i.e. programs for accounting sales and marketing support programs, and human resources management (HRM) programs), ERP and CRM solutions, or none of these.

**IT infrastructure**

A well-designed information technology infrastructure of the organization or IT infrastructure is a prerequisite for the use of software solutions that form the basis for data to be captured, processed, exchanged and stored. It is a prerequisite for the operation and management of the company's IT services and business processes, which are supported by various information systems (Jabbouri et al., 2016).

During the literature review, it is possible to detect different definitions of what IT infrastructure is and what elements are needed to describe the IT infrastructure.

According to (Jabbouri et al., 2016) an IT infrastructure represents the basis for computer technology, communications, and data systems that helps organization to meet management needs and can be understood as a foundation for services delivered through central information system.

(Al-Sabaawi & Alyouzbak, 2022) defines an IT infrastructure as the foundation for IT capabilities that enable the development of technical applications and support organizations' activities. (Al-Sabaawi & Alyouzbak, 2022) also adds that IT infrastructure can include flexibility, where human aspect must be included – i.e. the knowledge and experience of information technology personnel and not only a technical view such as the use of a hardware, software, and communication technologies. According to (Al-Sabaawi & Alyouzbak, 2022) IT infrastructure flexibility can be understood as an ability of IT infrastructure to adapt to environmental changes to develop and implement technologies rapidly.

The similar definition can be found in (Widajanti & Ratnawati, 2020), where authors define the IT infrastructure as the basic foundation of information technology capabilities which includes internal equipment, software and cabling as well as human expertise needed to provide reliable services.

Based on the definitions provided, we understand an IT infrastructure as the integration of hardware, software, and communication technologies, information system elements and network equipment (i.e. computers, servers) as well as to include the human knowledge and expertise to provide services, necessary for the operation and management of the company's IT services and business processes.

**Data architecture**

Closely related to IT infrastructure is also data architecture. Data architecture represents the logical and physical structure of data sources and data management systems in an organization (Kaidalova et al., 2018; TOGAF, 2018). It is part of the enterprise architecture, which includes models, policies, rules and standards, which prescribe the collection, storage, transfer, integration and use of data in the organization (Iyamu, 2019; van den Hoven, 2003).

The goal of data architecture is to translate business requirements into data and system requirements and manage the flow of data through business processes (Iyamu, 2019). In other words, a data architecture represents a blueprint of how the data is managed throughout the organization to support entire data lifecycle (from collection through transformation, distribution and consumption) (IBM, 2023a; Iyamu, 2019; van den Hoven, 2003).

The starting point of data architecture represents the data architecture frameworks, which help the organization to design its own data architecture and to include all the necessary elements for data architecture design (Leist & Zellner, 2006) (Dumitriu & Popescu, 2020). The most well-known data architecture frameworks are TOGAF (TOGAF, 2018), DAMA-DMBOK2 (Gichohi, 2020), and Zahman framework for enterprise architecture (Gerber et al., 2020).

According to TOGAF (TOGAF, 2018) there are four types of architectures:

Business architecture, which defines the enterprise's organizational structure, business strategy, and processes.

Data architecture, which describes the conceptual, logical, and physical data assets and how they are stored and managed throughout their lifecycle.

Applications architecture, which represents the application systems, and how they relate to key business processes and each other.

Technical architecture, which describes the technology infrastructure (hardware, software, and networking) needed to support mission-critical applications.

Based on the description and definitions above, we understand data architecture as a plan that describes how an organization translates business requirements into data and system requirements and manages the flow of data through business processes by taking into account the business strategy, and the available technologies, technical infrastructure and applications.

Modern data architectures often leverage cloud platforms to manage and process data. While it can be more costly, its compute scalability enables important data processing tasks to be completed rapidly. The storage scalability also helps to cope with rising data volumes, and to ensure all relevant data is available to improve the quality of training AI applications.

To assess how mature is an organization in the context of the data architecture, we defined four criteria values that describes what type of data architecture is established within the enterprise:

- No data architecture is present or established within the enterprise
- Basic data architecture is established within the enterprise – Basic data architecture element (i.e. databases, servers, computers) are established on-premise, no cloud infrastructure exists or is used within the enterprise
- Hybrid data architecture established within the enterprise – all the data infrastructure is established on-premise and in cloud to integrate data across domains, between departments or geographies and business functions, which allows us to break down data silos
- Cloud-based data architecture is established within the enterprise - Entire data infrastructure is established through cloud, which allows us to access, exchange and use the data across different geographies and business sites.

**Social media (i.e. Facebook, LinkedIn, Instagram)**

In addition to the software solutions with which the organization collects, exchanges, processes and manages data in order to support its business processes, an important part of a data mature organization is also the exchange of information and interaction with customers. With the development of digital technologies, the use of social media has expanded, which, in addition to basic communication through the use of e-mail, allow the company an additional way of communicating with customers and advertising its brand. In this way, the relationship between the company and its customers is also built. (Marolt, 2018) points out that before the development of social media, customers were passive recipients of messages, while with the use of social media, the communication between the company and the customer has become more active and two-way, where companies can encourage customers to support their brand by becoming its ambassador, thereby increasing the visibility of the company and its product and service offerings.

In the literature, we can find different definitions that describe what social media are and different purposes for which they can be used.

(Carr & Hayes, 2015) defines social media as Internet-based channels that allow users to opportunistically interact and selectively self-present, either in real-time or asynchronously, with both broad and narrow audiences who derive value from user-generated content and the perception of interaction with others.

Similar definition can be found in (Appel et al., 2020) where social media can be understood as a collection of software-based digital technologies, that are usually presented as apps and websites, which provide users with digital environments, where users can send and receive digital content or information over some type of online social network (i.e. Facebook, Instagram or Twitter). (Appel et al., 2020) adds that social media represents another type of digital marketing channel that is used by marketers to communicate with consumers (customers) through advertising in a form of social influence by the users who have a high social value, to influence others and effect on consumers attitudes and behaviors.

Other authors, as in (F. Li et al., 2021) focused on researching the social media in the context of social media marketing strategy. (F. Li et al., 2021) explains that social media can be used as a platform to expand geographic reach to buyers, strengthen the brand of the organization and build closer connections with customers, or to fully include customers in marketing communication process, where the customer becomes creator, collaborator and commentator of messages.

It is therefore important how the company uses the data it has available through the use of social media - whether the company uses social media only to advertise its brand or actively includes it as part of marketing, analyzes the data regarding messages and tries to offer to customers more personalized products or services.

In this context, we have defined 4 values for the social media criterion, where we want to assess whether the company uses social media and for what purpose.

We arranged the values from the least desirable value, where the company does not use social media, to the most desirable value, where social media is part of the company's strategy and a key channel of communication with customers.

**Cloud computing**

Cloud computing or its services have become an important part of the IT infrastructure of companies as it makes data processing more efficient on multiple computing and storage systems, where accessibility is executed through the internet (Golightly et al., 2022).

During the literature review, we found that the precise definition of the cloud computing is relatively difficult, as each author provides his own definition, which he understands by this term.

(Sunyaev, 2020) defines cloud computing as a model that enables access to computing resources that evolved in information technology and has become a dominant business model for delivering IT infrastructure, components, and applications. The author further explains that with cloud computing, individuals and organizations can gain on-demand network access to a shared pool of managed and scalable IT resources, such as servers, storage, and applications.

The similar definition can be found in (Hassan et al., 2022) where authors understand cloud computing as a utility, where users can store their data remotely in the cloud to enjoy on-demand services and high-quality applications from a shared pool of configurable computing resources.

In the literature a frequently mentioned is also a definition provided by the US National Institute of Standards and Technology (NIST), which defines cloud computing as a model that provides easy network access to a set of configurable computing resources (e.g. networks, servers, storage, disks, applications and services) that can be quickly provisioned and released (Mell & Grance, 2011).

We know three main models of cloud computing, namely public cloud, private and hybrid cloud. Public cloud is deployed and managed by a third-party organization (i.e. cloud service provider), where the cloud service provider enables public access to the infrastructure it offers in the cloud and takes care of the entire infrastructure. This form is the least secure, as it is based on complete trust in the cloud service provider, who, in addition to the infrastructure, is also responsible for the security of the user's data (Golightly et al., 2022; Njeh, 2014). The second type of model is private cloud, where the cloud is deployed and managed within a single organization and no third-party organization (i.e. cloud service provider) is included, while the third type is hybrid cloud, where it represents the combination of public and private cloud (Golightly et al., 2022).

The use of cloud computing is further divided by the type of service that user wants to implement or use, namely Infrastructure as a Service (IaaS), Platform as a Service (PaaS) and Software as a Service (SaaS). In the IaaS the end user has the ability to control and manage the storage space, installed applications and operating system offered by cloud service providers, but does not manage the underlying hardware (i.e. processors, memory). The second type of service (Platform as a service) represents the basis for the design of a web user interface or a web application and allows the user to develop and create applications according to his wishes. While SaaS gives users access to use the applications offered by the cloud service providers, where the user pays as much as they use (pay-as-you-go) and does not need to worry about the development of the applications and whether there will be enough resources available.

In the context of assessing the data maturity of the organization, we want to know how mature the organization is in using the cloud computing or not. To differentiate between the levels of data maturity regarding the use of cloud computing, we defined four levels to cloud computing criterion. The least desirable value is that enterprise does not use any of cloud computing services. The second value indicates that cloud computing is used, but only minimally to provide either the additional safety of organizational data, due to standards, that requires that data must be stored in the cloud or due to the business area in which the enterprise operates. As the third value, we have defined that cloud computing is not only used for providing the additional safety of data, but to extent the use of cloud when cooperating with the suppliers and business partners to provide easier data sharing and communication. The last value represents the use of cloud computing as a part of the organizations' strategy where most of the business processes are also supported by access to the cloud.

**Artificial intelligence, Internet of Things, robotics, digital twins and blockchain**

One of the indicators of a data-mature organization is also the use of advanced technologies, such as the use of artificial intelligence, Internet of Things, robotics, digital twins, blockchain and others. With this, the organization communicates that it has high technological development and is constantly following technological progress.

The mentioned technologies can serve the company as an additional data source for data collection (use of artificial intelligence, Internet of Things, robotics), as a virtual snapshot of the company's working environment - e.g. simulating the operation of the production line and analyzing defect in machine operation through the use of digital twins or providing greater data security and traceability of data as provided by the use of blockchain technology.

**Artificial intelligence**

According to (Sadiq et al., 2021) the artificial intelligence can be defined as the ability of a system to correctly interpret external data, to produce knowledge to accomplish specific goals and tasks through constant adaptation and to solve engineering and industrial problems. While (Canhoto & Clear, 2019, pp. 184) defines artificial intelligence as an assemblage of technological components that collect, process, and act on data in ways that simulate human intelligence.

According to (Canhoto & Clear, 2019) it is able to use unstructured inputs, such as images, speech, or conversations, in addition to structured inputs, like transaction data (i.e. to detect payment fraud or use data collected in real time, either via physical sensors) or by tracking online activity (i.e. to monitor shoppers in the store) to decide to offer them a discount or what product to recommend to them.

**Internet of Things and robotics**

In order to be a data mature organization, an organization must first capture the data in some way before it can process it.

Internet of Things and other technological developments allow companies to gather a considerable amount and variety of data (Babu et al., 2021). A typical IoT deployment contains heterogeneous devices (mobile devices, computers, manufacturing machines) that has embedded sensors that are interconnected through a network (i.e. Internet), by measuring the factors such as temperature, vibrations, speed, fuel consumption, electricity use, and location (Ahmad Khan & Khaled, 2018; Gimpel, 2020). As stated by (Gimpel, 2020), the implementation of Internet of Things represents several benefits as for example sounding alarms when machine temperatures rise too high, notifying supervisors when machines slow below a target speed, and accounting for fuel and energy use. In this way the overall equipment efficiency can be improved, operating expenses reduced.

Robotics is another technology that can be used to collect data and is directly connected with Internet of Things as it contains different sensors and cameras used to capture the data. In the context of a business operations robotics is often used to automate tasks in manufacturing plants, such as assembly line tasks, painting, and welding (Soori et al., 2023). Robotics is also directly connected to artificial intelligence and machine learning algorithms which are used to optimize the robotic operations, such as improving the efficiency and accuracy of movements, for which we need to provide accurate and quality data (Soori et al., 2023).

**Digital twin**

Digital twin can be defined as a virtual representation of a physical product, that represents all the states and functions of that physical product (Jones et al., 2020; Weber et al., 2017). According to (H.-J.Uhlemann et al., 2017) the digital twin is a prerequisite for the development of cyber-physical production system, which allows enterprise centralized analysis and control of production system.

The concept of digital twin was first introduced by the authors (Grieves & Vickers, 2017), where the authors define the digital twin as a set of virtual information constructs that fully describes a potential or actual physical manufactured product from the micro atomic level to the macro geometrical level. As stated by (H.-J.Uhlemann et al., 2017) organizations are often challenged with the heterogenous and insufficient quality data, which is a prerequisite to establish a digital twin within the enterprise. The supplement for data acquisition in this case represent the use of sensor-based tracking systems and machine vision. Despite the fact that digital twins are often mentioned in business area related to the production, it can also be utilized in other business areas such as sales and in the context of innovation processes and activities (Holopainen et al., 2022).

According to (Holopainen et al., 2022) in an innovation process, a digital twin facilitate visualization, enables collaboration and decision-making throughout the value chain, not only in the integration and sharing of data within the company, but also between companies, and with external parties in collaborative product development, manufacturing, operation, and maintenance. Users can take part in the innovation and development processes of future products, services, processes, and business innovations.

**Blockchain**

The guiding principle of a data-driven organization is that data must be organized, structured and secure. Data is therefore key resource of the enterprise to operate and support the business processes (Xu et al., 2019). It is becoming important to ensure appropriate security and traceability of the data, because in this way we have greater control over the data and manage them more easily. In this context, a blockchain technology is becoming important among digital technologies.

A blockchain can be defined as a collection of data sets which are composed of a chain of data packages (blocks) where a block comprises multiple transactions (Nofer et al., 2017). The blockchain is extended by each additional block and hence represents a complete ledger of the transaction history. Each block contains a timestamp, the hash value of the previous block ("parent"), and a nonce, which is a random number for verifying the hash (Nofer et al., 2017).

This concept ensures the integrity of the entire blockchain through to the first block ("genesis block"). Hash values are unique and fraud can be effectively prevented since changes of a block in the chain would immediately change the respective hash value (Nofer et al., 2017).

Blockchain ensures decentralization, where information are distributed by individual block of information and the enterprise can avoid the single point of failure situation (Zheng et al., 2017). Furthermore it provides anonymity and traceability of information by removing the problem of tracing back ownership in long transaction chains and provides high level of security, where transaction cannot be tampered once it is packed into the blockchain (Zheng et al., 2017). Blockchain plays an increasingly important role in the field of smart contracts, where enterprises can automate transactions without manual confirmation (i.e. automatic filling of taxes under smart contracts) (Xu et al., 2019).

**Data analytics**

One of the key abilities to become a data-driven enterprise represents the ability to analyze the data. According to (Monino, 2021) data always included strategic value, where due to the magnitude of the data it has become important how to treat them. (Monino, 2021) adds that we are witnessing the explosion of sensors and smart devices, where the data in enterprises has become complex as we have variety of structured, semi-structured and unstructured data. The need to analyze the data has therefore become necessary, if we want to discover new knowledge and hidden patterns that data can provide.

Data analytics can be defined as the process of analyzing any format of data like structural, semi-structural, and unstructural to generate valuable information (Vijesh Joe et al., 2020). Data analytics can be often interchanged with the term of data analysis. According to (Sarker, 2021), data analytics refers to the theories, technologies, instruments, and processes that allow an in-depth understanding and exploration of actionable data insight, where it consists of descriptive analytics, predictive analytics, and prescriptive analytics (Cao, 2017).

Descriptive analytics is used to interpret historical data to better understand the changes that have occurred in a business (i.e. what happened in the past). Predictive analytics examines data or content to answer the question what will happen in the future (i.e. to assess business risks, anticipate potential market patterns or to decide when maintenance is needed). Prescriptive analytics prescribe what action should be taken on recommending the best way forward, where the data are collected from several descriptive and predictive sources and applied to the decision-making process (Sarker, 2021).

While the data analysis refers to the processing of data by conventional (e.g., classic statistical, mathematical, or logical) theories, technologies, and tools for extracting useful information and for practical purposes (Cao, 2017).

Data analytics is thus a broader term that describes the use of data and tools to make business decisions, while data analysis is a subset of data analytics – i.e.

one of the processes or steps to follow to gain insights and information from the data.

**Data analytics tools**

If we want to extract and collect useful information and insights and to find hidden patterns from the data, organization must use a data analytics tool. Data analytic tools can be defined as an accessory that helps visualize and interpret the data to provide meaningful summaries of analyzed data, usually in the form of graphical representation such as chart, plot, histogram or other visualization (Sarker, 2021). For business purposes there has been developed a number of analytics tools, from basic tools i.e. Excel that provides statistical and mathematical calculations and visualization of the data in the form of charts, and histograms to more advanced data analytics and business intelligence tools, such as Microsoft Power BI, SAS Business Intelligence, QlikView, which provide a deeper analysis of data and techniques to acquire additional knowledge (i.e. mathematical modeling, simulation and scenario development, and interactive data visualization) (Mikalef et al., 2018).

**Digital channels**

Due to the technological development in recent years, a new form of engagement between customer and company has emerged in the form of digital channels that are replacing the traditional communication and interaction with the customers (Straker et al., 2015). Although communication with customers is moving to the Internet in the sense of the websites, social media (i.e. Facebook, LinkedIn, Instagram) or platforms (i.e. Amazon, eBay, YouTube) (Straker et al., 2015), in practice, in some companies it can be perceived that communication with customers is still limited to communication via e-mail (Chaparro-Peláez et al., 2022).

Digital channel can be defined as a media that allows a communication through digital or electronic media among businesses or consumers (Shankar et al., 2022). The more broader definition is related to digital marketing, which defines the practice and management of marketing through electronic media, such as web, e-mail or other type of media (Frausto-da-Silva et al., 2015). The use of web in the form of webpages or webstore and e-mail communication in this case represent the type of digital channel through which the information's are transferred to inform and to establish interaction with the customer.

The most basic form of communication with the customer is mouth-to-mouth or face-to-face communication (Stankovska et al., 2016). The communication has then moved to digital interaction with the customer with the use of electronic mail as a medium to communicate with the customers (Chaparro-Peláez et al., 2022; Lemon & Verhoef, 2016). The next technological development brought an online channels, which are presented through the use of websites of the enterprises and use of social media and mobile devices (Lemon & Verhoef, 2016; Wolf & Steul-Fischer, 2022). With the development of e-commerce, the digital channels were used as a digital platforms or electronic marketplaces, which can be described as a virtual place where multiple buyers and sellers conduct transactions by electronic means and can be physical, virtual, or conceptual (Grieger, 2003; Loukis et al., 2011; Wang & Archer, 2007).

**Paperless office (Digitalization level)**

One of the prerequisites for effective data management within the organization and also for the organization to become data-driven is to get rid of paper-based business and, where possible, digitalize business processes and operate entirely digital.

To assess at what stage of digitalization the organization is, or how much the organization has already digitalized its business processes, this can be achieved by assessing the degree of digitalization, through the assessment of three levels: digitization, digitalization and digital transformation as described by (Verhoef et al., 2019) and (Vial, 2019).

According to (Verhoef et al., 2019) digitization refers to the change of analog to digital tasks, to convert analog information into digital information. Typical task of digitization is to transform internal and external document processes into digital form.

Digitalization describes how information (IT) technologies or digital technologies can be used to alter existing business processes (i.e. creation of new online or mobile communication channels that allow all customers to easily connect with the enterprise). IT serves as a key enabler to seize new business possibilities by changing existing business processes.

The last step is digital transformation, which can be defines as an evolutionary process that leverages digital capabilities and technologies to enable business models, operational processes and customer experiences to create value (Morakanyane et al., 2017, pp. 437). It is a process where digital technologies create disruptions triggering strategic responses from organizations that seek to alter their value creation paths while managing the structural changes and organizational barriers (Vial, 2019, pp. 1)

**Document and data exchange with business partners and suppliers**

Part of a every organization is also the sharing and exchange of documents and data within the organization as well as outside it, where the organization exchanges its data with external business partners and suppliers. If there is no sharing of data and data exchange, we can be less informed, which means we cannot create knowledge. Data that are available within the company, other than support the business processes and operation of the enterprise can also be used to predict behavior, automate and improve relation with the customers, where data exchange is important from the view of the competition (Costa & Miguel, 2020).

Data sharing or data exchange can be described as the exchange of resources, where organizations provide data they have gathered to network partners (i.e. suppliers, distributors, partners) to facilitate collaboration in the broader ecosystem (Quach et al., 2022).

According to (Costa & Miguel, 2020) data exchange can be differentiated by three types:

1) Horizontal data exchange, where data is exchanged between the two firms, that are competing on the same market 2) independent data exchange, where data is exchanged between the two firms, that are competing on different market and 3) vertical data exchange when two firms are integrated in customer/supplier relations and exchange data (i.e. data exchange between Amazon and FedEx).

Data exchange is also directly connected to the type of digital channel used to share and exchange the information, which we have already described under the digital channel criterion. In the context of data maturity assessment, we want to assess in which way the enterprise exchanges the data with its business partners and suppliers. For this purpose, we have defined the following four criteria values that describes the maturity of the enterprise related to the data exchange, proposed by (Kljajić Borštnar & Pucihar, 2021).

The least desirable value represents the state, where all of the documents and data with the business partners and suppliers are shared and exchanged through the use of e-mail or in textual form.

The second value represents the case, where all the standard business documents, such as purchase order, invoice and delivery note are exchanged and shared electronically in digital form.

The third value represents the connected information system to the information system of a business partner or supplier, which enables organization to obtain insights into business partners IS systems – i.e. insights in product stock.

The fourth value indicates that enterprise has an information system, connected with the entire supply chain to provide seamless electronic data exchange with entire ecosystem of business partners and suppliers.

**Data storage arrangement within the enterprise**

Before we can access the data, we must ensure adequate data storage. Data in companies can be stored in different places (computers, servers, NAS systems, use of the cloud) and in different formats (PDF, XML) and forms (structured data (i.e. transaction information, customer name, e-mail addresses), unstructured data (i.e. audio and video files, social media posts, satellite images, ...) or semi-structured data (i.e. call center log, spreadsheets, folders organized by topic, ...).

Data storage refers to a collective methods and technologies that are used to capture and retain digital information on electromagnetic, optical or silicon-based storage media (Sriramoju, 2019). Similar definition was proposed by large enterprise IBM (IBM, 2023b) where data storage refers to magnetic, optical or mechanical media that records and preserves digital information for ongoing or future operations.

According to (Blumzon & Pănescu, 2020) data can be stored in three types of locations (i.e. local storage, storage at institutional level (or network storage) and stored off-site in specialized facilities).

As described by (Blumzon & Pănescu, 2020) local storage means that data are stored on a local machine (i.e. computer) where it allows to quickly access the data, but represents and obstacle, when we want to share the data with others. The owner of that machine is responsible for the data preservation.

The data storage at the institutional level (also known as network storage), enables the data to be stored on additional network device, such as storage area network (SAN) system or network area storage (NAS) system (Blumzon & Pănescu, 2020).

The third type of data storage (i.e. off-site data storage) represents the data storage location, where the data are stored outside of the organization on the cloud in a specialized facilities at the cloud provider (i.e. Amazon, Microsoft, Google) (Blumzon & Pănescu, 2020). This type of storage is suitable, when enterprise does not have the required resources or when the data must be shared across a network of collaborators. In this case a privacy and legal need to be considered as usually a third party is responsible for handling of the data storage.

In this context, we assigned to the criterion data storage arrangement within the enterprise four values. We want to assess how the data is stored within the enterprise, where the least desirable value refers to the paper storage (i.e. the data are stored on paper), and most desirable value to the storage in the cloud. We have also added values that are slightly better than the first one and worse than the last, namely the data are stored on a local device (i.e. computer) and no network attached storage (NAS) system or on the local servers, NAS system and cloud, which represents a hybrid type of data storage.

The similar criterion values apply for the criterion access to business data within the enterprise.

**E-archiving (also known as electronic or digital archiving)**
Archiving is the last step of data management cycle. When the data are put to the archive it means that they were removed from the production and are maintained for a period of time, depending on enterprise or legal requirements (Hornick, 2020). Based on this description, we have defined three criteria values: the paper archive, where organization does not have implemented any electronic archiving and the data are still stored in physical folders. Digital archiving where the data is stored electronically through the use of document systems or dedicated internal organization archive software. The third value represent certified digital archiving where the archived stored documents are legally compliant and have the same evidentiary value as paper originals.

## 5. Discussion

Data as a source of information and knowledge is becoming an important part of digital transformation and strategic source for new value creation. In this context, a transformation to an organization driven by data or data-driven organization is becoming an important goal to achieve.

If we want to know what level of data maturity the organization currently has, we need to measure it in some way, which can be achieved by establishing a proper measurement scale. One is the measuring the level of data maturity (scale of the overall criteria) and the other is the scale of individual criteria, which we address in this paper. So, we are interested in measurement scales for individual criteria, which are used to describe data maturity. For this purpose, we have reviewed the literature of existing data maturity models and measurement scales.

The literature review showed, that although many models have been proposed and developed in the past to assess the data maturity, most of the reviewed models only provide an assessment levels, derived from the CMMI model and lacks a clear and systematic development methodology, as observed by (Helmy et al., 2022). Helmy et al. (2022) did an analytical study of the existing big data management frameworks and models available in the literature. Authors found that most of the maturity assessment models do not have a clear and systematic development methodology. Another critique applies to the models such as the one proposed by (Comuzzi & Patel, 2016), whose model only describes the maturity of capabilities implicitly-to-levels, diagnosing "As-is" states of big data adoption capabilities, but does not define explicitly, what improvement practices should be applied to those states. Based on the observations from the literature review, we have not found a sufficiently comprehensive model that would be consistent with the needs and specifics of the SMEs. For a comprehensive assessment of data maturity, we need to have a set of criteria, such as leadership, skills, strategy, data quality, data security and privacy and others and a clear definition of measurement scales, which the existing data maturity models often lacks. Existing maturity models are less transparent when measuring data maturity. When defining the measurement scales that existing models provide, it is often difficult to quickly and easily understand in which level of data maturity the evaluated company can be placed.

## 6. Conclusion

In this paper, we addressed the problem of data maturity assessment of SMEs. The aim of this paper was to define a set of measurement scales, based on which we will be able to assess how mature the SMEs are in utilization of their data, and what is their current data maturity level. The measurement scales proposed in this paper will be used in the development process of a data maturity model for SMEs, using the DEX method. The final aim is to build a comprehensive multi-criteria model for evaluating the different levels of data maturity achieved by small and medium-sized enterprises. Based on the assessment the SMEs will be able to plan their actions towards data maturity better.

## Acknowledgments

This research was supported by the Slovenian Research and Innovation Agency: Program No. P5-0018 "Decision Support Systems in Digital Business" and postgraduate research funding for Young Researchers No. 54752-0586-21.

## Bibliography

Accenture. (2018). *Becoming a data-driven enterprise: Data Industrialization.* https://www.accenture.com/us-en/insights/technology/data-industrialization

Ahmad Khan, M., & Khaled, S. (2018). IoT security: Review, blockchain solutions, and open challenges. *Future Generation Computer Systems, 82*, 395–411. https://doi.org/10.1016/j.future.2017.11.022

Akaegbu, J. B., & Usoro, A. A. (2017). THE PLACE OF ORGANISATIONAL CAPABILITIES IN STRATEGY FORMULATION AND IMPLEMENTATION: AN EXPLORATORY ANALYSIS. *GLOBAL JOURNAL OF SOCIAL SCIENCES, 16*, 39–48. https://doi.org/10.4314/gjss.v16i1.5

Al-Ansi, A. M., Jaboob, M., Garad, A., & Al-Ansi, A. (2023). Analyzing augmented reality (AR) and virtual reality (VR) recent development in education. *Social Sciences & Humanities Open, 8*(1), 100532. https://doi.org/10.1016/j.ssaho.2023.100532

Al-Ruithe, M., Benkhelifa, E., & Hameed, K. (2018). Key Issues for Embracing the Cloud Computing to Adopt a Digital Transformation: A study of Saudi Public Sector. *Procedia Computer Science, 130*, 1037–1043. https://doi.org/10.1016/j.procs.2018.04.145

Al-Ruithe, M., Benkhelifa, E., & Hameed, K. (2019). A systematic literature review of data governance and cloud data governance. *Personal and Ubiquitous Computing, 23*(5), 839–859. https://doi.org/10.1007/s00779-017-1104-3

Al-Sabaawi, M. Y. M., & Alyouzbak, B. A. (2022). The Impact of Information Technology Infrastructure Flexibility and Behavioral Biases on Investment Decision Making. *International Journal of Enterprise Information Systems, 18*(1). https://doi.org/10.4018/IJEIS.313050

Alazie, G., & Tsigie, S. (2019). *Data management practice in 21 st century: systematic review.* https://www.emerald.com/insight/content/doi/10.1108/XJM-08-2020-0096/full/html

Almazmomi, N., Ilmudeen, A., & Qaffas, A. A. (2021). The impact of business analytics capability on data-driven culture and exploration: achieving a competitive advantage. *Benchmarking*, 1–20. https://doi.org/10.1108/BIJ-01-2021-0021

Appel, G., Grewal, L., Hadi, R., & Stephen, A. T. (2020). The future of social media in marketing. *Journal of the Academy of Marketing Science, 48*(1), 79–95. https://doi.org/10.1007/s11747-019-00695-1

Ardagna, D., Cappiello, C., Samá, W., & Vitali, M. (2018). Context-aware data quality assessment for big data. *Future Generation Computer Systems, 89*, 548–562. https://doi.org/10.1016/j.future.2018.07.014

Arnold, M., Goldschmitt, M., & Rigotti, T. (2023). Dealing with information overload: a comprehensive review. *Frontiers in Psychology, 14.* https://doi.org/10.3389/fpsyg.2023.1122200

Babu, M. M., Rahman, M., Alam, A., & Dey, B. L. (2021). Exploring big data-driven innovation in the manufacturing sector: evidence from UK firms. *Annals of Operations Research*, 1–28. https://doi.org/10.1007/S10479-021-04077-1

Baesens, B., Bapna, R., Marsden, J. R., Vanthienen, J., & Zhao, J. L. (2016). TRANSFORMATIONAL ISSUES OF BIG DATA AND ANALYTICS IN NETWORKED BUSINESS. *MIS Quarterly, 40*(4), 807–818. https://pdfs.semanticscholar.org/0fc1/5b775475b97c5e29d1422af5df6afef8e446.pdf

Becker, J., Knackstedt, R., & Pöppelbuß, J. (2009). Developing Maturity Models for IT Management – A Procedure Model and its Application. *Business & Information Systems Engineering, 1*, 213–222. https://doi.org/10.1007/s12599-009-0044-5

Blumzon, C. F. I., & Pănescu, A.-T. (2020). *Data Storage BT - Good Research Practice in Non-Clinical Pharmacology and Biomedicine* (A. Bespalov, M. C. Michel, & T. Steckler (eds.); pp. 277–297). Springer International Publishing. https://doi.org/10.1007/164_2019_288

Bohanec, M. (2006). Measurement scales and stocks of parameter values. In *DECISION MAKING AND MODELS* (p. 127).

Bohanec, M., Martin, Ž., Vladislav, R., Ivan, B., & Blaž, Z. (2013). DEX Methodology: Three Decades of Qualitative Multi-Attribute Modeling. *Informatica*, *37*(1), 49–54. https://www.informatica.si/index.php/informatica/article/viewFile/433/437

Brinkhues, R. A., Carlos Gastaud Maçada, A., & D'Agostini Oliveira Casalinho, G. (2014). Information Management Capabilities: Antecedents And Consequences. *Twentieth Americas Conference on Information Systems*, 1–11. https://www.researchgate.net/profile/Rafael-Brinkhues/publication/263272671_Information_Management_Capabilities_Antecedents_And_Consequences_Completed_Research_Paper/links/564a11b908ae44e7a28d9146/Information-Management-Capabilities-Antecedents-And-Conseq

Briscoe, M. D. (2022). The paperless office twenty years later: Still a myth? *Sustainability: Science, Practice and Policy*, *18*(1), 837–845. https://doi.org/10.1080/15487733.2022.2146370

Canhoto, A. I., & Clear, F. (2019). *Artificial intelligence and machine learning as business tools: A framework for diagnosing value destruction potential*. https://doi.org/10.1016/j.bushor.2019.11.003

Cao, L. (2017). Data Science: A Comprehensive Overview. *ACM Computing Surveys*, *50*(3). https://doi.org/10.1145/3076253

Carillo, K. D. A. (2017). Let's stop trying to be "sexy" – preparing managers for the (big) data-driven business era. *Business Process Management Journal*, *23*(3), 598–622. https://doi.org/10.1108/BPMJ-09-2016-0188

Carr, C. T., & Hayes, R. A. (2015). Social Media: Defining, Developing, and Divining. *Atlantic Journal of Communication*, *23*(1), 46–65. https://doi.org/10.1080/15456870.2015.972282

Cech, T. G., Spaulding, T. J., & Cazier, J. A. (2018). Data competence maturity: developing data-driven decision making. *Journal of Research in Innovative Teaching & Learning*, *11*(2), 139–158. https://doi.org/10.1108/JRIT-03-2018-0007

Chandler, A. D. J. (1962). *Strategy and Structure: Chapters in the History of the Industrial Enterprise*. https://s3.amazonaws.com/arena-attachments/705027/a973f694aaaee073aeb1cfce037f3b11.pdf

Chao, C. (2015). *Implementing a Paperless System for Small and Medium-Sized Businesses (SMBs)* [University of Oregon]. https://core.ac.uk/download/pdf/36693527.pdf

Chaparro-Peláez, J., Hernández-García, Á., & Lorente-Páramo, Á.-J. (2022). May I have your attention, please? An investigation on opening effectiveness in e-mail marketing. *Review of Managerial Science*, *16*(7), 2261–2284. https://doi.org/10.1007/s11846-022-00517-9

Chen, L., & Nath, R. (2018). Business analytics maturity of firms: an examination of the relationships between managerial perception of IT, business analytics maturity and success. *Information Systems Management*, *35*(1), 62–77. https://doi.org/10.1080/10580530.2017.1416948

Chen, W., Liu, C., Xing, F., Peng, G., & Yang, X. (2022). Establishment of a maturity model to assess the development of industrial AI in smart manufacturing. *Journal of Enterprise Information Management*, *35*(3), 701–728. https://doi.org/10.1108/JEIM-10-2020-0397

Chen, Y., Wang, Q., Chen, H., Song, X., Tang, H., & Tian, M. (2019). An overview of augmented reality technology. *Journal of Physics: Conference Series*, *1237*(2), 22082. https://doi.org/10.1088/1742-6596/1237/2/022082

CMMI. (2014). *CMMI Institute - Data Management Maturity (DMM)*. https://stage.cmmiinstitute.com/dmm

CMMI Institute. (2019). *Data Management Maturity Model (DMM)*. https://stage.cmmiinstitute.com/getattachment/cb35800b-720f-4afe-93bf-86ccefb1fb17/attachment.aspx

Coleman, S., Göb, R., Manco, G., Pievatolo, A., Tort-Martorell, X., & Reis, M. S. (2016). How Can SMEs Benefit from Big Data? Challenges and a Path Forward. *Quality and Reliability Engineering International*, *32*(6), 2151–2164. https://doi.org/10.1002/QRE.2008

Collins, C., Dennehy, D., Conboy, K., & Mikalef, P. (2021). Artificial intelligence in information systems research: A systematic literature review and research agenda. *International Journal of Information Management*, *60*, 102383. https://doi.org/10.1016/j.ijinfomgt.2021.102383

Comuzzi, M., & Patel, A. (2016). How organisations leverage Big Data: a maturity modl. *Industrial Management & Data Systems*, *116*(8), 1468–1492. https://doi.org/10.1108/IMDS-12-2015-0495

Costa, O., & Miguel, A. (2020). A Model of Data and Data Exchange in Competitive Markets. *SSRN Electronic Journal*. http://dx.doi.org/10.2139/ssrn.3564361

Davenport, T. H., & DalleMule, L. (2017). The 2 Types of Data Strategies Every Company Needs. *Harvard Business Review*. https://hbr.org/2017/05/whats-your-data-strategy

Davids, E. L., Roman, N. V., & Leach, L. (2016). Decision Making Styles: A Systematic Review of Their Associations with Parenting. *Adolescent Research Review*, *1*(1), 69–90. https://doi.org/10.1007/s40894-015-0003-y

De Silva, D., & Alahakoon, D. (2022). An artificial intelligence life cycle: From conception to production. *Patterns*, *3*(6), 100489. https://doi.org/10.1016/j.patter.2022.100489

Deloitte. (2021). *Demystifying data 2021 - Unlocking the benefits of data maturity and machine learning in Australia and New Zealand*. https://www2.deloitte.com/content/dam/Deloitte/au/Documents/Economics/deloitte-au-dae-demystifying-data-2021-301121.pdf

Dravis, F. (2004). Data Quality Strategy: A Step-by-Step Approach. *Proceedings of the Ninth International Conference on Information Quality (ICIQ-04)*. https://api.semanticscholar.org/CorpusID:30552791

Dumitriu, D., & Popescu, M. A.-M. (2020). Enterprise Architecture Framework Design in IT Management. *Procedia Manufacturing*, *46*, 932–940. https://doi.org/10.1016/j.promfg.2020.05.011

Elsaify, M., & Hasan, S. (2021). Data exchanges among firms. *Digital Business*, *1*(2), 100010. https://doi.org/10.1016/j.digbus.2021.100010

Eroğlu, Ş., & Çakmak, T. (2018). Information as an organizational asset: assessment of a public organization's capabilities in Turkey: *36*(1), 58–77. https://doi.org/10.1177/0266666918811004

Farah, B. (2017). A Value Based Big Data Maturity Model. *Journal of Management Policy and Practice*, *18*(1), 11–18. http://www.na-businesspress.com/JMPP/FarahB_Web18_1_.pdf

Faroukhi, A. Z., El Alaoui, I., Gahi, Y., & Amine, A. (2020). Big data monetization throughout Big Data Value Chain: a comprehensive review. *Journal of Big Data*, *7*(1), 1–22. https://doi.org/10.1186/s40537-019-0281-5

Farzaneh, M., Mozaffari, F., Ameli, S. P., Karami, M., Mohamadian, A., & Arianyan, E. (2019). Designing an Organizational Readiness Framework for Big Data Adoption. In M. Farzaneh, F. Mozaffari, S. P. Ameli, M. Karami, A. Mohamadian, & E. Arianyan (Eds.), *9th International Symposium on Telecommunication: With Emphasis on Information and Communication Technology, IST 2018* (pp. 387–391). IEEE. https://doi.org/10.1109/ISTEL.2018.8661073

Frausto-da-Silva, T., Grilo, A., & Cruz-Machado, V. (2015). *Selection of Digital Marketing Channels: Application of Modern Portfolio Theory BT - Industrial Engineering, Management Science and Applications 2015* (M. Gen, K. J. Kim, X. Huang, & Y. Hiroshi (eds.); pp. 585–597). Springer Berlin Heidelberg.

Gajdzik, B. (2022). Frameworks of the Maturity Model for Industry 4.0 with Assessment of Maturity Levels on the Example of the Segment of Steel Enterprises in Poland. In *Journal of Open Innovation: Technology, Market, and Complexity* (Vol. 8, Issue 2). https://doi.org/10.3390/joitmc8020077

Gandhi, S., Thota, B., Kuchembuck, R., & Swartz, J. (2018). Demystifying data monetization. *MIT Sloan Management Review*. https://sloanreview.mit.edu/article/demystifying-data-monetization/

Gartner. (2008). *Gartner data governance maturity model*. https://www.lightsondata.com/data-governance-maturity-models-gartner/

Gartner. (2018). *Gartner Survey Shows Organizations Are Slow to Advance in Data and Analytics*. https://www.gartner.com/en/newsroom/press-releases/2018-02-05-gartner-survey-shows-organizations-are-slow-to-advance-in-data-and-analytics

Gašperlin, B., Pucihar, A., & Kljajić Borštnar, M. (2023). *NABOR KRITERIJEV ZA OCENJEVANJE PODATKOVNE ZRELOSTI V MALIH IN SREDNJEVELIKIH PODJETJIH = A SET OF DATA MATURITY ASSESSMENT CRITERIA FOR SMALL AND MEDIUM-SIZED ENTERPRISES*. In Press

Gašperlin, B., Pucihar, A., & Kljajič Borštnar, M. (2021). SMEs READINESS IN UTILIZING DIGITAL TECHNOLOGIES AND DATA IN DIGITAL TRANSFORMATION. *SOR '21- The 16th International Symposium on Operations Research in Slovenia*, 107–112. http://fgg-web.fgg.uni-lj.si/~/sdrobne/sor/SOR'21-Proceedings.pdf

Geissdoerfer, M., Vladimirova, D., & Evans, S. (2018). Sustainable business model innovation: A review. *Journal of Cleaner Production*, *198*, 401–416. https://doi.org/10.1016/j.jclepro.2018.06.240

Gerber, A., le Roux, P., Kearney, C., & van der Merwe, A. (2020). *The Zachman Framework for Enterprise Architecture: An Explanatory IS Theory BT - Responsible Design, Implementation and Use of Information and Communication Technology* (M. Hattingh, M. Matthee, H. Smuts, I. Pappas, Y. K. Dwivedi, & M. Mäntymäki (eds.); pp. 383–396). Springer International Publishing.

Gichohi, B. (2020). Leveraging on big data and advanced technologies to enhance domestic revenue mobilization. *Statistical Journal of the IAOS*, *36*, 111–119. https://doi.org/10.3233/SJI-200706

Gierlich-Joas, M., & Hess, T. (2020). *Towards an Understanding of Data's Influence on Leadership*. https://doi.org/10.30844/wi_2020_q3-gierlich

Gil-Gomez, H., Guerola-Navarro, V., Oltra-Badenes, R., & Lozano-Quilis, J. A. (2020). Customer relationship management: digital transformation and sustainable business model innovation. *Economic Research-Ekonomska Istraživanja*, *33*(1), 2733–2750. https://doi.org/10.1080/1331677X.2019.1676283

Gill, S. S., Kumar, A., Singh, H., Singh, M., Kaur, K., Usman, M., & Buyya, R. (2022). Quantum computing: A taxonomy, systematic review and future directions. *Software: Practice and Experience*, *52*(1), 66–114. https://doi.org/10.1002/spe.3039

Gimpel, G. (2020). Bringing dark data into the light: Illuminating existing IoT data lost within your organization. *Business Horizons*, *63*(4), 519–530. https://doi.org/10.1016/j.bushor.2020.03.009

Godoy, J. de, Otrel-Cass, K., & Toft, K. H. (2021). Transformations of trust in society: A systematic review of how access to big data in energy systems challenges Scandinavian culture. *Energy and AI*, *5*, 1–15. https://doi.org/10.1016/J.EGYAI.2021.100079

Gökalp, Mert O, Kayabay, K., Gökalp, E., Koçyiğit, A., & Eren, P. E. (2021). Assessment of process capabilities in transition to a data-driven organisation: A multidisciplinary approach. *IET Software*, *15*(6), 376–390. https://doi.org/10.1049/sfw2.12033

Gökalp, Mert Onuralp, Gökalp, E., Gökalp, S., & Koçyiğit, A. (2021). The development of data analytics maturity assessment framework: DAMAF. *Journal of Softwate: Evolution and Process*. https://doi.org/10.1002/smr.2415

Gökalp, Mert Onuralp, Gökalp, E., Kayabay, K., Koçyiğit, A., & Eren, P. E. (2021). Data-driven manufacturing: An assessment model for data science maturity. *Journal of Manufacturing Systems*, *60*, 527–546. https://doi.org/10.1016/j.jmsy.2021.07.011

Gökalp, Mert Onuralp, Gökalp, E., Kayabay, K., Koçyiğit, A., & Eren, P. E. (2022). The development of the data science capability maturity model: a survey-based research. *Online Information Review*, *46*(3), 547–567. https://doi.org/10.1108/OIR-10-2020-0469

Golightly, L., Chang, V., Xu, Q. A., Gao, X., & Liu, B. S. C. (2022). Adoption of cloud computing as innovation in the organization. *International Journal of Engineering Business Management*, *14*, 18479790221093990. https://doi.org/10.1177/18479790221093992

Gölzer, A. A., & Philipp, P. (2018). The IoT and Digital Transformation: Toward the Data-Driven Enterprise. *IEEE Pervasive Computing*, *17*(1), 87–91. https://doi.org/10.1109/MPRV.2018.011591066

Grieger, M. (2003). Electronic marketplaces: A literature review and a call for supply chain management research. *European Journal of Operational Research*, *144*(2), 280–294. https://doi.org/10.1016/S0377-2217(02)00394-6

Grieves, M., & Vickers, J. (2017). *Digital Twin: Mitigating Unpredictable, Undesirable Emergent Behavior in Complex Systems* (pp. 85–113). https://doi.org/10.1007/978-3-319-38756-7_4

Grossman, R. L. (2018). A framework for evaluating the analytic maturity of an organization. *International Journal of Information Management*, *38*(1), 45–51. https://doi.org/10.1016/j.ijinfomgt.2017.08.005

Guangming, C., Yao, L., Zhiwei, G., & Xiaoyin, L. (2017). Cloud Data Governance Maturity Model. *8th IEEE International Conference on Software*

*Engineering and Service Science (ICSESS)*, 517–520. https://doi.org/10.1109/ICSESS.2017.8342968

Günther, L. C., Colangelo, E., Wiendahl, H.-H., & Bauer, C. (2019). Data quality assessment for improved decision-making: a methodology for small and medium-sized enterprises. *Procedia Manufacturing*, *29*, 583–591. https://doi.org/10.1016/j.promfg.2019.02.114

Gür, I., Guggenberger, T., & Altendeitering, M. (August 9, 2021). Towards a Data Management Capability Model. *Twenty-Seventh Americas Conference on Information Systems*. https://www.researchgate.net/publication/351225130_Towards_a_Data_Management_Capability_Model

Gür, I., Spiekermann, M., Arbter, M., & Otto, B. (2021). Data Strategy Development: A Taxonomy for Data Strategy Tools and Methodologies in the Economy. *Wirtschaftsinformatik 2021 Proceedings*, 1–16. https://aisel.aisnet.org/cgi/viewcontent.cgi?article=1015&context=wi2021

H.-J.Uhlemann, T., Lehmann, C., & Steinhilper, R. (2017). The Digital Twin: Realizing the Cyber-Physical Production System for Industry 4.0. *Procedia CIRP*, *61*, 335–340. https://doi.org/10.1016/j.procir.2016.11.152

Hagen, J., & Hess, T. (2020). Linking Big Data and Business: Design Parameters of Data-Driven Organizations. *Conference of the Association-for-Information-Systems (AMCIS)*, 1–10. https://www.researchgate.net/profile/Janine-Hagen/publication/343549422_Linking_Big_Data_and_Business_Design_Parameters_of_Data-Driven_Organizations/links/5f3137ff458515b729123254/Linking-Big-Data-and-Business-Design-Parameters-of-Data-Driven-Organization

Halper, F. (2020). *TDWI Analytics Maturity Model Assessment Guide TDWI RESEARCH Introduction 4*. https://go.tdwi.org/rs/626-EMC-557/images/TDWI_Analytics-Maturity-Model-Assessment-Guide_2020.pdf

Halper, F., & Krishnan, K. (2014). *TDWI BIG DATA MATURITY MODEL GUIDE*. https://tdwi.org/~/media/3BF039A2F7E1464B8290D8A9880FEC22.pdfma

Hanafizadeh, P., & Harati Nik, M. R. (2020). Configuration of Data Monetization: A Review of Literature with Thematic Analysis. *Global Journal of Flexible Systems Management*, *21*(1), 17–34. https://doi.org/10.1007/s40171-019-00228-3

Harie, H. (2021). *Data management a necessity, not a nice to have*. https://it-online.co.za/2021/07/19/data-management-a-necessity-not-a-nice-to-have/

Harwood, I. (2006). *Revisiting the "paperless office": A case of values, power and (in)action*.

Hassan, J., Shehzad, D., Habib, U., Aftab, M. U., Ahmad, M., Kuleev, R., & Mazzara, M. (2022). The Rise of Cloud Computing: Data Protection, Privacy, and Open Research Challenges—A Systematic Literature Review (SLR).

*Computational Intelligence and Neuroscience, 2022*, 8303504. https://doi.org/10.1155/2022/8303504

Helmy, M., Mazen, S., Helal, I. M., & Youssef, W. (2022). Analytical Study on Building a Comprehensive Big Data Management Maturity Framework. *International Journal of Information Science and Management, 20*(1), 225–255. https://ijism.ricest.ac.ir/index.php/ijism/article/view/2348/563

Hevner, A. R. (2007). A Three Cycle View of Design Science Research. *Scandinavian Journal of Information Systems, 19*(2), 1–6. https://aisel.aisnet.org/cgi/viewcontent.cgi?article=1017&context=sjis

Hevner, A. R., March, S. T., Park, J., & Ram, S. (2004). Design Science in Information Systems Research. *MIS Quarterly, 28*(1), 75–105. https://doi.org/10.2307/25148625

Höck, H., Toussaint, F., & Thiemann, H. (2020). Fitness for use of data objects described with quality maturity matrix at different phases of data production. *Data Science Journal, 19*(1). https://doi.org/10.5334/DSJ-2020-045/METRICS/

Høj Brasen, L. P., Groos, O. F., & Tambo, T. (2021). Comparison between data maturity and maintenance strategy: A case sutdy. *Procedia CIRP, 104*, 1918–1923. https://doi.org/10.1016/j.procir.2021.11.324

Holopainen, M., Saunila, M., Rantala, T., & Ukko, J. (2022). Digital twins' implications for innovation. *Technology Analysis & Strategic Management*, 1–13. https://doi.org/10.1080/09537325.2022.2115881

Hornick, M. (2020). *A Data Science Maturity Model for Enterprise Assessment.* https://www.oracle.com/a/devo/docs/data-science-maturity-model.pdf

Huang, F. (2019). *Data Processing.* https://doi.org/10.1007/978-3-319-32001-4_314-1

Humphrey, W. S. (1988). Characterizing the Software Process: A Maturity Framework. *IEEE Software, 5*(2), 73–79. https://doi.org/10.1109/52.2014

IBM. (2007). *IBM data governance maturity model.* https://www.lightsondata.com/data-governance-maturity-models-ibm/

IBM. (2023a). *What is a data architecture?* https://www.ibm.com/topics/data-architecture

IBM. (2023b). *What is data storage?* https://www.ibm.com/topics/data-storage

Iqbal, M., Kazmi, S. H. A., Manzoor, A., Soomrani, A. R., Butt, S. H., & Shaikh, K. A. (2018). A study of big data for business growth in SMEs: Opportunities & challenges. *2018 International Conference on Computing, Mathematics and Engineering Technologies (ICoMET)*, 1–7. https://doi.org/10.1109/ICOMET.2018.8346368

Iqbal, R., Yuda, P., Aditya, W., Hidayanto, A. N., Wuri Handayani, P., & Harahap, N. C. (2019). Master data management maturity assessment: Case study of XYZ company. *2nd International Conference on Applied Information Technology and Innovation (ICAITI)*, 133–139. https://doi.org/10.1109/ICAITI48442.2019.8982123

Ishizaka, A., Bhattacharya, A., Gunasekaran, A., Dekkers, R., & Pereira, V. (2019). Outsourcing and offshoring decision making. *International Journal of Production Research, 57*(13), 4187–4193. https://doi.org/10.1080/00207543.2019.1603698

Iyamu, T. (2019). The architectures of data and information: Their confounded confusion. In *South African Journal of Information Management* (Vol. 21, pp. 1–9). scieloza.

Jabbouri, N. I., Siron, R., Zahari, I., & Khalid, M. (2016). mpact of Information Technology Infrastructure on Innovation Performance: An Empirical Study on private Universities In Iraq. *Procedia Economics and Finance 39*, 861– 869. https://doi.org/10.1016/S2212-5671(16)30250-7

Jones, D., Snider, C., Nassehi, A., Yon, J., & Hicks, B. (2020). Characterising the Digital Twin: A systematic literature review. *CIRP Journal of Manufacturing Science and Technology, 29*, 36–52. https://doi.org/10.1016/j.cirpj.2020.02.002

Kaidalova, J., Sandkuhl, K., & Seigerroth, U. (2018). How Digital Transformation affects Enterprise Architecture Management-a case study. *International Journal of Information Systems and Project Management, 6*(3), 5–18. https://doi.org/10.12821/ijispm060301

Karaboga, H. A., Zehir, C., & Karaboga*, T. (2019). Big Data Analytics And Firm Innovativeness: The Moderating Effect Of Data-Driven Culture. In M. Özşahin & T. Hıdırlar (Eds.), *Proceedings of the 14th International Strategic Management Conference & 8th International Conference on Leadership, Technology, Innovation and Business Management (Joint Conference ISMC & ICLTIBM 2018)* (pp. 526–535). Future Academy. https://doi.org/10.15405/EPSBS.2019.01.02.44

Kemppainen, T., Frank, L., Makkonen, M., & Kallio, A. (2022). Barriers to Data-Driven Decision-Making Among Online Retailers. *35 ThBled EConference – Digital Restructuring and Human (Re)Action - Conference Proceedings*. https://doi.org/10.18690/um.fov.4.2022.20

Kerr, K. (2000). *The Development of a Data Quality Framework and Strategy for the New Zealand Ministry of Health. 8*. https://www.researchgate.net/publication/228866986_The_Development_of_a_Data_Quality_Framework_and_Strategy_for_the_New_Zealand_Ministry_of_Health

Kerr, K., Norris, T., & Stockdale, R. (2009). The strategic management of data quality in healthcare. *Health Informatics Journal, 14*, 259–266. https://doi.org/10.1177/1460458208096555

Kilkenny, M. F., & Robinson, K. M. (2018). Data quality: "Garbage in – garbage out." *Health Information Management Journal, 47*(3), 103–105. https://doi.org/10.1177/1833358318774357

Kljajič Borštnar, M., Gašperlin, B., & Pucihar, A. (2022). *DEJAVNIKI PODATKOVNE ZRELOSTI IN PODATKOVNOVODENA ORGANIZACIJA = DATA MATURITY FACTORS AND DATA-DRIVEN ORGANIZATION.* Znanstveno-Raziskovalni Izzivi Na Poti Digitalne Preobrazbe. https://doi.org/10.18690/um.fov.6.2022

Kljajić Borštnar, M., & Pucihar, A. (2021). Multi-Attribute Assessment of Digital Maturity of SMEs. In *Electronics* (Vol. 10, Issue 8). https://doi.org/10.3390/electronics10080885

Kljajić Borštnar, M., & Pucihar, A. (2022). Večkriterijski model za ocenjevanje digitalne zrelosti malih in srednje velikih podjetij. In *Znanstveno-raziskovalni izzivi na poti digitalne preobrazbe.* https://doi.org/10.18690/um.fov.6.2022

Koltay, T. (2016). Data governance, data literacy and the management of data quality. *IFLA Journal, 42*(4), 303–312. https://doi.org/10.1177/0340035216672238

Kraus, S., Durst, S., Ferreira, J. J., Veiga, P., Kailer, N., & Weinmann, A. (2022). Digital transformation in business and management research: An overview of the current status quo. *International Journal of Information Management, 63,* 102466. https://doi.org/10.1016/j.ijinfomgt.2021.102466

Lavalle, S., Lesser, E., Shockley, R., Hopkins, M. S., & Kruschwitz, N. (2011). "Big data, analytics and the path from insights to value." *MIT SLOAN MANAGEMENT REVIEW, 52*(2), 20–32. https://tarjomefa.com/wp-content/uploads/2017/08/7446-English-TarjomeFa.pdf

Lee, J., Suh, T., Roy, D., & Baucus, M. (2019). Emerging Technology and Business Model Innovation: The Case of Artificial Intelligence. *Journal of Open Innovation: Technology, Market, and Complexity, 5*(3). https://doi.org/10.3390/joitmc5030044

Leist, S., & Zellner, G. (2006). Evaluation of Current Architecture Frameworks. *Proceedings of the ACM Symposium on Applied Computing, 2.* https://doi.org/10.1145/1141277.1141635

Lemon, K. N., & Verhoef, P. C. (2016). Understanding Customer Experience Throughout the Customer Journey. *Journal of Marketing, 80*(6), 69–96. https://doi.org/10.1509/jm.15.0420

Li, F., Larimo, J., & Leonidou, L. C. (2021). Social media marketing strategy: definition, conceptualization, taxonomy, validation, and future agenda. *Journal of the Academy of Marketing Science, 49*(1), 51–70. https://doi.org/10.1007/s11747-020-00733-3

Li, J., Greenwood, D., & Kassem, M. (2019). Blockchain in the built environment and construction industry: A systematic review, conceptual models and practical use cases. *Automation in Construction*, *102*, 288–307. https://doi.org/10.1016/j.autcon.2019.02.005

Limpeeticharoenchot, S., Cooharojananone, N., Chavarnakul, T., Charoenruk, N., & Atchariyachanvanich, K. (2022). Adaptive big data maturity model using latent class analysis for small and medium businesses in Thailand. *Expert Systems with Applications*, *206*, 117965. https://doi.org/10.1016/j.eswa.2022.117965

Lismont, J., Vanthienen, J., Baesens, B., & Lemahieu, W. (2017). Defining analytics maturity indicators: A survey approach. *International Journal of Information Management*, *37*(3), 114–124. https://doi.org/10.1016/j.ijinfomgt.2016.12.003

Loukis, E., Spinellis, D., & Katsigiannis, A. (2011). Barriers to the Adoption of B2B e-Marketplaces by Large Enterprises: Lessons Learned From the Hellenic Aerospace Industry. *Information Systems Management*, *28*(2), 130–146. https://doi.org/10.1080/10580530.2011.562129

Mach-Król, M. (2022). Conceptual Framework for Implementing Temporal Big Data Analytics in Companies. In *Applied Sciences* (Vol. 12, Issue 23). https://doi.org/10.3390/app122312265

Marchildon, P., Bourdeau, S., Hadaya, P., & Labissière, A. (2018). *Data governance maturity assessment tool: A design science approach*. https://www.cairn.info/revue-projectique-2018-2-page-155.htm

Marolt, M. (2018). *Social CRM adoption and its influence on customer relationship performance – SMEs perspective = Sprejetje družbenega upravljanja odnosov s strankami in njegov vpliv na učinkovitost odnosov s strankami – vidik malih in srednje velikih podjetij* [Fakulteta za organizacijske vede]. https://dk.um.si/Dokument.php?id=126488

Mazumdar, S., Seybold, D., Kritikos, K., & Verginadis, Y. (2019). A survey on data storage and placement methodologies for Cloud-Big Data ecosystem. *Journal of Big Data*, *6*(1), 15. https://doi.org/10.1186/s40537-019-0178-3

Mell, P., & Grance, T. (2011). *The NIST Definition of Cloud Computing - Recommendations of the National Institute of Standards and Technology*. https://nvlpubs.nist.gov/nistpubs/legacy/sp/nistspecialpublication800-145.pdf

Mikalef, P., Pappas, I. O., Krogstie, J., & Giannakos, M. (2018). Big data analytics capabilities: a systematic literature review and research agenda. *Information Systems and E-Business Management*, *16*(3), 547–578. https://doi.org/10.1007/s10257-017-0362-y

Milavec Kapun, M., Drnovšek, R., Rajkovič, V., & Rajkovič, U. (2022). A multi-criteria decision model for assessing health and self-care ability. *Central European Journal of Operations Research*. https://doi.org/10.1007/s10100-022-00823-3

Mitra, A., Gaur, S. S., & Giacosa, E. (2019). Combining organizational change management and organizational ambidexterity using data transformation. *Management Decision*, *57*(8), 2069–2091. https://doi.org/10.1108/MD-07-2018-0841

Mohamed, M., & Weber, P. (2020). Trends of digitalization and adoption of big data analytics among UK SMEs: Analysis and lessons drawn from a case study of 53 SMEs. *International Conference on Engineering, Technology and Innovation (ICE/ITMC 2020)*, 1–6. https://doi.org/10.1109/ICE/ITMC49519.2020.9198545

Molina-Castillo, F.-J., Rodríguez, R., López-Nicolas, C., & Bouwman, H. (2022). The role of ERP in business model innovation: Impetus or impediment. *Digital Business*, *2*(2), 100024. https://doi.org/10.1016/j.digbus.2022.100024

Monino, J.-L. (2021). Data Value, Big Data Analytics, and Decision-Making. *Journal of the Knowledge Economy*, *12*(1), 256–267. https://doi.org/10.1007/s13132-016-0396-2

Moonen, N., Baijens, J., Ebrahim, M., & Helms, R. (2019). *Small Business, Big Data: An Assessment Tool for (Big) Data Analytics Capabilities in SMEs*. https://remhelms.files.wordpress.com/2019/05/small-business-big-data-an-assessment-framework-for-big-data-analytics-capabilities-in-smes.pdf

Morakanyane, R., Grace, A., & O'Reilly, P. (2017). Conceptualizing Digital Transformation in Business Organizations: A Systematic Review of Literature. In A. Pucihar, M. Kljajić Borštnar, C. Kittl, P. Ravesteijn, R. Clarke, & R. Bons (Eds.), *30TH BLED ECONFERENCE: DIGITAL TRANSFORMATION – FROM CONNECTING THINGS TO TRANSFORMING OUR LIVES* (pp. 427–444). https://doi.org/10.18690/978-961-286-043-1.30

Muller, P., Ladher, R., Booth, J., Mohamed, S., Gorgels, S., Priem, M., Blagoeva, T., Martinelle, A., & Milanesi, G. (2022). *Annual Report on European SMEs 2021/2022: SMEs and environmental sustainability*. https://www.ggb.gr/sites/default/files/basic-page-files/SME AR 2021_22_Final Report %282%29.pdf

Nda, R. M., Tasmin, R., & Hamid, A. A. (2020). Assessment of Big Data Analytics Maturity Models: An Overview. *Proceedings of the 5th NA International Conference on Industrial Engineering and Operations Management*, 1681–1690. http://www.ieomsociety.org/detroit2020/papers/399.pdf

Nijzink, H. J. (2020). *Data-driven Decision-making Maturity*. http://essay.utwente.nl/85376/

Njeh, F. N. (2014). *Cloud Computing: An Evaluation of the Cloud Computing Adoption and Use Model* [Graduate School Bowie State University]. https://search-proquest-com.ezproxy.lib.ukm.si/pqdtglobal/docview/1667768864/87F7FAD2D64E473DPQ/6?accountid=28931

Nofer, M., Gomber, P., Hinz, O., & Schiereck, D. (2017). Blockchain. *Business & Information Systems Engineering, 59*(3), 183–187. https://doi.org/10.1007/s12599-017-0467-3

O'Donovan, P., Bruton, K., & O'Sullivan, D. T. J. (2016). IAMM: A Maturity Model for Measuring Industrial Analytics Capabilities in Large-scale Manufacturing Facilities. *International Journal of Prognostics and Health Management,* 1–11. https://cora.ucc.ie/bitstream/handle/10468/5396/4005.pdf?sequence=3&isAllowed=y

OECD. (2022). Artificial intelligence, digital technology and advanced production. *The Digitalisation of Science, Technology and Innovation.* https://doi.org/10.1787/B9E4A2C0-EN

Okuyucu, A., & Yavuz, N. (2020). Big data maturity models for the public sector: a review of state and organizational level models. *Transforming Government: People, Process and Policy, 14*(4), 681–699. https://doi.org/10.1108/TG-09-2019-0085

Olszak, C. M., & Mach-Król, M. (2018). A Conceptual Framework for Assessing an Organization's Readiness to Adopt Big Data. *Sustainability, 10*(10), 3734. https://doi.org/10.3390/SU10103734

Omar, R., Takim, R., & Nawawi, A. H. (2012). Measuring of Technological Capabilities in Technology Transfer (TT) Projects. *Asian Social Science, 8*(15), 211–221. https://doi.org/10.5539/ASS.V8N15P211

Otto, B., & Jarke, M. (2019). Designing a multi-sided data platform: findings from the International Data Spaces case. *Electronic Markets, 29*(4), 561–580. https://doi.org/10.1007/s12525-019-00362-x

Palmiero, M., Nori, R., Piccardi, L., & D'Amico, S. (2020). Divergent Thinking: The Role of Decision-Making Styles. *Creativity Research Journal, 32*(4), 323–332. https://doi.org/10.1080/10400419.2020.1817700

Parashar, M., AbdelBaky, M., Rodero, I., & Devarakonda, A. (2013). Cloud Paradigms and Practices for Computational and Data-Enabled Science and Engineering. *Computing in Science & Engineering, 15*(4), 10–18. https://ieeexplore-ieee-org.ezproxy.lib.ukm.si/stamp/stamp.jsp?tp=&arnumber=6530588

Parra, X., Tort-Martorell, X., Ruiz-Viñals, C., & Álvarez-Gómez, F. (2019). A Maturity Model for the Information-Driven SME. *Journal of Industrial Engineering and Management (JIEM), 12*(1), 154–175. https://doi.org/10.3926/jiem.2780

Pascucci, F., Savelli, E., & Gistri, G. (2023). How digital technologies reshape marketing: evidence from a qualitative investigation. *Italian Journal of Marketing, 2023*(1), 27–58. https://doi.org/10.1007/s43039-023-00063-6

Paunović, K. (2008). *Data Processing and Storage Data processing and storage BT - Encyclopedia of Public Health* (W. Kirch (ed.); pp. 210–213). Springer Netherlands. https://doi.org/10.1007/978-1-4020-5614-7_691

Peña, A., Bonet, I., Lochmuller, C., Tabares, M. S., Piedrahita, C. C., Sánchez, C. C., Giraldo Marín, L. M., Góngora, M., & Chiclana, F. (2018). A fuzzy ELECTRE structure methodology to assess big data maturity in healthcare SMEs. *Soft Computing, 23*(20), 10537–10550. https://doi.org/10.1007/S00500-018-3625-8

Perales-Manrique, J., Molina-Chirinos, J., & Shiguihara-Juarez, P. (2019). A Data Analytics Maturity Model for Financial Sector Companies. *2019 IEEE Sciences and Humanities International Research Conference (SHIRCON)*, 1–4. https://doi.org/10.1109/SHIRCON48091.2019.9024885

Proença, D., & Borbinha, J. (2016). Maturity Models for Information Systems - A State of the Art. *Procedia Computer Science, 100*, 1042–1049. https://doi.org/10.1016/j.procs.2016.09.279

Quach, S., Thaichon, P., Martin, K. D., Weaven, S., & Palmatier, R. W. (2022). Digital technologies: tensions in privacy and data. *Journal of the Academy of Marketing Science*. https://doi.org/10.1007/s11747-022-00845-y

Rachinger, M., Rauter, R., Müller, C., Vorraber, W., & Schirgi, E. (2019). Digitalization and its influence on business model innovation. *Journal of Manufacturing Technology Management, 30*(8), 1143–1160. https://doi.org/10.1108/JMTM-01-2018-0020

Ragaisis, S., Birstunas, A., Mitasiunas, A., & Stockus, A. (2012). Electronic Archive Information System. In A. Čaplinskas, G. Dzemyda, A. Lupeikienė, & O. Vasilecas (Eds.), *Tenth International Baltic Conference on Databases and Information Systems* (pp. 107–114). https://citeseerx.ist.psu.edu/document?repid=rep1&type=pdf&doi=d88aa8766d30b55ab43e65775b4696a27ced29e2#page=123

Rahaman, D. M., & Arif, M. Z. U. (2018). *Framework of Information Technology Infrastructure in Practices of Management Information Systems at Customer-Centric Service Organization: Case-Based Approach. 7*, 21–39. https://doi.org/10.15410/aijm/2018/v7i2/121503

Rath, D. K., & Kumar, A. (2021). Information privacy concern at individual, group, organization and societal level - a literature review. *Vilakshan - XIMB Journal of Management, 18*(2), 171–186. https://doi.org/10.1108/XJM-08-2020-0096

Rietsche, R., Dremel, C., Bosch, S., Steinacker, L., Meckel, M., & Leimeister, J.-M. (2022). Quantum computing. *Electronic Markets, 32*(4), 2525–2536. https://doi.org/10.1007/s12525-022-00570-y

Rogers, K. (2020). Creating a Culture of Data-Driven Decision-Making [ProQuest LLC]. In *ProQuest Dissertations and Theses*. https://search-proquest-com.ezproxy.lib.ukm.si/pqdtglobal/docview/2461428896/fulltextPDF/337FD22C0C5B433BPQ/1?accountid=28931#

Ruivo, P., Mestre, A., Johansson, B., & Oliveira, T. (2014). Defining the ERP and CRM Integrative Value. *Procedia Technology, 16*, 704–709. https://doi.org/10.1016/j.protcy.2014.10.019

Ruivo, P., Oliveira, T., & Mestre, A. (2017). Enterprise resource planning and customer relationship management value. *Industrial Management & Data Systems, 117*(8), 1612–1631. https://doi.org/10.1108/IMDS-08-2016-0340

Sadiq, R. B., Safie, N., Abd Rahman, A. H., & Goudarzi, S. (2021). Artificial intelligence maturity model: a systematic literature review. *PeerJ Computer Science, 7*, e661. https://doi.org/10.7717/peerj-cs.661

Sais, M., Rafalia, N., & Abouchabaka, J. (2022). Intelligent Approaches to Optimizing Big Data Storage and Management: REHDFS system and DNA Storage. *Procedia Computer Science, 201*, 746–751. https://doi.org/10.1016/j.procs.2022.03.101

Saputra, D. A., Handika, D., & Ruldeviyani, Y. (2018). Data Governance Maturity Model (DGM2) Assessment in Organization Transformation of Digital Telecommunication Company: Case Study of PT Telekomunikasi Indonesia. *2018 International Conference on Advanced Computer Science and Information Systems (ICACSIS)*, 325–330. https://doi.org/10.1109/ICACSIS.2018.8618255

Sarker, I. H. (2021). Data Science and Analytics: An Overview from Data-Driven Smart Computing, Decision-Making and Applications Perspective. *SN Computer Science, 2*(5), 377. https://doi.org/10.1007/s42979-021-00765-8

Saura, J. R., Palacios-Marqués, D., & Ribeiro-Soriano, D. (2023). Digital marketing in SMEs via data-driven strategies: Reviewing the current state of research. *Journal of Small Business Management, 61*(3), 1278–1313. https://doi.org/10.1080/00472778.2021.1955127

Schmidt, D. H., van Dierendonck, D., & Weber, U. (2023). The data-driven leader: developing a big data analytics leadership competency framework. *Journal of Management Development, 42*(4), 297–326. https://doi.org/10.1108/JMD-12-2022-0306

Shah, S. I. H., Peristeras, V., & Magnisalis, I. (2021). DaLiF: a data lifecycle framework for data-driven governments. *Journal of Big Data, 8*(89), 1–44. https://doi.org/10.1186/S40537-021-00481-3

Shankar, V., Grewal, D., Sunder, S., Fossen, B., Peters, K., & Agarwal, A. (2022). Digital marketing communication in global marketplaces: A review of extant research, future directions, and potential approaches. *International*

*Journal of Research in Marketing, 39*(2), 541–565. https://doi.org/10.1016/j.ijresmar.2021.09.005

Sherman, R. (2015). Data Architecture. In *Business Intelligence Guidebook* (pp. 107–142). Morgan Kaufmann. https://doi.org/10.1016/b978-0-12-411461-6.00006-x

Soori, M., Arezoo, B., & Dastres, R. (2023). Artificial intelligence, machine learning and deep learning in advanced robotics, a review. *Cognitive Robotics, 3*, 54–70. https://doi.org/10.1016/j.cogr.2023.04.001

Spiekermann, M. (2019). Data Marketplaces: Trends and Monetisation of Data Goods. *Intereconomics, 54*(4), 208–216. https://doi.org/10.1007/s10272-019-0826-z

Spruit, M., & Pietzka, K. (2015a). MD3M: The master data management maturity model. *Computers in Human Behavior, 51*, 1068–1076. https://doi.org/10.1016/j.chb.2014.09.030

Spruit, M., & Pietzka, K. (2015b). MD3M: The master data management maturity model. *Computers in Human Behavior, 51*, 1068–1076. https://doi.org/10.1016/J.CHB.2014.09.030

Srilakshmi, M., Veenadhari, C. L., & Pradeep, I. K. (2013). Deployment models of Cloud Computing: Challenges. *International Journal of Advanced Research in Computer Science, 4*(9), 137. https://www.researchgate.net/publication/328628558_Deployment_models_of_Cloud_Computing_Challenges

Sriramoju, S. (2019). A Comprehensive Review on Data Storage. *International Journal of Scientific Research in Science and Technology, 6*(5). https://doi.org/10.32628/IJSRST

Stahl, F., Schomm, F., Vossen, G., & Vomfell, L. (2016). A classification framework for data marketplaces. *Vietnam Journal of Computer Science, 3*(3), 137–143. https://doi.org/10.1007/s40595-016-0064-2

Stanford. (2013). *Data Governance Maturity Model. Thesis.* https://hnu.edu/wp-content/uploads/2020/03/Data-Governance-Maturity-Model.pdf

Stankovska, I., Josimovski, S., & Edwards, C. (2016). Digital channels diminish SME barriers: the case of the UK. *Economic Research-Ekonomska Istraživanja, 29*(1), 217–232. https://doi.org/10.1080/1331677X.2016.1164926

Stoiber, C., Stöter, M., Englbrecht, L., Schönig, S., & Häckel, B. (2023). Keeping Your Maturity Assessment Alive. *Business & Information Systems Engineering.* https://doi.org/10.1007/s12599-023-00805-y

Straker, K., Wrigley, C., & Rosemann, M. (2015). The role of design in the future of digital channels: Conceptual insights and future research directions. *Journal of Retailing and Consumer Services, 26*, 133–140. https://doi.org/10.1016/j.jretconser.2015.06.004

Sundblad, W. (2018). *Data Is The Foundation For Artificial Intelligence And Machine Learning*. Forbes. https://www.forbes.com/sites/willemsundbladeurope/2018/10/18/data-is-the-foundation-for-artificial-intelligence-and-machine-learning/?sh=5b50e9fe51b4

Sunyaev, A. (2020). *Cloud Computing BT - Internet Computing: Principles of Distributed Systems and Emerging Internet-Based Technologies* (A. Sunyaev (ed.); pp. 195–236). Springer International Publishing. https://doi.org/10.1007/978-3-030-34957-8_7

Sutanto, & Nuryani, E. (2020). *Management of the Electronic Archives for Optimizing Services at Banten Jaya University BT - Proceedings of the 1st International Multidisciplinary Conference on Education, Technology, and Engineering (IMCETE 2019)*. 82–86. https://doi.org/10.2991/assehr.k.200303.021

Tabesh, P., Mousavidin, E., & Hasani, S. (2019). Implementing big data strategies: A managerial perspective. *Business Horizons*, *62*(3), 347–358. https://doi.org/10.1016/j.bushor.2019.02.001

Thomke, S. (2001). Enlightened Experimentation: The New Imperative for Innovation. *Harvard Business Review*. https://hbr.org/2001/02/enlightened-experimentation-the-new-imperative-for-innovation

TOGAF. (2018). *TOGAF® Standard, Version 9.2 - Core Concepts*. https://pubs.opengroup.org/architecture/togaf9-doc/arch/chap02.html

van den Hoven, J. (2003). Data Architecture: Blueprints for Data. *Information Systems Management*, *20*(1), 90–92. https://doi.org/10.1201/1078/43203.20.1.20031201/40089.12

Verhoef, P. C., Broekhuizen, T., Bart, Y., Bhattacharya, A., Dong, J. Q., Fabian, N., & Haenlein, M. (2019). Digital transformation: A multidisciplinary reflection and research agenda. *Journal of Business Research*, *122*, 889–901. https://doi.org/10.1016/j.jbusres.2019.09.022

Vial, G. (2019). Understanding digital transformation: A review and a research agenda. *The Journal of Strategic Information Systems*, *28*(2), 118–144. https://doi.org/10.1016/j.jsis.2019.01.003

Vidgen, R., Shaw, S., & Grant, D. B. (2017). Management challenges in creating value from business analytics. *European Journal of Operational Research*, *261*(2), 626–639. https://doi.org/10.1016/j.ejor.2017.02.023

Vijesh Joe, C., Raj, J. S., & Smys, S. (2020). Big Data Analytics: Tools, Challenges, and Scope in Data-Driven Computing. In J. S. Raj (Ed.), *International Conference on Mobile Computing and Sustainable Informatics* (pp. 709–719). Springer International Publishing. https://doi.org/10.1007/978-3-030-49795-8_67

Wang, S., & Archer, N. P. (2007). Electronic marketplace definition and classification: literature review and clarifications. *Enterprise Information Systems*, *1*(1), 89–112. https://doi.org/10.1080/17517570601088380

Weber, C., Königsberger, J., Kassner, L., & Mitschang, B. (2017). M2DDM – A Maturity Model for Data Driven Manufacturing. *Procedia CIRP*, *63*, 173–178. https://doi.org/10.1016/j.procir.2017.03.309

Widajanti, E., & Ratnawati, T. (2020). INFORMATION TECHNOLOGY INFRASTRUCTURE OPTIMIZATION FOR ACHIEVING INNOVATION-BASED COMPANY PERFORMANCE. *International Journal of Business, Economics and Law*, *22*(1), 180–187. https://www.ijbel.com/wp-content/uploads/2020/11/IJBEL22_247.pdf

Wilkinson, M. D., Dumontier, M., Sansone, S.-A., Bonino da Silva Santos, L. O., Prieto, M., Batista, D., McQuilton, P., Kuhn, T., Rocca-Serra, P., Crosas, M., & Schultes, E. (2019). Evaluating FAIR maturity through a scalable, automated, community-governed framework. *Scientific Data*, *6*(174), 1–12. https://doi.org/10.1038/s41597-019-0184-5

Wilkinson, M. D., Sansone, S.-A., Schultes, E., Doorn, P., Bonino da Silva Santos, L. O., & Dumontier, M. (2018). A design framework and exemplar metrics for FAIRness. *Scientific Data*, *5*(1), 180118. https://doi.org/10.1038/sdata.2018.118

Windt, B., Borgman, H., & Amrit, C. (2019). Understanding Leadership Challenges and Responses in Data-driven Transformations. *Proceedings of the 52nd Hawaii International Conference on System Sciences*, 4987–4996. https://aisel.aisnet.org/cgi/viewcontent.cgi?article=1615&context=hicss-52

Wolf, L., & Steul-Fischer, M. (2022). Factors of customers' channel choice in an omnichannel environment: a systematic literature review. *Management Review Quarterly*. https://doi.org/10.1007/s11301-022-00281-w

Xu, M., Chen, X., & Kou, G. (2019). A systematic review of blockchain. *Financial Innovation*, *5*(1), 27. https://doi.org/10.1186/s40854-019-0147-z

Yablonsky, S. (2021). AI-driven platform enterprise maturity: from human led to machine governed. *Kybernetes*, *50*(10), 2753–2789. https://doi.org/10.1108/K-06-2020-0384

Yousufi, M. K. (2023). Exploring paperless working: A step towards low carbon footprint. *European Journal of Sustainable Development Research*, *7*(4), 1–8. https://doi.org/10.29333/ejosdr/13410

Zheng, Z., Xie, S., Dai, H.-N., Chen, X., & Wang, H. (2017). *An Overview of Blockchain Technology: Architecture, Consensus, and Future Trends*. https://doi.org/10.1109/BigDataCongress.2017.85

Rok Bojanc*, Andreja Pucihar** and Gregor Lenart***

# E-invoicing as a driver for digital transformation of Slovene economy

**Abstract:** This chapter examines the evolution of e-invoicing in Slovenia, a small country in the European Union (EU), over the past two decades. It provides a comprehensive overview of the relevant regulations, legislation, and policies that have shaped the development of e-invoicing in Slovenia, both domestically and at the EU level. The chapter draws on empirical findings from a survey of 284 organizations in Slovenia, which revealed that while mandatory e-invoicing for the public sector has been implemented, uptake among other business sectors remains limited. To further accelerate digital transformation, the chapter proposes the introduction of legislation mandating the standardized exchange of e-invoices among all business entities, similar to practices in other European countries. The chapter argues that the widespread adoption of e-invoices can serve as a catalyst for broader digital transformation initiatives within organizations. This comprehensive digitization of business processes is expected to enhance productivity, competitiveness, and sustainability at both organizational and national levels. The chapter concludes by providing insights into the current state of e-invoicing in Slovenia, outlining the opportunities and challenges for further digital transformation of Slovene organizations. It also discusses the benefits, barriers, and incentives associated with e-invoicing and other electronic business documents, emphasizing the importance of appropriate measures and incentives from policymakers and public administrations to support digital transformation initiatives, particularly for micro and small businesses.

**Keywords:** E-invocing, adoption, digital business transformation, Slovenia

## 1. Introduction

The current market conditions, characterised by globalisation, increasing competition, the rapid growth of start-ups and the accelerating development of emerging technologies, are pushing companies towards digital transformation (Nadkarni & Prügl, 2020; Pucihar, Mohar Bastar, & Lenart, 2022; Zammuto, Griffith, Majchrzak, Dougherty, & Faraj, 2007). Digital transformation is defined as the

* ZZI d.o.o.,Ljubljana Slovenia; e-mail: rok.bojanc@zzi.si

** University of Maribor Faculty of Organizational Sciences, Kranj, Slovenia; e-mail: andreja.pucihar@um.si

*** University of Maribor Faculty of Organizational Sciences, Kranj, Slovenia; e-mail: gregor.lenart@um.si

strategic use of digital technologies and accompanying organisational capabilities to enable effective use (Kljajić Borštnar & Pucihar, 2021; Pucihar, Marolt, Lenart, & Vidmar, 2021; Vial, 2019).

Many enterprises are starting their digital transformation journey by digitising their business documents and related processes (Verhoef et al., 2021). Electronic business documents are documents related to the processes of ordering, procurement, shipping, invoicing and payment. Digitisation of business documents is not new. It dates back to the 1980s, when companies sent electronic business documents to each other via electronic data interchange (EDI), replacing paper-based business documents. In Slovenia, EDI was introduced at that time mainly by companies involved in international supply chains, such as suppliers in the automotive industry, due to the requirements of their main customers - the German automotive manufacturers. Due to the large number of companies and documents involved, EDI quickly spread to large retail chains in Slovenia, which adopted a standardised exchange of electronic business documents at an early stage (Marolt, Lenart, Vidmar, & Pucihar, 2021). The use of EDI brings several benefits, ranging from faster delivery and processing, reduced human errors and lower operational costs (Horák, Bokšová, & Strouhal, 2020; Marolt et al., 2021).

Among the most widely used electronic business documents are electronic invoices (hereafter e-invoices). The issuance and receipt of e-invoices between companies, public administrations and individuals is becoming increasingly important due to the recognised positive effects of the digitisation of business and the growing need for efficiency in a highly competitive business environment. In this context, an e-invoice is an invoice that has been issued, transmitted and received in a structured electronic format (e.g. XML) which allows for its automatic and electronic processing. The benefits of electronic invoicing are maximised when the generation, sending, transmission, reception and processing of an invoice can be fully automated, which can only be achieved by using structured machine-readable invoices that can be processed automatically and digitally by the recipient (European Parliament, 2014).

The European Commission outlined the benefits of electronic invoicing in its report "Reaping the benefits of electronic invoicing for Europe" (European Commission, 2010). The report estimates potential savings from electronic invoicing at around EUR 240 billion over six years. In addition, electronic invoicing brings significant environmental benefits. The EU can reduce $CO_2$ emissions by 1 million tonnes per year by reducing paper and energy consumption in transport. These estimates are based on the assumption that 30 billion invoices are exchanged annually in the EU. The European Commission's Directorate General for Informatics (DG DIGIT) points out that the introduction of e-invoicing in the public sector could make a significant contribution to economic prosperity, as the introduction of e-invoicing supports public policy priorities (Connecting Europe Facility Stakeholder Management Office, 2019).

These include reducing the public sector deficit, increasing financial transparency and supporting sustainable development. It also makes an important contribution to reducing costs and improving efficiency in the public sector. E-invoicing also benefits private service providers, which can act as a catalyst for the wider adoption of digital processes in the public and private sectors (European Commission, n.d.). The European Commission has made the use of e-invoicing mandatory for the public sector in EU Member States through Directive 2014/55/EU on electronic invoicing in public procurement (European Commission, 2014).

To accelerate the transition to electronic commerce, Slovenia started in 2001 the eSLOG project. This project started the development of a national eSLOG standard for electronic business documents. In 2003, the eSLOG 1.3 standard for e-invoicing was developed, which has been upgraded over the years in line with the legislation and the guidelines of other standards (Zupančič et al., 2016). In 2005, the initiative for the establishment of the project "Issuing and receiving e-invoices in the e-region: an initiative for the establishment of a project in Slovenia" was established based on the initiative of the E-Centre (at the Faculty of Organisational Sciences of the University of Maribor) (Bjelica et al., 2005). Slovenia has joined the mandatory use of e-invoices among enterprises and the public sector as of January 1, 2015, using the national standard eSLOG 1.6 (RS, 2016). Today, the latest version of eSLOG is 2.0. The government is also preparing a law to make e-invoicing mandatory for all enterprises (RS, 2021).

Despite the recognised positive effects of using digital technologies and digitalization, many organisations are not yet achieving the desired results. This is also indicated by the Digital Index, which is measured by the EU Member States within their National Statistical Offices. In Slovenia, the majority of enterprises with 10 or more employees and self-employed people had a low digital index in 2022 (35%) (Statistični urad Republike Slovenije, 2022). E-invoices in a standardised structured format are exchanged by about 60% of enterprises with 10 or more employees in 2022, or 57% of small, 74% of medium-sized and 86% of large enterprises.

Many stakeholders expected that after the introduction of mandatory e-invoicing for the public sector, the use of e-invoicing would easily extend to business-to-business transactions. Especially considering that those companies that issue e-invoices to the public sector already have the necessary software for preparing and issuing e-invoices, as well as the knowledge to implement e-invoicing. The software and procedures for issuing e-invoices are identical, regardless of whether the recipient of the e-invoice is in the public sector or the economy.

Unfortunately, the predictions of stakeholders did not come true, because after the legal introduction of e-invoicing to the public sector, the e-invoicing among enterprises did not significantly increase. Although e-invoicing is increasing among enterprises, this is far from the initial expectations.

To better understand the reasons for the current state of e-invoicing in Slovenia and why e-invoicing has not become more established among enterprises, we conducted a survey among enterprises in cooperation with key Slovenian stakeholders. The research was carried out in cooperation with the Slovenian National eBusiness Centre at the Chamber of Commerce and Industry of Slovenia, the Horizontal ICT Network, the Digital Innovation Hub of Slovenia and the Faculty of Organizational Sciences of the University of Maribor. 284 organisations participated in the survey.

In this paper, we provide an in-depth review of the literature in the field of e-invoicing and an overview of the current development of e-invoicing in the EU and Slovenia. The research methodology and research findings are presented, detailing the use of e-invoicing, perceived benefits, barriers and incentives for wider use. The results provide valuable insight for decision-makers and policymakers, as they address open questions about increasing the widespread use of e-invoicing among enterprises.

## 2. Literature review

### 2.1 Digitisation, digitalisation and digital transformation

There are several stages in the digital transformation journey: digitisation, digitalisation and digital transformation (Verhoef et al., 2021). Digitisation refers to the transformation of analogue data and information into digital form (Loebbecke & Picot, 2015; Venkatraman, 2017). Some authors also define digitisation as the transformation of analogue into digital tasks (F. Li, Nucciarelli, Roden, & Graham, 2016; Sebastian et al., 2017) or as the integration of information technologies (IT) into existing tasks, which helps to use resources more cost-effectively through the use of IT (Lai, Wong, & Cheng, 2010; Vendrell-Herrero, Bustinza, Parry, & Georgantzis, 2017). Simplified, digitisation refers to the process of digitising internal and external documents, but it does not contribute to the creation of new value for customers (Verhoef et al., 2021).

Digitalisation is the next step in the digital transformation of organisations. It defines the use of IT or digital technologies to transform existing ways of doing business (F. Li et al., 2016). These activities can include, for example, the creation of new online and mobile channels for communicating with customers. In such cases, digital technologies are key enablers for achieving new business opportunities by transforming and digitalizing existing business processes such as communication, sales, distribution or other forms of business and collaboration (Verhoef et al., 2021). In addition to optimising and coordinating processes more efficiently (reducing operating costs), digitalization enables the creation of new value for customers and, as a consequence, improves customer experience (Pagani & Pardo, 2017). The impact of digitisation and digitalisation is reflected in the reduction of material and operational costs (W. Li, Liu, Belitski, Ghobadian, & O'Regan, 2016).

The highest level of digital technology adoption is leading to the digital transformation of organisations. Digital transformation refers to the use of (a combination of) digital technologies that redefine organisational capabilities. In the context of digital transformation, digital technologies are used to: simplify and change established ways of doing business, increase efficiency and change the way business processes are implemented, change the way employees work and collaborate, create new ways of engaging with customers, suppliers and partners in value chains, create new (or digitalized) products and services, and change or create new (digitalized) business models (Jeansson & Bredmar, 2019; Pucihar, 2020; Pucihar et al., 2021, 2022; Van Veldhoven & Vanthienen, 2021; Vial, 2019; Warner & Wäger, 2019).

The exchange of standardised structured electronic business documents is placed in the first two tiers on the path towards digital transformation. The first stage is the digitisation of documents. The use of structured (standardised) formats of digitalized documents also enables the automation of processes from the generation to the exchange and further processing of documents and their archiving. This involves the use of information technologies from external providers as well as the organisations' business information systems. The holistic view of this process leads from digitization to the digitalisation stage.

## 2.2 Definition of e-invoices and the impact of their use

European Directive 2014/55/EU defines an e-invoice as an invoice that has been issued, transmitted and received in a structured electronic format which allows for its automatic and electronic processing (European Parliament, 2014). In practice, this means faster processes, less manual work, fewer human errors and lower costs. Additional benefits and positive impacts are accessibility, as e-invoices can be accessed virtually anywhere and at any time, the possibility of real-time reporting, the positive impact on the company's reputation, the tracking and recording of events, greater geographical independence and better decision support.

Another widespread form of digitised invoices is invoices in visualised electronic formats such as PDF, JPG and HTML (European Commission, 2014). These formats are not considered e-invoices because they are not in a structured format and do not allow for the automation of processes and procedures. These formats only represent savings for enterprises in terms of printing, postage, intra-organisational routing and archiving. Nevertheless, PDF invoices are widespread among enterprises because they are easy to use (Koch, 2016, 2019).

The potential savings from e-invoicing are discussed in various reports, which cite savings of up to 64% from using e-invoices (Koch, 2016). However, these estimates mostly only take into account the financial benefits of e-invoicing, and are multiplied when non-financial benefits are taken into account. The Billentis report publishes an indication of the potential savings from the use of e-invoicing in the public sector of some European countries (Koch, 2016). For countries such as Austria and Switzerland, the potential savings are estimated at around EUR 600–700 million per year and even EUR 6,500 million per year for Germany. The calculations are made for the public sector only, where 60% of e-invoices and 40% of PDF invoices would be exchanged.

However, when Italy introduced mandatory e-invoicing for all businesses in early 2019, it became clear that the savings in this area could be significantly higher (Haack, 2021; Viry Christophe, 2019). According to the Italian Ministry of Finance, 2.1 billion e-invoices were issued by 3.6 million legal entities in 2019, of which 54% were business-to-business, 44% business-to-consumer and 2% business-to-government. Before the roll-out, it was estimated that the roll-out would generate an additional EUR 1.4 billion per year in the area of tax payments alone. Following the introduction of mandatory e-invoicing, the difference in tax payments in 2019 is set to increase by EUR 3.5 billion. This amount represents only a benefit for the government, but the savings for individual enterprises should also be considered.

## 2.3 E-invoicing in Europe

Over the past decade, the European Commission has set itself the goal of making e-invoicing the dominant invoicing method. However, Member States have to overcome many difficulties arising from the lack of interoperability of existing e-invoicing systems (European Commission, 2010). European Directive 2014/55/EU on electronic invoicing in public procurement was adopted to remove market and trade barriers arising from different national rules and technical standards (European Commission, 2014). The main objective of the Directive is to reduce paper-based transactions and to simplify, streamline and automate e-commerce. To ensure these objectives, CEN has developed a single European standard for e-invoicing, EN 16931 (CEN, 2017). This standard ensures interoperability between different Member States and supports cross-border procurement and e-commerce.

The Directive places a strong emphasis on interoperability, which aims to enable data and information to be referenced and processed consistently across all business information systems, regardless of their technology, application or platform. It is about the ability to seamlessly execute business processes across organisational boundaries, which is achieved by understanding how business processes across different enterprises can be interconnected. To make this possible, it is necessary to standardise the data and information exchanged in terms of the content of the invoice (semantics), the format or language used (syntax), and the method of transmission. This means that the e-invoice contains a certain amount of the necessary data and information and that the precise meaning of the exchanged information is preserved and unambiguously understood, independently of how it is physically represented or transmitted (European Commission. Directorate-General for Internal Market, 2020). At the same time, the data elements of an e-invoice are presented in a format which can be exchanged directly between the sender and recipient and processed automatically. This can be ensured in one of two ways, either by using a common syntax or using mapping between different syntaxes (European Commission, 2014).

Directive 2014/55/EU makes e-invoicing commonplace in EU countries (European Commission, 2023). Most countries have made the receipt of e-invoices mandatory for public administration organisations, and some also make the issuance of e-invoices mandatory. However, the use of e-invoicing among enterprises in Europe is growing at a much slower pace. This is likely to change in the coming years as more and more European countries (Poland, France, Germany, Spain, Belgium) announce the introduction of mandatory e-invoicing for all businesses in the near future (VAT Update, 2023).

In December 2022, the European Commission also published a proposal for legislative changes to the "VAT in the digital age - ViDA" initiative, which addresses three separate areas: digital VAT reporting and e-invoicing obligations, the VAT treatment of digital platform models and the introduction of a single VAT registration in all Member States (Proposal for a COUNCIL DIRECTIVE amending Directive 2006/112/EC as regards VAT rules for the digital age, 2022). In the area of e-invoicing, the ViDA proposal e-invoicing is becoming the default invoicing method in the EU and includes mandatory e-reporting and e-invoicing for intra-EU transactions.

## 2.4 E-invoicing in Slovenia

According to the European Commission, Slovenia is one of the most advanced countries in Europe in the field of e-invoicing. According to the DESI 2022 (The Digital Economy and Society Index), which summarises important indicators of the development of digitalisation in EU Member States and their digital competitiveness, Slovenia is ranked fourth among Member States in the e-invoicing category (European Commission, 2021). The DESI e-Invoicing Index for Slovenia, which stood at just 2.33% in 2015, has jumped to 58.4% in 2022.

The beginnings of the standardisation of electronic business documents in Slovenia date back to 2001, when the Chamber of Commerce and Industry of Slovenia, on the initiative of companies, launched the eSLOG project, which aimed to develop and implement standard electronic business documents for enterprises (Slovenian National eBusiness Centre., 2023). The project, which involved experts from more than 90 companies, resulted in the development of electronic business documents for purchase orders, despatch advice and invoices. Over the following years, the eSLOG standards for business documents have been continuously upgraded and updated and are now used by both the government and private sector.

Among eSLOG documents, e-invoices have become the most widely used. They were first used by mass invoicing companies such as communication operators, energy companies and retailers. The Slovenian Public Payments Administration (PPA) introduced the exchange of e-invoices between public sector organisations in 2010, and since 2012 has been facilitating the exchange of e-invoices between the public sector, business entities (companies) and individuals through interbank system integration or through e-invoicing service providers (Bojanc et al., 2018).

Since 2015, the e-invoicing in eSLOG format has been mandatory for the entire public sector in Slovenia. The exchange of e-invoices with public sector users is exclusively through the single entry-exit point of the PPA. Issuers can choose to send e-invoices through an e-invoicing service provider contracted with the PPA or through the banking system, while smaller issuers can manually enter invoices on the PPA's web portal (Uprava Republike Slovenije za javna plačila, 2023).

Between 2017 and 2020, the Slovenian Chamber of Commerce and Industry and the Public Payments Administration, together with their partners, implemented the ambitious ROSE ("Readiness Of Slovenian E-invoicing") and ROSE 2 projects. The projects resulted in the support of the EU Directive 2014/55 in Slovenia, the introduction of a European standard for e-invoicing, the introduction of the national registry of e-invoice recipients, the inclusion of Slovenia in the European Peppol network for the exchange of business electronic documents, the upgrade of the technological environment for the exchange of e-invoices, the raising of awareness and user competencies for the use of e-invoicing and the upgrade of the eSLOG documents purchase order, despatch advice and invoice to version 2.0 (Bojanc et al., 2020).

The widespread use of e-invoicing has been greatly facilitated by the mass adoption of eSLOG documents by business software providers in their software solutions (ERP solutions, accounting software and other solutions). This has enabled users to easily use e-invoices and other electronic business documents in existing software solutions without the need to use additional dedicated solutions.

The challenge of ensuring the reliable and secure exchange of e-invoices and other electronic business documents is being addressed by e-invoicing service providers. For Slovenia, it is particularly positive that the 4-corner model has been adopted by service providers, where the issuer and the recipient can use different service providers, and the providers take care of interconnection and interoperability (European Multi-Stakeholder Forum on E-Invoicing (EMSFEI), 2018). In addition to document exchange, service providers can provide various value-added services to their users, such as technical validation of documents before delivery to the user, or conversion of documents between different syntaxes and standards if the issuer and the recipient do not use the same electronic document syntax, which is often the case in cross-border e-invoice exchange.

Slovenia's strong e-invoicing performance is due to the uniform application of standards, broad support for e-invoicing in IT solutions, the exchange of e-invoices through e-invoicing service providers and the broad involvement of various stakeholders. Software solution providers have integrated e-invoice exchange services offered by service providers into their software (Figure 1), thus enabling their users to fully automate the processes of sending and receiving e-invoices and other electronic business documents. This automation eliminates the need to use additional software solutions to manually copy, import or export documents, allowing users to carry out the entire process of issuing, sending, receiving and processing e-invoices via existing software solutions already in use in the enterprise. In this way, e-invoicing is greatly simplified and facilitated, especially for small and medium-sized enterprises (SMEs).

The Slovenian National e-Invoicing Forum is an important stakeholder in the Slovenian e-invoicing ecosystem. To promote the use of e-invoicing in the EU, the European Commission has established the European e-Invoicing Forum, to which it has also invited representatives of the National Forums. At the initiative of the European Commission in 2012, the Chamber of Commerce and Industry of Slovenia and the PPA, established the Slovenian National e-Invoicing Forum to take an active leadership and coordination role in promoting and implementing the positive effects of e-invoicing. The two main objectives of the National e-Invoicing Forum are to promote the use of e-invoicing and to achieve a critical mass of users in the process of exchanging e-invoices adapted to a more modern and simplified way of doing business. The National Forum brings together more than 170 experts from business, public administration, academia and the banking sector (Slovenian National eBusiness Centre, 2023b).

In 2019, the Slovenian National eBusiness Centre (EPOS) was launched under the auspices of the Slovenian Chamber of Commerce and Industry to provide enterprises, other organisations and individuals with a one-stop shop for all the relevant information and assistance for the introduction and effective implementation of e-invoicing and e-business. The National eBusiness Centre has an ambitious goal to ensure that Slovenia remains among the leading countries in the EU in the field of e-business. The goal is supported by the introduction of e-commerce standards and effective support and promotion in the business sector (Slovenian National eBusiness Centre, 2023a). Figure 1 presents the national e-invoice adoption framework, which is based on EU initiatives and regulations, national initiatives, supporting ecosystem of various institutions and providers and a 4-corner delivery framework.

However, despite good results and a mature e-invoicing ecosystem, the uptake of e-invoicing among enterprises is still low in Slovenia. Our research therefore aimed to find out why enterprises are not using e-invoicing more and what needs to be done to increase the uptake of e-invoicing among enterprises. As in many EU countries, the introduction of mandatory e-invoicing for businesses is being announced in Slovenia, but it is not yet known when this will happen.

## 3. Research method

In order to analyse the development and current state of e-invoicing in Slovenia, a questionnaire was created in cooperation between the Slovenian National eBusiness Centre, the Slovenian Chamber of Commerce and Industry, the

*Figure 1: Slovenian E-invoice adoption framework.*

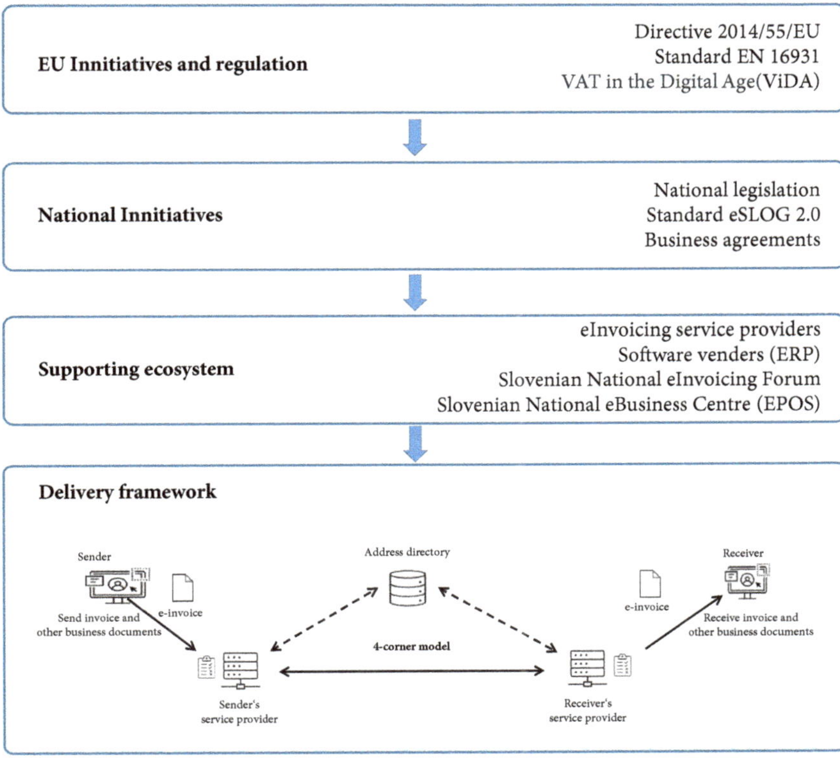


Horizontal ICT Network, the Digital Innovation Hub of Slovenia and the Faculty of Organisational Sciences University of Maribor. The questionnaire was prepared with participation of experts from the field of e-invoicing and the members of national eSLOG standards group, as well as experts from the field of digital business and digital transformation.

The research intent was to investigate the adoption of e-invoicing in a wider range of organizations, we decided to use the survey method. We opted for an online survey, which allows us to capture and obtain the views of a wider population in a relatively short time and in a cost-effective (Lefever, Dal, & Matthíasdóttir, 2007). In addition, the data can be processed more quickly and easily for subsequent statistical analysis in this way (Bakla, Çekiç, & Köksal, 2013).

The questionnaire consisted of 22 questions divided into four sections: Organisational Demographics, E-Invoicing Use, Perceived Advantages, Impacts, Barriers and Incentives to E-Invoicing Use, and Respondent Demographics. Prior to distribution, the questionnaire was tested with 10 professionals.

The survey was distributed to their members by organizations and associations that support the digital transformation (Digital Innovation Hub Slovenia, Chamber of Commerce and Industry, e-invoicing service providers). The survey was conducted between April 18 and May 2, 2023 via the online service 1ka.arnes.si and reached 1638 respondents, of which 901 started the survey. A total of 284 (17%) of respondents completed the survey.

The survey used the definition of organization size based on the European Commission regulations, i.e. micro organization with 1–9 employees, small organizations with 10–49 employees, medium-sized organizations with 50–249 employees and large organizations with more than 250 employees.

The collected survey data was transferred to SPSS 28 software to perform a frequency analysis and descriptive statistics to calculate the mean scores to assess the importance on a 5-point Likert scale from 1 not at all important to 5 very important) of the identified advantages, barriers and incentives for e-invoicing usage.

## 4. Survey results

284 representatives of organizations (enterprises and public institutions) from 75 different locations in Slovenia and 19 different industries took part in the survey. The size structure of the participating organisations in terms of the number of employees was 117 (41.2%) micro organizations, 115 small (40.5%), 45 medium (15.8%) and 7 (2.5%) large organisations. The respondents were employed in the following positions: 62 (22.2%) general managers, 26 (9.2%) finance managers, 12 (4.2%) IT managers, 51 (18%) accounting managers, 31 (10.9%) other business managers, 18 (6.3%) IT officers and 77 (27.1%) employees in other positions.

Figure 2 shows an analysis of the sending and receiving of invoices by form and organizations' size. Majority of micro (89.7%), small (90.4%), medium (86.7%) and large (85.7%) organisations receive invoices in paper form. A little lower is proportion of micro (73.3%), small (73.9%), medium (86.7%) and large (71.4%) organisations which sends invoices in paper form. Figure 2 shows that a similar proportion of organisations which receive and send invoices in paper form also receive and send invoices in PDF format via e-mail. A much smaller proportion of organisations receive (39.7% of micro, 45.2% of small, 40% of medium-sized,

42.9% of large organizations) and send (28.4% of micros, 27% of small, 24.4% of medium-sized and 28.6% of large organizations) invoices in PDF format with electronic signature.

*Figure 2: Sending and receiving of invoices by form and organisation's size.*

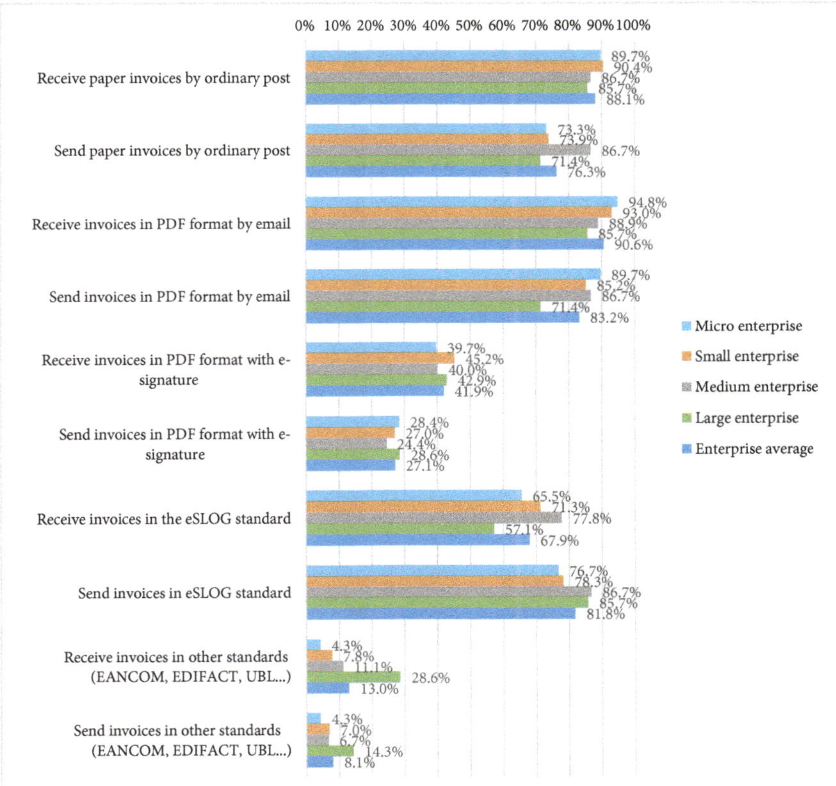


The most commonly used for e-invoicing standard is national eSLOG standard. eSLOG standard is used for receiving 65.5% for micro, 71.3% for small, 77.8% for medium and 57.1% for large organisations and sending 76.7% for micro, 78.3% for small, 86.7% of medium and 85.7% for large organisations shares of e-invoices. Other e-invoicing standards such as EANCOM, EDIFACT, and UBL are used to a lower extent which is higher for large organisations (28.6% for receiving and 14.3% for sending e-invoices).

An analysis of the sending and receiving of e-invoices by partner (Figure 3) shows that organisations mainly exchange e-invoices with suppliers 85.2% and buyers 82.7%. The proportion of e-invoices exchanged with the public administration is slightly lower (70.4%). An even smaller proportion of e-invoices is exchanged with logistics providers (28.5%), retailers (37.7%) and consumers (20.4%). A further analysis of sending and receiving of e-invoices by domestic and foreign partners (Figure 3) shows that organisations exchange e-invoices to a much greater extent with domestic partners compared to exchanges of e-invoices with foreign partners.

*Figure 3: Proportions of e-invoice exchanges by domestic and foreign partners.*

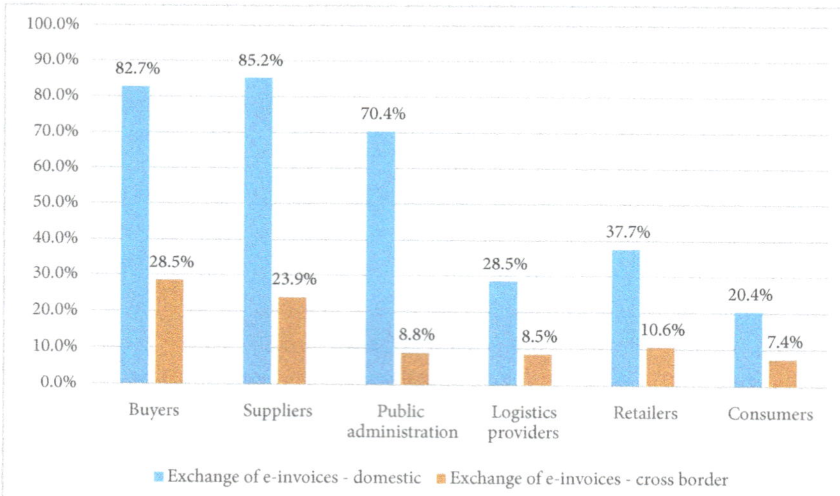


We also analysed the proportion of e- invoices received and sent compared to other forms of invoices (Figure 4). The results show that, on average, organisations receive 18.3% of invoices in eSLOG format and send 23.22% of invoices in eSLOG format, while they receive only 0.9% and send 0.82% of e-invoices in other e-invoicing standards. The highest average share of invoices received (40.73%) and invoices sent (36.62%) is in paper format. The average proportion of received invoices in PDF format with an electronic signature is 4.36% for received and 5.34% for sent. On average, organizations receive 35.71% of invoices in PDF format and send 33.99% of invoices in PDF format.

*Figure 4: Percentages of invoices received and sent by the form of occurrence.*

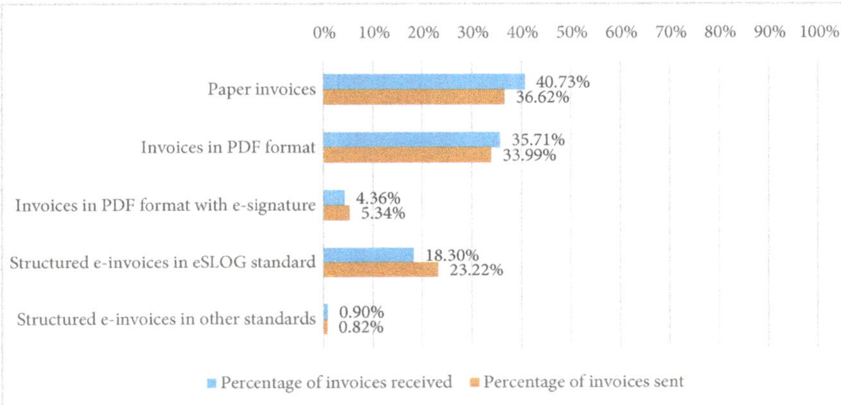


We were also interested in how organizations create e-invoices (Figure 5). The majority of organisations use an ERP (Enterprise Resource Planning) solution for e-invoicing, 57.8%, 27.4% use a dedicated software application, 22.6% use the PPA (Public Payment Agency) portal, 17.8% use a web application, 13.5% have developed their own customised e-invoicing software solution, 11.5% use a software solution from a business partner and 4.4% use a web service from a business partner.

*Figure 5: Ways of preparing e-invoices.*

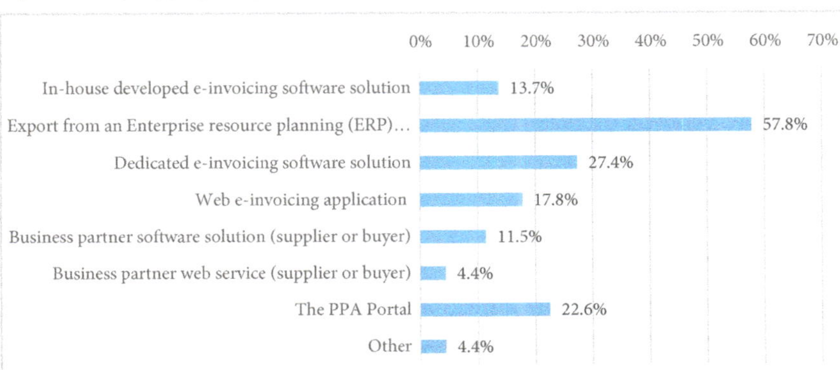

To analyse how the e-invoicing usage relates to the electronic exchange of other business documents, we asked organisations which of following business documents price/sales catalogue, request for quotation, quotation, purchase order, recall, order response, arrival notice, despatch advice and receiving advice they already use, plan to use or want to use in the future (see Figure 6). We identified four business which are most often related with usage of e-invoices: Quotation, Purchase order, Order response and Despatch advice.

Quotation is exchanged by 27.46% of organizations, 11.27% of them plan to use it and 15.49% of organizations want to use it in the future. A purchase order is exchanged by 32.39% of organizations, 9.86% plan to use it and 15.85% of organizations want to use it in the future. Order response is exchanged by 25.7% of organizations, 11.97% of them plans to use and 13.38% of organizations wants to use it in the future. Despatch advice is exchanged by 26.41% or organizations, planned to be used by 13.03% of them and would like to be used in the future by 17.96% of organizations.

*Figure 6: Use and development plans for e-exchange of other business documents.*

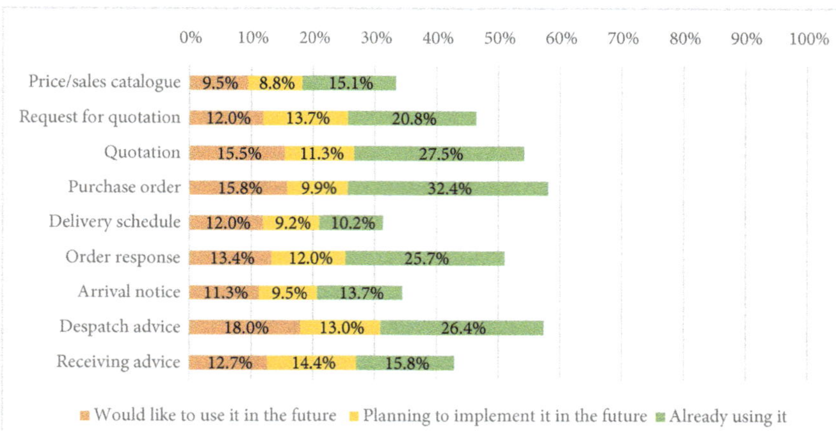


Table 1 presents the mean scores on a Likert scale 1–5 for the perceived importance of e-invoicing usage advantages. The highest mean score (4.48) was observed for Business process automation, followed by Faster processing of invoices and 'Faster delivery of invoices' with mean scores of 4.47 and 4.45. The advantages 'Improved business effectiveness' and 'Reduction of employee time' also received high mean scores of 4.36 and 4.31 respectively, indicating their significant importance in the context of e-invoicing usage.

On the lower end of the scale, 'Better relationships with customers and suppliers' and 'Better business process compliance' had mean scores of 3.98 and 3.97 respectively. The least important advantage, as perceived by the respondents, was 'Improved cash flow and finances' with a mean score of 3.80.

It is noteworthy that the standard deviations for all the advantages were less than 1.14, indicating a relatively low level of variability in the responses. The standard error means were also low (less than 0.072), suggesting a high level of accuracy for the mean values. These findings provide valuable insights into the perceived importance of various e-invoicing usage advantages.

*Table 1: Means for importance of e-invoicing usage advantages*

| **e-invoicing usage advantages** | **N** | **Mean** | **Std. dev.** | **Std. err. mean** |
|---|---|---|---|---|
| Business process automation | 270 | 4.48 | 0.887 | 0.054 |
| Faster processing of invoices | 273 | 4.47 | 0.903 | 0.055 |
| Faster delivery of invoices | 275 | 4.45 | 0.880 | 0.053 |
| Improved business effectiveness | 257 | 4.36 | 0.851 | 0.053 |
| Reduction of employee time | 271 | 4.31 | 0.924 | 0.056 |
| Reduction of costs | 274 | 4.30 | 1.022 | 0.062 |
| Business process tracking | 272 | 4.29 | 0.952 | 0.058 |
| Increase of productivity | 268 | 4.27 | 1.014 | 0.062 |
| Lower error rate | 272 | 4.27 | 1.004 | 0.061 |
| Better relationships with customers and suppliers | 256 | 3.98 | 1.051 | 0.066 |
| Better business process compliance | 262 | 3.97 | 1.059 | 0.065 |
| Improved cash flow and finances | 250 | 3.80 | 1.136 | 0.072 |

Table 2 provides the mean scores on Likert scale 1–5 of the perceived importance of barriers for e-invoicing usage. The barrier 'Suppliers do not send e-invoices' had the highest mean score of 3.98, followed by 'Customers do not receive e-invoices' with a mean score of 3.96. Barriers 'Unawareness of the benefits of using e-invoices' and 'Lack of knowledge to implement e-invoicing' also had relatively high mean scores of 3.89 and 3.88, suggesting that these are also significant barriers to e-invoicing usage.

Barrier 'Not aware of e-invoicing providers and solutions' had the lowest mean score of 2.89, indicating that this was perceived as the least important barrier. The standard deviations for all the barriers were less than 1.31, suggesting a relatively low level of variability in the responses. The standard error means were also low (less than 0.088), indicating a high level of accuracy for the mean values.

*Table 2: Means for importance of e-invoicing usage barriers*

| e-invoicing usage barriers | N | Mean | Std. dev. | Std. err. mean |
|---|---|---|---|---|
| Suppliers do not send e-invoices | 245 | 3.98 | 0.954 | 0.061 |
| Customers do not receive e-invoices | 243 | 3.96 | 0.964 | 0.062 |
| Unawareness of the benefits of using e-invoices | 240 | 3.89 | 0.905 | 0.058 |
| Lack of knowledge to implement e-invoicing | 242 | 3.88 | 1.023 | 0.066 |
| The complexity of implementing e-invoicing | 238 | 3.69 | 1.033 | 0.067 |
| High costs of e-invoicing IT implementation | 227 | 3.67 | 1.168 | 0.078 |
| Information security concerns | 238 | 3.47 | 1.085 | 0.070 |
| Lack of management support | 230 | 3.35 | 1.271 | 0.084 |
| Limited IT capabilities in the organisation | 231 | 3.31 | 1.197 | 0.079 |
| Low level of e-business adoption | 221 | 3.27 | 1.310 | 0.088 |
| Not aware of e-invoicing providers and solutions | 224 | 2.89 | 1.250 | 0.083 |

The Table 3 presents the mean scores of perceived importance for e-invoicing adoption incentives on Likert scale 1–5. The perceived highest mean score has incentive for reduced initial costs of implementation (4.35), followed by increased awareness of the benefits (4.31), and business software providers integrating e-invoicing into their solutions (4.30) incentive.

Other notable incentives include customer requirements for e-invoicing (4.23), education on e-invoicing (4.23), digitalization financial grants (4.22), and incentives from the government and institutions (4.11). The least perceived important incentives are public catalogue of service providers and their solutions (3.88), and competitors using e-invoicing (3.81).

The standard deviations for all the barriers were less than 1.271, suggesting a relatively low level of variability in the responses. The standard error means were also low (less than 0.088), indicating a high level of accuracy for the mean values.

*Table 3: Means for importance of e-invoicing usage incentives*

| e-invoicing usage incentives | N | Mean | Std. dev. | Std. err. mean |
|---|---|---|---|---|
| Reduced initial costs of implementing e-invoicing | 255 | 4.35 | 0.828 | 0.052 |
| Increased awareness of the benefits of e-invoicing | 257 | 4.31 | 0.812 | 0.051 |
| Business software providers integrate e-invoicing into their solutions | 247 | 4.30 | 0.870 | 0.055 |
| Customer requirements for the use of e-invoicing | 254 | 4.23 | 0.845 | 0.053 |
| Education on e-invoicing | 256 | 4.23 | 0.828 | 0.052 |
| Digitalization financial grants | 247 | 4.22 | 1.052 | 0.067 |
| Incentives from the government and institutions | 249 | 4.11 | 1.030 | 0.065 |
| Calls for tenders for digitalization | 244 | 4.10 | 1.051 | 0.067 |
| Publicly presented examples of good practice | 246 | 4.04 | 0.976 | 0.062 |
| Public directory of business entities for the exchange of e-invoices | 243 | 4.03 | 1.034 | 0.066 |
| Government to legislate mandatory e-invoicing for all companies | 249 | 3.95 | 1.115 | 0.071 |
| Public catalogue of service providers and their solutions | 243 | 3.88 | 1.028 | 0.066 |
| Competitors use e-invoicing | 254 | 3.81 | 1.087 | 0.068 |

## 5. Discussion

Survey results have shown that majority of organizations still receive and send invoices in PDF (receive 90.6%, send 83.2% of organizations) and paper format (receive 88.1%, send 76.3% of organizations) (see Figure 2). However, the third most common type of invoice exchange is electronic format based on national standard eSLOG (receive 67.9% and send 81.1%). We may notice that there is a difference between organizations receiving e-invoices in the eSLOG standard (67.9%) and sending those in the same format (81.8%). This is most likely because since 2015, it has become obligatory to exchange invoices in eSLOG electronic format, while doing business with public institutions. Therefore, many organisations are able to send eSLOG invoices to public sector; however, they still may not be able to receive e-invoices themselves.

According to the Statistical Office of the Republic of Slovenia, 89.8% of organizations send paper invoices, 80.4% send PDF invoices and 60.5% send structured e-invoices (Statistical office of the Republic of Slovenia, 2023). A comparison of the data in our survey with the Statistical Office's data suggests that the proportion of organisations sending PDF invoices is consistent, but the actual rate of e-invoice use in the wider population of organisations is lower than that shown in the sample of participating organisations in our survey. It is also noticeable that the proportion of paper invoices sent in the wider population is higher. Again, the reasons for these results are partly because the survey participants were active organisations that are following the digital business and digital transformation agenda and have already taken some steps in this direction.

It is noticeable that the proportion of organisations receiving paper and PDF invoices decreases with the size of the organisation. Micro and small enterprises receive the most paper and PDF invoices, while medium-sized and large enterprises receive the least. The situation is exactly the opposite for structured electronic invoices (eSLOG, EANCOM, EDIFACT, UBL and other standards), where medium-sized and large enterprises receive the highest number of e-invoices (except for of eSLOG e-invoices in large enterprises), while micro and small enterprises receive the lowest number of e-invoices. This distribution is to be expected, as medium-sized and larger enterprises are generally better IT-supported for receiving e-invoices, while many smaller enterprises, and especially micro enterprises, do not have the appropriate IT solutions and expertise to deal with e-invoices. In addition, larger enterprises are also more involved into global supply chains where they have to adapt industry standards and supply chain practices.

According to the data shown in Figure 4, paper invoices are the predominant format for exchanging invoices, with 40.73% of invoices received and 36.62% of invoices sent being in paper format. The second most common type of invoice exchange is PDF format, with 35.71% of invoices received and 33.99% of invoices sent. The third most common form of invoices exchange is the structured form in eSLOG standard (18.30% of invoices received and 23.22% of invoices sent). Only a smaller proportion of invoices are exchanged in PDF format with electronic signature (4.36% of invoices received and 5.34% of invoices sent). This is probably because the legislation does not require the invoice to be signed and its use is left to the discretion of the individual organization. Although the use of electronic signature is not legally required, it can have a positive impact, as electronic signatures are an effective mechanism to ensure the authenticity of the origin and integrity of the content of the invoice, which is something that the organisation needs to ensure. An electronic signature may also be included in the eSLOG invoice format, but its use is not mandatory. Less than one per cent of invoices are exchanges in other structured formats. The results of our survey are also in line with the findings of the Billentis report, where paper and PDF are the dominant formats for exchanging invoices (Koch, 2016).

For invoices in eSLOG format, there is a higher proportion of invoices sent (23.22%) than received (18.30%). The reason for this is that the vast majority of the surveyed organisations exchange invoices with the public sector (70.4%), as shown in Figure 2. However, the use of eSLOG format is mandatory for sending invoices to the Slovenian public sector.

As expected, the eSLOG format is by far the most widespread among structured e-invoice formats, as it is legally required for the exchange of e-invoices for the public sector, widely supported in various business software solutions and by e-invoicing service providers (Figure 4). Other structured formats (e.g. EANCOM and EDIFACT) are used most in the retail and supply chains of different industries (e.g. automotive) and together present less than 1% of all exchanged invoices. This can also be seen in Figure 1, where the proportion of organisations receiving other structured invoice formats is by far the highest for large organisations. On the other hand, large organisations have the lowest share among all organisations in receiving invoices in the eSLOG standard.

28.5% of the surveyed organisations send e-invoices to their buyers abroad (Figure 2). Given that majority of all e-invoices sent (96.5%) are in eSLOG format (calculated based on the data in Figure 4), which is a national standard and is not used abroad, we emphasise the importance of e-invoicing service providers for ensuring cross-border interoperability. Based on the dominant use of the eSLOG standard in sending e-invoices, it is necessary to translate the eSLOG invoice into one of the international standards used by the foreign buyer. Such translations between different standards are in turn carried out by the e-invoicing service providers.

The same applies to foreign suppliers sending e-invoices to Slovenian organisations (23.9% of such organisations in the survey), where service providers translate the received invoice from the international standard into the eSLOG standard and then forward it to the Slovenian recipient. As many as 8.8% of organisations exchange e-invoices with foreign government bodies, with Italy and Croatia likely to have the highest volume of e-invoice exchanges. Again, e-Invoicing providers are involved in this case, providing the exchange with public authorities in other countries and at the same time translating the invoices from the eSLOG standard to the FatturaPA standard for the Italian and the UBL standard for the Croatian public administration.

The majority of e-invoices (57.8%) are prepared by respondents with enterprise resource planning (ERP) solutions, ranging from global vendors such as SAP and Dynamics NAV to various Slovenian vendors such as Datalab Pantheon, Vasco, SAOP and others (Figure 5). This is to be expected, as the issuance of e-invoices has been massively supported by ERP solution providers. This means that almost any organisation using an ERP solution in its business operations can issue e-invoices. An additional reason for the mass support of e-invoices in ERP solutions is that all major Slovenian ERP business software solution providers have enabled the automation of sending and receiving e-invoices in their solutions through integration with the services of e-invoicing providers. This has enabled their end-users to conduct their entire e-invoicing process within a single software solution without the need for unnecessary manual copying, importing or storing of documents.

For enterprises, who only issue small number of invoices in a year, various online portals are available for the preparation of e-invoices. For micro and small organisations, the introduction of e-invoicing should take into account their cost sensitivity and the fact that they have fewer IT staff, IT support and financial resources available. For generating and issuing e-invoices to the public sector, the Public Payments Administration of the Republic of Slovenia (PPA) provides free use of the UJP (national) web portal, which is used by almost a quarter of the respondents. As the number of invoices issued via the UJP portal is limited to a hundred per year, this method is mainly available for smaller issuers or those organisations that do not have another software solution for e-invoicing. Although it was expected that the use of the UJP portal would be predominantly by micro and small organisations, it turned out that the highest share of use of the UJP portal is among medium-sized organisations, followed by small and micro organisations. This is because only a minority of micro and small organisations do business with the public sector. If organisations using the UJP portal want to issue e-invoices to other enterprises, they would have to use a different software solution or service provider to do so. UJP portal can only be used by organizations to issue e-invoices to the public sector.

The potential future use of other electronic business documents is led by purchase orders, order response, despatch advice and quotation (Figure 6). The interest in introducing other electronic business documents is fairly even across all the documents listed in the survey, with more than 20% of respondents expressing a desire or plan to introduce other business electronic structured documents. The despatch advice has the highest potential for adoption, with more than 30% of respondents wanting or planning to adopt it. Another positive signal for digitisation is that more than 30% of respondents indicated that they would like to use or already use all the electronic business documents mentioned. The electronic document with the lowest interest for adoption is the electronic recall document, which is linked to manufacturing enterprises or supply chains and is not used more widely. It is important to mention, that the Technical committee of eSLOG (national standards) carries out the development and maintenance of electronic business documents that are established in Slovenia: purchase order, order response, dispatch advice, invoice, payment reminder, statement of account and response to statement of account (Slovenian National eBusiness Centre., 2023). All these documents are available for implementation in standardized electronic form.

An important part of the research carried out is how the surveyed organisations identify statistically significant important advantages (Table 1), barriers (Table 2), and incentives (Table 3) related to e-invoicing. Respondents perceived most of the advantages of using e-invoicing as important, with business process automation, faster processing of invoices, faster delivery of invoices and improved business effectiveness highlighted as the most important advantages. In addition to these, the following advantages of e-invoicing were also identified as important: reduction of employee time, reduction of costs and lower error rates resulting in increased productivity and better business process compliance with standards. Improved cash flow and finances was not identified as a statistically important advantage of e-invoicing, meaning that simplification and optimisation of business processes is more important to the organisations surveyed than payment and financial discipline. In addition, better relationships with customers and suppliers were also not identified as a statistically important advantage of e-invoicing, which is most likely related to the fact that the invoice is the last business document in the buyer-supplier business transaction process and that other factors lead towards sustainable and trustworthy buyer-supplier relationship.

The two most important barriers (see Table 2) identified by the respondent organisations were: Suppliers do not send e-invoices and Customers do not receive e-invoice. Both barriers are interlinked and reflect the low willingness to use e-invoicing among all stakeholders. The very similar scores for both barriers mean that the low willingness to use e-invoicing is approximately the same for Purchase-2-Pay as for Order-2-Cash processes. Other important barriers include Unawareness of the benefits of using e-invoices and Lack of knowledge to implement e-invoicing. This is understandable as lack of awareness and knowledge are also among the most important barriers to the adoption of other IT or business innovations. To overcome these barriers, Slovenian National eBusiness Centre (EPOS), in cooperation with various stakeholders, aims to raise awareness and knowledge of the use of e-invoicing and possibilities of digitisation.

Respondents' recognition of the importance of various incentives leading to wider use of e-invoicing is noteworthy (see Table 3). These incentives are closely linked to existing government funding schemes, in particular those established for digital transformation through entities such as the Digital Innovation Hub of Slovenia and similar programmes. Emphasis is also placed on the need to create regulatory frameworks that will require mandatory e-invoicing between enterprises. In addition, the establishment of a public directory of business entities to facilitate the exchange of e-invoices and public catalogue of service and solution providers is seen as a benefit. The recognition of the need for training, education and the learning of best practices is seen as crucial to acquire the necessary knowledge that is indispensable for the successful implementation of e-invoicing. Finally, the integration of e-invoicing into the wider business ecosystem and supply chain is highlighted as a key driver.

### 5.1 E-invoicing and AI

Artificial intelligence (AI) has transformed business processes and industries and will therefore also have an impact on e-invoicing. With the help of AI, e-invoicing systems can analyse and extract relevant information from e-invoices to predict payment behaviour, optimise invoice delivery times, accelerate payments and even fully automate invoice processing. By using machine learning (ML) algorithms, AI-enabled e-invoicing systems can increase the effectiveness of e-invoicing systems, as they can process large volumes of invoices instantly and ensure much higher accuracy than manual processes through process automation (Malladhi, 2023).

AI can not only improve the efficiency and processing of e-invoices, but can also detect and prevent frauds and make the invoicing processes more resilient to errors and oversights. Through deep cognitive insights, pattern analysis and anomaly detection, AI can immediately and accurately detect fraudulent invoices, discrepant amounts or inconsistencies in customer data and issue an alert (Bruin, 2023).

## 6. Conclusions

This chapter provides a comprehensive overview covering more than two decades of the development of e-invoicing in Slovenia, a small country in the European Union. The theoretical framework presented in this chapter includes an outline of relevant regulations, legislation and policies at both Slovenian and EU level that have a significant impact on the development of e-invoicing. According to international surveys, Slovenia ranks among the most developed countries in the EU in the field of e-invoicing, which is the result of a well-functioning ecosystem of cooperation between different stakeholders. The high level of interoperability for the electronic exchange of documents is due to the unified use of standards and appropriate national legislation adopted.

The empirical findings presented in the main body of the paper are drawn from a survey of 284 organisations in Slovenia. Despite the existing legal provisions mandating the electronic exchange of invoices with the public sector, the uptake of e-invoicing among most other business entities remains limited, with a significant prevalence of paper and PDF invoicing practices.

In order to stimulate further digitisation and digital transformation, the introduction of legislation requiring the standardised exchange of e-invoices among all business entities is proposed as an incentive, as is already the case in many other European countries. Italy and Serbia have already been introduced legal regulation of mandatory exchange of e-invoices between organisations. Several countries including, Belgium, France, Poland, Spain and Romania are preparing to introduce it in the near future. Slovenia is already preparing for this step.

The paper argues that the widespread use of e-invoices is a foundation and potential catalyst for widespread digitisation and digital transformation of enterprises. More than 50% of the organisations surveyed express current or future intentions to exchange electronically additional electronic business documents beyond e-invoices, such as purchase orders, order responses and despatch advices. The envisaged comprehensive digitisation of all business documents is aligned with the digitisation of related business processes, which will increase productivity, competitiveness and sustainability at both organisational and national economic levels in Slovenia.

It is important that the paper, in highlighting the benefits of exchanging e-invoices and other electronic business documents, not only addresses the time and financial savings for organisations, but also the reduced impact on the environment. The shift to e-invoicing significantly reduces carbon dioxide emissions, at the expense of reduced paper consumption and associated energy costs for transport. For 30 billion invoices per year, which is the estimate for the EU area, this would be a reduction of one million tonnes of emissions per year. While these statistics are remarkable, the wider potential of digital transformation in businesses and societies remains latent and poised to make a significant contribution to sustainability.

The paper and the results of our research provide important information on the development of the use of e-invoices in Slovenia, the current situation and the possibilities for further development of this area, which also includes the wider exchange of other electronic business documents. The paper also discusses the benefits, barriers and incentives associated with e-invoices and other electronic business documents, thus contributing to a better understanding of the path towards digital transformation. It provides important information for decision-makers and public administrations to take appropriate measures and incentives to support the functioning of an appropriate ecosystem for digital transformation in the country. For micro and small businesses in particular, it is important that the government provides adequate co-financing and appropriate solutions.

While the study provides valuable insights into the evolution of the use of e-invoicing and the potential for advancing the electronic exchange of other business documents, it is not without limitations. The biggest limitation is the sampling method inherent in surveying organisations already involved in digitisation efforts. Comparative analysis with national digitisation results mitigates this bias, but further research opportunities are recognised. Future research should use a variety of data sources and research methods to provide a nuanced understanding of the development of the field.

## Acknowledgements

This research was partially supported by the Slovenian Research and Innovation Agency; Program No. P5-0018 – Decision Support Systems in Digital Business.

## Bibliography

Bakla, A., Çekiç, A., & Köksal, O. (2013). Web-based surveys in educational research. *International Journal of Academic Research Part B*, *5*(1), 5–13. https://doi.org/10.7813/2075-4124.2013/5-1/B.1

Bjelica, B., Bogataj Habjan, K., Bohnec, D., Bračun, F., Domanjko, T., Gričar, J., … Triplat, M. (2005). *Izdajanje in prejemanje e-računov v e-regiji: pobuda za vzpostavitev projekta v Sloveniji.*

Bojanc, R., Zorko, I., Adlešič, A., Zorko, A., Zupančič, D., Šinkovec, T., … Boh, M. (2020). Digitalization of business from order to payment. Retrieved April 25, 2023, from https://www.epos.si/assets/docs/ROSE_Zbornik2020_EN_Web.pdf

Bojanc, R., Zupančič, D., Miklavčič, A., Pilih, D. A., Bertalanič, J., & Anka Zorko. (2018). *e-Invoicing in Slovenia*. Retrieved from http://www.roseslovenia.eu/e_files/news/ROSE_Zbornik_SLO_Webcompressed.pdf

Bruin, K. de. (2023). AI-driven e-Invoicing: Embracing Disruption and Unleashing Opportunity Amidst Change & Compliance. Retrieved November 15, 2023, from https://www.linkedin.com/pulse/ai-driven-e-invoicing-embracing-disruption-unleashing-kim-de-bruin/

CEN. (2017). *EN 16931-1:2017, Electronic invoicing - Part 1: Semantic data model of the core elements of an electronic invoice.*

Connecting Europe Facility Stakeholder Management Office. (2019). *D05.01 eInvoicing Benefits' Analysis.*

European Commission. Directorate-General for Internal Market, I. (2020). *Interoperability in end-to-end eProcurement.* Retrieved from https://op.europa.eu/en/publication-detail/-/publication/1c578b32-4c82-11ea-b8b7-01aa75ed71a1

European Commission. (2010). *Reaping the benefits of electronic invoicing for Europe.* Retrieved from https://eur-lex.europa.eu/legal-content/HR/TXT/?uri=CELEX:52010DC0712

European Commission. *Directive 2014/55/EU of the European Parliament and of the Council of April 16, 2014 on electronic invoicing in public procurement.*, (2014).

European Commission. (2021). DESI by components — Digital Scoreboard - Data & Indicators. Retrieved April 25, 2023, from https://digital-agenda-data.eu/charts/desi-components#chart=%7B%22indicator%22:%22desi%22,%22breakdown-group%22:%22desi%22,%22unit-measure%22:%22egov_score%22,%22time-period%22:%222020%22%7D

European Commission. (2023). DIGITAL - eInvoicing. Retrieved April 25, 2023, from https://ec.europa.eu/digital-building-blocks/wikis/display/DIGITAL/eInvoicing

European Multi-Stakeholder Forum on E-Invoicing (EMSFEI). (2018). *Report on interoperability and transmission of e-invoices with a special focus on the needs of Small and Medium-sized Enterprises (SMEs).* Retrieved from https://ec.europa.eu/cefdigital/wiki/download/attachments/80184632/FINAL EMSFEI report on Interoperability and transmission.pdf?version=1&modificationDate=1552920931958&api=v2

European Parliament. (2014). *Directive 2014/55/EU of the European Parliament and of the Council of 16 April 2014 on electronic invoicing in public procurement.*

Haack, D. (March 10, 2021). Two Years of Mandatory E-Invoicing in Italy. Retrieved June 2, 2023, from https://www.xsuite.com/en/blog/mandatory-e-invoicing-in-italy/

Horák, J., Bokšová, J., & Strouhal, J. (September 2020). Electronic Invoicing Adoption within the European Union. *International Advances in Economic Research*, Vol. 26, pp. 449–450. https://doi.org/10.1007/s11294-020-09802-3

Jeansson, J., & Bredmar, K. (2019). Digital Transformation of SMEs: Capturing Complexity. In A. Pucihar, M. Kljajić Borštnar, R. Bons, J. Seitz, H. Cripps, & D. Vidmar (Eds.), *32nd Bled eConference. Humanizing technology for a sustainable society* (pp. 523–541). University of Maribor Press.

Kljajić Borštnar, M., & Pucihar, A. (2021). Multi-Attribute Assessment of Digital Maturity of SMEs. *Electronics, 10*(8). https://doi.org/10.3390/electronics10080885

Koch, B. (2016). *Billentis: E-Invoicing / E-Billing Digitisation & Automation 2016.* Retrieved from www.billentis.com

Koch, B. (2019). *Billentis: The e-invoicing journey 2019–2025.* Retrieved from www.billentis.com

Lai, K., Wong, C. W. Y., & Cheng, T. C. E. (2010). Bundling digitized logistics activities and its performance implications. *Industrial Marketing Management*, *39*(2), 273–286. https://doi.org/10.1016/j.indmarman.2008.08.002

Lefever, S., Dal, M., & Matthíasdóttir, Á. (2007). Online data collection in academic research: advantages and limitations. *British Journal of Educational Technology*, *38*(4), 574–582. https://doi.org/10.1111/j.1467-8535.2006.00638.x

Li, F., Nucciarelli, A., Roden, S., & Graham, G. (2016). How smart cities transform operations models: a new research agenda for operations management in the digital economy. *Production Planning & Control*, *27*(6), 514–528. https://doi.org/10.1080/09537287.2016.1147096

Li, W., Liu, K., Belitski, M., Ghobadian, A., & O'Regan, N. (2016). e-Leadership through strategic alignment: An empirical study of small- and medium-sized enterprises in the digital age. *Journal of Information Technology*, *31*(2). https://doi.org/10.1057/jit.2016.10

Loebbecke, C., & Picot, A. (2015). Reflections on societal and business model transformation arising from digitization and big data analytics: A research agenda. *The Journal of Strategic Information Systems*, *24*(3), 149–157. https://doi.org/10.1016/j.jsis.2015.08.002

Malladhi, A. (2023). AI-Embedded E-Invoicing: The Future of Business. Retrieved November 15, 2023, from https://www.linkedin.com/pulse/ai-embedded-e-invoicing-future-business-avinash-malladhi/

Marolt, M., Lenart, G., Vidmar, D., & Pucihar, A. (2021). Uporaba e-računov v Sloveniji. *40th International Conference on Organizational Science Development Values Competencies and Changes in Organizations*, 603–616. https://doi.org/10.18690/978-961-286-442-2.41

Nadkarni, S., & Prügl, R. (2020). Digital transformation: a review, synthesis and opportunities for future research. *Management Review Quarterly*. https://doi.org/10.1007/s11301-020-00185-7

Pagani, M., & Pardo, C. (2017). The impact of digital technology on relationships in a business network. *Industrial Marketing Management*, *67*, 185–192. https://doi.org/10.1016/j.indmarman.2017.08.009

*Proposal for a COUNCIL DIRECTIVE amending Directive 2006/112/EC as regards VAT rules for the digital age.*, (2022).

Pucihar, A. (2020). The digital transformation journey: content analysis of Electronic Markets articles and Bled eConference proceedings from 2012 to 2019. *Electronic Markets*, *30*(1). https://doi.org/10.1007/s12525-020-00406-7

Pucihar, A., Marolt, M., Lenart, G., & Vidmar, D. (2021). Digitalna preobrazba in njeno stanje v organizacijah v Sloveniji. In U. Rajkovič & A. Baggia (Eds.), *Znanstveno-raziskovalni trendi na področju digitalne preobrazbe*. https://doi.org/10.18690/978-961-286-509-2

Pucihar, A., Mohar Bastar, K., & Lenart, G. (2022). Organizacije v Sloveniji na poti digitalne preobrazbe. In M. Kljajić Borštnar & A. Pucihar (Eds.), *Znanstveno-raziskovalni izzivi na poti digitalne preobrazbe* (pp. 1–20). https://press.um.si/index.php/ump/catalog/book/712

RS, U. list. *Zakon o opravljanju plačilnih storitev za proračunske uporabnike (ZOPSPU-1).*, (2016).

RS, U. list. *Zakon o izmenjavi elektronskih računov in drugih elektronskih dokumentov.*, (2021).

Sebastian, I. M., Moloney, K. G., Ross, J. W., Fonstad, N. O., Beath, C., & Mocker, M. (2017). How big old companies navigate digital transformation. *MIS Quarterly Executive*, *16*(3), 197–213.

Slovenian National eBusiness Centre. (2023). eSLOG. Retrieved April 25, 2023, from https://www.epos.si/en/eslog

Slovenian National eBusiness Centre. (2023a). Slovenian National eBusiness Centre. Retrieved April 25, 2023, from https://epos.si/en

Slovenian National eBusiness Centre. (2023b). Slovenian National eInvoicing Forum. Retrieved April 25, 2023, from https://epos.si/en/slovenian-national-einvoicing-forum

Statistical office of the Republic of Slovenia. (2023). SiStat Database. Retrieved August 22, 2023, from https://pxweb.stat.si/sistat/en

Statistični urad Republike Slovenije. (2022). *Digitalno podjetništvo, podrobni podatki.Digitalno preobrazbo poslovanja podjetij ovira pomanjkanje ustreznega kadra ali znanja.*

Uprava Republike Slovenije za javna plačila. (2023). Pošiljanje e-računov in e-dokumentov proračunskim uporabnikom. Retrieved April 25, 2023, from https://www.gov.si/zbirke/storitve/posiljanje-eracunov/

Van Veldhoven, Z., & Vanthienen, J. (2021). Digital transformation as an interaction-driven perspective between business, society, and technology. *Electronic Markets*. https://doi.org/10.1007/s12525-021-00464-5

VAT Update. (2023). Timeline of B2B E-Invoicing & E-Reporting mandates in the European Union. Retrieved September 25, 2023, from https://www.vatupdate.com/2023/09/25/timeline-of-e-invoicing-e-reporting-mandates-in-the-european-union-2-2-2-2-2/

Vendrell-Herrero, F., Bustinza, O. F., Parry, G., & Georgantzis, N. (2017). Servitization, digitization and supply chain interdependency. *Industrial Marketing Management*, *60*, 69–81. https://doi.org/10.1016/j.indmarman.2016.06.013

Venkatraman, V. (2017). The Digital Matrix. New rules for business transformation through technology. In *Escritos Contables y de Administración* (Vol. 8). LifeTree.

Verhoef, P. C., Broekhuizen, T., Bart, Y., Bhattacharya, A., Qi Dong, J., Fabian, N., & Haenlein, M. (2021). Digital transformation: A multidisciplinary reflection and research agenda. *Journal of Business Research*, *122*(July 2018), 889–901. https://doi.org/10.1016/j.jbusres.2019.09.022

Vial, G. (2019). Understanding digital transformation: A review and a research agenda. *The Journal of Strategic Information Systems*, *28*(2). https://doi.org/10.1016/j.jsis.2019.01.003

Viry Christophe. (October 8, 2019). Assessing the implementation of the Clearance model in Italy. Retrieved June 2, 2023, from https://www.generix-group.com/en/blog/clearance-model-italy

Warner, K. S. R., & Wäger, M. (2019). Building dynamic capabilities for digital transformation: An ongoing process of strategic renewal. *Long Range Planning*, *52*(3), 326–349. https://doi.org/10.1016/j.lrp.2018.12.001

Zammuto, R. F., Griffith, T. L., Majchrzak, A., Dougherty, D. J., & Faraj, S. (2007). Information Technology and the Changing Fabric of Organization. *Organization Science*, *18*(5), 749–762. https://doi.org/10.1287/orsc.1070.0307

Zupančič, D., Bastl, A., Ružič, A., Lunar Peček, B., Bertalanič, J., Bratušek, M., … Gaberc, B. (2016). Priporočila za uporabo standarda GZS eSlog 1.6.1 za enostavni račun. *Verzija 2016/1*, pp. 1–85.

Marjeta Marolt*

# Exploring consumer online purchase behaviour

**Abstract:** The rapid development of digital technology and the growing preference for online shopping have transformed the Slovenian retail market. Today, consumers are more willing to embrace these changes and focus on the benefits that online retailers offer. For businesses using digital commerce as a distribution channel, it is crucial to understand who is buying online, what they are buying, why they choose to shop online, and what their online purchase behaviour looks like to realise its full potential. This chapter aims to provide an in-depth analysis of the differences in online purchase behaviour among Slovenian consumers. To achieve this goal, a questionnaire was developed based on the relevant literature and data was collected through a survey of 324 individuals aged 15 years or older who had made at least one online purchase. The results of the survey show significant differences in consumers' online behaviour before, during, and after the purchase with regard to various characteristics such as gender, digital literacy, decision-making factors, type of products purchased online and frequency of online purchases. These findings highlight the complex landscape of Slovenian customers' online purchase behaviour and encourage businesses to further optimise their marketing efforts to ultimately drive growth and success in the competitive world of digital commerce. To keep pace with rapid changes in digital technologies, social trends and consumer experiences, businesses need to adopt artificial intelligence approaches and mechanisms for big data analytics to closely monitor consumer behaviour and deliver better experiences.

**Keywords:** online purchase behaviour, consumers characteristics, digital commerce, consumer experiences, artificial intelligence

## 1. Introduction

Every business must aim to create a product or service that is desired by the consumer, both in terms of tangible characteristics (colours, size, functionality, etc.) and intangible characteristics (transport, sales services, etc.). It is important to know the difference between the perceived characteristics of the physical product and the product presented in the digital world. Online products lose important characteristics (tangibility, smell, taste), so the online retailer has to ensure that there is enough content and visual information. Branding and consumer loyalty play an important role in maintaining long-term relationships

* University of Maribor, Faculty of Organizational Sciences, Kranj, Slovenia; e-mail: marjeta.marolt@um.si

(Marolt et al., 2020). The key to excellent online presentation of a product is its identified attractiveness and usability. Attractiveness and usability can be translated into emotional value and functional value that consumers expect from the products and services presented (Kato, 2021).

Furthermore, the price of the product and the terms of sale are also important, as consumers' purchase decisions usually depend on certain offers, the price and attractiveness of discounts, and the way and ease of payment (Zhao et al., 2021). The lower cost of online marketing and selling often allows the online retailer to set a lower price, which is a key competitive advantage. Consumers have access to a large amount of information about prices, delivery and business terms, complaint policies or consumer reviews via the internet. With this information, they can make a more informed decision. Pricing policies have many advantages in the online environment and are constantly adapting to the dynamics of supply and demand (Ampountolas et al., 2019).

In addition to technological advancements, the Covid-19 pandemic has had a significant impact on consumer behaviour (Donthu & Gustafsson, 2020; Eger et al., 2021). Research conducted after the first wave of the Covid-19 pandemic suggests that people around the world are approaching products and brands in a new way (Accenture, 2020; McKinsey&Company, 2020). The pandemic has forced them to change their buying habits and even learn new ones (Sheth, 2020). They have started shopping online, getting home delivery and paying cashless, which they had never considered before the Covid-19 pandemic (Pantano et al., 2020). These changes have had a profound impact on businesses, which have become aware of the need to monitor consumer behaviour in all the interactions a consumer has with a brand at the different stages of the consumer journey (Richardson, 2010). The different stages of the journey represent the touch points between the consumer and the brand.

This chapter focuses on consumers, who are an essential part of any business. As understanding consumer purchase behaviour is crucial, especially in the digital environment where they behave differently than in real life, we present recent research on Slovenian consumers' online purchase behaviour. In the last part, we discuss the main findings of the study and provide concluding remarks.

## 2. Digital consumer

The digital environment has a major impact on the way consumers are informed about different products and services and encouraged to buy. The success of digital marketing and online sales depends not only on understanding the technology, but also on understanding the digital consumer. Through a deeper understanding of the consumer, companies can provide a better online experience that leads to greater customer loyalty and retention (Rasool et al., 2020). Therefore, to achieve their goals, companies need a clearly defined strategy that uses paid, owned and earned media to reach their target audience and drive interactions, subscriptions and leads through a website, blog and interactive tools (Marolt et al., 2018). These activities can lead to consumers visiting a digital commerce website and taking the desired action. After conversion, businesses need to engage consumers to cultivate loyalty and advocacy.

Integrating marketing and sales has become essential in the age of digital marketing and commerce, where consumer interactions can be tracked and analysed. To achieve this, the traditional marketing funnel and the sales funnel have been combined into a single funnel with six phases. Figure 1 illustrates the different phases and how marketing and sales work together in each stage.

*Figure 1: Marketing and sales funnel (adapted from Hopper (2022)).*

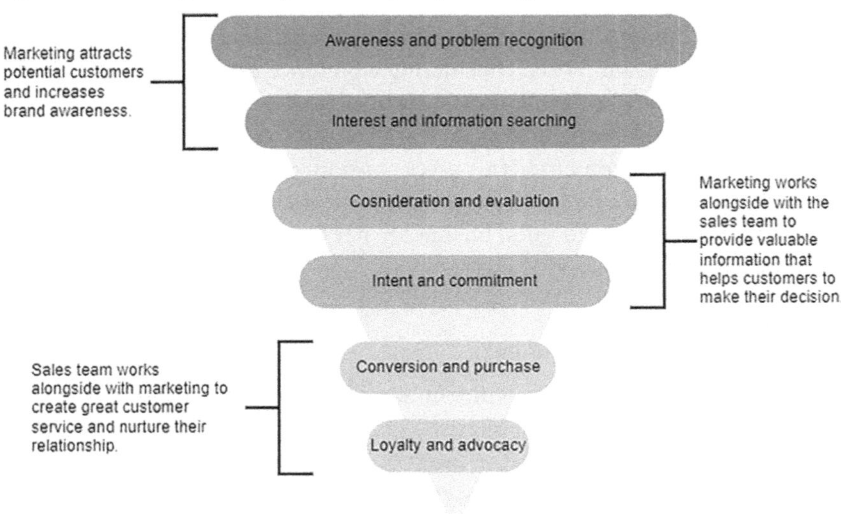


Digital marketing is essential for online sales (Djakasaputra et al., 2021) and is an increasingly effective and popular approach to marketing around the world. Businesses can use various digital marketing channels to reach potential consumers with information about their brands, products or services. The most commonly used digital marketing channels by businesses are email, website, mobile, social media, display ads, organic search and paid search (Peter & Dalla Vecchia, 2021). Email is one of the most personal digital channels for communicating with consumers, while the website is an ideal channel for content. While the number of mobile users is increasing, mobile websites and apps are becoming profitable marketing channels. Social media also offers great potential for marketing as it enables consumer engagement. To increase traffic to websites, businesses place ads on host websites, improve search engine optimisation and invest in search engine marketing. Typically, businesses use more than one digital marketing channel. The combination of digital channels businesses use depends on their goals, budget, competition and, most importantly, consumers' channel preferences (Dzyabura & Jagabathula, 2017).

The success of digital marketing activities reflects conversion and sales. Businesses can sell their products and services through marketplaces, social media and their web shop. To sell products and services online, businesses can use different channels, including marketplaces, social media and web shops. Depending on their objectives, businesses may prefer to invest in a web shop to build their brand or sell through social media channels such as Facebook, Pinterest or Instagram. When considering a presence on online marketplaces, you can choose between general marketplaces such as Amazon and Walmart, handmade and craft marketplaces such as Etsy and Craftsy, or auction marketplaces such as eBay and eBid. This gives consumers multiple options to learn more about products or services and purchase them through different sales channels. After successful sales, businesses need to engage with customers to build loyalty and advocacy.

## 2.1 Digital consumer journey

Digital consumers are more confident and demanding than traditional consumers before the dawn of the internet. Many of them are comfortable online because they have been using the internet and other digital technologies for years. When searching, they are fast, efficient and have high expectations (Ryan & Jones, 2012). As such, they are dictating a paradigm shift in marketing that is transforming transactional marketing into relationship-based marketing (Marolt et al., 2022). This means that consumers expect interactions with the brand as they go through different stages on the path to loyalty towards a brand, product or service. This so-called consumer journey is a more detailed representation of the consumer purchase process. The traditional consumer journey has evolved significantly with the development of digital touchpoints (Tueanrat et al., 2021).

*Figure 2: Modern consumer journey (own elaboration based on Kotler & Armstrong (2018) and current trends).*

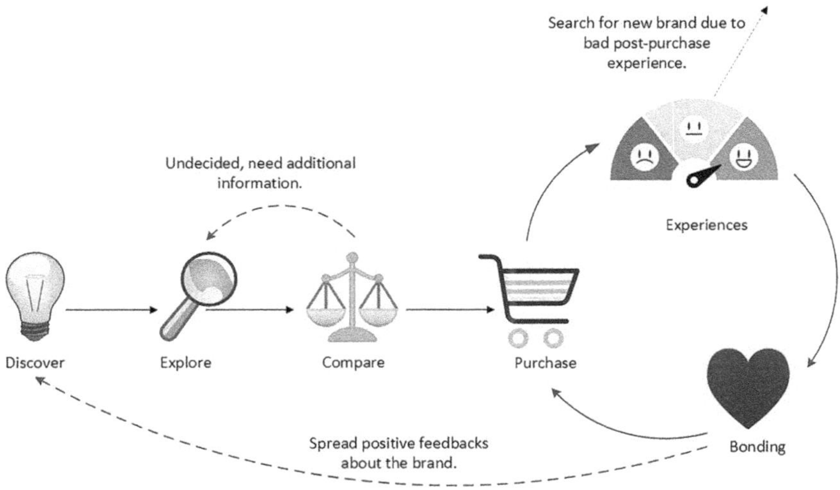


The initial step for consumers is to identify their need for a particular product or service and then gather information from various online sources, including interaction with other consumers, to form an opinion about it. They then compare their opinion with other options available in the market, and if they are unsure, they search online for additional information. Finally, they decide whether they are interested or not. However, mere interest is not enough to turn a potential consumer into a potential buyer. To achieve this, companies need to provide compelling content that demonstrates the value of the product or service they offer. This can be done through various marketing techniques such as advertising, sales promotion, public relations, direct marketing, etc. that demonstrate the benefits and advantages of the product or service (Dabbous & Barakat, 2020). In addition, it is crucial to engage in two-way communication with consumers. This interaction allows businesses to share information and content with consumers, which in turn provides them with valuable insights into consumer behaviour. By gaining a deeper understanding of their target audience, companies can effectively engage consumers to make a final purchase decision and maintain their loyalty after the purchase (Wang, 2021). In addition, good product quality, exceptional service and support show consumers that they are valued, which ultimately leads to stronger loyalty to the brand. Regular proactive engagement with the brand also encourages the development of an emotional connection with consumers, leading to repeat purchases and electronic word of mouth (eWOM) (Gvili & Levy, 2018).

## 2.2 Consumer purchase behaviour

In the digital landscape, consumer behaviour differs from their behaviour in the physical world, making it critical for businesses to understand their purchasing patterns. A comprehensive understanding of consumer purchase behaviour encompasses several characteristics, such as cultural, social, personal and psychological attributes, which companies should consider when interacting with their target audience (Kotler & Armstrong, 2018).

### *2.2.1 Cultural characteristics*

British anthropologist Edward Taylor defined culture as a pattern of behaviour that includes knowledge, beliefs, arts, morals, laws, customs, and all other skills and habits learned by an individual as a member of society and passed on from one generation to the next (Tylor, 1871). There is a close relationship between culture and purchase behaviour, so knowledge of culture is extremely important for marketers. Culture influences the way, place and purpose of the purchase, what criteria consumers consider when shopping, whether they negotiate on price, etc. (Kotler & Armstrong (2018) consider culture as a fundamental determinant of a person's preferences and behaviour. Every culture consists of subcultures that its members accept based on common life experiences and situations. Nationalities, religions, racial groups and geographical regions are considered subcultures. Marketers can consider these subcultures as important market segments. Similarly, marketers also need to consider different social classes, as consumers from the same social class tend to have similar purchasing behaviour (Abdellatif et al., 2018). The main indicators of social class membership are occupation, education and income.

### *2.2.2 Social characteristics*

The family as a group is often the most important factor in decision-making, as family members often make decisions together (Kurdi et al., 2022). Women, in particular, remain the main decision-makers when it comes to household purchases and other daily necessities (Rehman et al., 2020). Husbands and wives make joint decisions, especially when buying durable goods, and children also play an increasingly important role. When shopping together, family members usually take on different roles in the buying process, e.g. brainstorming, gathering information, evaluating alternatives, choosing a brand and finally deciding whether to buy the product. A single person can also take on several roles. Marketers are therefore very interested in understanding the roles of each family member and their interactions during the buying process. Cultural differences have a strong impact on these roles, which is why market-specific research is necessary.

In general, individuals belong to different groups (McKinsey & Company, 2018) with different positions and roles that define their status (Kotler & Armstrong, 2018). Depending on their position and status, individuals may choose products and brands that reflect their identity. For example, high status individuals buy expensive cars to show their social status, which is why CEOs are often associated with luxury cars. Marketers need to consider that certain products and brands can serve as status symbols for certain groups of people.

### *2.2.3 Personal characteristics*

A person's characteristics, such as age, occupation and lifestyle, play an important role in shaping their buying behaviour. As people progress through different stages of life, their needs, attitudes, preferences, tastes and values change, which in turn affects the products and services they buy. Marketers identify groups of people with similar professional interests and offer them appropriate products, such as smartphones and laptops for managers. A person's lifestyle also determines their purchase behaviour, as it influences how they divide their time between work and leisure, as well as their perceptions, needs and desires. To understand the characteristics that drive purchase behaviour, marketers must also consider the influence of a person's unique personality, which makes them unique and distinctive (Kotler & Armstrong, 2018).

### *2.2.4 Psychological characteristics*

To understand consumer behaviour, it is crucial to know how individuals process information and make decisions during the buying process (Furaiji et al., 2012). Unmet needs and motives play a crucial role in all stages of the purchase decision, but are particularly important in the initial stage. Unmet needs drive consumers to actively seek satisfaction. Therefore, a motive can only arise when a need is present and strong enough. A motive can be defined as an inner driving force or reason that drives a person towards a certain goal. For this reason, various theories of human motivation have been developed by psychologists, such as the theories of Maslow, Freud and Herzberg (Kotler & Armstrong, 2018). When consumers make a purchase, they may have several motives in mind, including price, service, location, honesty and friendliness of the salesperson (Furaiji et al., 2012). By understanding which motives are prevalent in consumers' minds and why, marketers can leverage these attributes in their sales strategies to gain a competitive advantage.

To influence consumer behaviour and purchase decisions, marketers need to thoroughly understand the learning process. Learning is the result of information processing, which is closely linked to consumer involvement in the purchase. When involvement is high, information processing occurs consciously; when involvement is low, it occurs unintentionally or even unconsciously. Learning consists of changes in a person's behaviour that result from previous experiences. Theories state that learning is the result of an interplay of drives, stimuli, cues, responses and reinforcement (Kotler & Armstrong, 2018). Marketers could therefore increase demand for their products by linking them to strong stimuli, using cues and reinforcing satisfaction. The results of learning are reflected in consumer knowledge and behaviour change. For learning to be effective, it needs to be stored in long-term memory so that consumers can recall product knowledge when they purchase again.

Individuals have a certain attitude towards almost everything, based on their own experiences and relationships with other people. Consumer attitudes are a major contributor to the success or failure of a product or brand, and marketers strive to maintain or improve positive consumer attitudes toward their brand. Consumers with negative attitudes may stop buying products and spread their negative opinions among family, friends and acquaintances (Bhandari & Rodgers, 2017). Changing attitudes is one of the main goals of marketers, but it is important to understand that changing attitudes that have already been formed can be challenging.

## 3. Methodology

This study draws on previous studies in an attempt to shed light on the differences between individuals in their online purchasing behaviour. More specifically, this study considers online consumers' behaviour before, during and after purchase, focusing on differences in gender, age, status, place of residence, digital literacy, frequency of online purchase, factors that influenced their decision to purchase online, products purchased and time taken to make the online purchase decision.

A quantitative research method was used for data collection. The unit of analysis was an individual aged 15 years or more who has made at least one purchase online. The survey was conducted among Slovenian citizens. As it was not possible to obtain a database of all citizens, the snowball method was used. The data collection period was from May 13 to June 2, 2022. Emails, social media and forums were used for data collection in order to obtain a sufficient number of responses in a relatively short time frame.

The questionnaire used to collect quantitative data was designed based on the relevant literature. The first section of the questionnaire was related to information technology use and related skills, followed by six sections related to consumer purchasing behaviour. The remaining two sections collected data on the respondent. The online questionnaire was created on the 1ka platform and distributed along with a brief introduction to the survey. The data was analysed using Microsoft Excel and IBM SPSS version 28.

A total of 386 responses were received. The data was downloaded from 1ka and cleaned for further analysis. Of the total 386 responses received, 56 were not complete and were therefore excluded. The final number of complete responses was 330. Descriptive analysis was conducted to summarise the sample and identify emerging patterns in the data. The majority of respondents (hereafter referred to as consumers) were female (85%). Consumers were divided into five age groups. As shown in Figure 3, the majority of participants were younger than 50 years and only 6% were older than 66 years. Participants lived in urban areas (50%), suburban areas (26%) and rural areas (24%).

*Figure 3: Respondents by age group.*

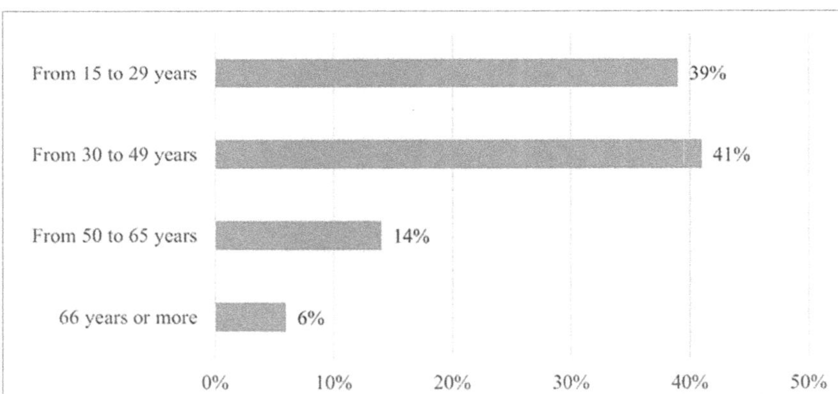


## 4. Findings

The responses of the participating consumers indicated that they use information and communication technology regularly. In particular, a large proportion of respondents reported using a mobile phone (94%), followed by a laptop (78%), a desktop computer (42%) and a tablet (39%). On average, they spend about three hours per day using their mobile phones (M=3.2, S.D.=1.25), while the time spent using desktop computers and laptops is about one and a half hours (M=1.6, S.D.=1.07) and (M=1.5, S.D.=0.92) respectively. The average time spent using a tablet was about one hour. When asked about their digital skills, more than half of the respondents (51%) said they had basic digital skills, while 27% said they had advanced digital skills and 22% said they had low digital skills.

## 4.1 Overview of online purchasing behaviour

The majority of participating consumers (52%) shop online less than once a month, followed by 40% who shop online one to three times a month. As shown in Figure 4, only a small percentage of consumers shop online at least once a week. Interestingly, a higher percentage of men (11%) than women (8%) shop online at least once a week. In addition, 61% of participating consumers reported that they increased their online shopping frequency after the Covid 19 pandemic, while 39% reported that their online shopping habits remained unchanged.

*Figure 4: Online buying frequency.*

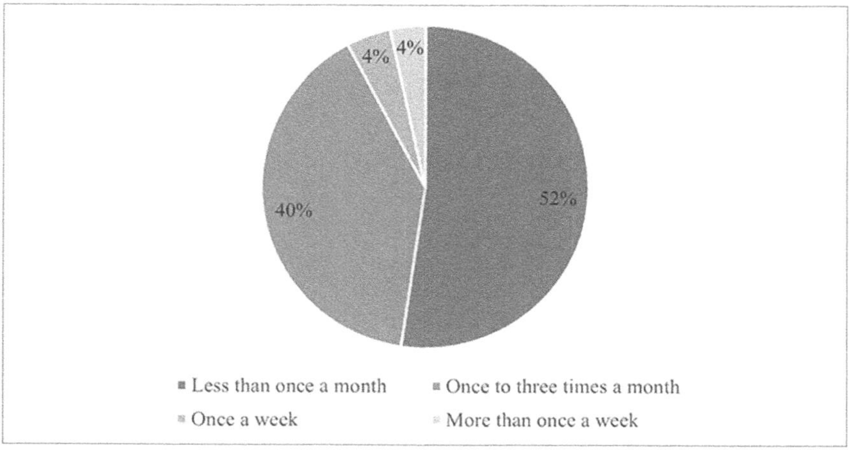


The majority of participating consumers (81%) purchase clothes, shoes and accessories, while cosmetics and beauty products follow closely behind (35%). Other product categories, such as sports equipment, electronic devices, books, food and beverages, children's toys, furniture and home accessories, are less popular among consumers. A detailed analysis by gender and age groups was conducted (see Table 1). Women tend to purchase clothes, shoes and accessories more often than men (85% vs. 67%), while men are more interested in electronic devices (46% vs. 13%). All age groups primarily buy clothes, shoes and accessories, although younger consumers (under 50) are more likely to purchase electronic devices and sports equipment, while older consumers (50 or older) are more likely to buy furniture, home accessories and children's toys.

*Table 1: Purchase of different product categories by gender and age*

| | Gender | | Age | | | |
|---|---|---|---|---|---|---|
| **Product categories** | **Women** | **Men** | **From 15 to 29 years** | **From 30 to 49 years** | **From 50 to 65 years** | **Over 66 years** |
| Clothing, shoes, and accessories | 67% | 85% | 92% | 79% | 67% | 80% |
| Electronic equipment (audio-video, mobile phones, cameras) | 46% | 13% | 19% | 19% | 12% | 0% |
| Sports equipment | 15% | 22% | 20% | 25% | 14% | 0% |
| Furniture and home accessories | 20% | 18% | 12% | 20% | 26% | 30% |
| Children's toys | 11% | 10% | 5% | 12% | 21% | 20% |
| Food and drink | 4% | 10% | 6% | 14% | 10% | 0% |
| Books, CDs, and other physical media | 4% | 14% | 9% | 18% | 7% | 0% |
| Cosmetics, beauty products, relaxation products | 15% | 40% | 38% | 35% | 38% | 10% |

The main factors that influenced participating consumers' decision to buy online were better price (72%), previous buying experience (51%), convenience (50%) and better choice (25%). Better price is the most important factor for both women and men to buy online (70% for women, 80% for men). Women placed more emphasis on previous purchase experience (54% for women and 41% for men), while men placed more emphasis on convenience (67% for men and 49% for women). As shown in Table 2, price was also the most important factor for all age groups. Consumers under 30 placed more value on convenience, while those over 30 placed more value on previous purchasing experience.

*Table 2: Drivers that swayed consumers' decision to buy online by gender and age*

| | Gender | | Age | | | |
|---|---|---|---|---|---|---|
| **Drivers to buy online** | **Women** | **Men** | **From 15 to 29 years** | **From 30 to 49 years** | **From 50 to 65 years** | **Over 66 years** |
| Better price | 70% | 80% | 75% | 71% | 60% | 80% |
| Past purchase experience | 54% | 41% | 50% | 56% | 50% | 50% |
| Convenience | 49% | 67% | 64% | 42% | 45% | 40% |
| Better selection | 26% | 33% | 29% | 27% | 19% | 30% |

Of the participating consumers, 51% spend less than €49 per month on online purchases and 32% spend between €50 and €99. A smaller percentage, 14%, spend between €100 and €199, and even fewer, only 3%, spend between €200 and €499. Only 1% of consumers said they spend more than €500 on purchases. The breakdown by gender and age in Table 3 shows similar results. Further analysis shows that 16% of men under 50 spend at least €200 per month, but only 2% of women in the same age group.

*Table 3: Average monthly amount spent on online purchases by gender and age*

| | Gender | | Age | | | |
|---|---|---|---|---|---|---|
| **Average monthly amount spent on online purchases** | **Women** | **Men** | **From 15 to 29 years** | **From 30 to 49 years** | **From 50 to 65 years** | **Over 66 years** |
| Less than 49€ | 46% | 54% | 50% | 40% | 57% | 60% |
| Between 50 and 99€ | 35% | 30% | 37% | 33% | 29% | 40% |
| Between 100 and 199€ | 19% | 11% | 12% | 25% | 14% | 0% |
| Between 200 and 499€ | 4% | 4% | 3% | 6% | 0% | 0% |
| More than 500€ | 0% | 1% | 0% | 1% | 0% | 0% |

The majority of participating consumers tend to make their purchase decisions quickly, either the same day (40%) or the next day (41%), while only 10% take three to five days and 9% more than five days. Table 4 shows that men are more likely to make impulsive purchase decisions than women, with a higher percentage of men making a purchase decision within two days of going online. In addition, the majority of consumers over 50 years old make their purchase decisions on the same day.

*Table 4: Time needed to make online purchase decisions by gender and age*

| | Gender | | Age | | | |
|---|---|---|---|---|---|---|
| **Needed time to make an online purchase decision** | **Women** | **Men** | **From 15 to 29 years** | **From 30 to 49 years** | **From 50 to 65 years** | **Over 66 years** |
| Same day | 38% | 48% | 47% | 40% | 57% | 70% |
| 1-2 days | 42% | 39% | 49% | 42% | 24% | 20% |
| 3-5 days | 11% | 9% | 10% | 12% | 10% | 10% |
| More than 5 days | 9% | 4% | 10% | 7% | 10% | 0% |

Participating consumers also indicated their preferred payment method. More than half of the consumers (52%) prefer to pay cash on delivery, 42% pay with a credit card, 9% with PayPal and 7% by invoice. As shown in Table 5, women and men have similar preferences when it comes to payment methods. However, consumers over the age of 66 prefer to pay exclusively by cash on delivery or credit card.

*Table 5: Payment methods used by gender and age*

| | Gender | | Age | | | |
|---|---|---|---|---|---|---|
| **Payment method** | **Women** | **Men** | **From 15 to 29 years** | **From 30 to 49 years** | **From 50 to 65 years** | **Over 66 years** |
| Payment on delivery | 50% | 48% | 47% | 48% | 57% | 80% |
| Credit card | 33% | 35% | 38% | 32% | 24% | 20% |
| PayPal | 9% | 11% | 11% | 10% | 7% | 0% |
| Payment by invoice | 7% | 7% | 4% | 9% | 12% | 0% |

## 4.2 Online pre-purchase behaviour

Before making an online purchase, consumers perform various actions. As shown in Figure 5, the majority of participating consumers agree with the statement that they check product information online before buying a product ($\overline{x} = 3.8$), followed by the statements that they compare different prices on several websites before buying a product ($\overline{x} = 3.7$) and check the reviews of other consumers who have already bought the product before buying it ($\overline{x} = 3.7$).

*Figure 5: Average agreement with statements about online pre-purchase behaviour.*

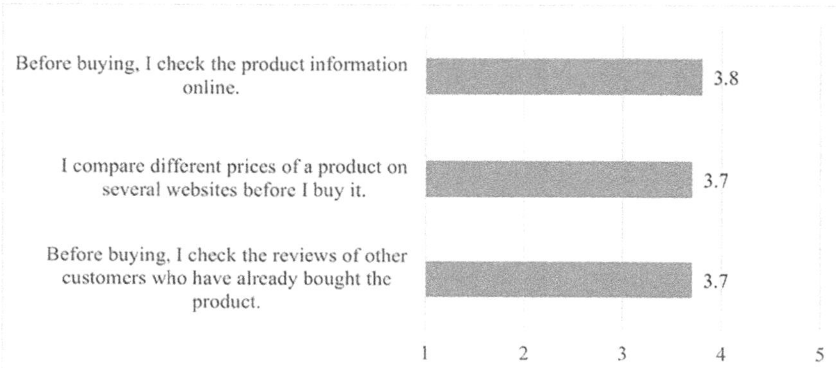


Men are generally more engaged before purchase than women (Table 6), but the statistically significant differences only show up when they check the reviews of other consumers who have already bought the product ($t = 2.356$, $p = 0.002 < 0.05$).

*Table 6: Descriptive statistics and t-test results for online pre-purchase behaviour by gender*

| | Gender | | | | | | t-test | |
|---|---|---|---|---|---|---|---|---|
| | Men | | | Women | | | | |
| | N | Mean | SD | N | Mean | SD | t | p |
| Before buying, I check the product information online. | 46 | 4.02 | 1.256 | 278 | 3.74 | 1.281 | 1.362 | 0.174 |
| I compare different prices of a product on several websites before I buy it. | 46 | 3.61 | 1.273 | 278 | 3.74 | 1.307 | -0.638 | 0.524 |
| Before buying, I check the reviews of other consumers who have already bought the product. | 46 | 4.15 | 1.010 | 278 | 3.65 | 1.371 | 2.356 | 0.002 |

The study found no significant differences in online pre-purchase behaviour between different age groups, consumer status and areas of residence. However, the results suggest that there are significant differences in online pre-purchase behaviours according to on consumers' digital skills. Table 7 shows that there are statistically significant differences in average agreement with all three statements for consumers with different digital skills. The results of the multiple comparison test indicate that there are significant differences between consumers with low digital skills and those with basic and advanced digital skills for all three online pre-purchase activities, while there are no significant differences between those with basic and advanced digital skills.

*Table 7: Descriptive statistics and ANOVA results for online pre-purchase behaviour by digital competencies*

| | Gender | | | | | | t-test | |
|---|---|---|---|---|---|---|---|---|
| | Men | | | Women | | | | |
| | N | Mean | SD | N | Mean | SD | t | p |
| Before buying, I check the product information online. | 46 | 4.02 | 1.256 | 278 | 3.74 | 1.281 | 1.362 | 0.174 |
| I compare different prices of a product on several websites before I buy it. | 46 | 3.61 | 1.273 | 278 | 3.74 | 1.307 | -0.638 | 0.524 |
| Before buying, I check the reviews of other consumers who have already bought the product. | 46 | 4.15 | 1.010 | 278 | 3.65 | 1.371 | 2.356 | 0.002 |

Furthermore, the results show significant differences in online pre-purchase behaviour in terms of the factors that consumers reported as influencing their online purchasing decision. Table 8 shows that consumers who indicated better price as an important factor had significantly higher agreement with the statement to compare prices on different websites before buying ($t = 3.323$, $p = 0.002 < 0.05$). Similarly, Table 9 shows that consumers who indicated previous purchase experience as an important factor had significantly higher agreement with the statement to check product information online before purchase ($t = -2.137$, $p = 0.033 < 0.05$) (Table 9). Finally, Table 10 shows that consumers who indicated "convenience" as an important factor had significantly higher agreement with the statements to check product information online ($t = 2.061$, $p = 0.020 < 0.05$) and to check the reviews of other consumers who have already bought the product ($t = 3.692$, $p = 0.000 < 0.05$).

*Table 8: Descriptive statistics and t-test results for online pre-purchase behaviour of groups of consumers who indicated whether or not the better price was an important factor*

| | Better price | | | | | | t-test | |
|---|---|---|---|---|---|---|---|---|
| | Important | | | Not important | | | | |
| | N | Mean | SD | N | Mean | SD | t | p |
| Before buying, I check the product information online. | 237 | 3.83 | 1.235 | 93 | 3.67 | 1.378 | 1.026 | 0.165 |
| I compare different prices of a product on several websites before I buy it. | 237 | 3.87 | 1.172 | 93 | 3.35 | 1.508 | 3.323 | 0.002 |
| Before buying, I check the reviews of other consumers who have already bought the product. | 237 | 3.76 | 1.339 | 93 | 3.58 | 1.330 | 1.094 | 0.275 |

*Table 9: Descriptive statistics and t-test results for online pre-purchase behaviour of groups of consumers who indicated whether or not past purchase experience was an important factor*

| | Past purchase experience | | | | | | t-test | |
|---|---|---|---|---|---|---|---|---|
| | Important | | | Not important | | | | |
| | N | Mean | SD | N | Mean | SD | t | p |
| Before buying, I check the product information online. | 88 | 3.53 | 1.231 | 242 | 3.87 | 0.083 | -2.137 | 0.033 |
| I compare different prices of a product on several websites before I buy it. | 88 | 3.56 | 1.258 | 242 | 3.79 | 0.084 | -1.445 | 0.150 |
| Before buying, I check the reviews of other consumers who have already bought the product. | 88 | 3.67 | 1.328 | 242 | 3.72 | 0.086 | -0.316 | 0.752 |

In addition, the results show that there are differences in online pre-purchase behaviour between consumers who have purchased a particular product and those who have not, but only for certain product categories such as electronic devices (audio-video, mobile phones, cameras), sports equipment and food and beverages. Specifically, consumers who purchase electronic devices or food and beverages are more likely to check the reviews of other consumers who have already purchased the product before making a purchase (($t = 2.175$, $p = 0.016 < 0.05$) and ($t = 2.826$, $p = 0.003 < 0.05$) respectively) (Table 11 and Table 13). In addition, consumers who buy sports equipment tend to check product information online before purchasing ($t = 2.034$, $p = 0.022 < 0.05$) (Table 12).

*Table 10: Descriptive statistics and t-test results for online pre-purchase behaviour of groups of consumers who indicated whether or not convenience was an important factor*

| | Convenience | | | | | | | |
|---|---|---|---|---|---|---|---|---|
| | Important | | | Not important | | | t-test | |
| | N | Mean | SD | N | Mean | SD | t | p |
| Before buying, I check the product information online. | 169 | 3.92 | 1.165 | 161 | 3.63 | 1.372 | 2.061 | 0.020 |
| I compare different prices of a product on several websites before I buy it. | 169 | 3.84 | 1.207 | 161 | 3.61 | 1.375 | 1.623 | 0.053 |
| Before buying, I check the reviews of other consumers who have already bought the product. | 169 | 3.97 | 1.197 | 161 | 3.43 | 1.422 | 3.692 | 0.000 |

*Table 11: Descriptive statistics and t-test results for online pre-purchase behaviour of groups of consumers who indicated whether or not they had bought electronic equipment*

| | Buy electronic equipment | | | | | | | |
|---|---|---|---|---|---|---|---|---|
| | Yes | | | No | | | t-test | |
| | N | Mean | SD | N | Mean | SD | t | p |
| Before buying, I check the product information online. | 58 | 3.93 | 1.183 | 272 | 3.75 | 1.296 | 0.980 | 0.328 |
| I compare different prices of a product on several websites before I buy it. | 58 | 3.79 | 1.120 | 272 | 3.71 | 1.330 | 0.426 | 0.670 |
| Before buying, I check the reviews of other consumers who have already bought the product. | 58 | 4.02 | 1.147 | 272 | 3.64 | 1.367 | 2.175 | 0.016 |

It is worth noting that the study found no statistically significant differences in online pre-purchase behaviour in terms of frequency of online purchases and time spent on purchase decisions.

## 4.3 Online behaviour during purchase

Figure 6 illustrates the different steps of the online purchase process. The data show that consumers strongly agree with the statement that they can easily enter all the information required to complete their order ($\overline{x} = 4.3$) and that they agree with the statements that they have no problems processing their shopping cart

*Table 12: Descriptive statistics and t-test results for online pre-purchase behaviour of groups of consumers who indicated whether or not they had bought sports equipment*

| | Buy sports equipment | | | | | | t-test | |
|---|---|---|---|---|---|---|---|---|
| | Yes | | | No | | | | |
| | N | Mean | SD | N | Mean | SD | t | p |
| Before buying, I check the product information online. | 68 | 4.04 | 1.165 | 262 | 3.71 | 1.298 | 2.034 | 0.022 |
| I compare different prices of a product on several websites before I buy it. | 68 | 3.71 | 1.328 | 262 | 3.73 | 1.288 | -0.153 | 0.879 |
| Before buying, I check the reviews of other consumers who have already bought the product. | 68 | 3.87 | 1.348 | 262 | 3.67 | 1.333 | 1.098 | 0.273 |

*Table 13: Descriptive statistics and t-test results for online pre-purchase behaviour of groups of consumers who indicated whether or not they had bought food and drinks*

| | Buy food and drink | | | | | | t-test | |
|---|---|---|---|---|---|---|---|---|
| | Yes | | | No | | | | |
| | N | Mean | SD | N | Mean | SD | t | p |
| Before buying, I check the product information online. | 32 | 3.81 | 1.230 | 298 | 3.78 | 1.284 | 0.143 | 0.887 |
| I compare different prices of a product on several websites before I buy it. | 32 | 3.78 | 1.128 | 298 | 3.72 | 1.313 | 0.248 | 0.804 |
| Before buying, I check the reviews of other consumers who have already bought the product. | 32 | 4.16 | 0.884 | 298 | 3.66 | 1.369 | 2.826 | 0.003 |

($\overline{x} = 4.1$), verifying the legitimacy of the website where they want to buy the product they have selected ($\overline{x} = 3.9$), and that shipping costs might prevent them from buying the product they want ($\overline{x} = 3.8$).

Women are more assertive when it comes to actually buying (Table 14), although there are statistically significant differences only when shipping costs might deter them from buying the desired product ($t = -1.087$, $p = 0.048 < 0.05$).

The study found no significant differences in online purchasing behaviour between different age groups and consumer status. However, significant differences in online pre-purchase behaviour were found among consumers with different digital competencies. Since the assumption of homogeneity of variances

*Figure 6: Average agreement with statements about online behaviour during purchase.*

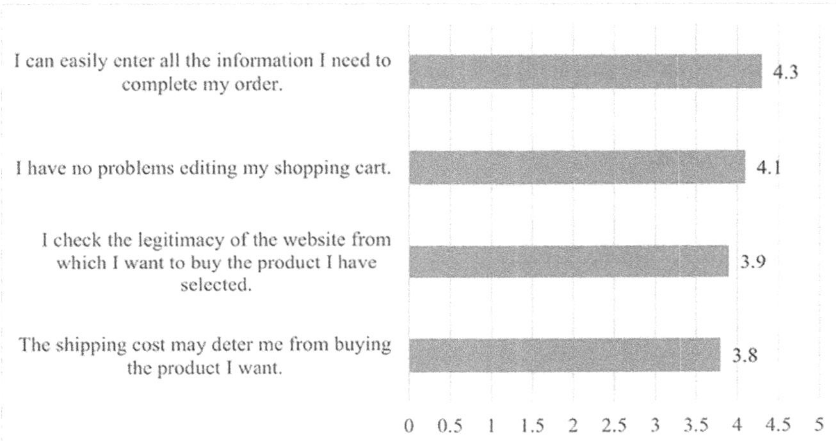


*Table 14: Descriptive statistics and t-test results for online behaviour during purchase by gender*

| | Gender | | | | | | t-test | |
|---|---|---|---|---|---|---|---|---|
| | Men | | | Women | | | | |
| | N | Mean | SD | N | Mean | SD | t | p |
| I have no problems editing my shopping cart. | 46 | 4.20 | 0.910 | 277 | 4.27 | 1.126 | -0.409 | 0.683 |
| I can easily enter all the information I need to complete my order. | 46 | 4.59 | 0.686 | 276 | 4.39 | 1.019 | 1.685 | 0.278 |
| The shipping cost may deter me from buying the product I want. | 46 | 3.67 | 1.506 | 276 | 3.91 | 1.309 | -1.087 | 0.048 |
| I check the legitimacy of the website from which I want to buy the product I have selected. | 46 | 3.98 | 1.164 | 275 | 3.99 | 1.225 | -0.056 | 0.955 |

was violated, Welch and Brown-Forsythe's tests were used to assess three online activities during the purchase process. As shown in Table 15, for one online activity where homogeneity of variance was not violated, there were no statistically significant differences between levels of digital literacy. However, significant differences were found for the other three activities. The multiple comparison test showed that consumers with low levels of digital literacy differed significantly from those with basic and advanced digital literacy when it came to processing their shopping cart and entering all the information required to complete an order. In addition, there were statistically significant differences between consumers with basic and advanced digital skills in terms of checking the legitimacy of the website.

*Table 15: Descriptive statistics and ANOVA results of online behaviour during the purchase by digital competencies*

| | Digital competencies | N | Mean | SD | Test | F | p |
|---|---|---|---|---|---|---|---|
| I have no problems editing my shopping cart. | Low digital skills | 56 | 4.02 | 1.136 | Welch | 5.304 | 0.006 |
| | Basic digital skills | 176 | 4.17 | 1.149 | Brown-Forsythe | 4.719 | 0.010 |
| | Advanced digital skills | 95 | 4.52 | 0.932 | | | |
| I can easily enter all the information I need to complete my order. | Low digital skills | 56 | 4.09 | 1.116 | Welch | 5.515 | 0.005 |
| | Basic digital skills | 176 | 4.40 | 0.998 | Brown-Forsythe | 5.295 | 0.006 |
| | Advanced digital skills | 94 | 4.63 | 0.790 | | | |
| The shipping cost may deter me from buying the product I want. | Low digital skills | 56 | 3.82 | 1.478 | ANOVA | 0.171 | 0.843 |
| | Basic digital skills | 175 | 3.85 | 1.287 | | | |
| | Advanced digital skills | 95 | 3.94 | 1.359 | | | |
| I check the legitimacy of the website from which I want to buy the product I have selected. | Low digital skills | 56 | 3.55 | 1.451 | Welch | 3.171 | 0.045 |
| | Basic digital skills | 175 | 4.08 | 1.090 | Brown-Forsythe | 3.710 | 0.027 |
| | Advanced digital skills | 94 | 4.05 | 1.221 | | | |

In addition, statistically significant differences were found between consumers with different online purchase frequencies. Welch and Brown-Forsythe's tests were conducted for three online activities during purchase, as the assumption of homogeneity of variances was violated. As can be seen in Table 16, for the one online activity where homogeneity of variance was not violated, there are also no statistically significant differences between online purchase frequencies, while for the other three Welch's and Brown-Forsythe tests showed significant differences between online purchase frequencies. The results of the multiple comparison test show that there are statistically significant differences in average agreement with all three statements between consumers who shop online less than once a month and consumers who shop online once a week.

*Table 16: Descriptive statistics and ANOVA results for online behaviour during the purchase by buying frequencies*

| | Online buying frequency | N | Mean | SD | Test | F | p |
|---|---|---|---|---|---|---|---|
| I have no problems editing my shopping cart. | Less than once a month | 171 | 4.08 | 1.163 | Welch | 3.939 | 0.017 |
| | Once to three times a month | 131 | 4.39 | 1.004 | Brown-Forsythe | 3.677 | 0.019 |
| | Once a week | 14 | 4.71 | 0.726 | | | |
| | More than once a week | 11 | 4.55 | 1.214 | | | |
| I can easily enter all the information I need to complete my order. | Less than once a month | 171 | 4.23 | 1.112 | Welch | 6.126 | 0.002 |
| | Once to three times a month | 130 | 4.61 | 0.731 | Brown-Forsythe | 4.720 | 0.009 |
| | Once a week | 14 | 4.79 | 0.426 | | | |
| | More than once a week | 11 | 4.45 | 1.293 | | | |
| The shipping cost may deter me from buying the product I want. | Less than once a month | 171 | 4.23 | 1.112 | ANOVA | 0.525 | 0.665 |
| | Once to three times a month | 130 | 4.61 | 0.731 | | | |
| | Once a week | 14 | 4.79 | 0.426 | | | |
| | More than once a week | 11 | 4.45 | 1.293 | | | |
| I check the legitimacy of the website from which I want to buy the product I have selected. | Less than once a month | 170 | 3.81 | 1.273 | Welch | 3.785 | 0.020 |
| | Once to three times a month | 130 | 4.12 | 1.125 | Brown-Forsythe | 3.420 | 0.025 |
| | Once a week | 14 | 4.50 | 0.760 | | | |
| | More than once a week | 11 | 4.36 | 1.286 | | | |

## 4.4 Online post-purchase behaviour

Consumers perform various activities after purchase, such as returning the product or giving a positive review. Figure 7 shows that consumers generally agree with the statement that they return unsuitable products ($\overline{x} = 4.1$), while their agreement with the statement that they share information about their purchase online is neutral ($\overline{x} = 2.8$).

*Figure 7: Average agreement with statements about online post-purchase behaviour.*

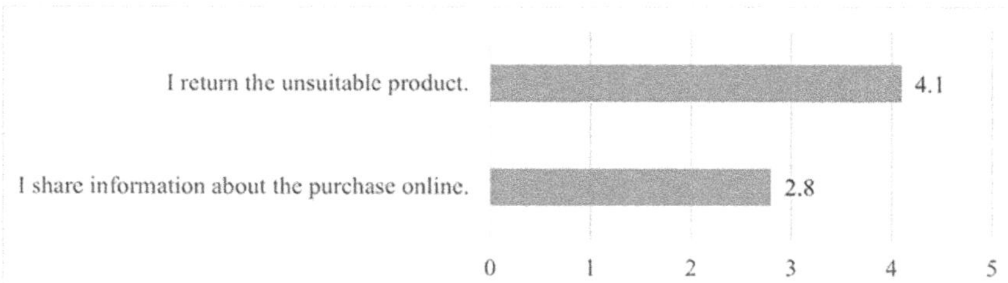


Women are more likely to share information about the purchase online (Table 14), while men are more likely to return the unsuitable product. Statistically significant differences were found for the latter statement ($t = 2.410$, $p = 0.009 < 0.05$).

*Table 17: Descriptive statistics and t-test results for online post-purchase behaviour by gender*

| | Gender | | | | | | | |
|---|---|---|---|---|---|---|---|---|
| | Men | | | Women | | | t-test | |
| | N | Mean | SD | N | Mean | SD | t | p |
| I return the unsuitable product. | 46 | 4.41 | 0.909 | 276 | 4.04 | 1.245 | 2.410 | 0.009 |
| I share information about the purchase online. | 46 | 3.02 | 1.358 | 276 | 2.78 | 1.444 | 1.061 | 0.289 |

Again, there were no statistically significant differences in online post-purchase behaviour across age groups and consumer status. However, there were significant differences in online post-purchase behaviour between consumers who consider convenience an important factor in their decision-making process and those who do not. Table 18 shows that there were statistically significant differences between these two consumer groups in terms of returning unsuitable products ($t = 3.696$, $p = 0.000 < 0.05$).

*Table 18: Descriptive statistics and t-test results for online post-purchase behaviour of groups of consumers who indicated whether or not convenience is an important factor*

| | Convenience | | | | | | | |
|---|---|---|---|---|---|---|---|---|
| | Important | | | Not important | | | t-test | |
| | N | Mean | SD | N | Mean | SD | t | p |
| I return the unsuitable product. | 166 | 4.33 | 1.035 | 158 | 3.84 | 1.324 | 3.696 | 0.000 |
| I share information about the purchase online. | 166 | 2.93 | 1.457 | 158 | 2.70 | 1.399 | 1.495 | 0.136 |

Furthermore, the results show differences in online post-purchase behaviour between consumers who have purchased a particular product and those who have not. Statistically significant differences are only observed for two product groups, namely children's toys and food and beverages. Consumers who bought these products online differed significantly from those who did not buy these products online in terms of sharing purchase information (($t = 2.517$, $p = 0.008 < 0.05$) and ($t = 1.944$, $p = 0.049 < 0.05$) respectively) (Tables 19 and 20).

*Table 19: Descriptive statistics and t-test results for online post-purchase behaviour of groups of consumers who indicated whether or not they had bought children's toys*

| | Buy children toys | | | | | | | |
|---|---|---|---|---|---|---|---|---|
| | Yes | | | No | | | t-test | |
| | N | Mean | SD | N | Mean | SD | t | p |
| I return the unsuitable product. | 34 | 4.03 | 1.314 | 290 | 4.10 | 1.197 | -0.322 | 0.748 |
| I share information about the purchase online. | 34 | 3.41 | 1.459 | 290 | 2.75 | 1.415 | 2.517 | 0.008 |

*Table 20: Descriptive statistics and t-test results for online post-purchase behaviour in groups of consumers buying food and drink or not*

| | Buy food and drink | | | | | | | |
|---|---|---|---|---|---|---|---|---|
| | Yes | | | No | | | t-test | |
| | N | Mean | SD | N | Mean | SD | t | p |
| I return the unsuitable product. | 30 | 3.83 | 1.234 | 294 | 4.12 | 1.204 | -1.235 | 0.218 |
| I share information about the purchase online. | 30 | 3.30 | 1.489 | 294 | 2.77 | 1.419 | 1.944 | 0.049 |

Interestingly, there are no statistically significant differences in online post-purchase behaviour in terms of age, online purchasing frequency and digital literacy.

## 5. Discussion and conclusion

The buying behaviour of individuals is influenced by various characteristics. The combination of these characteristics determines the purchase behaviour and decision. By recognising and understanding these characteristics, brands can develop a more effective strategy that meets the needs of their consumers and leads to higher sales. While the results presented here are not comprehensive, they do highlight the differences in online consumer behaviour among Slovenian consumers.

The results of our study show that slightly less than half of Slovenian consumers shop online at least once a month. The majority of them mainly buy clothes, shoes and accessories and spend less than 100€ per month on online purchases. Moreover, they make their purchase decisions on the same or the next day and usually pay either on delivery or by credit card. Statistically significant differences in consumers' online behaviour before, during and after purchase were found for gender, digital literacy, common factors that influenced consumers' decision to buy online (price, better choice, convenience and previous experience), the products they buy online and frequency of online purchase. Surprisingly, no statistically significant differences were found for age and status, although there are more and more older people who have different needs than younger people. Moreover, young people start a family later and live alone until then (Sheth, 2020).

Consumer online purchase behaviour is a very complex process and it is almost impossible to predict how consumers will behave in a given situation. In the future, consumer online behaviour can be expected to be influenced to a large extent by the policies of individual countries and the European Union. We can only hope that these policies will encourage rather than inhibit consumption, as this can have a major impact on economic development. The development of digital technology will certainly also have an important influence on consumer behaviour. Today we cannot imagine life without mobile phones, the internet is as important as electricity and more important than television. This has implications for the development of new habits such as online information search, online shopping and information exchange. It is also expected that individuals will continue to change their habits. While family members used to spend a lot of time together, many families now have the habit of retreating to their private spaces after having lunch or dinner together and instead spend their time on social media, watching TV, playing games, etc. It can be said that collective consumption is decreasing and individual consumption is coming to the fore, tailored to each family member individually (Sheth, 2020).

Customer experience is becoming an important brand differentiator. Therefore, businesses need to invest in customer experience as customers have more decision-making power than ever before. Businesses are already undertaking many activities to improve the customer experience, but more than 70% of businesses are encountering difficulties (Gartner, 2019). In particular, they are finding it difficult to deliver personalised messages to consumers because they are underutilising their customer data. Businesses have large amounts of data stored in back-office systems, but they can extract even more data from social media and other digital media. However, some data analysis techniques still need to be developed. For example, natural language processing has already been developed, but analysing video content will require similar advances. Machine learning and artificial intelligence will play a key role in these areas and will have a significant impact on enhancing the customer experience through personalization, automation, and data-driven insights (Ameen et al., 2021; Calvo et al., 2023; Chen et al., 2021).

To keep pace with rapid changes in digital technologies, social trends, and consumer experiences, businesses need to adopt new approaches to monitor consumer behaviour and provide better experiences. Businesses need to effectively integrate these new approaches into their processes, considering secondary sources such as employees who can provide additional insights and explain consumer behaviour. In this way, businesses can quickly adapt to changes in consumer behaviour, improve the customer experience and remain competitive even in turbulent times (Gartner, 2021).

## Acknowledgments

The data analysed in this publication were collected by Viktorija Đukić, who carried out the research under my supervision and gave permission for further analysis.

## Bibliography

Abdellatif, M., Auf, A., Meddour, H., Saoula, O., Halim, A., & Majid, A. (2018). Consumer buying behaviour: the roles of price, motivation, perceived culture importance, and religious orientation. *A Journal of the Academy of Business and Retail Management*, *12*(4), 177–187. www.jbrmr.com

Accenture. (April 28, 2020). *COVID-19: Impact on Consumer Behavior Trends*. https://www.accenture.com/us-en/insights/consumer-goods-services/coronavirus-consumer-behavior-research

Ameen, N., Tarhini, A., Reppel, A., & Anand, A. (2021). Customer experiences in the age of artificial intelligence. *Computers in Human Behavior*, *114*, 106548. https://doi.org/10.1016/j.chb.2020.106548

Ampountolas, A., Shaw, G., & James, S. (2019). The role of social media as a distribution channel for promoting pricing strategies. *Journal of Hospitality and Tourism Insights*, *2*(1), 75–91. https://doi.org/10.1108/JHTI-07-2018-0040/FULL/PDF

Bhandari, M., & Rodgers, S. (2017). What does the brand say? Effects of brand feedback to negative eWOM on brand trust and purchase intentions, *37*(1), 125–141. https://doi.org/10.1080/02650487.2017.1349030

Bravo, R., Segura, M. G., Temowo, O., & Samaddar, S. (2022). How Does a Pandemic Disrupt the Benefits of eCommerce? A Case Study of Small and Medium Enterprises in the US. *Journal of Theoretical and Applied Electronic Commerce Research 2022, Vol. 17, Pages 522–557*, *17*(2), 522–557. https://doi.org/10.3390/JTAER17020028

Calvo, A. V., Franco, A. D., & Frasquet, M. (2023). The role of artificial intelligence in improving the omnichannel customer experience. *International Journal of Retail & Distribution Management*, *51*(9/10), 1174–1194. https://doi.org/10.1108/IJRDM-12-2022-0493

Casaló, L. v., Flavián, C., & Ibáñez-Sánchez, S. (2020). Influencers on Instagram: Antecedents and consequences of opinion leadership. *Journal of Business Research*, *117*, 510–519. https://doi.org/10.1016/J.JBUSRES.2018.07.005

Chen, J.-S., Le, T.-T.-Y., & Florence, D. (2021). Usability and responsiveness of artificial intelligence chatbot on online customer experience in e-retailing. *International Journal of Retail & Distribution Management*, *49*(11), 1512–1531. https://doi.org/10.1108/IJRDM-08-2020-0312

Dabbous, A., & Barakat, K. A. (2020). Bridging the online offline gap: Assessing the impact of brands' social network content quality on brand awareness and purchase intention. *Journal of Retailing and Consumer Services*, *53*, 101966. https://doi.org/10.1016/J.JRETCONSER.2019.101966

Djakasaputra, A., Wijaya, O. Y. A., Utama, A. S., Yohana, C., Romadhoni, B., & Fahlevi, M. (2021). Empirical study of indonesian SMEs sales performance in digital era: The role of quality service and digital marketing. *International Journal of Data and Network Science*, *5*(3), 303–310. https://doi.org/10.5267/J.IJDNS.2021.6.003

Donthu, N., & Gustafsson, A. (2020). Effects of COVID-19 on business and research. *Journal of Business Research*, *117*, 284–289. https://doi.org/10.1016/J.JBUSRES.2020.06.008

Dzyabura, D., & Jagabathula, S. (2017). Offline Assortment Optimization in the Presence of an Online Channel, *64*(6), 2767–2786. https://doi.org/10.1287/MNSC.2016.2708

Eger, L., Komárková, L., Egerová, D., & Mičík, M. (2021). The effect of COVID-19 on consumer shopping behaviour: Generational cohort perspective. *Journal of Retailing and Consumer Services, 61*, 102542. https://doi.org/10.1016/J.JRETCONSER.2021.102542

Furaiji, F., Łatuszyńska, M., & Wawrzyniak, A. (2012). An Empirical Study of the Factors Influencing Consumer Behaviour in the Electric Appliances Market. *Journal of Consumer Research, 18*(2), 251. https://doi.org/10.1086/209257

Gartner. (2019). *Creating a High-Impact Customer Experience Strategy*. https://www.gartner.com/en/marketing/research/creating-a-high-impact-customer-experience-strategy

Gartner. (2021). *How Marketing Can Better Respond to Customer Needs*. https://www.gartner.com/en/marketing/insights/articles/how-marketing-can-better-sense-respond-to-customer-needs

Gvili, Y., & Levy, S. (2018). Consumer engagement with eWOM on social media: the role of social capital. *Online Information Review, 42*(4), 482–505. https://doi.org/10.1108/OIR-05-2017-0158/FULL/PDF

Hopper, D. (2022). *How a Marketing and Sales Funnel Works to Attract and Convert More Customers*. https://www.business2community.com/sales-management/how-a-marketing-and-sales-funnel-works-to-attract-and-convert-more-customers-02313179

Kato, T. (2021). Functional value vs emotional value: A comparative study of the values that contribute to a preference for a corporate brand. *International Journal of Information Management Data Insights, 1*(2), 100024. https://doi.org/10.1016/J.JJIMEI.2021.100024

Kotler, P., & Armstrong, G. (2018). *Principles of Marketing* (17th global edition). Pearson.

Kurdi, B. al, Alshurideh, M., Akour, I., Alzoubi, H. M., Obeidat, B., & Alhamad, A. (2022). The role of digital marketing channels on consumer buying decisions through eWOM in the Jordanian markets. *International Journal of Data and Network Science, 6*(4), 1175–1185. https://doi.org/10.5267/J.IJDNS.2022.7.002

Marolt, M., Zimmermann, H.-D., & Pucihar, A. (2018). Exploratory study of social CRM use in SMEs. *Engineering Economics, 29*(4). https://doi.org/10.5755/j01.ee.29.4.20246

Marolt, M., Zimmermann, H.-D., & Pucihar, A. (2020). Enhancing marketing performance through enterprise-initiated customer engagement. *Sustainability (Switzerland), 12*(9). https://doi.org/10.3390/su12093931

Marolt, M., Zimmermann, H.-D., & Pucihar, A. (2022). Social Media Use and Business Performance in SMEs: The Mediating Roles of Relational Social

Commerce Capability and Competitive Advantage. *Sustainability 2022, Vol. 14, Page 15029*, *14*(22), 15029. https://doi.org/10.3390/SU142215029

McKinsey & Company. (2018). *'True Gen': Generation Z and its implications for companies*. http://www.drthomaswu.com/uicmpaccsmac/Gen%20Z.pdf

McKinsey & Company. (October 26, 2020). *Consumer sentiment is diverging across countries | McKinsey*. https://www.mckinsey.com/business-functions/marketing-and-sales/our-insights/a-global-view-of-how-consumer-behavior-is-changing-amid-covid-19#

Pantano, E., Pizzi, G., Scarpi, D., & Dennis, C. (2020). Competing during a pandemic? Retailers' ups and downs during the COVID-19 outbreak. *Journal of Business Research*, *116*, 209–213. https://doi.org/10.1016/J.JBUSRES.2020.05.036

Peter, M. K., & Dalla Vecchia, M. (2021). The Digital Marketing Toolkit: A Literature Review for the Identification of Digital Marketing Channels and Platforms. *Studies in Systems, Decision and Control*, *294*, 251–265. https://doi.org/10.1007/978-3-030-48332-6_17/COVER

Rasool, A., Shah, F. A., & Islam, J. U. (2020). Customer engagement in the digital age: a review and research agenda. *Current Opinion in Psychology*, *36*, 96–100. https://doi.org/10.1016/J.COPSYC.2020.05.003

Rehman, H., Moazzam, Dr. A., & Ansari, N. (2020). Role of Microfinance Institutions in Women Empowerment: A Case Study of Akhuwat, Pakistan. *South Asian Studies*, *30*(1). http://journals.pu.edu.pk/journals/index.php/IJSAS/article/view/2987

Richardson, A. (2010). *Using Customer Journey Maps to Improve Customer Experience*. Harvard Bus. Rev. https://hbr.org/2010/11/using-customer-journey-maps-to

Ryan, D., & Jones, C. (2012). *Understanding digital marketing: marketing strategies for engaging the digital generation* (2nd ed.). Philadelphia, PA, Kogan Page.

Sheth, J. (2020). Impact of Covid-19 on consumer behavior: Will the old habits return or die? *Journal of Business Research*, *117*, 280–283. https://doi.org/10.1016/J.JBUSRES.2020.05.059

Tueanrat, Y., Papagiannidis, S., & Alamanos, E. (2021). Going on a journey: A review of the customer journey literature. *Journal of Business Research*, *125*, 336–353. https://doi.org/10.1016/J.JBUSRES.2020.12.028

Tylor, E. B. (1871). *Primitive culture: Researches into the development of mythology, philosophy, religion, art and custom* (Vol. 2). J. Murray.

Voramontri, D., Klieb, L., Voramontri, D., & Klieb, L. (2019). Impact of social media on consumer behaviour. *International Journal of Information and Decision Sciences*, *11*(3), 209–233. https://EconPapers.repec.org/RePEc:ids:ijidsc:v:11:y:2019:i:3:p:209-233

Wang, C. L. (2021). New frontiers and future directions in interactive marketing: Inaugural Editorial. *Journal of Research in Interactive Marketing, 15*(1), 1–9. https://doi.org/10.1108/JRIM-03-2021-270/FULL/PDF

Yuen, K. F., Wang, X., Ma, F., & Li, K. X. (2020). The Psychological Causes of Panic Buying Following a Health Crisis. *International Journal of Environmental Research and Public Health, 17*(10), E3513–E3513. https://doi.org/10.3390/IJERPH17103513

Zhao, H., Yao, X., Liu, Z., & Yang, Q. (2021). Impact of Pricing and Product Information on Consumer Buying Behavior With Customer Satisfaction in a Mediating Role. *Frontiers in Psychology, 12*. https://doi.org/10.3389/FPSYG.2021.720151

Alenka Brezavšček* and Doroteja Vidmar**

# Recent changes in the ISO 27000 series of information security standards

**Abstract:** The ISO 27000 series of standards represents the most comprehensive set of standards in the field of information security. Their advantage is their general applicability, as they can be implemented quickly and efficiently in any organization, regardless of its sector or size. The ISO 27000 series provides organizations with a practical and established framework for information security assessment and certification. Compliance with ISO 27000 mitigates risks associated with cyber threats and data breaches, preserving the availability, integrity and confidentiality of digital assets. Therefore, ISO 27001 certification is very important for digital transformation in organizations since it ensures robust information security practices, enhances trust among stakeholders, customers, and partners, facilitating smoother adoption of digital technologies. As a result, the use of these standards in practice is widespread globally. In 2022, the ISO 27000 series underwent significant changes, with two of the most important standards receiving new editions. A new edition of ISO/IEC 27002 was published in February 2022, and ISO/IEC 27001 in October 2022. The revisions are very important for organizations implementing the requirements of the standards as part of information security management. In this paper, we provide a comprehensive and detailed overview of the changes introduced by the 2022 editions of ISO/IEC 27001 and ISO/IEC 27002 compared to the 2013 editions. We found that most of the changes were made to ISO/IEC 27002, which required a completely new structure for the "Annex A" of the ISO/IEC 27001. We have summarized the impact of these changes on organizations applying these standards in their business operations and certification, as well as on other standards in the ISO 27000 series.

**Keywords:** Information security, Standards, ISO 27000 Series, Changes, Transition, Digital business transformation

## 1. Introduction

The ISO 27000 series of standards (also known as the ISO27K) represents the most comprehensive set of standards in the field of information security (OGCIO, 2022). Its main advantage is its general applicability, as the standards can be implemented

---

* University of Maribor, Faculty of organizational sciences, Kranj, Slovenia; e-mail: alenka.brezavscek@um.si

** University of Maribor, Faculty of organizational sciences, Kranj, Slovenia; e-mail: doroteja.vidmar@um.si

quickly and efficiently in a wide range of organizations, regardless of their industry sector or size. In addition, the ISO 27000 series of standards provides organizations with a useful and established framework for information security compliance assessment and subsequent certification. ISO 27001 certification is crucial for digital transformation in organizations because it ensures robust information security practices, safeguarding sensitive data and systems. It enhances trust among stakeholders, customers, and partners, facilitating smoother adoption of digital technologies. Compliance with ISO 27001 mitigates risks associated with cyber threats and data breaches, preserving the integrity and confidentiality of digital assets. Additionally, it provides a structured framework for continuous improvement, aligning security measures with evolving digital landscapes and regulatory requirements. For all these reasons, these standards are widely used in practice both worldwide and in Slovenia.[1] According to the latest survey from ISO,[2] the total number of valid ISO/IEC 27001:2013 certificates has exceeded 58.000 in 2021 and is up 19% from 2020.

In 2022, the ISO 27000 series of standards underwent significant changes, with two of the most important standards from the series receiving new editions.[3] In February, a new edition of ISO/IEC 27002 called "*ISO/IEC 27002:2022, Information security, cybersecurity, and privacy protection - Information security controls*" (ISO, 2022b) was published, and in October, a new edition of ISO/IEC 27001 called "*ISO/IEC 27001:2022, Information security, cybersecurity, and privacy protection - Information security management systems - Requirements*" (ISO, 2022a) was issued. The revision of both standards is of key importance to all organizations that rely on the provisions of these standards for their information security management. The organizations that have already certified their compliance with the previous edition of the standard, as well as the organizations that are implementing the standards more informally and may only be considering certification, will need to consider the changes in their operations in the near future.

The main objective of this paper is to provide a comprehensive and detailed overview of the changes introduced by the new editions of ISO/IEC 27001

---

1 In Slovenia, the English versions of the standards are used under the denotation SIST EN ISO/IEC 27001:2022 and SIST EN ISO/IEC 27002:2022. The denotation SIST means that the standard has been adopted in the Republic of Slovenia, while the denotation EN means that the standard has also been adopted by the European Union.

2 https://www.iso.org/the-iso-survey.html

3 Every ISO standard is subject to review every five years. Starting in Mar 2018, the ISO JTC1/SC27 proposed to update the standard, taking into account evolvement of new technologies, emerging risks, and the changing industrial practices.

(ISO, 2022a) and 27002 (ISO, 2022b) compared to the previous editions from 2013 (ISO, 2013a, 2013b). We will systematically present both major and minor changes in both standards. Under major changes, we classify controls that were newly added in the latest editions, as well as controls that represent a merger of existing controls. Minor changes include more "cosmetic" corrections such as renaming and/or renumbering of existing controls. The results of the paper will be of great help to all organizations applying the ISO 27000 series of standards, either in a formal way with a certificate of compliance or in an informal way as a code of good practice. Guidance is provided on how and in what time frame organizations should approach the transition process.

## 2. Preliminaries

### 2.1 ISO 27000 series of standards

ISO 27000 series is developed and published by the International Organization for Standardization - ISO,[4] and the International Electrotechnical Commission - IEC.[5] It is a set of international standards that provides guidelines and best practices for managing information risks by implementing security controls within the framework of an overall Information Security Management System (ISMS) which is a systematic approach to managing sensitive information and ensuring its confidentiality, integrity, and availability (see e.g., (Niemann, 2021)). The ISO 27000 series has established itself as the most prominent international standard adopted by enterprises (Meriah & Rabai, 2019) to help organizations establish, implement, maintain, and continually improve an effective ISMS.

The standards of the ISO 27000 series are divided into four main parts: vocabulary and overview, requirements, general guidelines, and sector-specific guidelines. An overview of the essential parts of the ISO 27000 series is presented in Table 1, while the complete list of standards in the ISO 27000 series, already published and adopted by organizations, can be found on the website https://www.isms.online/iso-27000/#published-iso-27000-standards.

ISO/IEC 27001 and 27002 are certainly among the most important standards in the series, so we will focus on the latter below.

4 https://www.iso.org/home.html
5 https://iec.ch/homepage

*Table 1: The structure of the ISO 27000 series of standards*

| | | |
|---|---|---|
| **Terminology** | **Vocabulary** | **ISO/IEC 27000: Overview and vocabulary** |
| **Normative** | **Requirements** | ISO/IEC 27001: ISMS requirements |
| | | ISO/IEC 27006: Requirements for bodies providing audit and certification of ISMS |
| | | ISO/IEC 27701: Privacy information management System |
| **Informative** | **General guidelines** | ISO/IEC 27002: ISMS Information security controls - Code of practice |
| | | ISO/IEC 27003: ISMS explanation and implementation guidance |
| | | ISO/IEC 27004: ISMS Monitoring, measurement, analysis and evaluation |
| | | ISO/IEC 27005: Guidance on managing information security risks |
| | | ISO/IEC 27007: Guidelines for ISMS auditing |
| | | ISO/IEC 27032: Guidelines for cybersecurity |
| | | ... other standards |
| | **Sector-specific guidelines** | ISO/IEC 27011: Guidelines for telecommunications organizations based on ISO/IEC 27002 |
| | | ISO/IEC 27017: Code of practice for information security controls based on ISO/IEC 27002 for cloud services |
| | | ISO/IEC 27018: Code of practice for protection of personally identifiable information (PII) in public clouds |
| | | ... other standards |

## 2.2 Chronological development of ISO/IEC 27001 and 27002

The evolution of ISO/IEC 27001 and 27002 up to 2013 is illustrated in Figure 1. It can be seen that the predecessor of today's standards ISO/IEC 27001 and 27002 is the British standard BS 7799, which was published by the British Standards Institute - BSI[6] in 1995. Since 2000, the development of these standards has been carried out under the auspices of the International Organization for Standardization - ISO. One of the most important turning points occurred in 2005, when the standard

6 https://www.bsigroup.com/

was split into two parts, or two separate standards, with the first standard (then ISO/IEC 17799:2005) representing the "Code of Practice for Information Security Management", and the second standard (then ISO/IEC 27001:2005) defining the "Information Security Management System (ISMS) Requirements". A similar "logic" is followed in the existing editions of both standards. ISO/IEC 27001:2005 is the immediate predecessor of today's ISO/IEC 27001:2022, while the code of practice ISO/IEC 17799:2005 was in 2007 renamed to ISO/IEC 27002:2007 and is thus the immediate predecessor of today's ISO/IEC 27002:2022.

*Figure 1: Evolution of ISO/IEC 27001 and ISO/IEC 27002.*

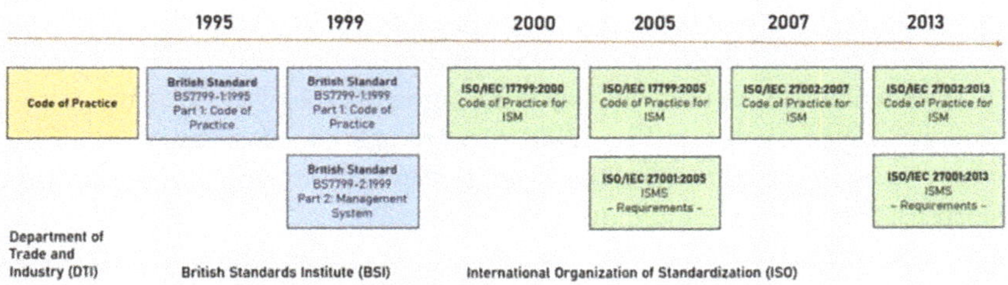


*Source: Volyntseva (2021)*

## 2.3 Understanding the differences between ISO/IEC 27001 and 27002

Both standards, ISO/IEC 27001 and ISO/IEC 27002, are closely related in both content and structure but also have important differences. Understanding these is crucial for implementing the standards into practice.

ISO/IEC 27001 introduces the concept of an ISMS, which is a complex management system for controlling and managing information security risks in an organization. ISMS comprises a set of policies, procedures, and practices that ensure both physical and logical security and compliance with existing regulations. Therefore, the primary purpose of ISO/IEC 27001 is to provide a framework to assist during the design, implementation, monitoring, maintenance and improvement of an organization's ISMS. ISO/IEC 27001 does not "mandate" specific information security controls but provides a set of requirements that an organization's ISMS should meet. As such, ISO/IEC 27001 also provides specifications for certifying an organization or its ISMS (Adams, 2021). Certification of compliance with ISO/IEC 27001 is an optional activity, not a mandatory one, but it does provide a number of benefits to the organization that chooses to become certified (see, e.g., Shojaie et al., 2016).

As shown in Figure 2 (left side), the standard ISO/IEC 27001 is divided into two parts: the main part "*Management System - Requirements*" and the appendix "*Annex A*". The main part defines the requirements for the ISMS in seven different areas (chapters 4 - 10): "*Context*", "*Leadership*", "*Planning*", "*Support*", "*Operations*", "*Performance*" and "*Improvement*". Moreover, "*Annex A*" provides a list of various security controls that can help an organization to meet the requirements from the main part of the standard. Figure 2 shows that the previous editions of the standards contained 114 controls, divided into 14 groups.

It should be noted that "*Annex A*" to ISO/IEC 27001 defines security controls sparsely (practically just lists them) and does not address the control implementation aspect. This aspect is the focus of another standard, ISO/IEC 27002, also known as the "*Code of Practice*" (see right panel of Figure 2). ISO/IEC 27002 can therefore serve as a supporting standard that provides fairly detailed guidance and instructions on the practical implementation of each of the security controls listed in "*Annex A*" to ISO/IEC 27001. An example of a security control listed from "*Annex A*" of ISO/IEC 27001 with guidance on its implementation from ISO/IEC 27002 is shown in Figure 3.

*Figure 2: Structure of ISO/IEC 27001 (left) and ISO/IEC 27002[7] (right).*

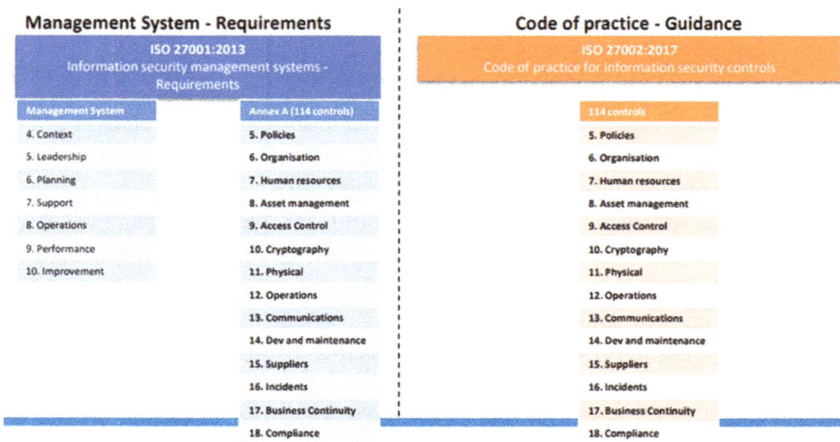


*Source: Volyntseva (2021)*

7 ISO/IEC 27001:2017 is an interim edition based on the 2013 edition and incorporating corrections from 2014 and 2015.

*Figure 3: Example of the security control* "Labelling of information" *from* "Annex A" *to ISO/IEC 27001:2013 with guidelines for its implementation in ISO/IEC 27002:2017.*

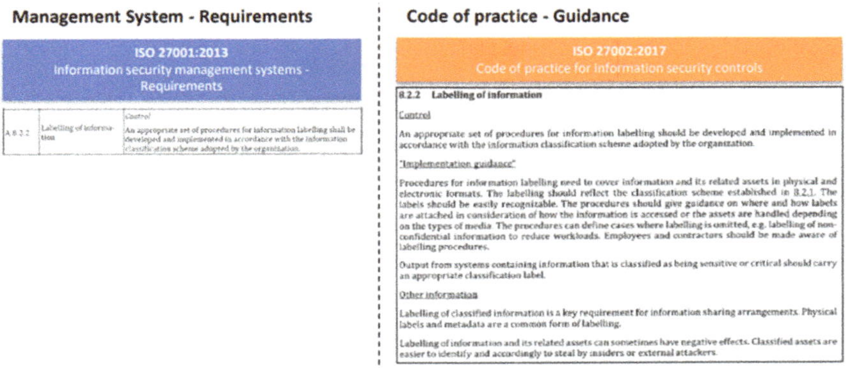
Management System - Requirements

ISO 27001:2013
Information security management systems - Requirements

| | | |
|---|---|---|
| A.8.2.2 | Labelling of information | *Control*<br>An appropriate set of procedures for information labelling shall be developed and implemented in accordance with the information classification scheme adopted by the organization. |

Code of practice - Guidance

ISO 27002:2017
Code of practice for information security controls

**8.2.2 Labelling of information**

Control

An appropriate set of procedures for information labelling should be developed and implemented in accordance with the information classification scheme adopted by the organization.

"Implementation guidance"

Procedures for information labelling need to cover information and its related assets in physical and electronic formats. The labelling should reflect the classification scheme established in 8.2.1. The labels should be easily recognizable. The procedures should give guidance on where and how labels are attached in consideration of how the information is accessed or the assets are handled depending on the types of media. The procedures can define cases where labelling is omitted, e.g. labelling of non-confidential information to reduce workloads. Employees and contractors should be made aware of labelling procedures.

Output from systems containing information that is classified as being sensitive or critical should carry an appropriate classification label.

Other information

Labelling of classified information is a key requirement for information sharing arrangements. Physical labels and metadata are a common form of labelling.

Labelling of information and its related assets can sometimes have negative effects. Classified assets are easier to identify and accordingly to steal by insiders or external attackers.

*Source: Volyntseva (2021)*

## 3. Novelties in the latest editions of ISO/IEC 27001 and 27002

As a result of an ever-changing global digital landscape and evolving cyber threats, cybercrime is growing more severe and sophisticated. To address this evolution and better tackle cybersecurity challenges, the International Organization for Standardization - ISO has updated the standards ISO/IEC 27001 and 27002 (KPMG, 2023). ISO/IEC 27002:2022 was published on February 15, 2022, followed by ISO/IEC 27001:2022 on October 25, 2022.

Based on a detailed review and comparison of the two editions (the last edition of 2013 and the new edition of 2022) of both standards (ISO /IEC 27001 and ISO /IEC 27002). The main changes will be systematically presented and described. In addition, we will discuss the impact of the changes on organizations implementing the standards and on other standards within the ISO 27000 series.

### 3.1 Broadening the focus from information security to cybersecurity and privacy protection

Global regulatory changes, such as the Protection of Personal Information Act (POPIA) in South Africa, the Australian Privacy Principles (APP), increasing cybersecurity risks, and the growing demands and needs to ensure business continuity and protect user privacy are all challenges faced by organizations around the world. All of these are just a few of the reasons that have led to the need to broaden the focus of the ISO 27000 series of standards, which previously focused primarily on information security assurance. As shown in Table 1, the new editions of the standards address a broader concept, including cybersecurity and user data protection. As shown in Table 2, these changes were also reflected in the new titles of both standards.

*Table 2: Old and new title of ISO/IEC 27001 in 27002 standards*

| | **Old title (2013)** | **New title (2022)** |
|---|---|---|
| **ISO/ IEC 27001** | ISO/IEC 27001:2013 Information technology - Security techniques - Information security management systems - Requirements | ISO/IEC 27001:2022 Information security, **cybersecurity and privacy protection** - Information security management systems –Requirements |
| **ISO/ IEC 27002** | ISO/IEC 27002:2013 Information technology — Security techniques — Code of practice for information security controls | ISO/IEC 27002:2022 Information security, **cybersecurity and privacy protection** — Information security controls |

## 3.2 What is new in ISO/IEC 27001:2022?

A summary of the main changes in the new edition of ISO /IEC 27001:2022 is presented in Figure 4. It can be seen that the changes affect It is clear that the changes affect both, the substantive part of the standard and its appendix "*Annex A*".

A detailed examination of the two editions of the standard shows that the changes in the substantive part of the standard are not extensive. It can be seen from Table 3 that the main chapters (i.e., clauses) have remained exactly the same, only the title of the "*Annex A*" has been changed.

The main part of ISO 27001 (i.e., clauses 4 to 10), has changed only slightly, especially in clauses 4.2, 6.2, 6.3, and 8.1 where additional new content has been added. Other updates include minor changes in the terminology and restructuring of sentences and clauses. The updates can be summarised as follows (BSI, n.d.)

- *Editorial changes:*
  - Full alignment with new ISO harmonized structure, used in other management system standards (e.g. ISO 31000).
  - Re-arranging of some English wording to allow for easier translation.
  - Minor numbering re-structure to align with the harmonized approach.
  - Removal of reference to control objectives as they no longer exist either in "*Annex A*" or ISO 27002.

*Figure 4: Summary of the main changes in the new edition of the standard ISO/IEC 27001:2022.*

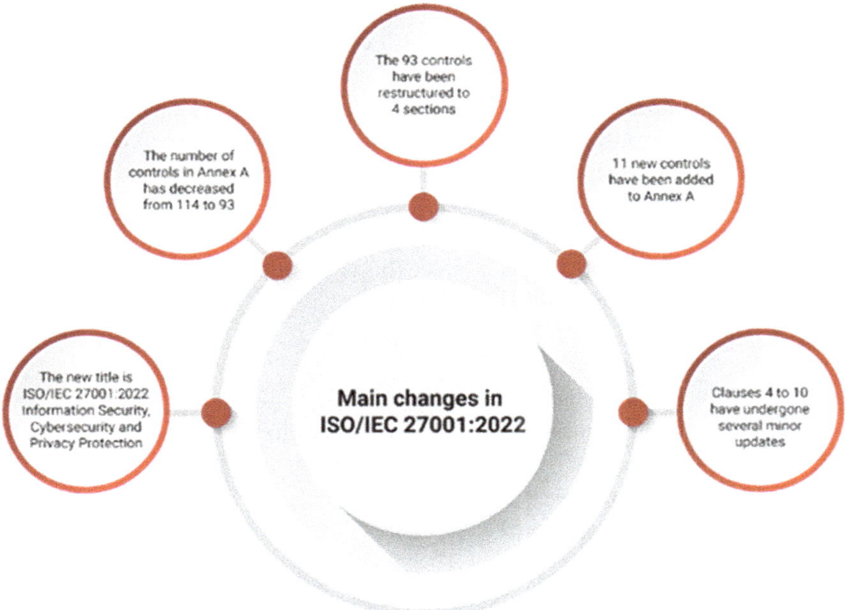


*Source: Hyseni (2022)*

*Table 3: Table of contents of ISO/IEC 27001:2013 and ISO/IEC 27001:2022*

| **ISO/IEC 27001:2013** | **ISO/IEC 27001:2022** |
|---|---|
| 0. Introduction | 0. Introduction |
| 1. Scope | 1. Scope |
| 2. Normative references | 2. Normative references |
| 3. Terms and definitions | 3. Terms and definitions |
| 4. Context of the organization | 4. Context of the organization |
| 5. Leadership | 5. Leadership |
| 6. Planning | 6. Planning |
| 7. Support | 7. Support |
| 8. Operation | 8. Operation |
| 9. Performance evaluation | 9. Performance evaluation |
| 10. Improvement | 10. Improvement |
| Annex A. Reference control objectives and controls | Annex A. Information security controls reference |

- *Changes in ISMS requirements:*
  - Define the processes and interactions needed to implement and maintain your ISMS.
  - Communicate organizational roles relevant to information security within the organization.
  - Monitor information security objectives.
  - Ensure the organization determines how to communicate as part of clause 7.4.
  - Establish criteria for operational processes and implementing control of the processes.
  - Some new sub-clauses are introduced:
    - "6.3 *Planning of changes*" (Note: This is a moderate change which needs to be controlled.)
    - "9.2 *Internal audit*" has been divided to
      - "9.2.1 *General*"
      - "9.2.2 *Internal audit programme*"
    - "9.3 *Management review*" has been divided to
      - "9.3.1 *General*"
      - "9.3.2 *Management review inputs*"
      - "9.3.3 *Management Review results*"

All changes in clauses 4 - 10 of ISO/IEC 27001:2022 in comparison to ISO/IEC 27001:2013 are explained in detail in SGS (SGS, 2022a).

The changes in "*Annex A*" of ISO/IEC 27001:2022 are moderate. As observed by Hyseni (2022) it contains changes in both, the number of controls, and their listing in groups (i.e., control categories). The title of this Annex has also changed from "Reference control objectives and controls" to "Information security controls reference". Therefore, the reference objectives of each control group that were present in the previous edition of the standard, now have been removed.

As can be seen from Table 4 and Figure 5, the changes made in "*Annex A*" can be summarised as follows:

- The total number of controls has been reduced from 114 to 93, where 11 controls are new, 57 of them have been merged, and 1 control has been split (see Figure 6).
- As can be seen from Table 4, 93 controls are divided into 4 groups A.5 – A.8 (unlike the 2013 edition, when the number of groups was 14).
- The newly added controls are highlighted in Figure 6 and described in more detail in section 3.3. It can be seen that most (7 out of 11) of the newly added controls are in group A.8 - "*Technological controls*".

*Table 4: Structure of* "Annex A" *in both editions of the standard*

| **Annex A ISO/IEC 27001:2013** | | **Annex A ISO/IEC 27001:2022** | |
|---|---|---|---|
| A.5 | Information security policies | A.5 | Organizational controls (37 controls) |
| A.6 | Organization of information security | A.6 | People controls (8 controls) |
| A.7 | Human resource security | A.7 | Physical controls (14 controls) |
| A.8 | Asset management | A.8 | Technological controls (34 controls) |
| A.9 | Access control | | |
| A.10 | Cryptography | | |
| A.11 | Physical and environmental security | | |
| A.12 | Operations security | | |
| A.13 | Communications security | | |
| A.14 | System acquisition, development and maintenance | | |
| A.15 | Supplier relationships | | |
| A.16 | Information security incident management | | |
| A.17 | Information security aspects of business continuity management | | |
| A.18 | Compliance | | |

*Figure 5: Summary of changes to ISO/IEC 27001:2022* "Annex A".

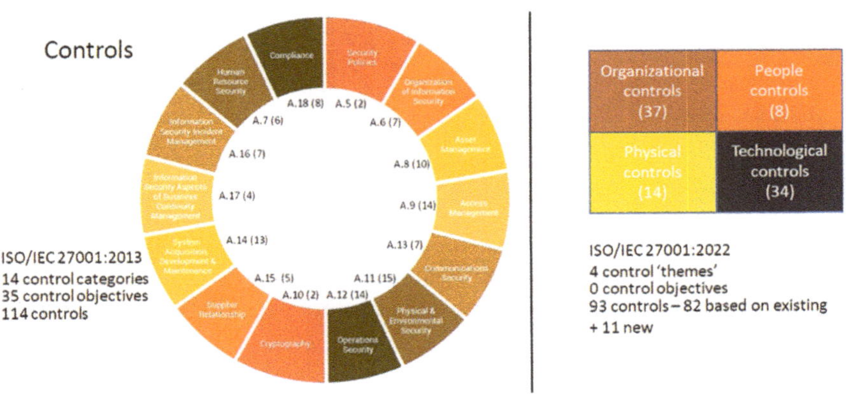


*Source: Green (2022)*

*Figure 6: Rearrangement of security controls in ISO/IEC 27002:2022* "Annex A".

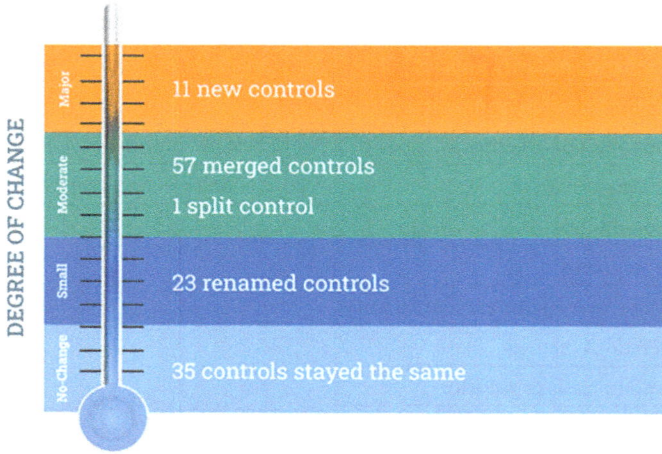


*Source: Kosutic (n.d.)*

*Figure 7: New security controls in* "Annex A" *of ISO/IEC 27001:2022.*

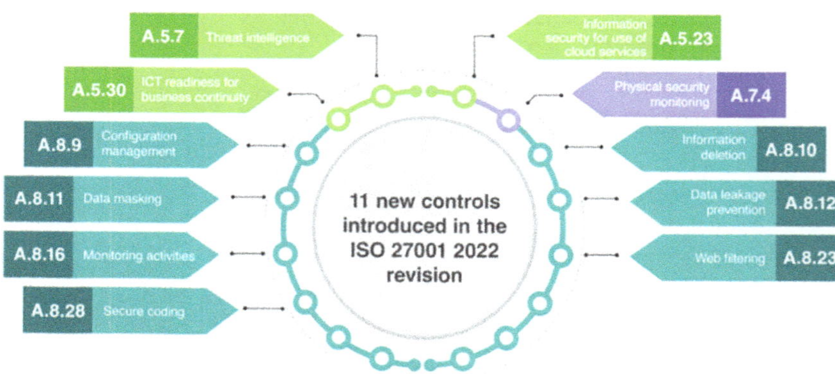


*Source: Kosutic (n.d.)*

"*Annex A*" needed to be revised to align with the information security controls in ISO/IEC 27002:2022. The changes are therefore presented in more detail in the next section.

### 3.3 What is new in ISO/IEC 27002:2022?

As we already explained, ISO/IEC 27002 is a guidance document and is designed to be used as a reference for selecting controls while implementing ISMS based on ISO/IEC 27001 or as a guidebook for organizations implementing commonly accepted information security controls. Organizations may use ISO /IEC 27002:2022 as a reference document in any case where their ISMS is based on ISO 27001 or another framework of their choice (Flores, 2022).

The current ISO/IEC 27002:2013 edition had been under review since 2018 by ISO/IEC JTC 1/SC27 and the new edition was officially published on 15 February, 2022. While part of the controls remains unchanged, there are significant changes in structure of control categories and the controls' layout.

The key changes in the 2022 edition as compared to the 2013 edition of ISO/IEC 27002 can be described as follows:

- *Changed title:* As we mentioned in section 3.1, the title of the 2022 edition is modified to "*Information security, cybersecurity and privacy protection – Information security controls*". It is important to emphasize that the term "*Code of Practice*" is removed to reflect that the document is a reference to generic information security controls.
- *The total number of controls has been reduced:* The 2022 edition are 93 controls in the 2022 edition versus 114 controls in the 2013 edition.
- *The structure of control categories has been simplified:* Controls are regrouped into 4 categories, instead of 14 themes and 35 categories in the 2013 edition (Table 5). The simplified control layout can make it easier for management to assign responsibilities within the organization for improving information security (SGS, 2022b).
- *Some controls are new*: 11 new controls are introduced to address the evolvement in technologies and industrial practices (see Table 5).
- *Some controls have been merged*: As can be seen from Table 7, 24 controls in the 2022 edition are the results of merging some controls from the 2013 edition. A list of merged controls can be also found in "*Annex B*" of ISO/IEC 27002:2022. Merging of controls results in a reduced number of controls and thus creates a leaner standard.
- *Some controls have been renamed and/or reassigned*: 12 controls have been renamed and/or reassigned to one of the 4 categories as appropriate (see Table 7).

- *One control has been split:* Control "18.2.3 *Technical compliance review*" has been split into "5.36 *Conformance with policies, rules and standards for information security*" and "8.8 *Management of technical vulnerabilities*".
- *New control layout:* New control layout is shown in Table 9. It can be seen that some elements (control title, control description, guidance and other information) remain unchanged from the 2013 edition. The biggest innovation is the so-called "*attribute table*", where each control is associated with five attributes with corresponding attribute values. The structure of the attribute table is presented in Table 10. Attributes are used to create different views of the controls. The use is demonstrated in "*Annex A*" of ISO/IEC 27002:2022. Nevertheless, the use of the attributes is not mandatory. Organizations can disregard one or more of the attributes or select other attributes, e.g. the maturity model (SGS, 2022b).
- *ISO/IEC 27000 is no longer the normative reference of ISO/IEC 27002:2022:* In the 2022 edition, the terms and definitions defined in clause 3 are applied. Users are recommended to refer to the terms and definitions to facilitate their understanding of the controls and the guidance in the document.

*Table 5: Structure of control categories in ISO/IEC 27002:2022 in comparison to 27002:2013*

| **ISO/IEC 27002:2013** | | | **ISO/IEC 27002:2022** |
|---|---|---|---|
| 5 Information security policies | 6 Organization of information security | 7 Human resource security | 5 Organizational controls |
| 8 Asset management | 9 Access control | 10 Cryptography | 6 People controls |
| 11 Physical and environmental security | 12 Operations security | 13 Communications security | 7 Physical controls |
| 14 System acquisition, development and maintenance | 15 Supplier relationships | 16 Information security incident management | 8 Technological controls |
| 17 Information security aspects of business continuity management | | 18 Compliance | |

*Table 6: New controls in ISO/IEC 27002:2022*

| **Control** | | | **Remark (summarized from SGS (2022b))** |
|---|---|---|---|
| **Organizational controls** | 5.7 | Threat intelligence | Organizations must remain vigilant and maintain awareness of the constantly evolving threat landscape. Threat intelligence can be categorized into three levels: strategic, tactical and operational. Tactical and operational threat intelligence can be drawn from sources such as special interest groups (Control 5.6: Contact with special interest groups), lessons learnt from information security incidents (Control 5.27: Learning from information security incidents) or the Security Operations Center (SOC).<br>In addition, organizations should monitor the evolving threat landscape not only in their own industry, but also across other industries. |
| | 5.23 | Information security for use of cloud services | It is clear that this new control was introduced to address the increasing reliance of organizations on cloud services over the last ten years. Although it is classified as an organizational control, its effective implementation requires technical expertise in cloud technology. Therefore, organizations should consider involving cloud specialists in the implementation process. |
| | 5.30 | ICT readiness for business continuity | The objective of this new control differs from control 5.29 (Information security during disruption). It focuses on ensuring the availability of the organization's information and related assets in the event of disruptions. An example of the implementation of this control is the Disaster Recovery Plan (DRP) developed by the IT department, provided it is consistent with the organization's business continuity requirements.<br>In contrast, control 5.29 (Information security during disruption) is used to ensure the confidentiality, integrity and availability (CIA) of information during disruptions. This may be the case, for example, if the physical access control systems are temporarily unavailable due to a power failure. |

*(Continued)*

*Table 6: (Continued)*

| Control | | | Remark (summarized from SGS (2022b)) |
|---|---|---|---|
| Physical controls | 7.4 | Physical security monitoring | Although this is a new control under Annex B of ISO/IEC 27002:2022, many organizations may have already implemented it on their premises. Examples include the installation of surveillance systems, intrusion detection systems or door access control systems. |
| Technological controls | 8.9 | Configuration management | Configuration management should be an ongoing process to control the configurations of hardware, software, services (e.g. cloud services) and networks throughout their lifecycle. An example of the implementation of this control is system hardening.<br>Configurations must be maintained to ensure their continued effectiveness. All changes should be implemented in a controlled manner by following the change management process (Control 8.32: Change management), with change records kept securely. |
| | 8.10 | Information deletion | The inclusion of these three controls reflects the focus of the 2022 edition entitled *Information security, cybersecurity, and privacy protection – Information security controls.* These controls are implemented largely in accordance with applicable data protection laws and international standards such as the GDPR and ISO/IEC 27701 to protect the rights of data subjects. |
| | 8.11 | Data masking | |
| | 8.12 | Data leakage prevention | |
| | 8.16 | Monitoring activities | This control is designed to monitor networks, systems and applications for anomalous behaviour and potential information security incidents. Organizations often use various monitoring methods to monitor their IT environment, such as the implementation of anti-virus software, firewalls or web philtres with logging functions. |
| | 8.23 | Web filtering | This control is relatively simple and many organizations have already implemented it in their IT networks. Although filtering more external websites reduces vulnerability to malicious content, organizations need to carefully balance information security risks with business requirements. |
| | 8.28 | Secure coding | The aim of this control to minimize potential information security vulnerabilities in newly developed or improved software. This control was omitted in the 2013 edition. |

*Table 7: Controls merged during the revision of ISO/IEC 27002*

| ISO/IEC 27002:2013 | | ISO/IEC 27002:2022 | | |
|---|---|---|---|---|
| 5.1.1 | Policies for information security | 5.1 | Policies for information security | Organizational controls |
| 5.1.2 | Review of the policies for information security | | | |
| 6.1.5 | Information security in project management | 5.8 | Information security in project management | |
| 14.1.1 | Information security requirements analysis and specification | | | |
| 8.1.1 | Inventory of assets | 5.9 | Inventory of information and other associated assets | |
| 8.1.2 | Ownership of assets | | | |
| 8.1.3 | Acceptable use of assets | 5.10 | Acceptable use of information and other associated assets | |
| 8.2.3 | Handling of assets | | | |
| 13.2.1 | Information transfer policies and procedures | 5.14 | Information transfer | |
| 13.2.2 | Agreements on information transfer | | | |
| 13.2.3 | Electronic messaging | | | |
| 9.1.1 | Access control policy | 5.15 | Access control | |
| 9.1.2 | Access to networks and network services | | | |
| 9.2.4 | Management of secret authentication information of users | 5.17 | Authentication information | |
| 9.3.1 | Use of secret authentication information | | | |
| 9.4.3 | Password management system | | | |
| 9.2.2 | User access provisioning | 5.18 | Access rights | |
| 9.2.5 | Review of user access rights | | | |
| 9.2.6 | Removal or adjustment of access rights | | | |
| 15.2.1 | Monitoring and review of supplier services | 5.22 | Monitoring, review and change management of supplier services | |
| 15.2.2 | Managing changes to supplier services | | | |
| 17.1.1 | Planning information security continuity | 5.29 | Information security during disruption | |
| 17.1.2 | Implementing information security continuity | | | |
| 17.1.3 | Verify, review and evaluate information security continuity | | | |

*(Continued)*

*Table 7: (Continued)*

| ISO/IEC 27002:2013 | | ISO/IEC 27002:2022 | | |
|---|---|---|---|---|
| 18.1.1 | Identification of applicable legislation and contractual requirements | 5.31 | Legal, statutory, regulatory and contractual requirements | |
| 18.1.5 | Regulation of cryptographic controls | | | |
| 18.2.2 | Compliance with security policies and standards | 5.36 | Conformance with policies, rules and standards for information security | |
| 18.2.3 | Technical compliance review | | | |
| 16.1.2 | Reporting information security events | 6.8 | Information security event reporting | People controls |
| 16.1.3 | Reporting information security weaknesses | | | |
| 11.1.2 | Physical entry controls | 7.2 | Physical entry | P Physical controls |
| 11.1.6 | Delivery and loading areas | | | |
| 8.3.1 | Management of removable media | 7.10 | Storage media | |
| 8.3.2 | Disposal of media | | | |
| 8.3.3 | Physical media transfer | | | |
| 11.2.5 | Removal of assets | | | |
| 6.2.1 | Mobile device policy | 8.1 | User end point devices | Technological controls |
| 11.2.8 | Unattended user equipment | | | |
| 12.6.1 | Management of technical vulnerabilities | 8.8 | Management of technical vulnerabilities | |
| 18.2.3 | Technical compliance review | | | |
| 12.4.1 | Event logging | 8.15 | Logging | |
| 12.4.2 | Protection of log information | | | |
| 12.4.3 | Administrator and operator logs | | | |
| 12.5.1 | Installation of software on operational systems | 8.19 | Installation of software on operational systems | |
| 12.6.2 | Restrictions on software installation | | | |
| 10.1.1 | Policy on the use of cryptographic controls | 8.24 | Use of cryptography | |
| 10.1.2 | Key management | | | |
| 14.1.2 | Securing application services on public networks | 8.26 | Application security requirements | |
| 14.1.3 | Protecting application services transactions | | | |

| **ISO/IEC 27002:2013** | | **ISO/IEC 27002:2022** | | |
|---|---|---|---|---|
| 14.2.8 | System security testing | 8.29 | Security testing in development and acceptance | |
| 14.2.9 | System acceptance testing | | | |
| 12.1.4 | Separation of development, testing and operational environments | 8.31 | Separation of development, test and production environments | |
| 14.2.6 | Secure development environment | | | |
| 12.1.2 | Change management | 8.32 | Change management | |
| 14.2.2 | System change control procedures | | | |
| 14.2.3 | Technical review of applications after operating platform changes | | | |
| 14.2.4 | Restrictions on changes to software packages | | | |

*Table 8: Controls renamed and/or reassigned during the revision of ISO/IEC 27002*

| **ISO/IEC 27002:2013** | | **ISO/IEC 27002:2022** | | |
|---|---|---|---|---|
| 9.2.1 | User registration and de-registration | 5.16 | Identity management | Organizational controls |
| 15.1.1 | Information security policy for supplier relationships | 5.19 | Information security in supplier relationships | |
| 15.1.2 | Addressing security within supplier agreements | 5.20 | Addressing information security within supplier agreements | |
| 15.1.3 | Information and communication technology supply chain | 5.21 | Managing information security in the ICT supply chain | |
| 16.1.1 | Responsibilities and procedures | 5.24 | Information security incident management planning and preparation | |
| 16.1.4 | Assessment of and decision on information security events | 5.25 | Assessment and decision on information security events | |
| 18.1.4 | Privacy and protection of personally identifiable information | 5.34 | Privacy and protection of PII | |

*(Continued)*

*Table 8: (Continued)*

| ISO/IEC 27002:2013 | | ISO/IEC 27002:2022 | | |
|---|---|---|---|---|
| 7.3.1 | Termination or change of employment responsibilities | 6.5 | Responsibilities after termination or change of employment | People controls |
| 6.2.2 | Teleworking | 6.7 | Remote working | |
| 11.1.1 | Physical security perimeter | 7.1 | Physical security perimeters | Physical controls |
| 11.2.9 | Clear desk and clear screen policy | 7.7 | Clear desk and clear screen | |
| 11.2.6 | Security of equipment and assets off-premises | 7.9 | Security of assets off-premises | |
| 9.2.3 | Management of privileged access rights | 8.2 | Privileged access rights | Technological controls |
| 9.4.5 | Access control to program source code | 8.4 | Access to source code | |
| 9.4.2 | Secure log-on procedures | 8.5 | Secure authentication | |
| 12.2.1 | Controls against malware | 8.7 | Protection against malware | |
| 13.1.1 | Network controls | 8.20 | Networks security | |
| 13.1.3 | Segregation in networks | 8.22 | Segregation of networks | |
| 14.2.1 | Secure development policy | 8.25 | Secure development life cycle | |
| 14.2.5 | Secure system engineering principles | 8.27 | Secure system architecture and engineering principles | |
| 14.3.1 | Protection of test data | 8.33 | Test information | |
| 12.7.1 | Information systems audit controls | 8.34 | Protection of information systems during audit testing | |

*Table 9: Structure of ISO/IEC 27002:2022 controls layout*

| | |
|---|---|
| ***Control title*** | The name of the control. |
| ***Attribute table*** | Values of five attributes associated with the control. |
| ***Control*** | A description of what needs to be accomplished to be compliant with the control. |
| ***Guidance*** | Tips on how the control should be implemented. |
| ***Other information*** | Complementary information to understand the control and references to other documents for consultation. |

*Table 10: Structure of ISO/IEC 27002:2022 controls attribute table*

| Attribute | Attribute value | Remark (summarized from SGS (2022b)) |
|---|---|---|
| **Control type** | #Preventive<br>#Detective<br>#Corrective | The control should be considered in terms of when and how it mitigates the risk of an information security incident occurring. |
| **Information security properties** | #Confidentiality<br>#Integrity<br>#Availability | The control should be considered from the point of view of which property of the information it helps to preserve, such as confidentiality, integrity or availability. |
| **Cybersecurity concepts** | #Identify<br>#Protect<br>#Detect<br>#Respond<br>#Recover | The control should be considered in the context of the concepts of cybersecurity as defined in ISO/IEC TS 27110 and the NIST Cybersecurity Framework. |
| **Operational capabilities** | #Governance<br>#Asset_management<br>#Information_protection<br>#Human_resource_security<br>#Physical_security<br>#System_and_network security<br>#Application_security<br>#Secure_configuration<br>#Identity_and_access_management<br>#Threat_and_vulnerability_management<br>#Continuity<br>#Supplier_relationships_security<br>#Legal_and_compliance<br>#Information_security_event management<br>#Information_security_assurance | This control should be considered from the perspective of the practitioner's information security skills. There are a total of 15 attribute values, most of which correspond to the control topics from the 2013 edition. |
| **Security domains** | #Governance_and_Ecosystem<br>#Protection<br>#Defense<br>#Resilience | The control should be considered from the perspective of the areas, expertise, services and products of information security. |

## 4. Discussion

A detailed analysis shows that the substantive part of ISO /IEC 27001 (clauses 1–10) has not undergone major changes. However, the rather extensive changes to ISO/ IEC 27002 have led to a significant reorganization of Annex A of ISO/IEC 27002.

Although the changes to ISO/IEC 27001 appear to be minor, they are significant to the professional community because this standard provides an established framework for certification. The changes will impact the certification process and, consequently, organizations whose ISMS is based on the requirements of 27001. Finally, the changes to two main standards in the ISO 27000 series may also influence other related standards in this series.

### 4.1 Impact of changes on the certification process

The requirements for transitioning to the new revision of ISO 27001 are detailed within a normative reference published by the International Accreditation Forum - IAF under Mandatory Document 26 (IAF MD 26:2023; see IAF (2023)).

The transition timeline for ISO/IEC 27001:2022 is set to be 3 years (36 months from the last day of the month published, i.e. from October 31, 2022). Therefore, the current 2013 certificates need to be transitioned to the new edition before November 2025.

All certification bodies that are accredited to issue certificates against ISO 27001 are required to conform to the transition procedures detailed within IAF MD 26 (IAF, 2023).

Accreditation Bodies (AB) (such United Kingdom Accreditation Service – UKAS, Deutsche Akkreditierungsstelle – DakkS, Swiss Accreditation Service - SAS, etc.) have six months of rulemaking time for Conformity Assessment Bodies (CAB) (such as BSI Group, TÜV SÜD, Bureau Veritas, etc.), starting from Oct 2022. Rulemaking covers the AB requirements on audit reports, other audit documentation, auditor training, auditor qualification etc.

Conformity Assessment Bodies (CAB) can then take six months to implement the new rules. Examples include internal procedures, audit time calculation methods, audit report template or tool changes, certificate template changes, the training of auditors, technical reviewers, and support staff.

As shown in Figure 8, certification against ISO/IEC 27001:2013 is still possible until October 31, 2023. After that, no new certifications will be issued against the 2013 edition.

Certification to the new edition ISO 27001:2022 is possible from the 2nd half of 2023 (NQA, 2022). As before, the ISO/IEC 27001:2022 compliance certificate will be valid for three years.

## 4.2 Impact of changes on organizations

Even though all changes are noteworthy, they will not have much impact on the organizations that have already implemented ISO 27001 and are already certified to ISO/IEC 27001:2013. Moderate efforts might be needed for revising the internal policies in accordance with the new sub-clauses and the modified requirements in accordance with ISO/IEC 27001:2022 "*Annex A*".

The transition period allows all organizations that already have a valid certificate of compliance with ISO/IEC 27001:2013 to upgrade and align their certificate with the new edition of ISO/IEC 27001:2022 (ControlCase, 2022). However, the new standard will require revision of risk assessment (ISO 27001 Clause 8.2) updates to the Statement of Applicability (SoA) document and risk treatment plan (ISO 27001 Clause 6.1.3), as well as Internal Audit schedules (ISO 27001 Clause 9.2.3). Additionally, the updates to clauses 4 through 10 will call for changes to ISMS documentation for most organizations. For a successful transition, a gap analysis of ISO 27001:2022 would be worthwhile. Moreover, organizations may need to provide additional training to staff to upgrade their awareness and competence.

Organizations seeking initial certification (for the first time) should consider that the ISO/IEC 27001:2013 will be valid for another three years. In addition, many certification bodies will not offer ISO 27001:2022 certification for at least six months after October 2022. Therefore, if the organization is currently planning or has already begun implementation to have its ISMS certified for the first time as early as 2022 or early 2023, it is advisable to proceed with the ISO 27001:2013 standard. However, if the certification process is at an early planning stage, we recommend starting with ISO 27001:2022, as the new standard is more streamlined and easier to follow.

All ISO/IEC 27001 compliance audits conducted by organizations after October 2025 must take into account the provisions of the new edition of ISO/IEC 27001:2022. Moreover, organizations should also be aware that all certificates of compliance with ISO/IEC 27001:2013 will expire at the end of the transition period.

## 4.3 Impact of changes on other standards in the ISO 27000 series

The new editions of ISO/IEC 27001:2022 and ISO/IEC 27002:2022 may affect also other related standards from ISO 27000 series, such as:

- ISO/IEC 27701:2019 Security techniques — Extension to ISO/IEC 27001 and ISO/IEC 27002 for privacy information management — Requirements and guidelines

*Figure 8: Estimated timeline for ISO/IEC 27001:2022 implementation.*

*Source: Kosutic (2022)*

- ISO/IEC 27017:2015: Information technology — Security techniques — Code of practice for information security controls based on ISO/IEC 27002 for cloud services
- ISO/IEC 27018:2019: Information technology — Security techniques — Code of practice for protection of personally identifiable information (PII) in public clouds acting as PII processors
- ISO/IEC 27006:2015: Information technology — Security techniques — Requirements for bodies providing audit and certification of information security management systems

We have no information on whether new editions of these standards are in preparation. However, a new edition of ISO/IEC 27005:2022 titled "*Information security, cybersecurity and privacy protection - Guidance on managing information security risks*" was published in October 2022, replacing the previous 2018 edition. The content of the 2022 edition has been aligned with ISO/IEC 27001:2022.

## 5. Conclusion

Nowadays, it is essential for organizations of every size, from critical infrastructure, small businesses to educational institutions, to protect intellectual property and critical data. The standards, ISO/IEC 27001 and ISO/IEC 27002 offer organizations a well-organized and flexible approach to building information security resilience in this age of modern cyberattacks and ever-changing information security risks.

In this paper, we have studied and systematically analysed the changes introduced by the new editions of standards ISO/IEC 27001:2022 and ISO/IEC 27002:2022 compared to the previous editions of 2013. We found that most of the changes were made to ISO/IEC 27002, which required a completely new structure for the "*Annex A*" of the ISO/IEC 27001.

The resulting changes affect all organizations that rely on the provisions of ISO/IEC 27001 and 27002 for their information security management. Due to the general applicability and widespread use of the standards in practice, the scope of these organizations is broad and includes both the public and private sectors. We have analysed the impact of the resulting changes to the certification process, as well as on other standards in the ISO 27000 series.

Given the scope of the treatment and the importance of the topics discussed, we believe that the content will be of great benefit to the entire professional community and, in particular, to chief information security officers in any organization. By incorporating the principles of ISO 27001 into the digital business transformation process, organizations can ensure that security, privacy, and compliance considerations are integrated into every step of the transformation process. In this way, a foundation is laid for secure and responsible digital operations.

Last but not least, one of the core digital transformation technologies helping organizations scale is artificial intelligence (AI). The rapid adoption of such systems is driving transformative advances across industries, from healthcare to logistics, education and finance. Companies are deploying AI tools more widely to enable data analytics and predict the future for effective decision-making strategies. According to a PwC study, about 86% of people recognize AI as a mainstream technology (USAII, 2022). According to the latest report from Research and Markets, AI is expected to achieve a compound annual growth rate of 52% by 2025, indicating its rapid adoption by global businesses (Hanif, 2022). However, this growth also brings significant cybersecurity challenges. As AI systems process large amounts of sensitive data and make critical decisions, they become prime targets for cyberattacks, data breaches, and algorithmic manipulation. In this landscape, the ISO 27000 series of standards plays a central role. These standards provide a comprehensive information security management framework that helps organizations protect AI systems from threats, ensure data integrity, manage access controls, and establish robust incident response mechanisms. By adhering to the ISO 27000 standards, organizations can strengthen their AI implementations and navigate the evolving cyber risk landscape with confidence.

## Bibliography


Adams, M. (April 7, 2021). *ISO 27001 Certification: Understanding the Process and Costs*. Businesstechweekly. https://www.businesstechweekly.com/legal-and-compliance/iso27001-certification/iso-27001-certification-process-costs/

BSI. (n.d.). *ISO/IEC 27001:2022 What's changed?* British Standards Institution - BSI. Retrieved May 9, 2023, from https://www.bsigroup.com/globalassets/localfiles/en-ph/isoiec27001/iso-iec-27001-2022-whats-changed.pdf

ControlCase. (2022). *Updates and Changes to ISO 27001:2022*. https://www.controlcase.com/updates-and-changes-to-iso-270012022/

Flores, M. (March 8, 2022). *What's New in ISO/IEC 27002: 2022 Updates*. Advantio. https://www.advantio.com/blog/whats-new-in-iso/iec-27002-2022-updates

Green, R. (2022). *ISO/IEC 27001 – What the latest edition means for you*. https://www.quality.org/sites/default/files/2022-12/Presentation.pdf

Hanif, B. (2022). The Role of Artificial Intelligence in Digital Transformation for Member-Based Organizations, GlueUp, https://www.glueup.com/blog/artificial-intelligence-in-digital-transformation

Hyseni, V. (October 25, 2022). *ISO/IEC 27001 - What are the main changes in 2022?* Professional Evaluation and Certification Board [PECB]. https://pecb.com/article/isoiec-27001---what-are-the-main-changes-in-2022

IAF. (2023). *IAF Mandatory Document - TRANSITION REQUIREMENTS FOR ISO/IEC 27001:2022, Issue 2 (IAF MD 26:2023)*. International Accreditation Forum, Inc. - IAF. https://iaf.nu/iaf_system/uploads/documents/IAF_MD26_Issue_2_15012023.pdf

ISO. (2013a). *ISO/IEC 27001:2013 Information technology — Security techniques — Information security management systems — Requirements*. International Organization for Standardization [ISO].

ISO. (2013b). *ISO/IEC 27002:2013 Information technology — Security techniques — Code of practice for information security controls*. International Organization for Standardization [ISO].

ISO. (2022a). *ISO/IEC 27001:2022 Information security, cybersecurity and privacy protection — Information security management systems — Requirements*. International Organization for Standardization [ISO].

ISO. (2022b). *ISO/IEC 27002:2022 Information security, cybersecurity and privacy protection — Information security controls*. International Organization for Standardization [ISO].

Kosutic, D. (n.d.). *What are the 11 new security controls in ISO 27001:2022?* Advisera. Retrieved February 22, 2023, from https://advisera.com/27001academy/explanation-of-11-new-iso-27001-2022-controls/

Kosutic, D. (October 25, 2022). *ISO 27001:2022 Revision: What has changed? 2013 vs. 2022 version.* Advisera. https://advisera.com/27001academy/blog/2022/02/09/iso-27001-iso-27002/

KPMG. (2023). *The ISO 27001:2022 - Understanding the "New ISO 27001 standard", a step-by-step journey for new certification or recertification.* Klynveld Peat Marwick Goerdeler – KPMG. https://assets.kpmg.com/content/dam/kpmg/cn/pdf/en/2023/02/iso-iec-27001-2022.pdf

Meriah, I., & Rabai, L. B. A. (2019). Comparative Study of Ontologies Based ISO 27000 Series Security Standards. *Procedia Computer Science, 160*, 85–92. https://doi.org/10.1016/J.PROCS.2019.09.447

Niemann, K.-H. (2021). *Abgrenzung der IT-Sicherheitsnormenreihen ISO 27000 und IEC 62443.* https://doi.org/10.25968/opus-1973

NQA. (2022). *ISO 27001:2022 Transition Guidance.* https://www.nqa.com/en-us/transitions/iso-27001-2022

OGCIO. (2022). *An Overview of ISO/IEC 27000 family of Information Security Management System Standards.* Office of the Government Chief Information Officer. https://www.ogcio.gov.hk/en/our_work/information_cyber_security/collaboration/doc/overview_of_iso_27000_family.pdf

SGS. (2022a). *Comparing ISO/IEC 27001:2022 to ISO/IEC 27001:2013. What are the changes? A guidance document.* SGS SA Corporate Headquarters. https://doi.org/10.1

SGS. (2022b). *Key Changes in ISO/IEC 27002:2022, White paper.* SGS Headquarters, Geneva, Switzerland. https://www.sgs.com/en/whitepapers/key-changes-in-iso-iec-27002-2022-form

Shojaie, B., Federrath, H., & Saberi, I. (2016). Getting the Full Benefits of the ISO 27001 to Develop an ISMS based on Organisations' InfoSec Culture. In N. Clarke & S. Steven Furnell (Eds.), *Proceedings of the Tenth International Symposium on Human Aspects of Information Security & Assurance (HAISA 2016).* Plymouth University.

USAII (2022). Impact of AI in Digital Transformation through 2023. United States Artificial Intelligence Institute, https://www.usaii.org/ai-insights/impact-of-ai-in-digital-transformation-through-2023

Volyntseva, Y. (April 7, 2021). *ISO 27001 & 27002: Understanding the difference between ISO27001 and ISO27002.* Businesstechweekly. https://www.businesstechweekly.com/legal-and-compliance/iso27001-certification/iso-27001-and-iso-27002/

Andrej Škraba* and Črtomir Rozman**

# Parametrization of the SI Epidemic Model for COVID-19: A Comparative Analysis Across Six Countries

**Abstract:** Present study provides comprehensive analysis of the Susceptible-Infected (SI) epidemic model application in the context of the COVID-19 pandemic across six diverse countries. Key parameters, primarily the transmission coefficient ($\beta$) and the proportion of the susceptible in population, were estimated using genetic algorithms and classical parametrization methods. Both observed and simulated numbers of infections at the end of the first wave were compared, shedding light on the model's predictive accuracy. Results revealed minor deviations between the predicted and actual numbers, emphasizing the model's robustness. However, nuances in the predictions were identified, indicating variations based on regional factors or data availability. This research accentuates the importance of accurate parametrization in epidemic modeling and offers insights for predictive analytics in potential future outbreaks applying the methods of artificial intelligence, in our case, the Genetic Algorithms.

**Keywords:** COVID-19, SI model, susceptible-Infected, simulation, parametrization, validation, epidemic, genetic algorithms, artificial intelligence

## 1. Introduction

COVID-19 pandemics (L. Yang et al., 2020) caused by severe acute respiratory syndrome coronavirus 2 (SARS-CoV-2) provided the challenge for many researchers in different fields. Never before in the history of mankind has data about the pandemic been collected worldwide (Sharma & Sharma, 2020) with such a remarkable precision on a daily basis. In the early days of the COVID-19 pandemic, it became painfully evident that, despite a well-established understanding of how pandemics spread, the ability to make accurate predictions and develop reliable models was strikingly scarce. This realization exposed significant gaps in our preparedness for dealing with a global health crisis of such magnitude. The COVID-19 pandemic generated an unprecedented wealth of data

* University of Maribor, Faculty of organizational sciences, Kranj, Slovenia; e-mail: andrej.skraba@um.si

** University of Maribor, Faculty of Agriculture and Life Sciences, Maribor, Slovenia; e-mail: crt.rozman@um.si

(Mathieu et al., 2020; OurWorldInData, 2023) that became crucial for understanding the virus's spread, and for devising effective public health responses. This abundant data stemmed from a variety of sources and covered numerous aspects of the pandemic, offering researchers and public health authorities a valuable resource for analysis and decision-making which is important particularly for providing the proper capacity of medical emergency departments (Gatto et al., 2020; Wynants et al., 2020). There are two aspects of analysing the COVID-19 pandemics. First is the modelling aspect, which should provide the assessment of the existing models to anticipate the pandemics spread. The second aspect is to analyse the dynamics of the spread, which could help us characterize the COVID-19 dynamic parameters such as the basic reproduction number R (D'Arienzo & Coniglio, 2020; Jones, 2007), the average number of people one person with an infectious disease will likely infect in particular timeframe (Alimohamadi et al., 2020; Samui et al., 2020; Sy et al., 2021; You et al., 2020). Regarding the methodological tools, the most reliable appear to be classical epidemiology models (Allen, 1994), such as SI (Susceptible-Infected) (Abadias et al., 2020; Pandit, 2020; Qi et al., 2020; Rocchi et al., 2020; Stanovov et al., 2022; Sun et al., n.d.). Although the SI model is the basic one it is important for understanding of the core epidemics spread mechanism (Demongeot et al., 2020; Kosmidis & Macheras, 2020). As such it's idea is present in all other, more sophisticated models. Having low complexity of only two compartments, it is also suitable for the first estimation for more complex models. In our previous research (Stanovov et al., 2022), the classical SI model was initialized according to the population of the country, for which the model was considered. This is important alteration, since the estimator of the proportion of the whole population that is susceptible is somehow universal and characterizes the spread of the epidemy in particular country. Susceptible-Infected-Recovered model (SIR) has also been applied at the modelling of the COVID-19 spread (Chen et al., 2021; Comunian et al., 2020; Cooper et al., 2020; Dutta, 2022; Engelbrecht & Scholes, 2021; Gounane et al., 2021; Kudryashov et al., 2021; Moein et al., 2021; Simha et al., 2020; Thank et al., 2020). However, SIR model might also be inefficient (Moein et al., 2021) for the prediction purposes which indicates that more sophisticated modelling strategies and detailed knowledge of the biomedical and epidemiological aspects of the disease would still be needed to efficiently forecast the pandemic. Adding additional compartment to the SIR model with Exposed, one gets the SEIR model, which has also been widely applied in it's original form (Annas et al., 2020; He et al., 2020; Mohajan et al., 2022a, 2022b; Mwalili et al., 2020; Pandey et al., n.d.; Rădulescu et al., 2020) as well as in the modified form (López & Rodó, 2021; Z. Yang et al., 2020). Small modifications might yield improvement in the model fit however, the establishment of new theories would take time. One of the important factors at the outbreak is the number of unreported cases. There might be quite a significant proportion of population, which would be asymptomatic as well as ill but not seeking medical treatment. These are potential carriers of the disease and their number might significantly influence the epidemics spread (Liu et al., 2020, 2021). There are many other approaches to modelling such as Artificial neural networks (Kofjač et 2003; Ferencek et al., 2020), Support vector machines, Nature inspired algorithms, Prophet algorithm, ARIMA Deep learning algorithms and others (Istaiteh et al., 2020; Odagaki, 2023; Rahimi et al., 2021; Wang et al., 2022). The COVID-19 epidemic has shown that the well-known SI, SIR, and SEIR models are not always capable of capturing the real dynamics of the disease. While these models are often used in epidemiological studies due to their flexibility, simplicity, and transparency, there are numerous modifications to these models that allow for the consideration of additional factors that influence the dynamics of infection spread (Stanovov et al., 2022). One of the interesting application of non-conventional models is Bass-diffusion model (F. Bass, 1969; F. M. Bass, 2004; Massiani & Gohs, 2015). The Bass-diffusion model incorporates important material flow between compartments that does not depend on the level of infected (sink level). In classical SI model, the material flow depends on the interaction between susceptible and infected. Therefore, the SI model would need at least one person to be infected at start while in the Bass diffusion model, the transitions could occur even, if there would be no infected at time $t=0$. This is rarely present in the classical theory of epidemiology, but the findings of the parametrization of the Bass diffusion model (Stanovov et al., 2022) might indicate, that this might be particularly suitable principle for modelling the spread of COVID-19 pandemics. At the time of the writing, the pandemics is well behind us, however, it might return in the following years. Therefore, it is important to enhance our knowledge about the modelling of the COVID-19 dynamics even after the pandemics since the developed models could indicate the hidden mechanism of the COVID-19 spread (Stanovov et al., 2022). Nevertheless, amid uncertainty about the pandemic's future, described models serve as essential tools for policymakers, clinicians, and public health practitioners. While epidemiological models come with constraints and uncertainties, they offer a systematic way to understand the implications of various scenarios in the face of a nonlinear and unpredictable nature of the pandemics, aiding decision-making when used appropriately (Holmdahl & Buckee, 2020).

In present work, it is our intention to parametrize the SI model of epidemics spread in order to contribute to the parameter determination based on simulation modelling. SI model could be used as the first step at the parameter estimation in the case of pandemics spread. There are many tools available to perform the parametrization. In our case, we will use MATLAB/Simulink Parameter estimation tool and Powersim Genetic Algorithm Solver.

Basic SI model will be augmented with the inclusion of the population data at the initialization of the Susceptible compartment. The performed analysis should contribute to our knowledge about the COVID-19 epidemy spread mechanisms.

## 2. Methodology and data

The SI model represents only two compartments: Susceptible (S) and Infected (I). It is described by the following set of equations:

$$\frac{dS}{dt} = -\beta \frac{IS}{N}$$
$$\frac{dI}{dt} = \beta \frac{IS}{N}$$

where $\beta$ is the parameter controlling the flow from susceptible to infected. N is the constant representing the total population, and it remains unchanged. N is computed as the sum of I and S.

Figure 1 illustrates an SI infectious disease spread model defined in Eq 1 implemented in MATLAB/Simulink. It has inputs for the disease's transmission rate (beta), total population, initial fraction of susceptible individuals (proportionOfPopulation), and the initial number of infected individuals (initInfected). The model calculates the initial susceptible population by multiplying the total population with the proportionOfPopulation. As the simulation progresses, the susceptible count reduces based on the number of new infections. An integration block accumulates the number of infected individuals over time. The block simout output block collects and logs data from the simulation, allowing users to analyze and visualize the results after the simulation completes. This Simulink model allows users to adjust various input parameters to simulate different disease spread scenarios, encapsulating the SI structure in a visually intuitive manner.

Figure 2 shows the SI model build by the principles of System Dynamics (Forrester, 1958; Sterman, 2000). The model consist of two compartments, S for susceptible and I for infected. Susceptible represents individuals who are not yet infected but can become infected if they come into contact with an infected person while infected represents individuals who are currently infected with the

*Figure 1: SI model in MATLAB/Simulink.*

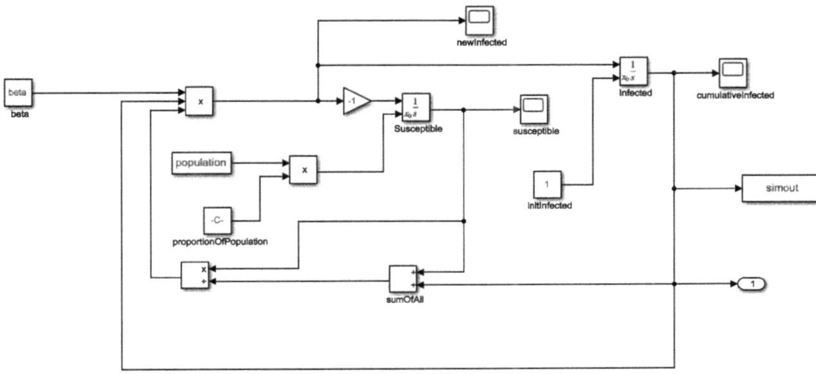


COVID-19 disease. In our case, for each country, the starting number of infected is 1. The infection rate depends on the parameter $\beta$, number of Susceptible, number of Infected and the size of the population which is determined as the sum of susceptible and infected. Infection rate is determined by the product of the effective contact rate ($\beta$), the number of susceptible individuals (S), and the number of infected individuals (I), all divided by the total population (N). The model has been augmented with the initialization of the number of susceptible according to the size of the population of particular country and the proportion of the population that is susceptible. There is also the level element named SSE as sum of squared errors. Here we consider the difference between simulated value for infected and the number of infected from the real data. Real data is inputted to the model via R parameter and transferred from the file with the data. The squared error is integrated on the SSE element. Here the final value represents the SSE for particular run. One would desire, that the SSE is as close to zero as it gets. If the SSE would be zero, there would be a perfect fit between actual and simulated dynamics.

The model dynamics could be expressed as (Rahmandad & Sterman, 2012; Sterman, 2000):

$$I(t) = I(0) + \int_0^t R(t)ds$$

$$S(t) = S(0) - \int_0^t R(t)ds$$

*Figure 2: SI model built by the principles of System Dynamics.*

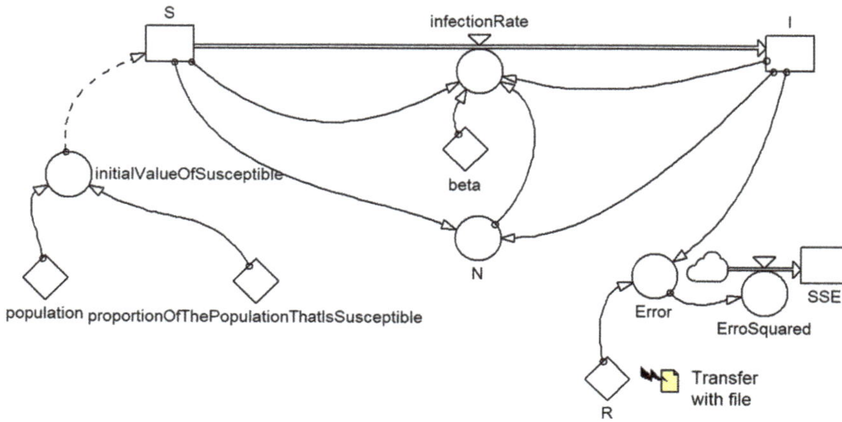


where $I$(t) represents the number of infected in time with units [person], $I$(0) initial number of infected, $R$(t) represents the newly infected with units [person/day], $S$(t) represents the number of susceptible which change over time. Rate of infected $R$(t) decreases the number of susceptible and on the other hand increases the number of infected. The Rate of infected $R$(t) is defined as:

$$R(t) = \frac{\beta S(t) I(t)}{S(t) + I(t)}$$

One could also express the variable $c$ as the concentration of susceptible people. Concertation $c$ could be computed as the ratio between the number of susceptible and the sum of susceptible and infected:

$$c = \frac{S(t)}{S(t) + I(t)}$$

Defined model provides an insight into the dynamics and key relationships between variables.

In the discrete form, where we perform the calculation with Euler's discrete numerical integration method, we write the equations as:

$$S(k+1) = S(k) + \Delta t(-\beta S(k) I(k)/N) \ I(k+1) = I(k) + \Delta t(\beta S(k) I(k)/N)$$

Where $\Delta t$ represents the time step and $k = 0, 1, 2, \ldots$ is the discrete step of the calculation.

The main difference between the two diagrams shown in Figure 1 and Figure 2 provided is in the visualization and layout, with the MATLAB/Simulink model offering a more direct visual representation of the mathematical relationships between the components.

Figure 3 shows the code of the simulation model developed by the SD principles.

*Figure 3: Simulation model developed by the SD principles.*

```
init   I = 1
flow   I = +dt*infectionRate
doc    I = Number of infected.
unit   I = person
init   S = initialValueOfSusceptible
flow   S = -dt*infectionRate
doc    S = Number of susceptible.
unit   S = person
init   SSE = 0
flow   SSE = +dt*ErroSquared
doc    SSE = Sum of Squared Errors as criteria function.
unit   SSE = dmnl
aux    ErroSquared = Error^2
doc    ErroSquared = Derivative of SSE as squared error of difference between actual and simulated data.
unit   ErroSquared = dmnl
aux    infectionRate = (beta*I*S)/N
doc    infectionRate = Infection rate at which susceptible become infected with unit person/day. | unit
       infectionRate = person/day
aux    Error = R-I | Diff. between Real data and simulated data.
unit   Error = person
aux    initialValueOfSusceptible = proportionOfThePopulationThatIsSusceptible*population
doc    initialValueOfSusceptible = According to the population and the proportion, the initialization of the
       Susceptible state is determined.
unit   initialValueOfSusceptible = person
aux    N = S+I
doc    N = Sum of Susceptible and Infected.
unit   N = person
const  beta = 0.11
doc    beta = Parameter, that determines the intensity of infection.
unit   beta = dmnl
const  population = 39355
doc    population = Population of particular country.
unit   population = person
const  proportionOfThePopulationThatIsSusceptible = 0.0099
doc    proportionOfThePopulationThatIsSusceptible = Proportion of the population that is susceptible.
unit   proportionOfThePopulationThatIsSusceptible = dmnl
const  R = 0
doc    R = Real world data, Total cases for each day, i.e. cumulative number of infected.
unit   R = person
spec   start = 0.00000
spec   stop = 88.00000
spec   dt = 0.50000
spec   method = Euler (fixed step)
```

According to our previous research (Stanovov et al., 2022), we have picked the six countries, where the initial, first wave could visibly be identified. The data exercise the indistinguishable S-shape and therefore it was our intention to parametrize the SI model to the data to extract key parameters. This would provide the initial parameters in the case of similar pandemics outbreak in the future.

The validation was performed on *n* points according to the following equations (Oliva, 1995; Sterman, 1984) where the coefficient of determination is defined as:

$$r^2 = \left( \left( \frac{1}{n} \sum_{t=1}^{n} (S_t A_t) - \overline{S}\overline{A} \right) / S_S A_A \right)^2$$

The coefficient of determination, $r^2$ is a statistical measure that represents the proportion of the variance in the dependent variable that is predictable from the independent variable. It provides a measure of how well the observed outcomes are replicated by the model, as the proportion of total variation of outcomes explained by the model. $S_t$ and $A_t$ are individual data points for two variables, simulated and actual at time t. $\overline{S}$ and $\overline{A}$ are the mean values of $S$ and $A$ respectively. $S_S$ and $A_A$ are standard deviations of simulation data and actual data respectively. Here we assume the standard deviation of the population and not sample.

Mean Absolute Percent Eror (MAPE) is a metric for understanding the accuracy of forecasting methods. It provides the average magnitude of errors between simulated and actual values expressed as a percentage, allowing for an easy-to-interpret scale-less measure of accuracy:

$$MAPE = \frac{1}{n} \sum_{t=1}^{n} \left| \frac{S_t - A_t}{A_t} \right| \times 100$$

MAPE provides an average of the absolute percentage discrepancies between simulated and actual values. Lower MAPE values indicate a better fit of the forecasted values to the actuals, while higher values suggest a poorer fit. One thing to note is that MAPE can be sensitive to situations where the actual value is close to zero, as this can lead to very large percentage errors.

Table 1 provides an interpretation of the Mean Absolute Percent Error (MAPE) value, which is commonly used to measure the accuracy of forecasting models (Lewis, 1982). The lower the MAPE value, the more accurate the forecasting model is, as it indicates that the model's predictions deviate less from the actual observed values. If MAPE value is less than 10% then the model is considered to be "Highly accurate." When the MAPE value is below 10%, it means that the forecasting errors are relatively small, indicating that the model has performed exceptionally well in predicting the observed data. The range between 10% and 20% is considered as "Good forecasting." While there's a moderate level of error, the predictions made by the model are still reasonably close to the observed values. MAPE values between 20% and 50% are considered as "Reasonable forecasting." A MAPE value in this range indicates a higher level of error, but the forecasting might still be acceptable depending on the context and the specific application. A MAPE value, that is greater than 50% indicates "Inaccurate forecasting" and suggests the model may be erroneous. Such a high error rate means the predictions made by the model are substantially off from the actual observed values, and there might be issues with the model's parameters, assumptions, or data used.

*Table 1: Interprestation of MAPE values adapted from* (Lewis, 1982)

| **MAPE value [%]** | **Interpretation** |
|---|---|
| <10 | Highly accurate forecasting |
| 10–20 | Good forecasting |
| 20–50 | Reasonable forecasting |
| >50 | Inaccurate forecasting (erroneous model) |

Table 1 offers a general guideline for evaluating the performance of developed models based on their MAPE values. This also enable us to perform validation. Since the MAPE values could easily be understood as the deviation from the real data in percentage, this is one of the main metrics at the simulation model validation.

Mean Squared Error (MSE) is a metric used to evaluate the accuracy of predictive models. It represents the average of the squares of the errors or deviations, that is, the difference between the simulation and actual data. Bias component of MSE (Mean Squared Error) captures the proportion of the MSE that can be attributed to the systematic deviation of the model's predictions from the actual values. It provides insight into whether a model's predictions are systematically too high or too low relative to the true values. Bias component of MSE is expressed as:

$$U^m = (\overline{S} - \overline{A})^2 / MSE$$

Variation component of MSE quantifies the portion of the MSE attributable to differences in the variability between the model's predictions and the actual values. If is close to 1, it suggests that the majority of the error in the model is due to variance, while a value close to 0 would indicate minimal variance-related error. This component helps to identify if the model's predictions have either too much or too little variability in comparison to the true data. Variation component of MSE is expressed as:

$$U^s = (S_S - A_A)^2 / MSE$$

Covariation component of MSE measures the extent to which the changes in simulated values deviate from the changes in actual values, adjusted for the overall level of error (MSE). A $U_c$ close to 1 would indicate that the majority of the model's error is due to this covariation discrepancy. Conversely, a $U_c$ close to 0 would suggest minimal error due to lack of the covariation between the simulated and the actual values. The equation for $U_c$ is:

$$U^c = 2(1-r)S_S A_A / MSE$$

where $A_t$ are actual numbers gained by the publically available data and $S_t$ are simulation results provided by the developed model. *r* epresents the correlation coefficient between the simulated values and the actual values of COVID-19 spread. Table 2 shows the initial and end dates of the considered first wave for particular country. The data was obtained from the Our World in Data web page (Mathieu et al., 2020; OurWorldInData, 2023). For each country, the table lists a) Initial date: this is the date marking the beginning of the first wave for that country, b) End date: the date marking the end of the first wave, c) No. of days: the duration, in days, of the first wave, calculated from the initial to the end date, d) Init. val.: the initial number of total cases recorded at the beginning of the first wave, e), End value: the total number of cases recorded by the end of the first wave, f) Population: The total population of the country is shown in the last column. Provided information about the used data is important fort the repetability of the conducted experiments. One could observe the variation of the population sizes as well as the length of the first wave with approximate ratio of 1:3½ for length of the first wave and 1:1300 for the size of the population. This speaks for the variety of the sample data as well as different dynamics of the COVID-19 epidemy spread.

*Table 2: The initial and end dates of the considered first wave for particular country. The number of days as well as initial and end value of total cases is provided. The population size of each country is shown in the last column*

| | **Initial date** | **End date** | **No. of days** | **Init. val.** | **End value** | **Population** |
|---|---|---|---|---|---|---|
| **NZL** | 2020-02-28 | 2020-06-15 | 109 | 1 | 1154 | 5185289 |
| IRL | 2020-03-02 | 2020-06-26 | 117 | 1 | 25396 | 5023108 |
| AUS | 2020-01-25 | 2020-06-11 | 139 | 1 | 7267 | 26177410 |
| SAU | 2020-03-04 | 2021-01-09 | 312 | 1 | 363582 | 36408824 |
| LIE | 2020-03-03 | 2020-05-30 | 89 | 1 | 83 | 39355 |
| KOR | 2020-01-19 | 2020-05-06 | 109 | 1 | 10806 | 51815808 |

Described data provided the basis for our work, where we would like to compare the real-world data to the output of the SI models and determine the key parameters, that determine the epidemiological dynamics.

## 3. Results

In the first step, the parametrization has been performed, where the MATLAB/Simulink model was applied with Parameter Estimation Tool. The SI model developed in Simulink was connected to the MATLAB workspace in order to perform post simulation analysis. We have implemented the algorithms for the key validation measures such as MAPE, RMSE, MSE and $r^2$. This implementation enabled us to quickly analyse the gathered data of the parametrization procedure. There were two parameters that were determined by the parameter estimation procedure, $\beta$ and the proportion of the population that is susceptible (p). Similar proceure was performed also with the model developed in Powersim with the Powersim Solver Genetic Algorithm tool.

Figure 4 shows the responses of the parametrized SI model for the six considered countries. One could observe the number of days on the x-axis, which goes from 0 to more than 300 days. On the y-axis the total number of cases is shown.

Orange line represents the actual data while the blue line shows the response of the parametrized model. For New Zealand, the actual orange curve starts gradually and then steeply increases until around day 50, where it stabilizes around 1000 total cases, with the blue simulation curve closely following this trajectory. In the case of Ireland, the actual curve rises steadily from the start, reaching just under 30,000 total cases by day 100, with the simulation closely matching this data. Australia's actual curve shows a gentle rise initially, which then becomes steeper around day 20, stabilizing near 5000 cases around day 70, and the simulation is almost identical to this. Saudi Arabia's actual curve depicts a gradual increase initially, followed by a sharp rise starting around day 100, reaching over 200,000 cases by day 300, while the simulation starts off similarly but deviates by consistently predicting higher cases after day 100. Liechtenstein's curve is relatively flat, showing a gentle rise to about 100 total cases by day 70, with a very close simulation match.

Lastly, South Korea's actual curve steeply rises initially, reaching about 8000 cases by day 50, after which it starts to stabilize, and the simulated curve aligns closely but slightly underestimates the cases around day 50. The speed of the epidemy spread is the fastest for the LIE – Liechtenstein, where the first wave was over in less than 50 days. The longest first wave between the considered countries was for the case of Saudi Arabia – SAU. One could also observe different terminal

*Figure 4: Actual (orange) and simulated (blue) dynamics of the COVID-19 pandemics first wave for NZL – New Zealand, IRL – Ireland, AUS – Australia, SAU – Saudi Arabia, LIE – Liechtenstein and KOR – South Korea. On x-axis the time in days is shown and on the y-axis the number of total cases are shown, i.e. the cumulative number of infected up to the certain day.*

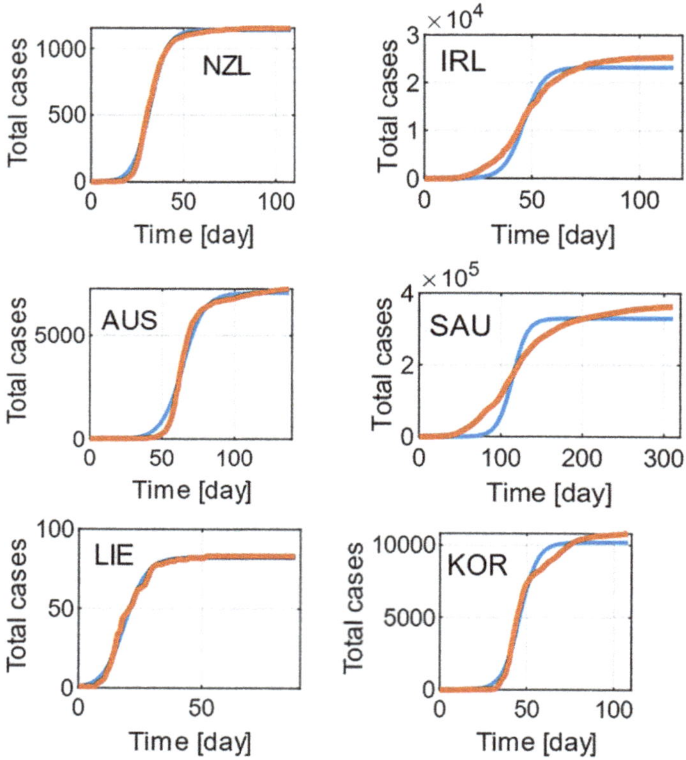


values of the total cases. In the case of Liechtenstein, the terminal value of the total cases in the first wave was 83 while for the case of Saudi Arabia – SAU, the terminal value of total cases was 363582. One can observe the distinguishable S-shaped curve which is the hallmark of the SI model response and captures the main mechanism of the epidemy spread, which is the transmission, that is dependent on the number of contacts between the susceptible and infected. For New Zealand – NZL, Australia – AUS and Liechtenstein one could observe better fit than for the cases of Ireland – IRL, Saudi Arabia – SAU and South

Korea – KOR. In the next steps, the quantification of the goodness of fit (Istaiteh et al., 2020; Nguyen et al., 2021; Turk et al., 2021) will be provided with MAPE and corresponding measures.

Figure 5 shows the scatter diagrams of the parametrization of the SI simulation model of the COVID-19 pandemics first the first wave. Here the Genetic Algorithms (GA) have been applied in order to search for the combination of the $\beta$ parameter and the percentOfPopulationThatIsSusceptible ($p$) parameter (expressed as the ratio). Distinctively, red dots depict values of the 'beta' parameter, while green dots signify values of the 'percentOfPopulationThat IsSusceptible' parameter. Analyzing these scatter points offers insights into how closely the simulation aligns with real-world data based on the chosen parameters.

For instance, in the SAU (Saudi Arabia) graph, the concentration of red dots around the 0.111 mark on the x-axis suggests that this beta value aligns the model response best with actual data, as it corresponds to the minimal deviation on the y-axis. Similarly, the cluster of green dots around the 0.009 value on the x-axis for 'percentOfPopulationThatIsSusceptible' indicates that this proportion results in the smallest deviation between the simulation and actual data for SAU. Through these diagrams, one can observe the convergence of the GA in the optimal parameter values search for each country.

The maximum number of the GA generations was set to 100 with 50 genes per generation. The target variable was SSE. Here we wanted to minimize the deviation between the actual data and the simulation. The boundaries of the parameters were $\beta \in [0.0001, 0.1]$ and $p \in [0.00001, 0.5]$. Red dots on the scatter diagram represent the value of the $\beta$ parameter, while the geen dots represent the value of the percentOfPopulationThatIsSusceptible (p) parameter (expressed as the ratio).

Table 3 Shows the results of the validation for the parameters determined with the MATLAB/Simulink parameter estimation tool. The Coefficient of Determination ($r^2$) provides insights into the goodness-of-fit of the model. Values closer to 1 denote that the model can explain a greater fraction of the variance in the observed data. Based on the presented values, all countries have a high $r^2$, with NZL and LIE boasting a perfect score of 1.00, indicating the model fits almost perfectly to the observed data for these countries. Mean Absolute Percent Error (MAPE) signifies the average magnitude of errors between predicted and observed values, expressed as a percentage. Lower MAPE values indicate better accuracy. Among the countries, LIE shows the smallest MAPE (19.48%), suggesting the most accurate predictions, whereas AUS and KOR have the highest MAPE values, hovering around 81%, signalling potential inaccuracies in model

*Figure 5: Scatter diagrams of the parametrization of the SI simulation model of the COVID-19 pandemics first wave for NZL – New Zealand, IRL – Ireland, AUS – Australia, SAU – Saudi Arabia, LIE – Liechtenstein and KOR – South Korea. On x-axis the parameter beta range is shown as well as percentOfPopulationThatIsSusceptible is shonw, expressed as a ratio. On the y-axis, the deviation between actual data and the model is shown. Red dots represent the value of beta parameter, while the geen dots represent the value of the percentOfPopulationThatIsSusceptible parameter.*

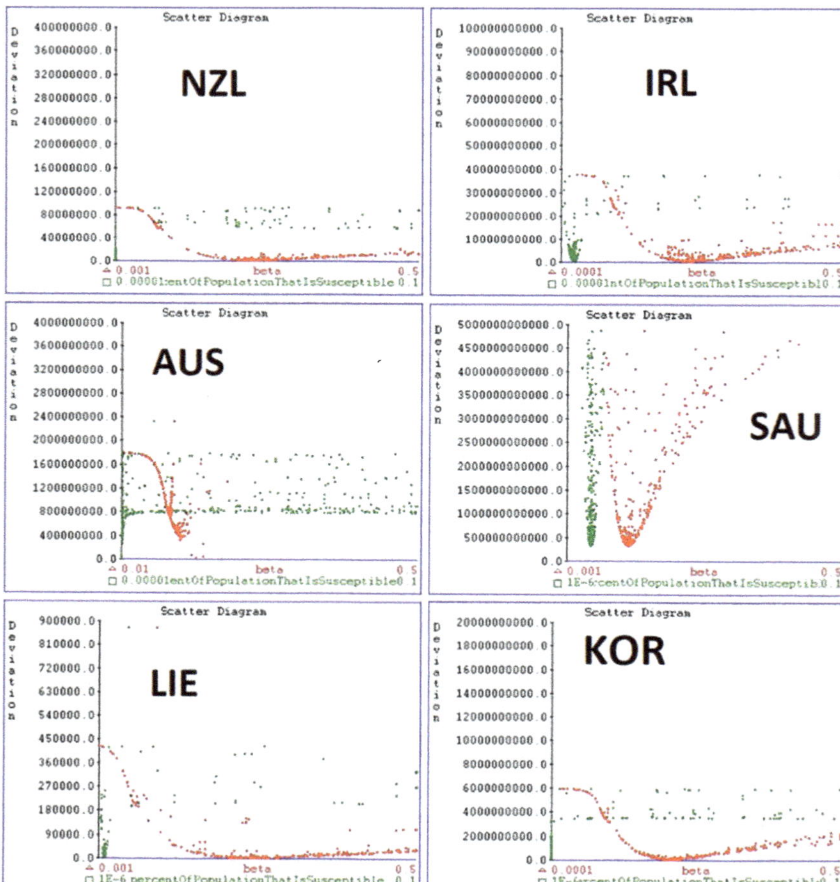


predictions for these countries. Values over 50% indicate, that special caution should be made in applying the model. Mean Square Error (MSE) and Root Mean Square Error (RMSE) are metrics that give insights into the model's prediction errors. They are particularly sensitive to outliers, so higher values suggest larger errors. Given the table, SAU has an especially high MSE and RMSE, pointing to significant discrepancies between the model and actual data. The components of MSE — Bias component (Um), Variation component (Us), and Covariation component (Uc) — shed light on the sources of error in the model. Specifically, Um gauges systematic error in predictions. For all countries, the bias component is quite low, which is encouraging as it suggests minimal systematic error in the model's predictions. Us represents the variability in errors, and it's relatively low for all countries, implying that the errors are consistent across data points. Uc denotes how much of the error is due to the joint behavior of predictions and observations. The high Uc values across all countries (especially for LIE and KOR with values close to 1) indicate that most of the error can be attributed to the proportional discrepancies between predicted and observed values. In summary, the validation results suggest that the simulation model offers a commendable fit to the real data for most countries, especially considering the $r^2$ values. While there are disparities in predictions (as seen with MAPE for AUS and KOR), the model's errors seem more proportional (high Uc) than systematic or variable. This is indicative of a reliable model, but some improvements might be necessary for countries with higher prediction errors.

*Table 3: Results of the validation for the parameters determined with the MATLAB/Simulink parameter estimation tool*

| | NZL | IRL | AUS | SAU | LIE | KOR |
|---|---|---|---|---|---|---|
| **N** | 109 | 117 | 139 | 312 | 89 | 109 |
| $r^2$ | 1.00 | 0.98 | 0.99 | 0.96 | 1.00 | 0.99 |
| MAPE | 34.79 | 29.16 | 80.97 | 35.56 | 19.48 | 81.17 |
| MSE | 470 | 2574979 | 82816 | 1019427143 | 4 | 243155 |
| RMSE | 22 | 1605 | 288 | 31928 | 2 | 493 |
| Um | 0.04 | 0.25 | 0.05 | 0.07 | 0.01 | 0.00 |
| Us | 0.13 | 0.00 | 0.08 | 0.07 | 0.06 | 0.02 |
| Uc | 0.83 | 0.75 | 0.87 | 0.86 | 0.94 | 0.98 |

Table 4 shows the results of the validation for the parameters determined with the Powersim GA Solver tool. In this case, MAPE values have changed, reflecting a shift in prediction accuracy. NZL and IRL see slight improvements, with decreased errors of 34.30% and 27.96% respectively. AUS also exhibits a reduction in MAPE from 80.97% to 72.26%. However, KOR's error surges noticeably from 81.17% to a staggering 103.06%, suggesting the model's predictions for

South Korea are even less accurate using the Powersim GA solver. MSE and RMSE show, that there are fluctuations in these metrics across countries. For instance, IRL witnesses a reduction in MSE, indicating that the Powersim GA solver reduces error magnitudes for this country. Conversely, AUS and KOR see an uptick in both MSE and RMSE, signifying increased discrepancies between the model's predictions and actual data for these nations. Regarding the Um (Bias component) the Powersim GA solver, the bias significantly increases from 0.05 to 0.30 for AUS, indicating the model now has a higher tendency to consistently over- or under-predict for Australia. Regarding the Us (Variation component) there's an observable shift for AUS; here's an increase from 0.08 to 0.15, while for IRL, the value decreases from 0.00 to 0.04. This suggests that the consistency of errors across data points varies with the solver, with AUS experiencing more variability in errors using the Powersim GA solver. Uc (Covariation component) drops noticeably for AUS from 0.87 to 0.55, indicating that with the Powersim GA solver, a smaller portion of the error can be attributed to proportional differences. In essence, when using the Powersim GA solver for validation, there are noticeable shifts in prediction accuracy and error components for certain countries. While some countries like NZL and IRL experience improved prediction accuracy (lower MAPE), others like AUS and especially KOR see less accurate results. Additionally, the nature and sources of the errors have adjusted, as reflected in the components of MSE, suggesting that the Powersim GA solver introduces different dynamics to the model's performance compared to the MATLAB/Simulink Parameter Estimation tool.

*Table 4: Results of the validation for the parameters determined with the Powerism GA Solver tool*

| | NZL | IRL | AUS | SAU | LIE | KOR |
|---|---|---|---|---|---|---|
| N | 109 | 117 | 139 | 312 | 89 | 109 |
| r^2 | 1.00 | 0.98 | 0.99 | 0.96 | 1.00 | 0.99 |
| MAPE | 34.30 | 27.96 | 72.26 | 35.17 | 20.33 | 103.06 |
| MSE | 476 | 2378863 | 234396 | 1041169246 | 5 | 323703 |
| RMSE | 22 | 1542 | 484 | 32267 | 2 | 569 |
| Um | 0.02 | 0.03 | 0.30 | 0.03 | 0.02 | 0.10 |
| Us | 0.12 | 0.04 | 0.15 | 0.06 | 0.12 | 0.02 |
| Uc | 0.86 | 0.93 | 0.55 | 0.91 | 0.86 | 0.88 |

Table 5 presents the results of a t-test comparing the RMSE accuracy of MATLAB Parameter estimation tool and Powersim solver GA. Hew, we would like to statistically determine whether there is a significant difference in the accuracy of these two tools. Key metrics from the table include Mean RMSE for MATLAB and Powersim. The Variance gives the spread of the RMSE values around their respective means. Observations indicate that the t-test is based on the six data points for each tool, for each country. The calculated t-value (t Stat) based on the sample data is shown in the table. This value helps determine whether there's a statistically significant difference between the two groups. The table provides the p-vaues for the one-tailed and two-tailed t-tests respectively. A p-value is a measure of the evidence against a null hypothesis. The smaller the p-value, the stronger the evidence to reject the null hypothesis. The table also provides the critical one-tail and two-tail t-values for the one-tailed and two-tailed t-tests. If the absolute value of the t Stat is greater than the critical t-value, we reject the null hypothesis. Given the presented data the p-value for the two-tailed test is 0.990452, which is much greater than the common alpha level of 0.05 used to determine statistical significance. This means that we do not have sufficient evidence to reject the null hypothesis. The calculated t Stat (–0.01227) is smaller in magnitude than both critical t-values (1.812461 for one-tail and 2.228139 for two-tail). Based on the t-test results presented in the table, there is no statistically significant difference in the RMSE accuracy between results obtained with MATLAB/Simulink Parameter estimation tool and Powersim solver GA. Hence, we can accept the hypothesis that there is no difference in accuracy whether using MATLAB or Powersim.

*Table 5: t-test Comparison of RMSE Accuracy between MATLAB and Powersim Simulations*

| | **RMSE MATLAB** | **RMSE Powersim** |
|---|---|---|
| Mean | 5722.963 | 5814.425 |
| Variance | 1.65E+08 | 1.68E+08 |
| Observations | 6 | 6 |
| Hypothesized Mean Difference | 0 | |
| **df** | 10 | |
| **t Stat** | −0.01227 | |
| **P(T<=t) one-tail** | 0.495226 | |
| **t Critical one-tail** | 1.812461 | |
| **P(T<=t) two-tail** | 0.990452 | |
| **t Critical two-tail** | 2.228139 | |

Table 6 shows similar results, this time considering the MAPE metrics. This time, the calculated t-value (t Stat) is –0.11625. This is the test statistic we get when comparing the MAPE means of MATLAB and Powersim. The p-value for the two-tailed test is 0.909755. Comparing the absolute value of the t Stat to the critical t-values, we see that |–0.11625| is much smaller than both 1.812461 (for one-tail) and 2.228139 (for two-tail). Considering these results, there is no statistically significant difference in the MAPE accuracy between MATLAB and Powersim. Thus, we can accept the hypothesis that there are no significant differences in accuracy between MATLAB and Powersim when considering MAPE values.

*Table 6: t-test Comparison of MAPE Accuracy between MATLAB and Powersim Simulations*

| | **MAPE MATLAB** | **MAPE Powersim** |
|---|---|---|
| Mean | 46.85414 | 48.8466 |
| Variance | 735.5109 | 1027.038 |
| Observations | 6 | 6 |
| Hypothesized Mean Difference | 0 | |
| **df** | 10 | |
| **t Stat** | –0.11625 | |
| **P(T<=t) one-tail** | 0.454878 | |
| **t Critical one-tail** | 1.812461 | |
| **P(T<=t) two-tail** | 0.909755 | |
| **t Critical two-tail** | 2.228139 | |

Table 7 shows the results of the parametrization of the SI model with MATLAB/Simulink Parameter Estimation tool for considered countries which are listed in the fist column. Other columns provide the estimated values for $\beta$ parameter, proportion of the population that is susceptible (prop), actual number of infected at the end of the first wave (I-actual), simulated number of infected at the end of the first wave (I-model), difference between the terminal values (Diff) and the percentage of deviation between the actual and simulated number of infected. For example, in the case of NZL (New Zealand), the estimated $\beta$ parameter is 0.21994, which determine the intensity of the epidemy spread. The proportion of the population that is susceptible is 0.00022. The actual number of infected people by the end of the first wave was 1,154, while the model predicted 1,141, which is a difference (Diff) of –13.07 individuals, translating to a –1% deviation from the actual number.

*Table 7: Results of the parametrization of the SI model with MATLAB/Simulink Parameter Estimation tool*

| | $\beta$ | **prop** | **I-actual** | **I-model** | **Diff** | [%] |
|---|---|---|---|---|---|---|
| **NZL** | 0.21994 | 0.00022 | 1154 | 1141 | −13.07 | −1 |
| IRL | 0.21758 | 0.00463 | 25396 | 23255 | −2140.59 | −8 |
| AUS | 0.13772 | 0.00027 | 7267 | 7077 | −189.86 | −3 |
| SAU | 0.11114 | 0.00907 | 363582 | 330364 | −33218.24 | −9 |
| LIE | 0.23129 | 0.00207 | 83 | 81 | −1.72 | −2 |
| KOR | 0.20019 | 0.00020 | 10806 | 10212 | −594.12 | −5 |

Table 8 shows the results of the parametrization of the SI model with Powersim Solver GA tool.

*Table 8: Results of the parametrization of the SI model with Powersim Solver GA tool*

| | **beta** | **prop** | **S-actual** | **S-model** | **Diff** | [%] |
|---|---|---|---|---|---|---|
| **NZL** | 0.21922 | 0.00022 | 1154 | 1141 | −13.24 | −1 |
| IRL | 0.22193 | 0.00475 | 25396 | 23865 | −1531.21 | −6 |
| AUS | 0.13413 | 0.00029 | 7267 | 7696 | 429.16 | 6 |
| SAU | 0.11378 | 0.00909 | 363582 | 330956 | −32625.79 | −9 |
| LIE | 0.23521 | 0.00206 | 83 | 81 | −1.97 | −2 |
| KOR | 0.20767 | 0.00020 | 10806 | 10208 | −598.29 | −6 |

Both, the Powersim Solver GA tool and MATLAB/Simulink Parameter Estimation tool produced comparable results for the countries listed, with deviations mostly ranging between −1% to −9%. However, there are slight differences in the estimated $\beta$ values and predicted cases. For instance, Powersim performed better for Ireland, while MATLAB had a closer prediction for Australia. Overall, the two tools are consistent in their estimations, with minor deviations indicating the nuances in the optimization algorithms and underlying assumptions of each software tool. These results can help in understanding the accuracy and potential areas of improvement for the SI model when predicting future outbreaks or assessing similar pandemics.

## 4. Discussion

Despite the availability of data on the COVID-19 pandemic, early models struggled to accurately predict the disease's spread. It is important to better understand two main aspects: the assessment of current models for predicting pandemic spread and analyzing the dynamics of disease spread. Classical epidemiological models, such as the Susceptible-Infected-Recovered (SIR) and Susceptible-Exposed-Infected-Recovered (SEIR) models, are highlighted, although they may not always reflect the pandemic's real dynamics. The SEIR model, which incorporates an "Exposed" compartment, and various other modifications and non-conventional models, like the Bass-diffusion model, are applied in several studies. A significant concern is the influence of unreported cases on disease spread. One of the main task in present paper was to parametrize the SI model using MATLAB/Simulink and the Powersim Genetic Algorithm Solver, integrating population data to enhance understanding of COVID-19 spread mechanisms.

The SI model offers a simplistic approach to understanding the spread of infectious diseases, notably those like COVID-19, where there's no recovery or immunity. This research presents two variations of the SI model – one implemented using MATLAB/Simulink and another based on the principles of System Dynamics. While the mathematical principles remain consistent, the visual representation differs, potentially impacting the user's understanding and accessibility to the model.

The MATLAB/Simulink representation provides an intuitive platform for simulation, which can be advantageous for users familiar with engineering simulation environments. This environment allows for the quick adjustment of parameters to study different disease spread scenarios. On the other hand, the System Dynamics model, being founded on principles from feedback control systems, emphasizes understanding the causality and feedback loops inherent in disease spread dynamics. This visualization is particularly effective for those in the policy and management fields, allowing for comprehensive insights into how different variables interplay.

The validation methodologies employed in this research, including MAPE, r2, and MSE, are robust and recognized in the literature. The distinction of bias, variation, and covariation components of MSE offers granular insights into the source of discrepancies between the simulated and actual data. This helps researchers fine-tune the model or adjust assumptions to improve model accuracy.

The dataset selected, focusing on the first wave from six varied countries, offers a diverse range for studying the model's applicability across different settings. The initial and end dates and the metrics used provide a clear understanding of the progression and magnitude of the first wave in these countries. By focusing on this specific time frame, the research aims to extract key parameters that could be invaluable in predicting or understanding the progression of similar pandemics in the future.

Understanding infectious disease spread is vital for both public health and policy-making, especially in the wake of global pandemics like COVID-19. By employing models like SI and using advanced simulation platforms, researchers can gain deeper insights into the disease dynamics, leading to better preparedness and response strategies. The presented research provides a detailed methodological approach, using varied tools and validation techniques, setting a precedent for future studies in the field.

The overview of the parametrization, simulation, and validation of the SI (Susceptible-Infected) model for six different countries, using two different toolsets: MATLAB/Simulink and Powersim GA Solver was successfully provided. The usage of MATLAB/Simulink in tandem with its Parameter Estimation Tool and connection to MATLAB's workspace offers the ability to swiftly evaluate and fine-tune the SI model. The usage of key validation measures such as MAPE, RMSE, MSE, and r^2 is commendable, as these measures offer a holistic perspective on the model's accuracy, variability, and overall fit. Having two parameters, $\beta$ (transmission rate) and p (proportion of susceptible population), allows for a simpler yet insightful representation of the model's dynamics. The S-shaped curve characteristic of the SI model response is evident, highlighting the transmission mechanics based on susceptible-infected interactions. The model showcases a close fit for countries like New Zealand, Australia, and Liechtenstein. However, there are noticeable deviations in countries like Saudi Arabia and South Korea, suggesting potential limitations or external factors affecting the epidemic dynamics in these countries.

Regarding the validation, the high $r^2$ values across all countries are encouraging, suggesting that the model explains a significant proportion of the variance in the actual data. The bias component, Um, is notably low for all countries, implying minimal systematic errors. However, countries like Australia and South Korea exhibit high MAPE values, signaling potential inaccuracies. The high Uc values across countries highlight that most of the error stems from proportional differences between predicted and actual values.

The Powersim GA solver results in varied model performance compared to MATLAB/Simulink. While some countries observe improvements, others like South Korea exhibit worsened prediction accuracy. Notably, the nature of errors, as reflected in the components of MSE (Um, Us, Uc), changes depending on the tool used. This suggests that the specific optimization algorithm and the manner in which it searches the parameter space can influence model outcomes.

One could conclude, that The SI model offers a good fit for representing the COVID-19 pandemic's first wave dynamics for most considered countries, especially when validated using the MATLAB/Simulink tool. The validation metrics employed provide a comprehensive assessment of the model's reliability, accuracy, and potential sources of error. The selection of tools and parameter estimation methods can influence model outcomes. The results using Powersim GA Solver highlight the importance of tool and method selection in simulation and model validation. The noticeable deviations in predictions for some countries suggest that while the SI model provides a generalized view, other external or country-specific factors might need to be considered for a more precise modeling.

Conducted analysis underlines the significance of model validation and the selection of appropriate tools when simulating complex epidemiological phenomena. Future steps might include investigating the factors causing deviations in countries like Saudi Arabia and South Korea, and potentially considering more complex models (like SEIR) that account for additional dynamics in epidemic spread.

For both RMSE and MAPE metrics, based on the t-test results presented in Table 5 and Table 6, there is no statistically significant difference in the accuracy of results obtained with MATLAB and Powersim. This implies that, from a statistical standpoint, either tool can be used without expecting a significant difference in the accuracy of the results for the given datasets.

Both MATLAB/Simulink Parameter Estimation tool and Powersim Solver GA tool offer reliable parametrization for the SI model, producing results with minor deviations for the considered countries. The variations between their predictions can serve as an indicator of the robustness of each tool and its sensitivity to the underlying data. Using both tools in tandem could provide a more holistic understanding and a comprehensive error margin for predictions in future epidemiological studies.

## Acknowledgement

The authors acknowledges the financial support from the Slovenian Research and Innovation Agency (research core funding No. P5-0018), the Ministry of Higher Education, Science, and Innovation of the Republic of Slovenia as part of the Next Generation EU National Recovery and Resilience Plan (Grants No. 3330-22-3515; NOO No: C3330-22-953012), and the Erasmus+ program of the European Union (Grant No. 2021-1-MK01-KA220-HED-000027646).

## Bibliography

Abadias, L., Estrada-Rodriguez, G., & Estrada, E. (2020). Fractional-order susceptible-infected model: Definition and applications to the study of COVID-19 main protease. *Fractional Calculus and Applied Analysis*, *23*(3), 635–655. https://doi.org/10.1515/fca-2020-0033

Alimohamadi, Y., Taghdir, M., & Sepandi, M. (2020). Estimate of the basic reproduction number for COVID-19: A systematic review and meta-Analysis. In *Journal of Preventive Medicine and Public Health* (Vol. 53, Issue 3, pp. 151–157). Korean Society for Preventive Medicine. https://doi.org/10.3961/JPMPH.20.076

Allen, L. J. S. (1994). Some discrete-time SI, SIR, and SIS epidemic models. *Mathematical Biosciences*, *124*(1). https://doi.org/10.1016/0025-5564(94)90025-6

Annas, S., Isbar Pratama, M., Rifandi, M., Sanusi, W., & Side, S. (2020). Stability analysis and numerical simulation of SEIR model for pandemic COVID-19 spread in Indonesia. *Chaos, Solitons and Fractals*, *139*. https://doi.org/10.1016/j.chaos.2020.110072

Bass, F. (1969). A new product growth for model consumer durables. *Management Science*, *15*(5), 215–227.

Bass, F. M. (2004). Comments on "A new product growth for model consumer durables." In *Management Science* (Vol. 50, Issue 12 SUPPL., pp. 1833–1840). https://doi.org/10.1287/mnsc.1040.0300

Chen, X., Li, J., Xiao, C., & Yang, P. (2021). Numerical solution and parameter estimation for uncertain SIR model with application to COVID-19. *Fuzzy Optimization and Decision Making*, *20*(2), 189–208. https://doi.org/10.1007/s10700-020-09342-9

Comunian, A., Gaburro, R., & Giudici, M. (2020). Inversion of a SIR-based model: A critical analysis about the application to COVID-19 epidemic. *Physica D: Nonlinear Phenomena*, *413*. https://doi.org/10.1016/j.physd.2020.132674

Cooper, I., Mondal, A., & Antonopoulos, C. G. (2020). A SIR model assumption for the spread of COVID-19 in different communities. *Chaos, Solitons and Fractals*, *139*. https://doi.org/10.1016/j.chaos.2020.110057

D'Arienzo, M., & Coniglio, A. (2020). Assessment of the SARS-CoV-2 basic reproduction number, R0, based on the early phase of COVID-19 outbreak in Italy. *Biosafety and Health*, *2*(2), 57–59. https://doi.org/10.1016/j.bsheal.2020.03.004

Demongeot, J., Griette, Q., & Magal, P. (2020). SI epidemic model applied to COVID-19 data in mainland China. *Royal Society Open Science*, *7*(12). https://doi.org/10.1098/rsos.201878

Dutta, A. (2022). COVID-19 waves: variant dynamics and control. *Scientific Reports*, *12*(1). https://doi.org/10.1038/s41598-022-13371-2

Engelbrecht, F. A., & Scholes, R. J. (2021). Test for Covid-19 seasonality and the risk of second waves. *One Health, 12.* https://doi.org/10.1016/j.onehlt.2020.100202

Ferencek, A., Kofjač, D., Škraba, A., Sašek, B., & Borštnar, M. K. (2020). Deep learning predictive models for terminal call rate prediction during the warranty period. Business Systems Research: International journal of the Society for Advancing Innovation and Research in Economy, 11(2), 36–50.

Forrester, J. W. (1958). Industrial dynamics: a major breakthrough for decision makers. *Harvard Business Review*, *36*(4), 37–66.

Gatto, M., Bertuzzo, E., Mari, L., Miccoli, S., Carraro, L., Casagrandi, R., & Rinaldo, A. (2020). *Spread and dynamics of the COVID-19 epidemic in Italy: Effects of emergency containment measures*, *117*(19). https://doi.org/10.1073/pnas.2004978117/-/DCSupplemental.y

Gounane, S., Barkouch, Y., Atlas, A., Bendahmane, M., Karami, F., & Meskine, D. (2021). An adaptive social distancing SIR model for COVID-19 disease spreading and forecasting. *Epidemiologic Methods*, *10*(s1). https://doi.org/10.1515/em-2020-0044

He, S., Peng, Y., & Sun, K. (2020). SEIR modeling of the COVID-19 and its dynamics. *Nonlinear Dynamics*, *101*(3), 1667–1680. https://doi.org/10.1007/s11071-020-05743-y

Holmdahl, I., & Buckee, C. (2020). Wrong but Useful — What Covid-19 Epidemiologic Models Can and Cannot Tell Us. *New England Journal of Medicine*, *383*(4), 303–305. https://doi.org/10.1056/nejmp2016822

Istaiteh, O., Owais, T., Al-Madi, N., & Abu-Soud, S. (2020). Machine Learning Approaches for COVID-19 Forecasting. *2020 International Conference on Intelligent Data Science Technologies and Applications, IDSTA 2020*, 50–57. https://doi.org/10.1109/IDSTA50958.2020.9264101

Jones, J. H. (2007). *Notes On R 0 1 The Basic Reproduction Number in a Nutshell.* https://web.stanford.edu/~jhj1/teachingdocs/Jones-on-R0.pdf

Kofjac, D., Skraba, A., & Kljajic, M. (2003). Neural network modeling by system dynamics methodology (Vol. 1, pp. 424–428). IEEE.

Kosmidis, K., & Macheras, P. (2020). A fractal kinetics SI model can explain the dynamics of COVID-19 epidemics. *PLoS ONE, 15*(8 August). https://doi.org/10.1371/journal.pone.0237304

Kudryashov, N. A., Chmykhov, M. A., & Vigdorowitsch, M. (2021). Analytical features of the SIR model and their applications to COVID-19. *Applied Mathematical Modelling, 90,* 466–473. https://doi.org/10.1016/j.apm.2020.08.057

Lewis, C. D. (1982). *Industrial and business forecasting methods: A practical guide to exponential smoothing and curve fitting.*

Liu, Z., Magal, P., Seydi, O., & Webb, G. (2020). Understanding unreported cases in the COVID-19 epidemic outbreak in Wuhan, China, and the importance of major public health interventions. *Biology, 9*(3). https://doi.org/10.3390/biology9030050

Liu, Z., Magal, P., & Webb, G. (2021). Predicting the number of reported and unreported cases for the COVID-19 epidemics in China, South Korea, Italy, France, Germany and United Kingdom. *Journal of Theoretical Biology, 509.* https://doi.org/10.1016/j.jtbi.2020.110501

López, L., & Rodó, X. (2021). A modified SEIR model to predict the COVID-19 outbreak in Spain and Italy: Simulating control scenarios and multi-scale epidemics. *Results in Physics, 21.* https://doi.org/10.1016/j.rinp.2020.103746

Massiani, J., & Gohs, A. (2015). The choice of Bass model coefficients to forecast diffusion for innovative products: An empirical investigation for new automotive technologies. *Research in Transportation Economics, 50*, 17–28. https://doi.org/10.1016/j.retrec.2015.06.003

Mathieu, E., Ritchie, H., Rodés-Guirao, L., Appel, C., Giattino, C., Hasell, J., Macdonald, B., Dattani, S., Beltekian, D., Ortiz-Ospina, E., & Roser, M. (2020). Coronavirus Pandemic (COVID-19). *Our World in Data.*

Moein, S., Nickaeen, N., Roointan, A., Borhani, N., Heidary, Z., Javanmard, S. H., Ghaisari, J., & Gheisari, Y. (2021). Inefficiency of SIR models in forecasting COVID-19 epidemic: a case study of Isfahan. *Scientific Reports, 11*(1). https://doi.org/10.1038/s41598-021-84055-6

Mohajan, H., Mohajan, D., & Kumar Mohajan, H. (2022a). *Munich Personal RePEc Archive Mathematical Analysis of SEIR Model to Prevent COVID-19 Pandemic Mathematical Analysis of SEIR Model to Prevent COVID-19 Pandemic.*

Mohajan, H., Mohajan, D., & Kumar Mohajan, H. (2022b). *Munich Personal RePEc Archive Mathematical Analysis of SEIR Model to Prevent COVID-19 Pandemic Mathematical Analysis of SEIR Model to Prevent COVID-19 Pandemic.*

Mwalili, S., Kimathi, M., Ojiambo, V., Gathungu, D., & Mbogo, R. (2020). SEIR model for COVID-19 dynamics incorporating the environment and social distancing. *BMC Research Notes, 13*(1). https://doi.org/10.1186/s13104-020-05192-1

Nguyen, H. M., Turk, P. J., & McWilliams, A. D. (2021). Forecasting COVID-19 hospital census: A multivariate time-series model based on local infection incidence. *JMIR Public Health and Surveillance, 7*(8). https://doi.org/10.2196/28195

Odagaki, T. (2023). New compartment model for COVID-19. *Scientific Reports*, *13*(1). https://doi.org/10.1038/s41598-023-32159-6

Oliva, R. (1995). A Vensim® module to calculate summary statistics for historical fit. *D-4584, System Dynamics Group, Massachusetts Institute of Technology, Cambridge, MA*.

OurWorldInData. (2023). *owid / covid-19-data*. https://github.com/owid/covid-19-data

Pandey, G., Chaudhary, P., Gupta, R., & Pal, S. (n.d.). *SEIR and Regression Model based COVID-19 outbreak predictions in India*.

Pandit, J. J. (2020). Managing the R0 of COVID-19: mathematics fights back. *Anaesthesia*, *75*(12), 1643–1647. https://doi.org/10.1111/anae.15151

Qi, C., Karlsson, D., Sallmen, K., & Wyss, R. (2020). *Model studies on the COVID-19 pandemic in Sweden*. http://arxiv.org/abs/2004.01575

Rădulescu, A., Williams, C., & Cavanagh, K. (2020). Management strategies in a SEIR-type model of COVID 19 community spread. *Scientific Reports*, *10*(1). https://doi.org/10.1038/s41598-020-77628-4

Rahimi, I., Chen, F., & Gandomi, A. H. (2021). A review on COVID-19 forecasting models. In *Neural Computing and Applications*. Springer Science and Business Media Deutschland GmbH. https://doi.org/10.1007/s00521-020-05626-8

Rahmandad, H., & Sterman, J. D. (2012). Reporting guidelines for simulation-based research in social sciences. *System Dynamics Review*, *28*(4), 396–411. https://doi.org/10.1002/sdr.1481

Rocchi, E., Peluso, S., Sisti, D., & Carletti, M. (2020). A Possible Scenario for the Covid-19 Epidemic, Based on the SI(R) Model. *SN Comprehensive Clinical Medicine*, *2*(5), 501–503. https://doi.org/10.1007/s42399-020-00306-z

Samui, P., Mondal, J., & Khajanchi, S. (2020). A mathematical model for COVID-19 transmission dynamics with a case study of India. *Chaos, Solitons and Fractals*, *140*. https://doi.org/10.1016/j.chaos.2020.110173

Sharma, M., & Sharma, S. (2020). The Rising Number of COVID-19 Cases Reflecting Growing Search Trend and Concern of People: A Google Trend Analysis of Eight Major Countries. *Journal of Medical Systems*, *44*(7). https://doi.org/10.1007/s10916-020-01588-5

Simha, A., Prasad, R. V., & Narayana, S. (2020). *A simple Stochastic SIR model for COVID 19 Infection Dynamics for Karnataka: Learning from Europe*. http://arxiv.org/abs/2003.11920

Stanovov, V., Grabljevec, S., Akhmedova, S., Semenkin, E., Stojanović, R., Rozman, Č., & Škraba, A. (2022). Identification of COVID-19 spread mechanisms based on first-wave data, simulation models, and evolutionary algorithms. *PLoS ONE*, *17*(12 December). https://doi.org/10.1371/journal.pone.0279427

Sterman, J. D. (1984). Appropriate Summary Statistics for Evaluating the Historical Fit of System Dynamics Models. *Dynamica, 10*(2), 51–66.

Sterman, J. D. (2000). *Business Dynamics: Systems thinking and modeling for a complex world*. McGraw Hill.

Sun, H., Qiu, Y., Yan, H., Huang, Y., Zhu, Y., & Chen, S. X. (n.d.). *Tracking and Predicting COVID-19 Epidemic in China Mainland*. https://doi.org/10.1101/2020.02.17.20024257

Sy, K. T. L., White, L. F., & Nichols, B. E. (2021). Population density and basic reproductive number of COVID-19 across United States counties. *PLoS ONE, 16*(4 April). https://doi.org/10.1371/journal.pone.0249271

Thank, I., Acemoglu, D., Avery, C., Chernozhukov, V., Clark, A., Dushoff, J., Ellison, S. F., Stock, J., Werning, I., Ackerman, C., Kim, B., & Ellison, G. (2020). *Implications of Heterogeneous SIR Models for Analyses of COVID-19* *. http://www.nber.org/papers/w27373

Turk, P. J., Tran, T. P., Rose, G. A., & McWilliams, A. (2021). A predictive internet-based model for COVID-19 hospitalization census. *Scientific Reports, 11*(1). https://doi.org/10.1038/s41598-021-84091-2

Wang, H., Jia, S., Li, Z., Duan, Y., Tao, G., & Zhao, Z. (2022). A Comprehensive Review of Artificial Intelligence in Prevention and Treatment of COVID-19 Pandemic. In *Frontiers in Genetics* (Vol. 13). Frontiers Media S.A. https://doi.org/10.3389/fgene.2022.845305

Wynants, L., Van Calster, B., Collins, G. S., Riley, R. D., Heinze, G., Schuit, E., Bonten, M. M. J., Damen, J. A. A., Debray, T. P. A., De Vos, M., Dhiman, P., Haller, M. C., Harhay, M. O., Henckaerts, L., Kreuzberger, N., Lohmann, A., Luijken, K., Ma, J., Andaur Navarro, C. L., … Van Smeden, M. (2020). Prediction models for diagnosis and prognosis of covid-19: Systematic review and critical appraisal. *The BMJ, 369*. https://doi.org/10.1136/bmj.m1328

Yang, L., Liu, S., Liu, J., Zhang, Z., Wan, X., Huang, B., Chen, Y., & Zhang, Y. (2020). COVID-19: immunopathogenesis and Immunotherapeutics. In *Signal Transduction and Targeted Therapy* (Vol. 5, Issue 1). Springer Nature. https://doi.org/10.1038/s41392-020-00243-2

Yang, Z., Zeng, Z., Wang, K., Wong, S. S., Liang, W., Zanin, M., Liu, P., Cao, X., Gao, Z., Mai, Z., Liang, J., Liu, X., Li, S., Li, Y., Ye, F., Guan, W., Yang, Y., Li, F., Luo, S., … He, J. (2020). Modified SEIR and AI prediction of the epidemics trend of COVID-19 in China under public health interventions. *Journal of Thoracic Disease, 12*(3), 165–174. https://doi.org/10.21037/jtd.2020.02.64

You, C., Deng, Y., Hu, W., Sun, J., Lin, Q., Zhou, F., Pang, C. H., Zhang, Y., Chen, Z., & Zhou, X. H. (2020). Estimation of the time-varying reproduction number of COVID-19 outbreak in China. *International Journal of Hygiene and Environmental Health, 228*. https://doi.org/10.1016/j.ijheh.2020.113555

Nejc Čelik* and Mirjana Kljajić Borštnar**

# Facial Recognition System Development

**Abstract:** In this paper we discuss the development and functionality of facial recognition systems. Besides the face recognition, facial recognition systems must be able to separate live or spoof faces for many different use cases such as access control. Without a solution to prevent face anti-spoofing facial recognition systems have big vulnerabilities from a security perspective. We explore the latest advancements in deep learning that allow for the creation of 2D facial recognition models and face anti-spoofing models. We present a method for training facial recognition models with limited data, eliminating the need for large, ethically questionable datasets. In addition, we also present the development of a face anti-spoofing model.

**Keywords:** face recognition, deep learning, artificial intelligence, anti-spoofing, limited data

## 1. Introuction

Facial recognition systems are systems that can, through the use of artificial intelligence, separate faces of different identity based on their facial characteristics. Facial recognition authentication is a type of biometric authentication. Biometric authentication is authentication based on recognizing physical traits unique to the individual like fingerprint, face, DNA, iris, voice etc. Facial recognition separates itself from other types of biometric authentication because for it to work we do not need any user input or physical contact which makes it possible to completely automate the process of authentication. Facial recognition systems can therefore be used to automate processes like access control and attendance management systems. Facial recognition systems are already in use for access control and for increasing security in infrastructures like airports. They are also extensively used to login in devices like mobile phones and computers. There are multiple approaches to the development of facial recognition systems with the use of computer vision (Adjabi et al., 2020).

In this paper we focus on the use of deep learning for development of 2D facial recognition system.

* University of Maribor, Faculty of Organizational Sciences, Kranj, Slovenia, e-mail: nejc.celik1@um.si

** University of Maribor, Faculty of Organizational Sciences, Kranj, Slovenia, e-mail: mirjana.kljajic@um.si

The use of computers to recognize faces started in 1960s where (Bledsoe, 1964) used method that compared hand measured face features like eye, mouth, nose and ear size end distances between facial points. In 1980s a breakthrough method of using artificial intelligence to recognize faces was developed by (Turk & Pentland, 1991) named Eigenfaces which used a Principal component analysis. Eigenfaces was the first reliable and usable method of recognizing faces. To improve and accelerate development and research in technology to recognize faces many face datasets were developed 1990s and 2000s like Face Recognition Technology (FERET) database (Phillips et al., 1998), Face Recognition Grand Challenge (FRGC) dataset (Phillips et al., 2005) and Labeled Faces in the Wild (LFW) dataset (Huang et al., 2007). In 2010s there were accelerated advances in development of deep learning methods driven by improvements in hardware, appearance of large datasets like ImageNet (Russakovsky et al., 2014) and breakthrough neural network architectures like AlexNet (Krizhevsky et al., 2012) and ResNet (He et al., 2015). Those advances lead to the use of deep learning for face recognition. In 2014 (Taigman et al., 2014) presented model named DeepFace which is a convolutional neural network trained on around 4 million images from Facebook internal dataset for which authors claimed to achieve near human level accuracy in recognizing faces (Adjabi et al., 2020).

First method of training neural networks to recognize faces like DeepFace (Taigman et al., 2014), used same methods used in classification where number of classes is fixed, and same classes are used in training and testing data. In face recognition every identity is basically its own class to classify so those approached did not generalize well on identities not seen by model during training. To improve performance on unseen identities new methods were developed like FaceNet (Schroff et al., 2015a), SphereFace (Liu et al., 2017), CosFace (H. Wang et al., 2018) and ArcFace (Deng et al., 2018).

To use deep learning to develop face recognition models there is a need for large amount of data. First successful deep learning-based face recognition models were trained on a large internal dataset of big corporations. For example, DeepFace (Taigman et al., 2014) was trained on Facebook's internal dataset of around 4.4 million images from 4000 persons and FaceNet (Schroff et al., 2015a) was trained with 200–300 million images from 8 million different persons from Google's internal dataset. To accelerate development of face recognition methods and to give researchers outside big corporations the ability to work on improving deep learning-based methods of face recognition many big and publicly accessible datasets were developed. Some of the most famous datasets include:

- CASIAWebFace (Yi et al., 2014) (494414 images of 10575 persons)
- MegaFace (Kemelmacher-Shlizerman et al., 2015) (1027060 images of 690572 persons)
- MS-Celeb-1M (Guo et al., 2016) (10 million images of 100000 persons)
- VGGFace (Parkhi et al., 2015) (2,6 million images of 2622 persons)
- VGGFace2 (Cao et al., 2017) (3,31 million images of 9131 persons)

Those datasets received a lot of criticism. Many images in datasets were copyrighted and used without the author's permission. In datasets there was a lot of bias as most images were of males of European roots. Those biases in data also extended to models trained on those datasets. Even though those datasets were opened only for non-commercial purposes they were extensively used in the development of commercial applications. Besides the use for commercial purposes those datasets were also used by government organizations (law enforcement and military) around the world for often ethically questionable purposes (Harvey Adam & LaPlace Jules., 2021)

To evaluate and compare different face recognition methods and models we measure their performance by ROC (Receiver Operating Characteristic) (Figure 1) analysis which assess relationship between TAR (True Accept Rate or True Positive Rate) (calculated as $TAR = TP/((TP + FN))$ where TP stands for number of true positive predictions and FN stands for false negative predictions) which in a context of face recognition describes a fraction of correctly classified pairs of face images where both images belong to same person and FAR (False Accept Rate or False Positive Rate) (calculated as $FAR = FP/((FP + TN))$ where FP stands for number of false positive predictions and TN stands for true negative predictions) which describes fraction of image pairs of different persons wrongly classified as same person (Adjabi et al., 2020).

Performance of face recognition models and methods is often also described by simplified metric the estimated mean accuracy (ACC) (calculated as $ACC = (TP + TN)/((TP + TN + FP + FN))$ where TP stands for number of true positive predictions, FN stands for false negative predictions, FP stands for false positive predictions and TN stands for true negative predictions). ACC represents fraction of correctly classified pairs (Adjabi et al., 2020).

Currently the best face recognition models are trained on large face datasets. Large face datasets are often very biased and not accessible for commercial use to most organizations and individuals. In this paper we explore fine tuning of networks trained on other task (like ImageNet (Russakovsky et al., 2014)) with very small training dataset (<5000 images). We derive from the proposition that it would be easier to control bias and quality of data in a smaller dataset

*Figure 1: ROC curve (Receiver Operating Characteristic - Wikipedia).*

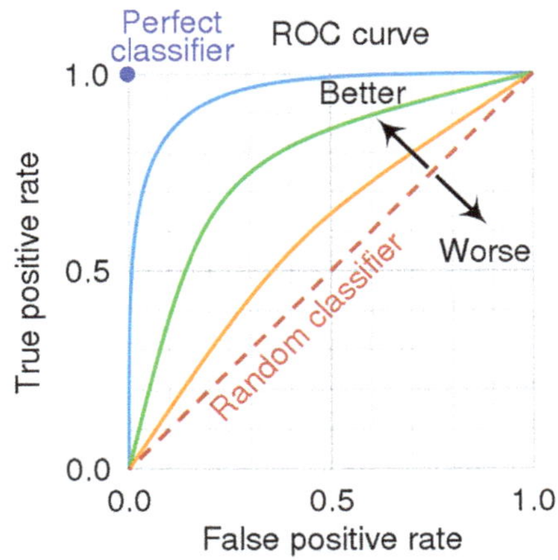


compared to large datasets, that way we could develop less biased models. Benefits from focusing on data quality were also found in recent study where Taylor et al. (2022) achieved better performance of large language models on scientific tasks while also observing less stereotypical bias and higher truthfulness when training models only on scientific corpus compared to other large language models available at the time. Similarly, Hong et al. (2022) observed better performance on domain specific tasks when training large language models on domain specific data and they did not find that increasing amount of training data necessary results in significant improvements in performance. We believe that development of face recognition systems without the use of large amounts of data, would also be cheaper and more accessible. Besides development of face recognition model, we also present development of face anti spoofing model because it is important part of face recognition systems as it is needed for most use cases.

## 2. Methodology

We followed the guidelines of design science research (Hevner et al., 2004) in the process of facial recognition model development. Within the design cycle we presented methods and guidelines for face recognition systems with the use of small datasets of faces. Through the development process we followed CRISP-DM (Cross Industry Standard Process for Data Mining) (Wirth & Hipp, 2000) process model for data mining projects. CRISP-DM model separates data mining project into 6 phases (Figure 2):

- Business/Problem understanding (Understanding of what is the value of facial recognition system, what are use cases and where will we use it)
- Data understanding (what information is in our data, how we expect for models to learn it and what problems can occur because of the data during modelling)
- Data preparation (Preparing the data for use by our models)
- Modelling (Training the models)
- Evaluation (Assessment of the performance and opportunity for improving performance by repeat development process with acquired knowledge)
- Deployment (Wirth & Hipp, 2000)

*Figure 2: CRISP-DM process model (Wirth & Hipp, 2000).*

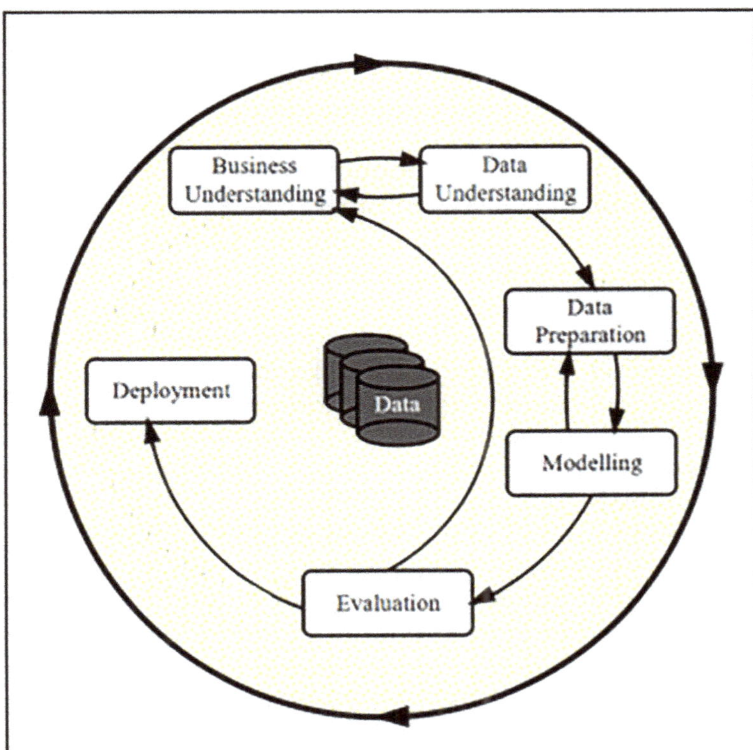

## 3. Results

In this paper we present development of face recognition system. Our system is composed of face detector, face recognition model and face anti-spoofing model. For face detector we used OpenCV's (Bradski, 2000) implementation of cascade classifiers (Viola & Jones, 2001) as the approach works very well for frontal face detection and requires very little computational resources. Both our face recognition model and face anti-spoofing model were developed by fine-tuning convolutional neural network. When developing face recognition model, we explored how number of identities, number of images per identity and data augmentation contribute to model performance.

Method, we used for development of face recognition model differs from normal classification method (Figure 3) with fixed number of classes (e.g. classifying cars and pedestrians (2 classes)) where SoftMax activation function is used on outputs of last (output) layer to get class probabilities. Weights are then optimised with the use of cross entropy loss (a.k.a. SoftMax loss) function (Bridle, 1990) between predicted class probabilities and ground truth labels. In face recognition because we want to be able to correctly recognise faces of any identity and not just the ones in our training data so we cannot use class probabilities to make decisions as we would in normal classification. To make decision outputs of last hidden layer are taken to compare between identities (images of same identity should have similar outputs). When optimising network to make correct class prediction as in normal classification, network can learn to produce enough discriminative outputs of last hidden layer to make predictions but requires very large dataset to generalize well on unseen identities (Parkhi et al., 2015).

To improve performance of using neural network for face recognition new approaches for training neural network were developed. Goal of those methods is to optimize network to produce discriminative embeddings between different identities. Examples of those methods are FaceNet (Schroff et al., 2015b), SphereFace (Liu et al., 2017), CosFace (H. Wang et al., 2018) and ArcFace (Deng et al., 2018). In our model we use ArcFace method.

Goal of ArcFace (Additive Angular Margin Loss) (Deng et al., 2018) when training is to optimise network to learn average face embedding in weights of output layer for every identity in dataset and produce face embeddings (output of last hidden layer) that have smaller angle (bigger cosine similarity) with weights belonging to neuron representing their identity (class) then to weights belonging to any other identity (Figure 4). To achieve that cosine similarity is calculated between weights and embeddings. Cosine similarities are then used as model outputs and like in normal classification used to calculate class probabilities using

*Figure 3: Learning using SoftMax and cross entropy loss (image by author).*

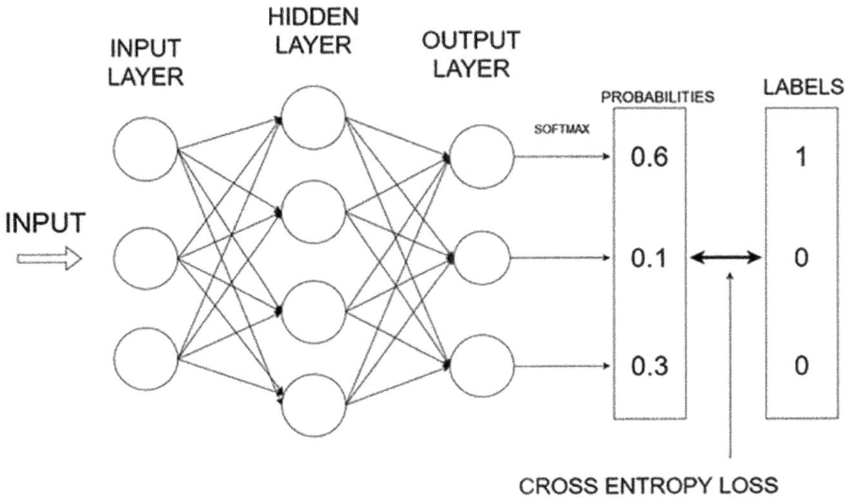


SoftMax. Higher cosine similarity therefore results to higher class probability. Cross entropy loss function (Bridle, 1990) is then used to calculate loss between predicted values and ground truth labels. To make bigger difference in cosine similarity, margin m is added to calculated angle between face embedding and weights for matching identity which means angle at ground truth needs to be additionally for $m$ smaller than other angles to still produce correct predictions.

We used (Chan Kha Vu, 2020) implementation of Additive Angular Margin Loss (ArcFace) (Deng et al., 2018) (Figure 5). When training the implemented layer, we first normalize inputs and weights using L2 normalization and then calculate cosine similarity between inputs and weights by multiplying the two tensors. During training we also feed labels into the layer in form of integers which represent class number that we then transform into 1-D tensor (n-dimensional matrices) that have one at the index equal to class number and zeroes at other indexes (one hot tensor). From cosine similarity we calculate angle $\theta$ between weights and inputs by using arccosine function. By using arccosine function we get values for angle $\theta$ between 0 and $\pi$. We then want to add margin $m$ to angle $\theta$ to weights at the same point as one in one hot tensor (labels) and where angle $\theta$ is not bigger than π – m as we do not want for calculated angle to be bigger than $\pi$ (because $cos\theta$ starts increasing for $\theta$ values between $\pi$ and $2\pi$). Then we multiple parameter s which we fixed to 60 and $cos\theta$ and output it. We then use SoftMax activation function and cross-entropy loss function to calculate loss and optimize trainable parameters.

*Figure 4: Difference between normal learning and ArcFace (Deng et al., 2018) approach (image by author).*

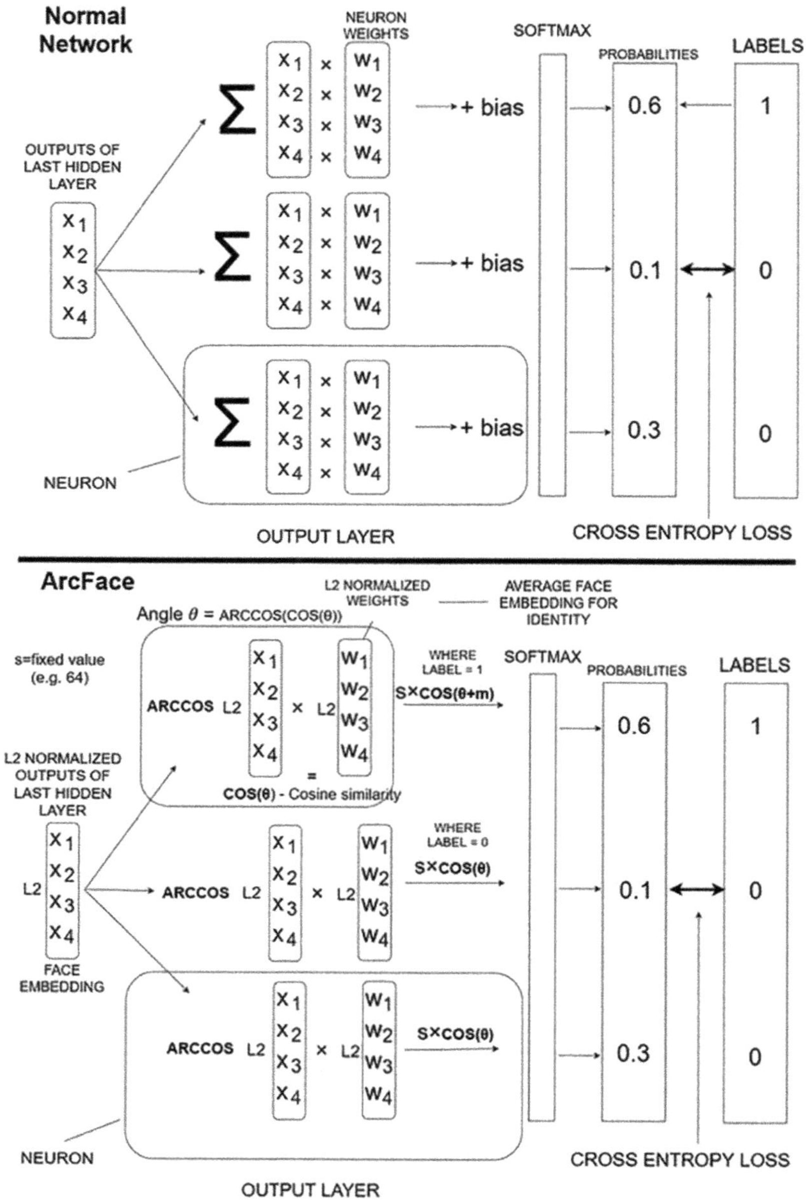

*Figure 5: Implementation of ArcFace layer (Chan Kha Vu, 2020).*

```
class ArcFace(Layer):

    def __init__(self,
                 num_classes,
                 s=64.0,
                 m=0.5,
                 regularizer=None,
                 name='arcface',
                 **kwargs):

        super().__init__(name=name, **kwargs)
        self._n_classes = num_classes
        self._s = float(s)
        self._m = float(m)
        self._regularizer = regularizer

    def build(self, input_shape):
        embedding_shape, label_shape = input_shape
        self._w = self.add_weight(shape=(embedding_shape[-1], self._n_classes),
                                  initializer='glorot_uniform',
                                  trainable=True,
                                  regularizer=self._regularizer,
                                  name='cosine_weights')

    def call(self, inputs, training=None):
        embedding, label = inputs
        label = tf.reshape(label, [-1], name='label_shape_correction')
        x = tf.nn.l2_normalize(embedding, axis=1, name='normalize_prelogits')
        w = tf.nn.l2_normalize(self._w, axis=0, name='normalize_weights')
        cosine_sim = tf.matmul(x, w, name='cosine_similarity')
        if not training:
            #return self._s * cosine_sim
            return x
        else:
            one_hot_labels = tf.one_hot(label,
                                        depth=self._n_classes,
                                        name='one_hot_labels')

            theta = tf.math.acos(K.clip(
                    cosine_sim, -1.0 + K.epsilon(), 1.0 - K.epsilon()))

            selected_labels = tf.where(tf.greater(theta, math.pi - self._m),
                                       tf.zeros_like(one_hot_labels),
                                       one_hot_labels,
                                       name='selected_labels')

            final_theta = tf.where(tf.cast(selected_labels, dtype=tf.bool),
                                   theta + self._m,
                                   theta,
                                   name='final_theta')

            output = tf.math.cos(final_theta, name='cosine_sim_with_margin')
            return self._s * output
```

To build our model (Figure 6) we used convolutional layers from MobileNetV3Small model trained on ImageNet dataset fully connected layer with 256 neurons which's outputs we then normalized using BatchNormalization (Ioffe & Szegedy, 2015) and then feed through GELU (Hendrycks & Gimpel, 2016) activation function. On top we added previously described layer.

*Figure 6: Model structure used for training.*

```
class MobileArc256(tf.keras.Model):
    def __init__(self, num_classes):
        super(MobileArc256, self).__init__()
        self.backbone = tf.keras.applications.MobileNetV3Small(
            input_shape=(112, 112, 3),
            include_top=False,
            weights="imagenet",
            pooling="avg",
        )
        self.bn1 = tf.keras.layers.BatchNormalization()
        self.fc2 = tf.keras.layers.Dense(256)
        self.bn2 = tf.keras.layers.BatchNormalization()
        self.arc = ArcFace(num_classes=num_classes)

    def call(self, inputs):
        x, label = inputs
        x = self.backbone(x)
        x = self.bn1(x)
        x = self.fc2(x)
        x = self.bn2(x)
        x = tf.keras.activations.gelu(x)
        x = self.arc([x, label])
        return x
```

For training we experimented with different hyper-parameters and find best settings with optimization method AdamW (Kingma & Ba, 2014; Loshchilov & Hutter, 2017) with leaning rate 1e-5, weight decay 1e-8 and batch size of 64.

To develop our face recognition model, we used Labeled Faces in the Wild (LFW) dataset (Huang et al., 2007). In this paper we explore fine-tuning of pre-trained convolutional neural networks on ImageNet (Russakovsky et al., 2014) for face recognition on a much smaller dataset (<5000 images). We were interested in answering the question of how many images and identities we need and how much augmentation we need to add to dataset to develop a face recognition model. For experimenting and testing we have decided to split our dataset in smaller datasets (Table 1). For testing we used images of identities where number of images per identity was equal to two. In LFW there are 776 identities with 2 images. From 1552 images belonging to those identities, we used 1521 images (in 31 images our face detector did not detect face correctly). For training we created 6 smaller datasets. In first one we put identities with 3 or 4 images per identity (478 identities and 1592 images). In second one we put identities with 5 to 20 images (366 identities and 2985 images). In third one we put identities with 20 to 100 images per identity (52 identities and 1751 images). In forth one we combined first and second one (from 3 to 20 images). In fifth one we put all identities from LFW with more than 2 images per identity (901 identities and 7453 images).

*Table 1: Datasets used for training*

| Dataset Name | Number of identities | Number of images |
|---|---|---|
| data-0 | 478 | 1592 |
| data-1 | 366 | 2985 |
| data-2 | 52 | 1751 |
| data-3 (data-0+data-1) | 844 | 4577 |
| data-4 (data-1+data-2) | 418 | 4736 |
| data-5 | 901 | 7453 |

In our experiments (Figures 8–12) looking at data-0 (3 images per identity) and data-2 (20–100 images per identity) we saw better performance with more images per identity then more identities with less images. When comparing data-1 and data-2 we observed similar final performance but much faster convergence on data-2. Combining data-0 and data-1 (i.e. data-3) only slightly outperformed data-2. Using data-5 (all identities with more than 2 images) we got worse performance than all but data-1. We got our best performance combining data-1 and data-2 (i.e. data-4) (Figure 12).

In our experiment we repeated training with 7 different data augmentation settings (Table 2) (Figure 7) for every dataset (Figure 8–12). First setting was no augmentation and without it we achieve up to 0.7 AUC score. By using random Contrast, brightness, saturation and hue (AUG-1) we observed ≈0.1 increase in AUC score in all datasets. When adding random horizontal flip to AUG-1 (AUG-2) we observed additional ≈0.05 increase in AUC score. By adding random erasing with 50% probability to AUG-2 (AUG-3) we observed another ≈0.05 increase AUC score. We observed similar increase by adding random rotation to AUG-2 (AUG-4). By adding both random erasing and random rotation to AUG-2 (AUG-5) we observed ≈0.02 additional increase compared to AUG-3 or AUG-4.

By increasing random erasing probability to 100% (AUG-6) we got slightly worse (≈0.005) AUC score. Best AUC score we achieved was 0.923 using AUG-5 and data-4 (Figure 12).

*Table 2: Used augmentation settings*

| | **Random b,C,H,S,B** | **Random horizontal flip** | **Random errasing** | **Random rotation (45°)** |
|---|---|---|---|---|
| No AUG | × | × | × | × |
| AUG-1 | ✓ | × | × | × |
| AUG-2 | ✓ | ✓ | × | × |
| AUG-3 | ✓ | ✓ | ✓ 50% probability | × |
| AUG-4 | ✓ | ✓ | × | ✓ |
| AUG-5 | ✓ | ✓ | ✓ 50% probability | ✓ |
| AUG-6 | ✓ | ✓ | ✓ 100% probability | ✓ |

*Figure 7: Examples of augmentation methods applied to images from Labeled Faces in the Wild dataset (Huang et al., 2007).*

Figure 8 shows AUC score and Figure 9 shows training loss for all datasets for all different augmentation (AUG) settings.

*Figure 8: AUC score through training for different augmentation settings and datasets.*

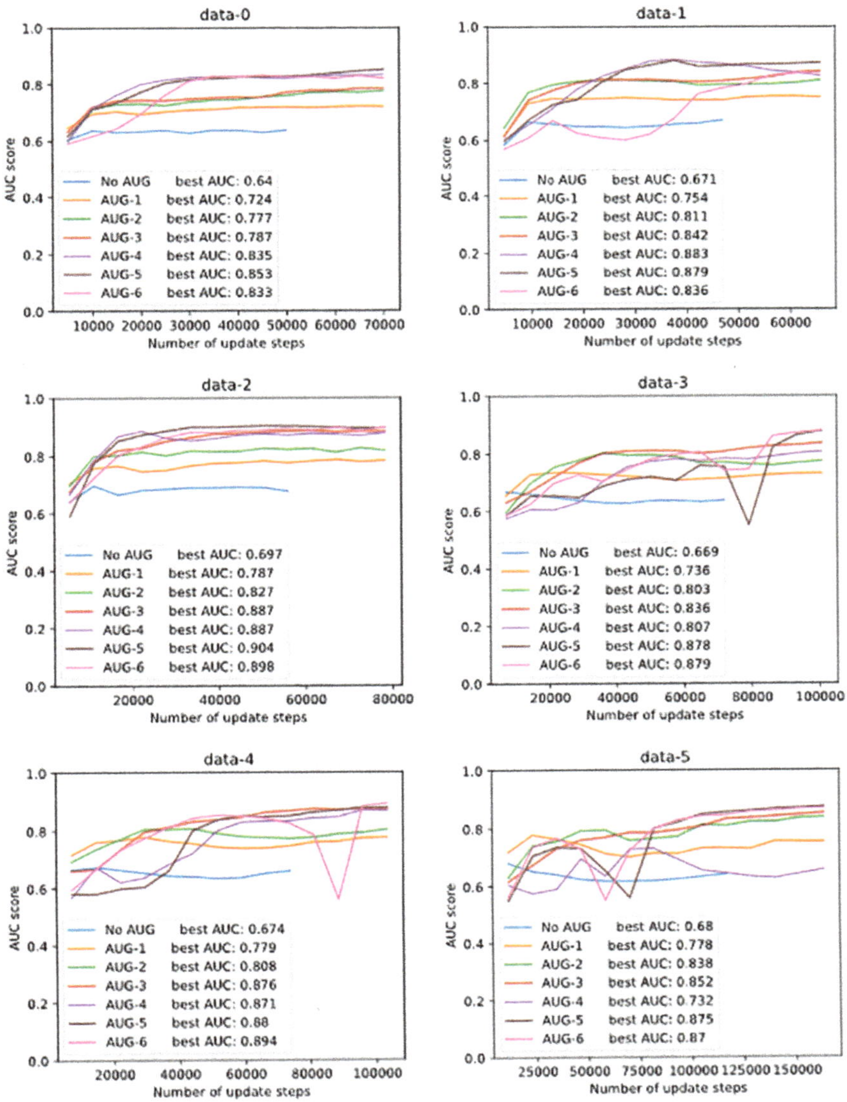

*Figure 9: Loss through training for different augmentation settings and datasets.*

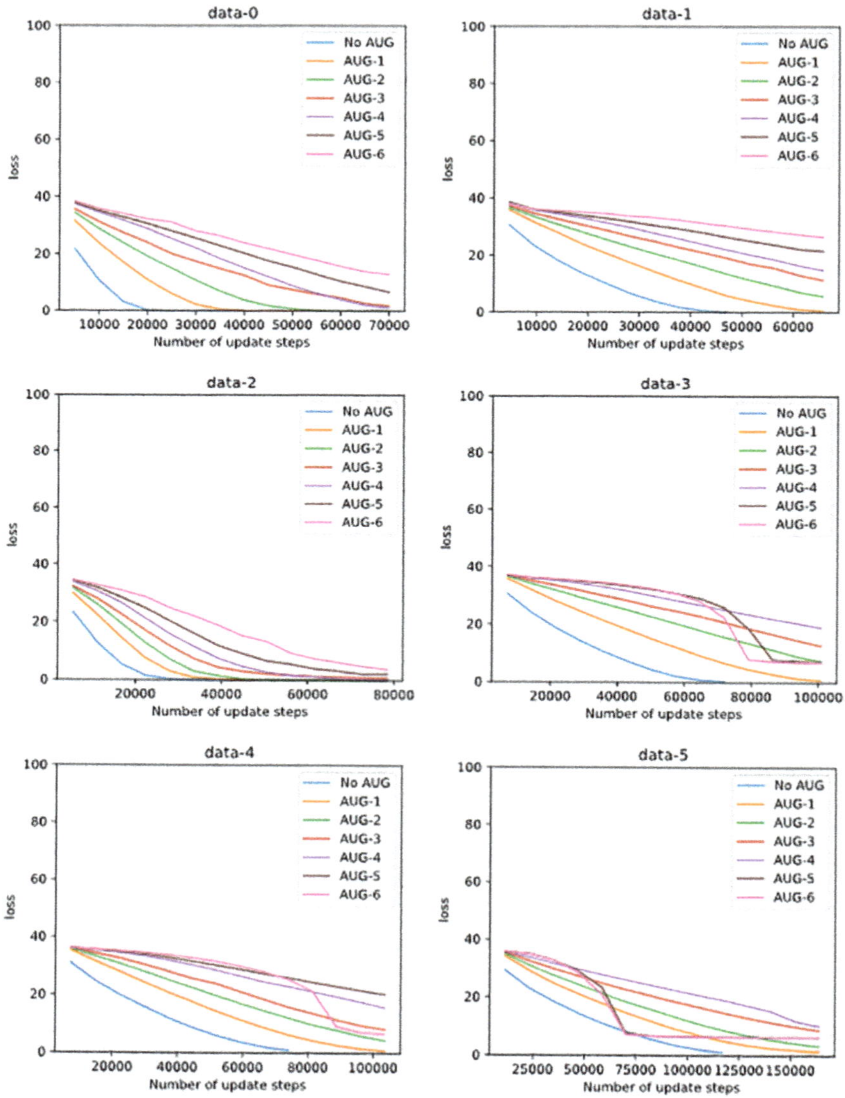

Figure 10 shows AUC score and Figure 11 shows training loss for all datasets for three best augmentation (AUG) settings with additional training steps.

*Figure 10: AUC score with extended training duration for best performing augmentation settings.*

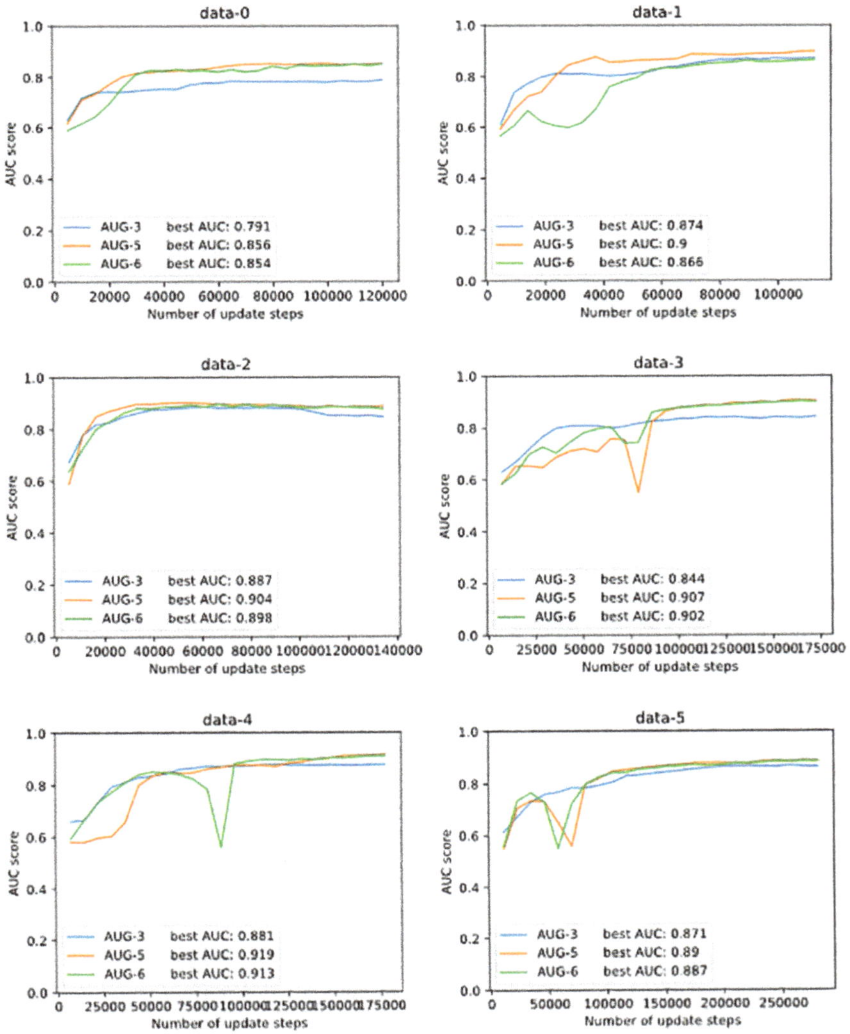

*Figure 11: Loss with extended training duration for best performing augmentation settings.*

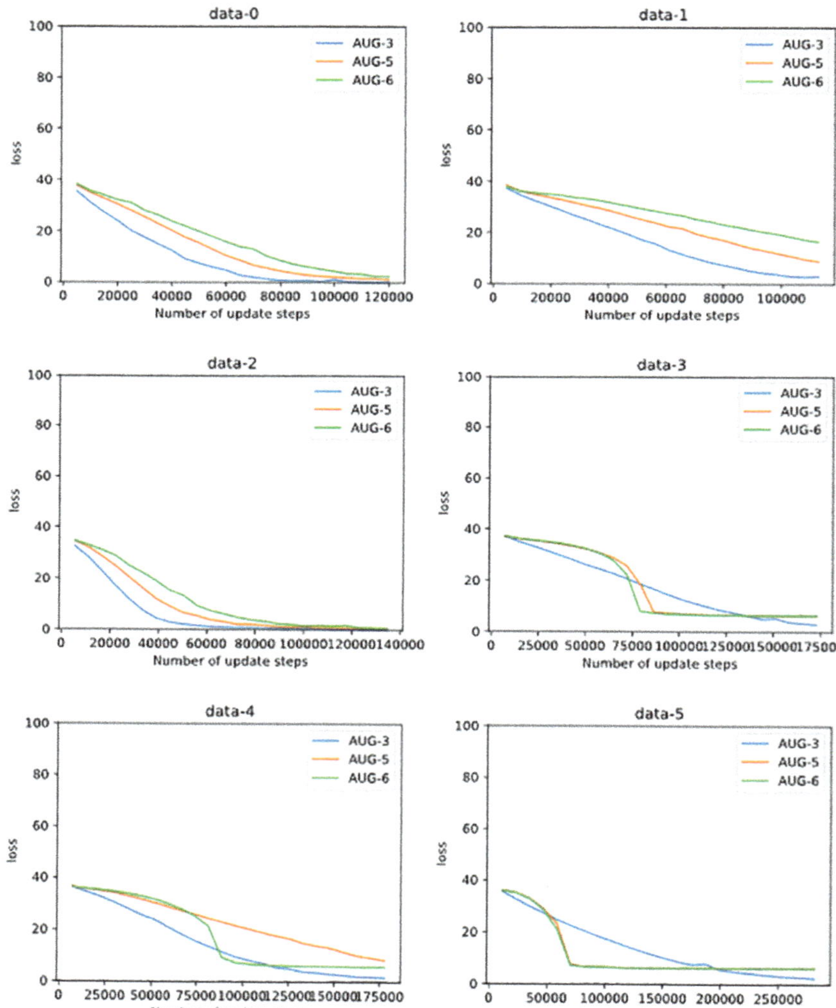


Figure 12 shows AUC score and training loss for best performing dataset for best two augmentation (AUG) settings with aditional training steps.

*Figure 12: AUC score and training loss for best performing dataset and augmentations with added additional training steps.*

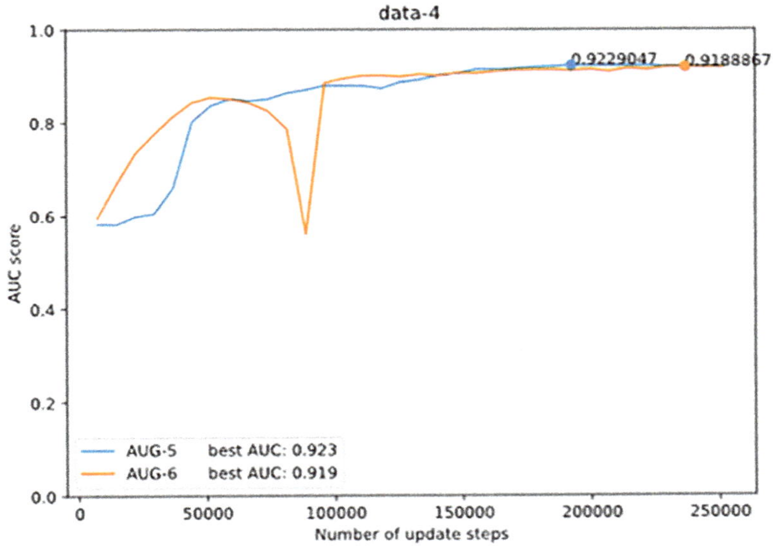


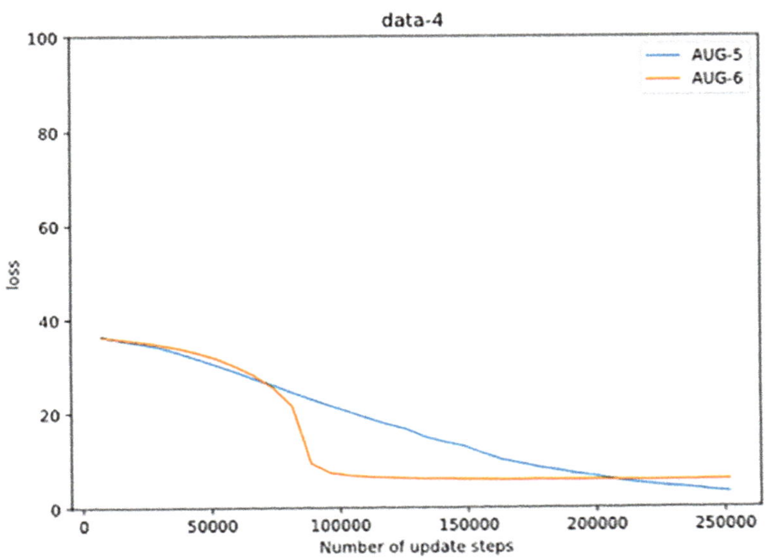

We tested our model on unused data from LFW dataset. For testing we took images of persons from dataset where number of their images equals to 2. When detecting faces in those images we removed those where our face detector did not successfully detect face and after that we were left with 1521 images of 776 different persons. For testing we used every possible image pair from our testing data which amounted to 1155960 different image pairs. During training we have observed AUC score, true positive rate, false positive rate and estimated mean accuracy. We have also graphed ROC curve (Figure 13). Our best model has achieved AUC score of 0.9229. We have compared different classification thresholds for classifying persons in image pairs as different or same based on cosine similarity between face embeddings and chosen two possible thresholds for use in our system. Threshold with which we achieved overall best mean estimated accuracy was at 0.18. At this threshold we achieve true positive rate of 0.812 and false positive rate of 0.109 which amounts to estimated mean accuracy of

*Figure 13: ROC curve for best performing model.*

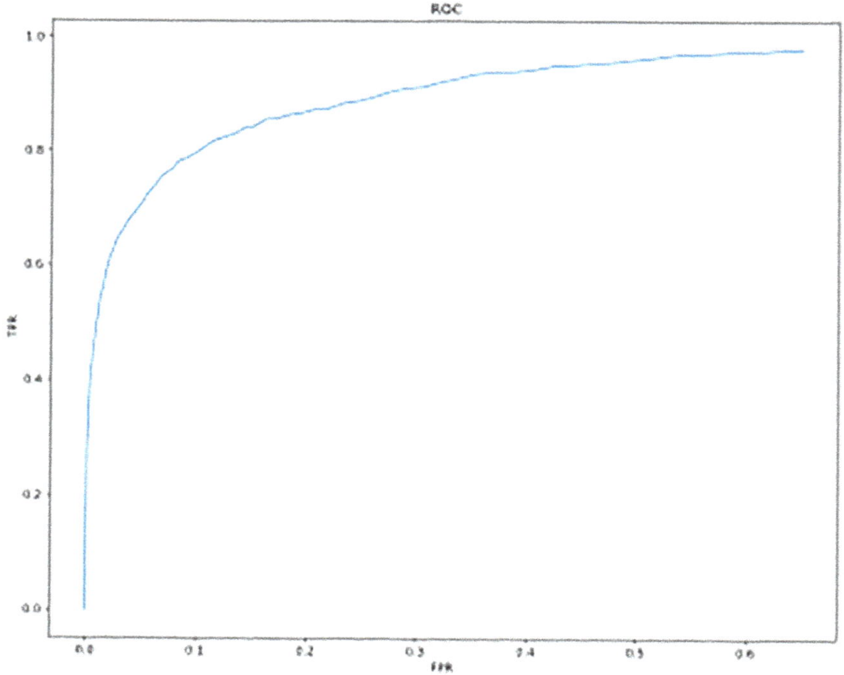

approximately 0.8515 in on data with equal number of positive and negative pairs. Another possible threshold could be 0.35 where we would achieve true positive rate of 0.4812 and false positive rate of 0.008. This threshold would better suit systems where not making false positive predictions would be more important than achieving best true positive rates. For better presentation we have also visualized cosine similarity between first 10 pictures from our testing dataset (Figure 14).

To develop our face anti spoof model, we used a method based on PatchNet (C. Y. Wang et al., 2022) with the difference in calculating loss by using ArcFace loss (Additive Angular Margin Loss) instead of Asymmetric AM-Softmax Loss

*Figure 14: Example of model performance (Code for visualization from (Learnopencv/Face-Recognition-with-ArcFace/Similarity.Py at Master · Spmallick/Learnopencv · GitHub, 2021)).*

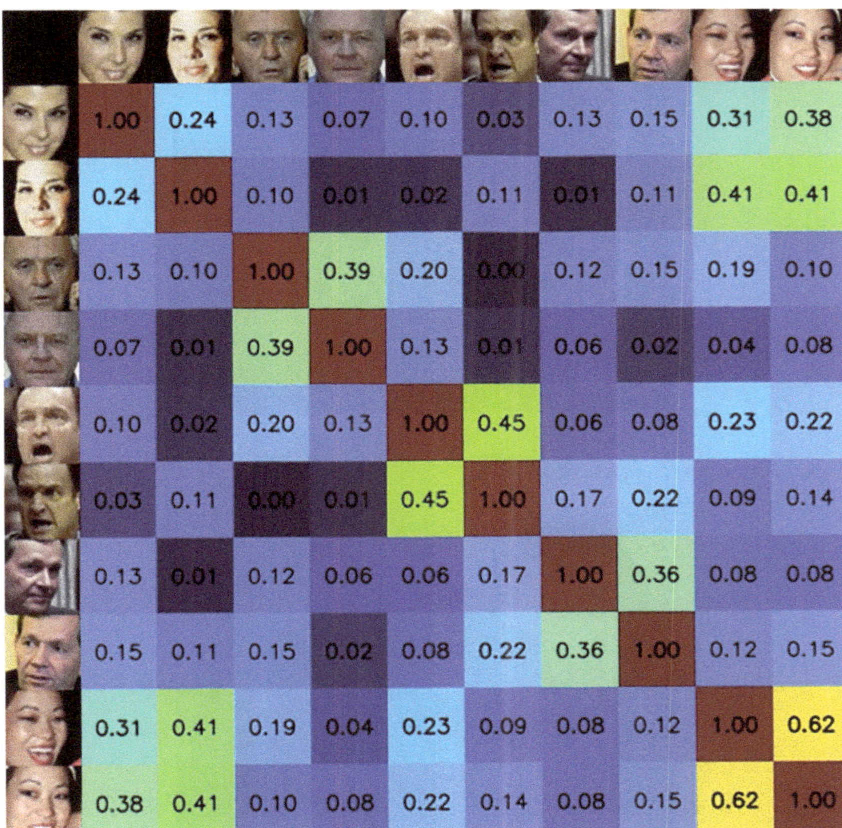

proposed by authors difference being that in proposed loss we use different margin for live and spoof classes and subtracting margin m from cos$\theta$ rather than adding m to $\theta$. We the combined it with proposed self-supervised similarity loss where we calculate mean squared error between two patches taken from same image.

To train our model we gathered our own data (Čelik, 2023). We gathered 25 images of the same face (author) taken from the same camera in the same place but under different lightning conditions (Figure 15). We then take those pictures and display them on a screen and retake them with a camera, so every image of live face has spoof counterpart (Figure 16). Our dataset is therefore comprised of 50 images equally split between real and spoof samples. We split our dataset in training (42 images of which 21 real and 21 spoof) and testing data (8 images of which 4 real and 4 spoof).

*Figure 15: Examples of live faces (Čelik, 2023).*

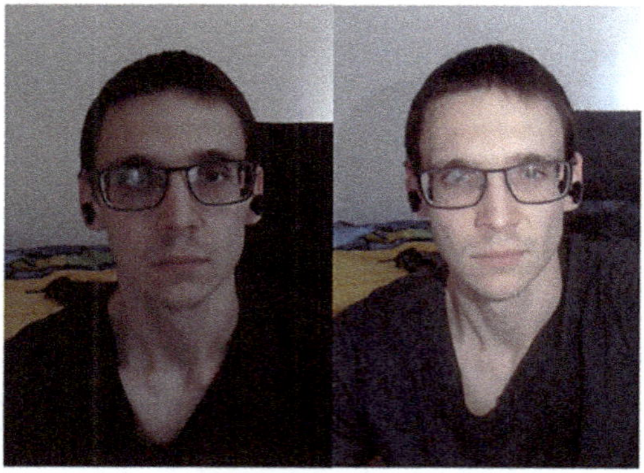

*Figure 16: Spoon examples (Čelik, 2023).*

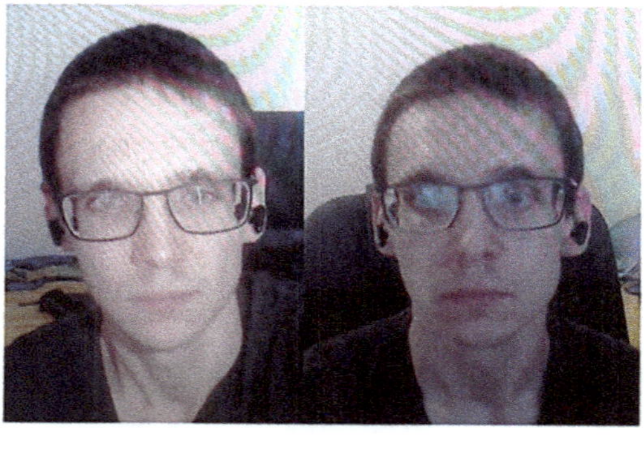

For training we use MobileNetV3Small architecture as a model backbone and then add structure in the same way as when implementing face recognition model but instead of using 512 neurons in fully connected layer we use only 128 and add them to the model outputs during training (Figure 17), to calculate mean squared error between 2 patches from same image (Figure 18).

*Figure 17: Structure of FAS model during training.*

```
class PatchNet(tf.keras.Model):
    def __init__(self,num_classes):
        super(PatchNet, self).__init__()
        self.backbone = tf.keras.applications.MobileNetV3Small(
            input_shape=(112,112,3),
            include_top=False,
            weights='imagenet',
            pooling='avg')
        self.drop1 = tf.keras.layers.Dropout(.5)
        self.bn1=tf.keras.layers.BatchNormalization()
        self.fc2=tf.keras.layers.Dense(128)
        self.bn2=tf.keras.layers.BatchNormalization()
        self.arc=ArcFace(num_classes=num_classes)

    def call(self, inputs):
        x1,x2,label=inputs

        x1 = self.backbone(x1)
        x1 = self.bn1(x1)
        x1 = self.drop1(x1)
        x1 = self.fc2(x1)
        x1 =self.bn2(x1)
        x1 = tf.keras.activations.gelu(x1)

        x2 = self.backbone(x2)
        x2 = self.bn1(x2)
        x2 = self.drop1(x2)
        x2 = self.fc2(x2)
        x2 =self.bn2(x2)
        x2 = tf.keras.activations.gelu(x2)

        x_arc1 = self.arc([x1,label])
        x_arc2 = self.arc([x2,label])
        x=tf.concat([x1,x2], 1, name='concat')
        return (x,x_arc1,x_arc2)
```

*Figure 18: Implementation of self-similarity loss.*

```
class PatchNetLossSim(tf.keras.losses.Loss):
    def __init__(self):
        super(PatchNetLossSim, self).__init__()

    def call(self, y_true, y_pred):
        x1,x2=tf.split(y_pred,2,1)
        mse = tf.keras.losses.MeanSquaredError()
        simloss=mse(x1, x2)
        return simloss
```

When training the model, we randomly rotate and flip the image and take 2 different patches in from face crop of size 112×112×3 that we use together as a training example at every epoch. During training model inputs are therefore B×P×112×112×3 (B=batch size, P=number of patches=2). We then calculate Mean squared error between two patches and cross entropy loss for outputs of ArcFace layer for both patches and combine it into total loss where both types of losses have same weight (total loss = 1x self-similarity loss + 2×0.5 ArcFace loss (Additive Angular Margin Loss)).

We trained our model for 10000 epochs with optimization method AdamW with hyper-parameters learning rate=1e-5 and weight decay=1e-8. When testing our model, we take single center crop from face of size 112×112 and calculate SoftMax for outputs of ArcFace layer (s* cos$\theta$, s=64) to check if the probabilities match our labels (Figure 19). On our testing data model achieves 100% accuracy.

To demonstrate the use of our models to build face recognition system we built prototype system (Figure 20). Our prototype captures images from camera and then detects faces inside every image using cascade classifiers. If face detector detects a face, it crops out 112×112 patch from its center. If a face is smaller than 112×112 we ignore it. We use face's center patch to classify face as live or spoof using build FAS model. Then we send the whole face crop to face recognition model which returns 512-dimensional normalized face embedding. We use that face embedding to calculate cosine similarity with saved face embeddings and if similarity is above certain threshold (for instance 0.35) we conclude that face belongs to same person. During testing we also observed how well our FAS model separates between live and spoof faces, and we saw that it was more often correct than wrong, but it was not 100% accurate like on our testing dataset.

*Figure 19: Structure of FAS model at inference.*

```
class PatchNetTest(tf.keras.Model):
    def __init__(self,num_classes):
        super(PatchNetTest, self).__init__()
        self.backbone = tf.keras.applications.MobileNetV3Small(
            input_shape=(112,112,3),
            include_top=False,
            weights='imagenet',
            pooling='avg')
        self.drop1 = tf.keras.layers.Dropout(.5)
        self.bn1=tf.keras.layers.BatchNormalization()
        self.fc2=tf.keras.layers.Dense(128)
        self.bn2=tf.keras.layers.BatchNormalization()
        self.arc=ArcFace(num_classes=num_classes)

    def call(self, inputs):
        x1,label=inputs

        x1 = self.backbone(x1)
        x1 = self.bn1(x1)
        x1 = self.drop1(x1)
        x1 = self.fc2(x1)
        x1 =self.bn2(x1)
        x1 = tf.keras.activations.gelu(x1)

        x_arc1 = self.arc([x1,label])
        return x_arc1
```

## 4. Discussion

With the developed models we showed that it is possible to develop face recognition system without the use of large datasets and computational power (we used consumer GPU (RTX 3060)). Our model developed on approximately 4736 images of 418 different persons achieved estimated mean accuracy of around 0.8515 and true positive rate of 0.8123 and false positive rate of 0.1092. Our model does not achieve accuracy of models trained on large dataset that achieve 0.99 accuracy (Deng et al., 2018) on LFW (Huang et al., 2007) test pairs (6000 evenly split positive and negative pairs) compared to around 0.85 which we would expect for our model to achieve (we tested our model on 1155960 non evenly split pairs so we cannot directly compare our performance). To compare our model with one also trained on smaller dataset we explored the literature and found work from (Yu & Liu, 2020) where they got accuracy on LFW test pairs of 0.9532 using

*Figure 20: Outputs of prototype system.*

120000 images of 2000 identities. Even though we can observe a visible relationship between accuracy and size of dataset our results suggest that it is possible to develop reliable models without using very large datasets. Further, the use of smaller balanced and unbiased datasets would make possible to developed reliable models for use in real world applications. In our experiment we did not try removing biases from the dataset, but it could be worth exploring deep learning-based approaches to detecting faces when developing face recognition systems. In our system FAS model was developed as a simple prototype. The production ready solution would require further research of a use case and collecting data of which complexity and amount would heavily depend on system's use case.

Recent EU AI Act (The Act | EU Artificial Intelligence Act, n.d.) has categorised biometric identification systems as high-risk AI systems and will put them under heavy regulations and supervision with some exceptions as is supposed to differentiate between different use cases for facial recognition technologies and categorise them differently. EU Act also explicitly bans use of face recognition for law enforcement in public spaces (except for few exceptions).

To improve performance in real time we do not need to completely rely on predictions from one image. To decide the identity of the face and detect spoof examples we could use prediction from few second video input and use more than one image to make decision and/or calculate average face embedding per identity to compare it to. Additionally, the use of multiple cameras that capture images under different angles might improve reliability of FAS model. System could also regularly update saved face embeddings by example from Apple FaceID (Apple, n.d.) to combat constant changes in appearance like hair growth, and ageing. Because we used smaller model architecture for backbone of our model it could be used in scenarios where we are limited by hardware capabilities. It would also be possible to use multiple models in ensemble what could add to better accuracy.

Because performance of the models in real time it is hard to predict solely by their performance on test data. There is a need to test such models in the real world. During testing we would observe when model makes mistakes and if possible, gather data and use it to improve model. Models should be consistently improved in line with CRISP-DM (Wirth & Hipp, 2000) guidelines.

## 5. Conclusion

In this paper we presented the development of a facial recognition system. Our goal was to train convolutional neural network on very small face dataset to be able to perform face recognition task. Further, our goal was also to train neural network to be able to classify between live and spoof faces and then combining both models in a facial recognition system that is besides performing face recognition also able to detect spoofing attacks. We presented a way of collecting and preparing data, preparing and training face recognition and face anti-spoofing models and combining them together with face detector in facial recognition system.

## Acknowledgement

The authors acknowledge the partial support from the Slovenian Research and Innovation Agency, research core funding No. P5-0018.

## Bibliography

Adjabi, I., Ouahabi, A., Benzaoui, A., & Taleb-Ahmed, A. (2020). Past, Present, and Future of Face Recognition: A Review. *Electronics 2020, Vol. 9, Page 1188*, *9*(8), 1188. https://doi.org/10.3390/ELECTRONICS9081188

Apple. (n.d.). *About Face ID advanced technology - Apple Support*. Retrieved August 25, 2023, from https://support.apple.com/en-lamr/102381

Bledsoe, W. W. (1964). *The Model Method in Facial Recognition*.

Bradski, G. (2000). The OpenCV Library. *Dr. Dobb's Journal of Software Tools*.

Bridle, J. S. (1990). Probabilistic Interpretation of Feedforward Classification Network Outputs, with Relationships to Statistical Pattern Recognition. *Neurocomputing*, 227–236. https://doi.org/10.1007/978-3-642-76153-9_28

Cao, Q., Shen, L., Xie, W., Parkhi, O. M., & Zisserman, A. (2017). VGGFace2: A dataset for recognising faces across pose and age. *Proceedings - 13th IEEE International Conference on Automatic Face and Gesture Recognition, FG 2018*, 67–74. https://doi.org/10.1109/FG.2018.00020

Čelik, N. (2023). *Razvoj sistema za prepoznavanje obrazov* [Master's Thesis]. University of Maribor.

Chan Kha Vu. (2020). *Keras Layers: ArcFace, CosFace, AdaCos | Kaggle*. https://www.kaggle.com/code/chankhavu/keras-layers-arcface-cosface-adacos

Deng, J., Guo, J., Yang, J., Xue, N., Kotsia, I., & Zafeiriou, S. (2018). ArcFace: Additive Angular Margin Loss for Deep Face Recognition. *IEEE Transactions on Pattern Analysis and Machine Intelligence*, *44*(10), 5962–5979. https://doi.org/10.1109/TPAMI.2021.3087709

Guo, Y., Zhang, L., Hu, Y., He, X., & Gao, J. (2016). MS-Celeb-1M: A Dataset and Benchmark for Large-Scale Face Recognition. *Lecture Notes in Computer Science (Including Subseries Lecture Notes in Artificial Intelligence and Lecture Notes in Bioinformatics), 9907 LNCS*, 87–102. https://doi.org/10.1007/978-3-319-46487-9_6

Harvey Adam, & LaPlace Jules. (2021). *Exposing.ai*. https://exposing.ai

He, K., Zhang, X., Ren, S., & Sun, J. (2015). Deep Residual Learning for Image Recognition. *Proceedings of the IEEE Computer Society Conference on Computer Vision and Pattern Recognition, 2016-December*, 770–778. https://doi.org/10.1109/CVPR.2016.90

Hendrycks, D., & Gimpel, K. (2016). *Gaussian Error Linear Units (GELUs)*. https://arxiv.org/abs/1606.08415v4

Hevner, A. R., March, S. T., Park, J., & Ram, S. (2004). Design science in information systems research. *MIS Quarterly: Management Information Systems, 28*(1), 75–105. https://doi.org/10.2307/25148625

Hong, Z., Ajith, A., Pauloski, J. G., Duede, E., Chard, K., & Foster, I. (2022). The Diminishing Returns of Masked Language Models to Science. *Proceedings of the Annual Meeting of the Association for Computational Linguistics*, 1270–1283. https://doi.org/10.18653/v1/2023.findings-acl.82

Huang, G. B., Ramesh, M., Berg, T., & Learned-Miller, E. (2007). *Labeled Faces in the Wild: A Database for Studying Face Recognition in Unconstrained Environments* (Issues 07–49).

Ioffe, S., & Szegedy, C. (2015). Batch Normalization: Accelerating Deep Network Training by Reducing Internal Covariate Shift. *32nd International Conference on Machine Learning, ICML 2015, 1*, 448–456. https://arxiv.org/abs/1502.03167v3

Kemelmacher-Shlizerman, I., Seitz, S. M., Miller, D., & Brossard, E. (2015). The MegaFace Benchmark: 1 Million Faces for Recognition at Scale. *Proceedings of the IEEE Computer Society Conference on Computer Vision and Pattern Recognition, 2016-December*, 4873–4882. https://doi.org/10.1109/CVPR.2016.527

Kingma, D. P., & Ba, J. L. (2014). Adam: A Method for Stochastic Optimization. *3rd International Conference on Learning Representations, ICLR 2015 - Conference Track Proceedings*. https://arxiv.org/abs/1412.6980v9

Krizhevsky, A., Sutskever, I., & Hinton, G. E. (2012). ImageNet Classification with Deep Convolutional Neural Networks. *Advances in Neural Information Processing Systems, 25*. http://code.google.com/p/cuda-convnet/

*learnopencv/Face-Recognition-with-ArcFace/similarity.py at master · spmallick/learnopencv · GitHub*. (2021). https://github.com/spmallick/learnopencv/blob/master/Face-Recognition-with-ArcFace/similarity.py

Liu, W., Wen, Y., Yu, Z., Li, M., Raj, B., & Song, L. (2017). SphereFace: Deep Hypersphere Embedding for Face Recognition. *Proceedings - 30th IEEE Conference on Computer Vision and Pattern Recognition, CVPR 2017, 2017-January*, 6738–6746. https://doi.org/10.1109/CVPR.2017.713

Loshchilov, I., & Hutter, F. (2017). Decoupled Weight Decay Regularization. *7th International Conference on Learning Representations, ICLR 2019*. https://arxiv.org/abs/1711.05101v3

Parkhi, O., Vedaldi, A., & Zisserman, A. (2015). Deep face recognition. *BMVC 2015-Proceedings of the British Machine Vision Conference 2015*.

Phillips, P. J., Flynn, P. J., Scruggs, T., Bowyer, K. W., Chang, J., Hoffman, K., Marques, J., Min, J., & Worek, W. (2005). Overview of the face recognition grand challenge. *Proceedings - 2005 IEEE Computer Society Conference on Computer Vision and Pattern Recognition, CVPR 2005, I*, 947–954. https://doi.org/10.1109/CVPR.2005.268

Phillips, P. J., Wechsler, H., Huang, J., & Rauss, P. J. (1998). The FERET database and evaluation procedure for face-recognition algorithms. *Image and Vision Computing, 16*(5), 295–306. https://doi.org/10.1016/S0262-8856(97)00070-X

*Receiver operating characteristic - Wikipedia*. (n.d.). Retrieved November 19, 2023, from https://en.wikipedia.org/wiki/Receiver_operating_characteristic

Russakovsky, O., Deng, J., Su, H., Krause, J., Satheesh, S., Ma, S., Huang, Z., Karpathy, A., Khosla, A., Bernstein, M., Berg, A. C., Fei-Fei, L., Russakovsky, O., Deng, J., Su, H., Krause, J., Satheesh, S., Ma, S., Huang, Z., … Fei-Fei, L. (2014). ImageNet Large Scale Visual Recognition Challenge. *International Journal of Computer Vision, 115*(3), 211–252. https://doi.org/10.1007/s11263-015-0816-y

Schroff, F., Kalenichenko, D., & Philbin, J. (2015a). FaceNet: A Unified Embedding for Face Recognition and Clustering. *Proceedings of the IEEE Computer Society Conference on Computer Vision and Pattern Recognition, 07-12-June-2015*, 815–823. https://doi.org/10.1109/CVPR.2015.7298682

Schroff, F., Kalenichenko, D., & Philbin, J. (2015b). FaceNet: A Unified Embedding for Face Recognition and Clustering. *Proceedings of the IEEE Computer Society Conference on Computer Vision and Pattern Recognition, 07-12-June-2015*, 815–823. https://doi.org/10.1109/CVPR.2015.7298682

Taigman, Y., Yang, M., Ranzato, M., & Wolf, L. (2014). DeepFace: Closing the gap to human-level performance in face verification. *Proceedings of the IEEE Computer Society Conference on Computer Vision and Pattern Recognition*, 1701–1708. https://doi.org/10.1109/CVPR.2014.220

Taylor, R., Kardas, M., Cucurull, G., Scialom, T., Hartshorn, A., Saravia, E., Poulton, A., Kerkez, V., & Stojnic, R. (2022). *Galactica: A Large Language Model for Science*. https://arxiv.org/abs/2211.09085v1

Turk, M., & Pentland, A. (1991). Eigenfaces for recognition. *Journal of Cognitive Neuroscience, 3*(1), 71–86. https://doi.org/10.1162/JOCN.1991.3.1.71

Viola, P., & Jones, M. (2001). Rapid object detection using a boosted cascade of simple features. *Proceedings of the IEEE Computer Society Conference on Computer Vision and Pattern Recognition, 1*. https://doi.org/10.1109/CVPR.2001.990517

Wang, C. Y., Lu, Y. D., Yang, S. T., & Lai, S. H. (2022). PatchNet: A Simple Face Anti-Spoofing Framework via Fine-Grained Patch Recognition. *Proceedings of the IEEE Computer Society Conference on Computer Vision and Pattern Recognition, 2022-June*, 20249–20258. https://doi.org/10.1109/CVPR52688.2022.01964

Wang, H., Wang, Y., Zhou, Z., Ji, X., Gong, D., Zhou, J., Li, Z., & Liu, W. (2018). CosFace: Large Margin Cosine Loss for Deep Face Recognition. *Proceedings of the IEEE Computer Society Conference on Computer Vision and Pattern Recognition*, 5265–5274. https://doi.org/10.1109/CVPR.2018.00552

Wirth, R., & Hipp, J. (2000). CRISP-DM: Towards a standard process model for data mining. *Proceedings of the 4th International Conference on the Practical Applications of Knowledge Discovery and Data Mining.*

Yi, D., Lei, Z., Liao, S., & Li, S. Z. (2014). *Learning Face Representation from Scratch.* https://arxiv.org/abs/1411.7923v1

Yu, L., & Liu, J. (2020). Face Recognition Based on Deep Learning of Small Data Set. *Journal of Physics: Conference Series, 1624*(5). https://doi.org/10.1088/1742-6596/1624/5/052004

www.ingramcontent.com/pod-product-compliance
Ingram Content Group UK Ltd.
Pitfield, Milton Keynes, MK11 3LW, UK
UKHW020714071026
15590UKWH00011B/597

9 783631 924327